THE DALLAS COWBOYS

By the same author

Martial Justice: The Last Mass Execution
in the United States

The Chicago Bears, An Illustrated History

Joe D

THE DALLAS COWBOYS

An Illustrated History

By Richard Whittingham

Foreword by Roger Staubach

1817

HARPER & ROW, PUBLISHERS, New York
Cambridge, Philadelphia, San Francisco, London
Mexico City, São Paulo, Sydney

Acknowledgements

There are many people who contributed graciously and substantially to the creation of this book. The author and publisher wish to extend their special thanks to:

The Dallas Cowboys Organization for their generous cooperation and assistance, especially Joe Bailey and Greg Aiello.

The Dallas Cowboys Cheerleaders, particularly Suzanne Mitchell, director.

The Pro Football Hall of Fame in Canton, Ohio, and its superb research library, and especially Joe Horrigan, curator and chief researcher, whose help and guidance were tremendous contributions.

Tex Schramm, Gil Brandt, Ernie Stautner. Roger Staubach, and all the others who shared their remembrances with the author.

The photographers who provided such a wide choice of photos for this book, especially Brad Bradley, Vernon Biever, Ron Scribner, Russ Russell, David Woo, and Frank Shankle.

FIRST EDITION

Designer: Sidney Feinberg

Library of Congress Cataloging in Publication Data

Paige, David, 1939–
    The Dallas Cowboys.
    Includes index.
    1. Dallas Cowboys—History. I. Title.

GV956.D3P26 1981   796.332′64′097642812   81–47241

ISBN 0–06–014901–9   AACR2

81 82 83 84 85 10 9 8 7 6 5 4 3 2 1

Contents

Color photographs follow page 96.

In Memory
Charles A. and Virginia M.
who would have been pleased

Foreword by Roger Staubach

THERE ARE MANY THINGS that come to mind when I think about the Cowboys and my association with them. Some of them are wonderful memories—like the feelings I had when I got to start in that first game back in 1969 against the Cardinals. And the thrill when I threw my first touchdown pass, which was in that same game. There were also some less exhilarating ones—like the last pass I completed, which unfortunately was to Herb Scott, our All-Pro guard. In between all that, it was quite an experience.

Actually, the first encounter I had with the Cowboys was when they drafted me as a junior in college, as a future, a very distant one at that. I still had another year at the Naval Academy and then a four-year active-duty commitment to the Navy, and I really hadn't been giving any thought to playing football beyond college.

Nothing more came of it until the summer of 1965. Lamar Hunt, owner of the Kansas City Chiefs, contacted me first. The NFL and AFL held two separate drafts in those days, and the Chiefs had also picked me in 1964. Now Hunt came to Annapolis with a contract proposal—some upfront money, a salary while I was on active duty, and a bonus if I played when my four years with the Navy were over.

I had some reservations. After all, back in 1965 the NFL was the predominant league and I had often thought that if I were to go into professional football, that's where it ought to be. But I hadn't heard from the Cowboys. Then Danny Peterson, an assistant basketball coach at Navy and a friend of Gil Brandt's, got hold of him to tell him about the Chiefs offer, and said that they had better act if they still had any interest in me.

As it turned out, the Cowboys were playing up in Philadelphia that year the same weekend as the Army-Navy game. The Cowboys were still interested, Brandt said, and so a meeting was set up in Philadelphia between Tex Schramm and Gil Brandt and Captain Paul Borden, a legal officer from Annapolis who was advising me. An offer was made and when Captain Borden told me the details—which were similar to but more generous than those offered by the Chiefs—I decided to accept it.

From that point on, even though it would be four years before I would become a rookie, I geared myself toward playing. I knew I wanted to; I just didn't know if I would be able to after a four-year lay-off. But during my entire tour with the Navy I worked out. Gil Brandt would send me films to study and a football to work out with—even when I was over in Vietnam [the summer of 1966 to the summer of 1967], I managed to find some football time.

When I got back to the United States I played with the base team down at Pensacola and then took leave in the summer of '68 and went out to the Cowboys' camp at Thousand Oaks. They wanted to take a look at me and I was anxious to see how the long lay-off had in reality affected me. The results out there would determine whether I stayed in the Navy or went to the pro game. As it turned out, I had a fine camp, better in fact than the one I would have the next year when I was about to join the team. I went back to the Navy ecstatic, and with a Cowboys playbook. I knew then I was going to play pro ball and I was pleased with where I'd be playing it.

It was out there that year when I first heard Tom Landry give a talk. It was a very impressive thing. He had a great football mind and that came across immediately. I could tell he was an incredible organizer. He had everything in control. Whatever it was—a guard blocking, a punter punting, a quarterback throwing, every facet of the game —he understood the details of each man's function.

To the rookies he made clear what he expected of them and then helped them set up their own goals. Everything was planning and precision to Landry whether it had to do with individual skills, game tactics, or motivation.

Tom Landry has always run the Cowboys like a fine machine, but not in an impersonal way. He was tough, but consistent, and that is a great trait for any leader. There was a formula there. I saw it at the very beginning. The approach was businesslike: objectives specified, analysis, grading, guidance, a complete follow-through. That's how Tom Landry structured it, and I guess all you have to do is look at the Cowboys' record for the last 15 or 16 years to judge its merits.

He himself has enormous self-discipline, and that is the pattern he expects the players to fall in with. You had to adjust to it, to pay the price, so to speak. For me, it was not all that difficult, probably because of my military training. For others it wasn't so easy. For some it was impossible. But you became a part of the pattern or you didn't stay around too long.

The organization itself is that way. All the major figures are part of the pattern. They are distinctly different types of people—Tex Schramm, Gil Brandt, Landry, Clint Murchison. Each is unique and especially good at what he is responsible for, but they mesh together very well. They have the same bottom line—winning and maintaining an image of quality. For the Cowboys, it was not always Super Bowls and filled stadiums. The team had to be built from nothing. They learned; they had the ability to learn quickly from their mistakes. They never looked for someone to heap the blame on, rather to find a way of turning the thing in the right direction.

I came along after the grim years, those first four or five. There was still a long way to go, a lot of things to work out. We hadn't been to the Super Bowl yet, much less won it.

Don Meredith retired just before my rookie season and I was stunned. So were a lot of other people, I think. It was the end of a Cowboys era and it presented a whole new challenge, not only for me because I'd be vying much more closely for the starting job but for the entire organization.

Together we had great highs and some awful lows. In fact, we went from the depths to the heights all within two years. I never saw Tom Landry so depressed, or the team so down as we were after the loss to Cleveland in the playoffs of 1969. We all were drained. Everybody was saying we were the team that couldn't win the big one, that something was dreadfully wrong somewhere. That was the bottom. Two years later we won the Super Bowl, and no one could say that about us anymore; that was carved into every smile on everyone's face after that game, especially Tom Landry's.

Seasons are only one thing. There are also the individual games. The Cowboys had more than their share of unforgettable football games. All the Super Bowls were that way, just by the nature of being the championship game. We had worked hard to get there and were joyful about the fact that we were in them. We won two of them and nothing beats the satisfaction you get from that. As a pro, it's what you play the game for. And there was nothing worse than losing there. It happened to us three times, and those were some dismal moments. At the same time, they were very dramatic—we never lost one by more than four points. In fact, with the difference of just one touchdown in each of those games, the Cowboys would be boasting today of five Super Bowl trophies.

And we had some really breathtaking games too. No one who was part of them could ever forget them. The conference playoff game up in Minnesota in 1975 was one, when Drew Pearson caught my Hail Mary pass and catapulted us toward Super Bowl X. Or the last game of my last regular season against the Redskins, the great comeback: two touchdowns in the last few minutes of the game, a last-second victory over an arch-rival. Or Danny White and Drew Pearson teaming up for those two spectacular touchdowns to win the 1980 playoff game against the Falcons.

That kind of thing is so much a part of the Cowboys' story. Their inherent strength has always been the ability to come back, whether it was turning a game around or a season. Other teams came to understand you could never count the Cowboys out, and that is a nice reputation to have around the league.

There are many other fond things that are also part of the experience. The great closeness among the players is an important one. You rely on other players and they rely on you; there is a fine interplay among athletes who are bound together as a team. You share the experiences, all of them, the good and the bad. And when you're gone from the game, you miss it.

There were other elements, too—the enemies and the feuds. I had my own with people like Diron Talbert of the Redskins and Mel Tom of the Eagles, even Clint Longley from our own team. There were also the eccentrics and the funny men who could make you laugh. But at the same time it was always a serious business with a definite goal and everyone knew that, and that is why you would meld together as a team.

I still feel you get out of it only what you put into it. The Cowboys have a tradition of winning. I contributed a share to it and, in turn, it contributed to me. It takes a lot of contributions from many people to sustain that tradi- tion. I'm grateful for having been part of the experience. All of us who were there have to be grateful for being part of that kind of tradition.

THE DALLAS COWBOYS

1 Opening Nights

It was sultry in Washington, D.C., the evening of September 8, 1980, when the Dallas Cowboys and the Washington Redskins trotted out on to the field at RFK Stadium. More than 55,000 fans, a sellout crowd, did not seem to mind, however, and greeted the teams tumultuously, while up in the press box Howard Cosell was telling several million TV viewers that this was the beginning of the second decade of the spectacle known as "ABC's Monday Night Football."

More significant, perhaps, was that with the launching of the 1980 regular season, the National Football League (NFL) was entering its *seventh* decade, conceived back with the flappers and bootleggers and other characters who came to life with the Roaring Twenties. Sixty-one years had elapsed since that day in 1920 when Ralph Hay of the Canton Bulldogs, George Halas of the Decatur Staleys, and representatives of other professional football teams from places like Massilon, Ohio, Hammond, Indiana, Rochester, New York, and Rock Island, Illinois, gathered in a Hupmobile agency in Canton, Ohio, to lay the foundation for an organized league of professional football teams.

Sitting in RFK Stadium that night with all the television cameras and crews, all the news writers and sportscasters, all the sophisticated communications between coaches in the press box and those on the field, all the pageantry and hype, it would be difficult to envision the meager beginnings of the sport. The game that was about to take place there that night was a world away from those played when pro teams carried rosters of 16, maybe 18, players who practiced during the week, usually after they had finished their regular jobs, and played on weekends for $50 to $100 a game—if the gate receipts that week permitted such largess. They traveled from town to town back then on rickety steam-engine trains, not chartered jets, and dressed in dingy locker rooms with cold cement floors, not the carpeted dressing rooms of today. Long before face guards or flak jackets were dreamed of, they taped only their ankles and wore soft helmets and mushy pads on their hips and shoulders

The sport, of course, grew steadily, establishing as it did its own exciting, often frustrating, sometimes amazing, and always interesting history, one that became jeweled with names like Jim Thorpe, George Halas, Curley Lambeau, Red Grange, Ernie Nevers, Bronko Nagurski, Don Hutson, Sammy Baugh, Otto Graham, Steve VanBuren, Chuck Bednarik, Johnny Unitas, Jim Brown, Vince Lombardi, and all the others who were the true luminaries of the game. Over the course of its existence, teams, even competing leagues, have come and gone, and ephemeral dynasties like the Chicago Bears of the 1930s and early 1940s, the Cleveland Browns of the 1950s, the Green Bay Packers of the 1960s, and the Miami Dolphins and Pittsburgh Steelers in the 1970s have risen and fallen.

By the 1980s, the sport of professional football was not only a sophisticated big business but practically a national institution. The Super Bowl, its yearly climax, had almost achieved the status of a legal holiday, even a holy day to some, and had earned the distinction of being the largest single attraction on TV each year, playing to an estimated audience of more than 100 million people and enabling sponsors to pay about $550,000 for each 60-second commercial. During the season that preceded that extravaganza, virtually tens of millions of people would swarm into the stadiums, stare at TV sets, or listen to radio broadcasts to share in it each week. Pro football had become as familiar an element of the modern era as the telephone, TV, and taxation.

The Dallas Cowboys became a part of it in 1960. A fledgling in terms of longevity in a league in which many of the teams trace their heritage back to the 1920s and 1930s, the Cowboys in a mere two decades had managed to become the most visible and publicized team in the NFL and the most vivid symbol of the game's modernity.

The team could legitimately lay claim to the largest and most loyal following in the history of the sport, with fans not just in Dallas, or even Texas, for that matter—people from all over the United States had adopted the Dallas Cowboys. They had even been dubbed "America's Team." It was only appropriate, therefore, to choose the Cowboys to kick off the second decade of "ABC's Monday Night Football."

Now, down on the field, the Cowboys were loosening up for their first regular-season game of the 1980 season. Frank Gifford, pro football Hall of Famer, former halfback and teammate of Tom Landry with the New York Giants, and now front-line sportscaster, had introduced the starting lineups, the national anthem was over, and the first round of television commercials was completed. It was nine P.M. Eastern Daylight Time, and the Cowboys ambled out to line up for the kickoff. On the sideline, Coach Tom Landry paced a few feet one way, then back. Over the years, he had become a tremendously familiar figure, head coach ever since that very first Dallas Cowboys game back in 1960. He was dressed, as always, neatly in a sport coat and tie and with his trademark flip-brim hat; the only thing noticeably different, perhaps, was the "Free the Hostages" badge he was wearing on his lapel that evening.

There was anxiety in all corners this summery night—in the Dallas organization, filtering among the fans, in the press booth. It had nothing to do with the onset of the 1980s or the inauguration of their third decade of existence; the era of Roger Staubach had just ended the year before, his last pass thrown in the divisional playoff game they lost to the Los Angeles Rams in 1979 postseason play. Danny White was now the quarterback, while the legendary Staubach sat back to enjoy his retirement, and everyone was wondering if White could indeed replace the legend. Landry himself had said, "There was the Meredith era in the 1960s and the Staubach era in the 1970s, and now we must put together a third team."

That "third team" was now on the field, facing the long-time rival Redskins, and the Cowboys on their sec-

THE DALLAS COWBOYS
DALLAS, TEXAS

TEXAS E. SCHRAMM
PRESIDENT

It is not the critic who counts, not the man who points out how the strong man stumbled or where the doer of deeds could have done them better. The credit belongs to the man who is actually in the arena; whose face is marred by dust and sweat and blood; who strives valiantly; who errs and comes up short again and again; who knows the great enthusiasms, the great devotions, and spends himself in a worthy cause; who at the best knows in the end the triumph of high achievements; and who at the worst, if he fails, at least fails while daring greatly; so that his place shall never be with those cold and timid souls who know neither defeat nor victory.

THEODORE ROOSEVELT
___April 10, 1899

This quotation from Theodore Roosevelt is framed and hangs in the office of Tex Schramm. It describes perfectly Schramm's own philosophy—as well, perhaps, as the one upon which the Dallas Cowboys were built.

ond possession were marching. Danny White lobbed a screen pass to fullback Ron Springs, and the first touchdown of the 1980 season was recorded, then unrecorded, brought back because of a clipping penalty. Two sparkling runs later by Tony Dorsett and the touchdown was re-recorded, and with Rafael Septien's extra point, the Cowboys led 7–0.

As the game moved on, television viewers were treated to the reality of just how the Dallas Cowboys dominate the pro football scene. There were not merely 11 Dallas players on the football field; they seemed to be everywhere. Don Meredith, the Dallas quarterback of the 1960s, was

*When the One Great Scorer comes
to write against your name—
He marks—not that you won or lost
—but how you played the game.*
          —Grantland Rice, 1880–1954

Bull.
          —Tex Schramm, 1921–

From the writings of Dallas Morning News *columnist
Bob St. John*

up in the press booth with Howard Cosell and Frank Gifford, offering his own brand of color to the telecast. Roger Staubach was a special feature that night, cameras keying to him in the den of his home down in Dallas where he was watching the game and occasionally offering his comments to the television audience. Even at commercial time, there was former Cowboy running back Walt Garrison drawling his pitch for smokeless tobacco.

On the field, Dallas's fabled defense was also proving to be predominant. The Redskins were having great difficulty moving against it, just as so many other teams had in the preceding 15 years.

In the second quarter, Danny White lined up for the first time in the shotgun formation, the one made famous by his predecessor. Watching White waiting for the snap from center, everyone had to think of Roger Staubach, something Danny White knew he would have to face. And when he threw his first interception of the season from that formation, there was a murmur of discontent from the Dallas fans in RFK Stadium. A little while later, however, the skeptics would forget it when he drilled a 37-yard pass to wide receiver Tony Hill, bringing the Cowboys all the way to the Redskins 9-yard line. Dallas, however, had to settle for a field goal, and the half ended with their lead at 10–0.

During the halftime intermission, Howard Cosell talked, and the commercials ran, and Roger Staubach from in front of his own TV set admitted he missed the game but thought he, at 38, had gotten out when he should have.

In the second half, Danny White threw another interception. More murmurs. But Washington quarterback Joe Theismann returned the favor almost immediately by tossing the ball into the hands of the Cowboys' All-Pro safety Charlie Waters at the goal line, and he raced with it back out to the 30-yard line.

As the fourth quarter started, Washington's Mark Moseley kicked a field goal to finally put the Redskins on the

Diminutive quarterback Eddie LeBaron tries to pick up a few yards on the ground in the Cowboys' first NFL regular season game. He did better in the air that night, throwing for 3 touchdowns and earning 345 yards on 15 completions. But the Cowboys lost anyway, the first of 11 defeats they would suffer that difficult first year. No. 60 on the Cowboys is guard Joe Bob Isbell.   (Bradley Photographers)

scoreboard, but Dallas came right back. Danny White engineered a march down the field that used up eight vital minutes and ended when Ron Springs bulled in for a touchdown. Septien's kick made it 17–3, and that is the way the game ended.

Howard Cosell summed up the events in his own inimitable way, saying, "We have seen tonight how thoroughly the Dallas team dominated this game, how impressive

---

"America's Team"

The sobriquet "America's Team" was bestowed on the Dallas Cowboys in 1978 when NFL Films chose it as the title for a motion picture about the team's highlights. As they were putting the movie together, the filmmakers discovered that, like country and western music and the urban cowboy, the popularity of the Dallas Cowboys had spread across the United States. They had become to professional football what Notre Dame is to the sport on the college level, what the New York Yankees are to baseball. Consider:

- The *Dallas Cowboys Weekly,* the team's own publication, boasts a circulation in excess of 102,000 (more than 30,000 of which subscribe from outside Texas borders). The circulation is almost four times more than any other team publication in the NFL.
- The Cowboys have by far the largest radio network system in the NFL, broadcasting Dallas games to almost 200 stations in 18 states (including Hawaii); 16 stations in 7 states broadcast the games in Spanish.
- Of the all-time top-rated sporting events on national TV, three of them are the Dallas Cowboys' appearances in Super Bowls X, XII, and XIII. In addition, Dallas also holds the TV record for the highest ratings on "ABC's Monday Night Football" and for Thanksgiving Day games.
- Of all the pennants, trinkets, articles of clothing, and other items that carry the emblem of professional football teams that are sold throughout the United States by NFL Properties Inc., approximately 30% carry the Dallas Cowboy logo, while the remaining 70% are divided up between the league's other 27 teams.
- The team has inspired the creation of two novels: Pete Gent's *North Dallas Forty* and Gary Cartwright's *Hundred Yard War.*
- The Dallas Cowboys Cheerleaders have become the most nationally well known group of performing young ladies since the Ziegfeld Follies. Their posters sell in the millions, and their authorized likenesses can be found on everything from T-shirts and playing cards to jigsaw puzzles, dolls, and costume jewelry. A made-for-TV movie achieved exceptionally high ratings, while an X-rated porno flick, obviously unauthorized and corporately loathed, has been equally successful in a more sordid marketplace.

they were in their season's debut." And then it was over, the TV screens around the country turned to the news of the day, and the Cowboys showered and dressed and went out to the airport for the flight back to Dallas, starting now to think of the Denver Broncos, who would be laying for them in Mile-High Stadium the next Sunday.

The Cowboys *were* impressive that 1980 Monday night, as they so often have been on national TV, and they did truly dominate the game, as they have so many games since the mid-1960s. They were, in fact, on the way to their 14th appearance in the NFL playoffs in a string of 15 seasons, an incredible NFL record (or, counting their 1965 invitation to the Playoff Bowl, their 15th postseason appearance in 16 seasons).

It had not always been that way, however. It began in a much different climate and on a much different note back in 1960. True, it was the same organization; Clint Murchison was the majority owner, Tex Schramm managed the operation, and Tom Landry coached the team back then. It was also an election year, but John F. Kennedy was running against Richard Nixon instead of Jimmy Carter against Ronald Reagan. And the names in the news were not Khomeini, Brezhnev, Sadat, or Begin. They were Eisenhower, Khruschev, Nasser, Lumumba, Mobutu, and Castro. It was a time, according to the city's statisticians, when the average Dallas wage earner reaped $80.42 a week after tax deductions. No human being had yet flown in space, much less landed on the moon. And the Vietnam War was still a half decade away for the United States. It was 1960, the year that civil rights' sit-ins began at a lunch counter in Greensboro, North Carolina; the year that Francis Gary Powers and his U-2 reconnaissance plane was shot down over Russia; the year moviegoers were spending their money to see *Ben Hur, Elmer Gantry,* and *The Apartment.*

The Dallas Cowboys of 1960 were as different from the team of 1980 as the city of Dallas where blacks drank from separate water fountains in 1960 was from the city that bore the same name in the 1980s. The Cowboys—unproven, unheralded, and for all practical purposes virtually unnoticed—were an expansion team made up of castoffs from the league's other 12 teams; they had not even been eligible to draft any of the top college players that year.

For the first game of the 1960 regular season, they were a decided underdog to a Pittsburgh Steeler team that had, the year before, finished fourth in its six-team conference. There was, of course, no Texas Stadium in 1960, but the Cowboys were able to use the 75,000-seat Cotton Bowl. There wasn't any TV coverage of Cowboy football that opening night, either. The Dallas TV stations the Saturday night of the game would be monopolized by *Perry Mason, Leave It to Beaver, Bonanza, The Lawrence Welk Show,*

Legendary Texan Bobby Layne lines up at quarterback for the Pittsburgh Steelers to initiate the Cowboys into the National Football League. In this 1960 regular season opener, Layne threw 4 TD passes. Still, it took a fourth-quarter touchdown to secure a 35–28 victory for the Steelers. The Cowboys in the picture are defensive back Fred Doelling (34) and linebacker Jack Patera (56).   (Bradley Photographers)

Have Gun Will Travel, and *Gunsmoke.*

Pete Rozelle, just starting his first year as commissioner of the NFL, flew to Dallas from New York in a show of support for the Cowboys' maiden game. Roy Rogers, his faithful horse Trigger, and the Sons of the Pioneers came from California to put on a pregame show to help entice fans into the stadium. Tickets for the game were a real bargain back then, only $4.60 for the best seat in the stadium, and there were deals for a block of tickets even beyond that. An end-zone ticket, for example, could be purchased by an adult for the grand total of $2, which then entitled that person to bring in as many as five children free of charge. Still, only about 30,000 people showed up, leaving some 45,000 seats in the cavernous Cotton Bowl empty—and of the gate total it was later estimated that only about 13,000 actually paid to get into the game.

Although the Pittsburgh Steelers were hardly the crème de la crème of the NFL, they were, according to the bookmakers, a 7-point favorite, and they came to Dallas confident. They had a native Texan at quarterback, Bobby Layne, who had joined the Steelers two seasons earlier as a result of a trade with the Detroit Lions. And they had another future Hall of Fame player in defensive tackle Ernie Stautner on their roster. There were a few other notables on the team: end Buddy Dial, running back John

Henry Johnson, and defensive end George Tarasovic; and their head coach, Buddy Parker, was one of the more respected names in the NFL.

Perhaps as an omen of the dismal Dallas season to come, it rained most of the morning that Saturday, and although the field was not what sportscasters would call a "quagmire," it was sloppy.

Question: *Did Roger Staubach really appear outside your 11th story window?*

Tex Schramm: *He was right there. I was facing around like I always do when I'm talking on the phone, and I put my feet up on that credenza there. I was on a conference call, and we had eight or nine people on the call. I'm just sitting there looking out the window and all of a sudden . . . Let's go back. He had been waiting for me, and he found out how to get out there—on the ledge—and he came around the corner, and then all of a sudden he just leaped and spread-eagled himself across that middle pane there. Ahhhghhh. I jumped a mile high. You know, you're in another world when you're on the phone, just sitting there looking out. Then I jumped the second time when I saw who the hell it was outside.*

The kickoff sailed into the air at eight P.M. Central Daylight Time that Saturday night, September 24, 1960, and the Dallas Cowboys officially became a part of NFL history.

The great Dallas defense that night was still only a dream in Tom Landry's football mind. Bobby Layne, comfortable in the familiar surroundings of the Cotton Bowl where years earlier as a collegian he had gone head to head with another Texas legend, S.M.U.'s Doak Walker, took full advantage of the novice Dallas defense. He threw four touchdown passes and gained a total of 288 yards passing.

On the other hand, the Cowboys made a game of it. Eddie Le Baron, the Cowboys' diminutive quarterback, kept them in hot competition all the way down to the last three minutes of the game. As it turned out, LeBaron threw for 345 yards and three touchdowns—two to wide receiver Jim Doran (75 and 54 yards, respectively) and a 7-yarder to end Fred Dugan. Running back Don McIlhenny contributed the other touchdown with a 5-yard run.

But it was not enough to win. The score was 28–28 in the fourth quarter, and it all went down the drain with 2:51 left in the game. Bobby Layne unleashed a bomb from his own 35-yard line to Steeler running back Tom Tracy. The final score was 35–28, a 7-point margin that showed the bookmakers could handicap a brand-new team as well as they could the veterans.

It was not that poor a start for a 1960 expansion team —four touchdowns and an exciting finish to boot. But it was the beginning of a season that would become eternally long and darkly depressing. It was a far cry from the kind of season the Dallas Cowboys of 1980 would have.

Why do the Cowboys attract and sustain such a following? Everyone has his theory. A sportswriter with the Chicago Sun-Times, Randy Harvey, speculated:

It could be because they have had so many colorful players (Don Meredith, Roger Staubach, Duane Thomas, Walt Garrison, Calvin Hill, Tony Dorsett, Bob Hayes, Pete Gent, Lance Rentzel, Bob Lilly, Lee Roy Jordan, Randy White . . .). It could be because you rarely can turn on your television without hearing the wonders of work tools from Lilly, iced tea from Meredith, air conditioners from Staubach, Uncola from Dorsett, and snuff from Garrison . . . It could be because they brought the modern era of professional football the Flex Defense, the Doomsday Defense, the Shotgun Offense (actually the San Francisco 49ers used it first back in 1960), the Kick Karavan, cheerleaders, and the computer . . . Or because they were the first expansion team to advance to the NFL championship game . . . Or because of the Texas mystique . . .

Another writer suggests that it is because they were "the underdog who overcame all odds to succeed . . . the quintessential American dream."

Tex Schramm put it succinctly and perhaps most realistically: "If we didn't win, we wouldn't have as many fans as we do."

Question: *The turnaround actually seemed to come around 1965. Then in 1966, suddenly you were in the playoffs. Was there anything in particular that kind of catapulted you into it?*

Tex Schramm: *No. I mean, we were getting good football players, and we were doing a lot more than other people. We knew we couldn't rely just on the draft. So we had to go out and get players from other sports. That's how we wound up with Cornell Green, a basketball player. We knew we had to get a distinctive edge over everybody else. We couldn't just follow the same pattern that everybody else was. So we brought in basketballs players and track men. We were taking all kinds of chances. It was just a matter of time before it all came together.*

2 The Very Beginning

ACTUALLY, THE NFL first came to Dallas back in 1952, but it was not in the form of the Cowboys. It was a team called the Texans, and the franchise was really that of the old New York Yanks (who had formerly been known as the Boston Yanks and then the New York Bulldogs). New York fans had given up on the Yanks after they won only one of their 12 regular-season games and finished in last place in the National Conference of the NFL the year before. (The team had also lost somewhere in the vicinity of $1 million for its owner during an eight-year existence.)

So Yanks owner Ted Collins sold his franchise to the NFL, and commissioner Bert Bell subsequently awarded it to a syndicate of businessmen in Dallas. The Dallas Texans, as they were renamed, would replace the Yanks and join the Detroit Lions, Los Angeles Rams, San Francisco 49ers, Green Bay Packers, and Chicago Bears in the NFL's rugged National Conference.

At the time, the city of Dallas seemed like the ideal locale for a professional football team. The sport of football was tremendously popular in a state where college teams like Texas, Southern Methodist, Texas Christian, Rice, Baylor, Texas A & M, and Texas Tech were lionized and where such Saturday's heroes as Bobby Layne, Doak Walker, and Kyle Rote had been subjects of almost pagan idolatry, where the Cotton Bowl on New Year's Day annually hosted one of the nation's most popular football events, where even high school football was followed with the same fervor as major league baseball in Brooklyn.

The Texans had a more than respectable slate of football names on its roster when they opened for business in Dallas: running backs Buddy Young, George Taliaferro, and Dick Hoerner; quarterback Frank Tripucka; ends Bar-

ney Poole and a rookie named Gino Marchetti; tackle Art Donovan; and defensive back Tom Keane. The backfield had the potential for some real dazzle, and the defense appeared to be a sturdy one. And so the Texans were launched with a great deal of hope and enthusiasm on the part of the new owners and the NFL, but that is where the excitement ended. Not a lot of people, it seems, were interested in coming out to take a look at them.

The New York Giants were the first to arrive at the Cotton Bowl to face the Texans, bringing along Charlie Conerly, Frank Gifford, Eddie Price, Emlen Tunnell, Arnie Weinmeister, Al DeRogatis, and a combination defensive back and third-string quarterback by the name of Tom Landry. They demolished the Texans 24–6 before a crowd of about 17,000, who were scattered throughout the 75,000 seats of the Cotton Bowl. The story was the same the following week when the San Francisco 49ers, with Y. A. Tittle, Hugh McElhenny, Joe Perry, and Leo Nomellini, invaded Texas, only fewer people showed up that Sunday to see the Texans drubbed 37–14. (The 17,000 who attended the home opener against the Giants would stand as the biggest crowd the Texans would attract to the Cotton Bowl.)

The Texans were consistent in their losing ways. So were the fans in their patronage. After six consecutive losses, the Texans faced the Los Angeles Rams in the Cotton Bowl before an especially sparse crowd. As Sam Blair, sports columnist for the Dallas *Morning News,* wrote:

"Jimmy Phelan, the Texans' head coach and general

Two former All-American running backs, Buddy Young (Illinois) and George Taliafero (Indiana) offered a little razzle-dazzle in the Dallas Texans' otherwise dismal 1952 season. Here, Buddy Young tries to escape the grasp of Green Bay Packer defensive end John Martinkovic in one game; in another, George Taliafero is about to put a move on Chicago Bear tackle Bob Cross before breaking into the clear on a 36-yard touchdown run. The other Texan in the picture with Taliafero is center Brad Ecklund; the other Bears, Fred Williams (75) and Jack Hoffman (82). The Texans folded at the end of the season, gaining the dubious distinction of being the last team to drop out of the NFL.   (Pro Football Hall of Fame)

manager, was resigned to his team's fate by then. He wasn't surprised to see only a handful of people huddling under umbrellas in the huge stadium. He shrugged, returned to the locker room and addressed his players before the kickoff.

" 'Gentlemen,' Phelan said, 'before each game the members of the starting lineup have been introduced by the public address announcer as they ran on the field. However, today we're going to change the format. I want all of you to go up in the stands and personally meet each fan.' "

The Texans then went out and made that game their seventh loss in a row (27–6). After the game, Phelan handed out the players' paychecks and said to them: "Gentlemen, it is my opinion that you should get to your banks with all due haste." That same week, the owners turned the franchise back to Bert Bell and asked him to run it for the rest of the season. The NFL did, setting up a temporary headquarters for the team in Hershey, Pennsylvania, and operating the Texans as a "road team," one that would play the remainder of its games away. The only highlight of the season perhaps was the Texans' lone victory; they defeated the Chicago Bears 27–23 before 3,000 spectators in Akron, Ohio. When the season was mercifully over, the Texans were out of business, and the NFL was out of Texas. It was, incidentally, the last time that a team would drop out of the NFL.

The experience of the short-lived Texans in the NFL

was not to prove a deterrent to the reentry of pro football into Dallas, however. Seven years later, in 1959, when the possibility of an NFL expansion franchise was dangled before the eyes of Texas multimillionaire Clint Murchison, Jr., he was ready to step right up and try it again. And he was not alone. Lamar Hunt, scion of another Texas megamillionaire family, the same year announced his plans to form a new pro circuit and call it the American Football League (AFL). His franchise would be in Dallas, and he stated he had no trepidation whatsoever about naming it the same as the luckless predecessor, the Texans.

But it was Clint Murchison who would bring the NFL back to Dallas. He had wanted to own a football team for a long time. His wish was a simple one, as he said years later: "I just wanted the fun of being able to see professional football in my home town." He had been a fan of the ill-fated Texans of 1952; in fact, he had bought a block of 20 season tickets for their games that year. When the owners of the Texans dropped out of the picture, he considered buying the franchise himself, but that did not work out. So, during the next seven years, he looked for another team to buy and ended up negotiating for the San Francisco 49ers, the Washington Redskins, and the Chicago Cardinals, in that order. In each case, however, the deal fell through. When word of expansion in the NFL leaked out in 1959, he made his interest clear and quickly found himself moving to the front of the line.

The NFL was not proposing anything drastic in the way of realignment, just tinkering with the idea of allowing two new teams to enter its vaulted domain. Houston had been under consideration, but it would lose out to the twin cities of Minneapolis–St. Paul. Dallas was the other choice. The proposed expansion in these two metropolises would be voted on at the annual meeting of NFL owners scheduled for late January 1960. Not all owners were in favor of expansion, and so the return of NFL football to Dallas was not a sure thing. But a number of owners were, including George Halas of the Chicago Bears, who had been a guiding force in the league for four decades and by 1960 was chairman of the NFL expansion committee. Odds were that expansion would occur and Dallas would be a part of it. After all, it would be an ideal place for the NFL to go head to head with Lamar Hunt's new upstart of a league, many of the NFL owners felt. Clint Murchison began making plans for watching football in his home town and announced that his team would be known as the Dallas Rangers.

Lamar Hunt did indeed get his new league established, too. AFL franchises went out to eight teams; besides Hunt's Dallas Texans, there came into being the Houston Oilers, New York Titans, Buffalo Bills, Boston Patriots, Los Angeles Chargers, Oakland Raiders, and the Denver Broncos. The AFL did not intimidate the well-entrenched NFL, but most knowledgeable men in the league realized that it was nothing to sneer at. There was solid money behind the new teams, there was a wealth of football talent to be bartered for in the pro ranks and upcoming from the colleges, and professional football was continuing to grow steadily and significantly in popularity.

Soon the sports headlines in the Dallas *Morning News* and the Dallas *Times-Herald* read: "Pro Grid War Building" and "NFL-AFL War in Dallas." It was a strange turn of events. Here was a city whose one previous pro football team had shown it could not draw more than 17,000 people into the Cotton Bowl, and now two teams were hoping to be accommodated there, battling each other for fans and customers whose existence neither team had any reason to count on. If history were to be any kind of barometer, neither team would make a go of it.

Clint Murchison was not worried, however, and in many ways took the challenge and the competition as a healthy, amusing sort of diversion. His first key act would be to hire the right man to run the team. As he had stated publicly, he wanted "to own it, not operate it." He said he wanted the best executive talent, that that was the only way a Dallas team would survive in the NFL. He asked George Halas for some advice on the subject. Halas suggested that he hire a young man who had formerly been the general manager of the Los Angeles Rams, a Californian by the name of Texas Schramm, whose ancestry, however, went back to the Lone Star State and who had graduated from the University of Texas. Schramm had left

Tex Schramm

"When we first came to Dallas, our office was an unpartitioned corner in the Texas Auto Club. People would crowd in there to map routes for trips, and I'd be over in a corner discussing player contracts on the phone. Sometimes they'd listen in. The noise was unbelievable."

the pro game three years earlier and was presently working for CBS-TV as an assistant director of sports programming in New York City. As everyone knows, Murchison took George Halas's advice.

Tex Schramm headed down to Dallas from New York in November 1959 to start what he later would term "an enormous challenge" and "the most exciting few years of my life." At the time, however, he was general manager of a team that existed only in the hopes of Clint Murchison.

Schramm knew he faced a difficult situation. The Dallas franchise, if it materialized, would only be offered the

Posing at the NFL Owners' meeting in January 1960, just after the Dallas "Rangers" were voted into the National Football League, are, from the left, Bedford Wynne and Clint Murchison, Jr., owners of the new franchise; George Preston Marshall, owner of the Washington Redskins; and Tex Schramm, Dallas's general manager. Marshall, one of the league's more colorful, if irascible, owners, had been the most outspoken opponent of league expansion in 1960.   (Pro Football Hall of Fame)

Question: *In the beginning, when you were first starting out, how did you go about judging football talent?*

Gil Brandt: *We didn't have a scientific way of doing it back then. We just wrote a report, and many times we didn't cover all areas of the players' strengths or weaknesses. Then we decided that we had to have a form of some type that encompassed the characteristics of all football players. We knew there were certain characteristics in a football player—mental alertness, strength and explosion, competitiveness, quickness, agility, and balance. So we set up a form that had those characteristics on it with a nine-to-one rating scale. And we included on the form position specifics, the seven different positions, so that we had different things for a wide receiver than we would for an offensive lineman, different things for quarterbacks than for defensive linemen.*

By 1961, we approached it with a semblance of organization. Before people just wrote things about a player, and that can be a bad thing. Some people are very talented writers, and other people are not, so what happens is the one who writes a real good report, well, his player is likely to be drafted over a player whose report was not well written. So by spelling everything out, charting things, rating characteristics, we developed a system.

bottom end of the other teams' personnel in an expansion draft. Some players would probably turn out fine, he felt, but many would be over the proverbial hill or simply not good enough. In addition, the Cowboys would not be eligible to participate in the 1960 NFL draft of college players—it had already taken place—and therefore they would be deprived of the best upcoming talent.

The only avenue left was to track down the most promising players who had *not* been signed by other NFL teams. The obvious problem was to determine who they were. So he went to his former employer, the Rams, to work out a deal. The Rams had compiled a vast amount of information about players who had been signed and those who had not and were now free agents. Schramm paid the Rams $5,000 for the information about the players who were then free agents. Then he turned that information over to two of the first people he hired, scout and former NFL coach Hampton Pool and a part-time scout and former baby photographer, Gil Brandt. Their mission: to go out and sign the best of the free agents to a team that might, just might, become a part of the NFL in 1960.

There were other ways to get players, too. Schramm and Murchison talked them over. Their most pressing need would be a quarterback, and Don Meredith, a senior

at S.M.U. over on Mockingbird Lane in Dallas and a 6 foot 3 inch, 200-pound, two-time All-American, was the most enticing. Tex Schramm was certain the AFL, and most probably Lamar Hunt's Texans, would try to sign him. So Schramm and Clint Murchison had a personal-services contract drawn up, offering Meredith $150,000 for five years, a very impressive amount for 1960, especially from a team that did not officially own an NFL franchise. Perhaps the most amazing part of it was that the contract was guaranteed. Even if the Dallas franchise for some reason failed to materialize, Meredith would still get his $30,000 a year for the next half decade.

The AFL Texans did indeed draft "Dandy" Don Meredith, as he liked being called. But Meredith decided to go along with the tried-and-true NFL and passed that word on to Lamar Hunt, owner of the Texans.

To ensure that no other NFL team acquired Meredith in the draft, Schramm and George Halas did a little be-

The first quarterback on the Cowboy roster was Don Heinrich, who had been a back-up to Charlie Conerly with the New York Giants from 1954 through 1959. The Cowboys acquired him in the expansion draft of 1960, but the starting job would go to Eddie LeBaron, whom the Cowboys talked out of retiring from the Washington Redskins. Heinrich served as LeBaron's back-up and also contributed substantially by working with rookie Don Meredith. (Dallas Cowboys)

The Dallas "Rangers" not only had to worry about competition from other NFL teams, but they would have to battle for paying customers with Lamar Hunt's Dallas Texans, who would also play their games at the Cotton Bowl. Hunt launched the Texans and the AFL the same year that the Cowboys entered the NFL. Here, Hunt poses with what the NFL owners back in 1960 referred to as the "renegades," the AFL team owners and directors. From the left: seated are Bud Adams (Houston Oilers) and Joe Foss (AFL Commissioner); standing: Bill Sullivan (Boston Patriots), Cal Kunz (Denver Broncos), Ralph Wilson (Buffalo Bills), Lamar Hunt (Dallas Texans), Harry Wismer (New York Titans), Wayne Valley (Oakland Raiders), and Barron Hilton (Los Angeles, later San Diego, Chargers). (Pro Football Hall of Fame)

hind-the-scenes maneuvering. Halas drafted Meredith for the Chicago Bears, then traded him to Dallas for a third-round draft pick in 1962 (actually not until the second draft, in which Dallas would participate).

The Cowboys were so pleased with getting Don Meredith's name on a personal-services contract that they proposed to do the same with a running back whom they coveted. Don Perkins was a highly touted halfback even though his school, the University of New Mexico, was not known as a football dynasty. Through an old friend of Clint Murchison's, Sen. Clinton Anderson of New Mexico, the idea of playing professional football in the NFL for the soon-to-be Dallas franchise was broached to Perkins, and he, too, signed a personal-services contract.

The Baltimore Colts drafted Don Perkins, but he signed with Dallas, and the Colts received a ninth-round draft choice in 1962 as compensation.

It did not end with Perkins, either. Fueled by his first

two successes, Schramm decided to go after what would be the biggest catch of the year. He explained it to Geoffrey Norman in *Esquire* magazine:

"Around Christmas, when I was still living in Connecticut, I got word that Billy Cannon was coming to New York for one of those television All-American things and that he might want to talk to me. [Cannon was the most highly regarded player coming out of college that year, an exceptional running back from Louisiana State University and winner of the 1959 Heisman trophy.] I called him and asked him if he wanted to play for Dallas. He said he did, and we talked money. We were pretty close to a figure, so I said I would meet him in New York. I had one of those personal services contracts, and I was going down there to sign him. Before I went to New York, though, I called Pete Rozelle. He was still general manager of the Rams. I knew the Rams were interested in Cannon. So I told Pete

Running back Don McIlhenny came to the Cowboys in the expansion draft for 1960, one of the three players chosen from the Green Bay Packer roster. McIlhenny, a 4-year NFL veteran, would team with L. G. Dupre to handle most of the 1960 rushing duties. With the recovery of Don Perkins in 1961, McIlhenny would move to the San Francisco 49ers.   (Dallas Cowboys)

what I had in mind. He told me that I had already taken two good players out of circulation and that if I did it with this one, I couldn't be sure of his vote (for a Dallas franchise) at the league meeting. That was one train I never caught." [Billy Cannon was the first player selected in the NFL draft that year, and he was chosen by the Rams, but he was also a first-round choice of the Houston Oilers in the AFL, the team he finally signed with.]

On January 28, 1960, the NFL, at its meeting in Miami Beach, officially and formally voted to award a franchise to Clint Murchison (and a minority stockholder, Bedford Wynne). The franchise fee of $50,000 was paid, and it was agreed that the Dallas team would pay another $550,000 to compensate the other 12 teams in the league for the three players from each that Dallas would be allowed to select. Dallas once again had a team in the NFL; the Dallas Rangers were an NFL reality.

January 28, 1960 was surely a significant date in the story of Dallas's professional football history, but a date a month earlier would prove to be equally important. That was December 28, 1959, the day Tex Schramm called a press conference in Dallas to announce that he had just hired a coach for the new Dallas team and introduced Tom Landry to the members of the media gathered there.

To accommodate the newly enfranchised team in Dallas, each of the other 12 NFL teams had to give up three players to the Cowboys. Each team was allowed to freeze 25 of the 36 players on its roster, and Dallas could then select from the 11 unfrozen names. Of all those selected, only 22 made the Cowboys in 1960 (they are identified with an asterisk), and only three would prove to be long-term residents of the Cowboys—Bob Fry played for five seasons, and Frank Clarke and Jerry Tubbs both stayed around for eight years.

St. Louis Cardinals:	Ed Hussmann*	DT
	Bob Cross	OT
	Jack Patera*	LB
Cleveland Browns:	Leroy Bolden	RB
	Frank Clarke*	WR
	Ed Modzelewski	FB
New York Giants:	Al Barry	OG
	Don Heinrich*	QB
	Buzz Guy*	OG
Philadelphia Eagles:	Dick Bielski*	TE
	Jerry DeLucca	OT
	Bill Striegel	OG
Pittsburgh Steelers:	Ray Fisher	DT
	Bobby Luna	DB
	Ray Mathews*	WR
Washington Redskins:	Tom Braatz*	LB
	Joe Nicely	OG
	Doyle Nix	DB
Baltimore Colts:	L. G. Dupre*	RB
	Ray Krouse	DT
	Dave Sherer*	P
Detroit Lions:	Charlie Ane	OT
	Gene Cronin*	DE
	Jim Doran*	WR
Green Bay Packers:	Nate Borden*	DE
	Bill Butler*	S
	Don McIlhenny*	RB
Los Angeles Rams:	Tom Franckhauser*	DB
	Bob Fry*	OT
	Duane Putnam*	G
San Francisco 49ers:	Fred Dugan*	WR
	John Gonzaga*	DE
	Jerry Tubbs*	LB
Chicago Bears:	Don Healy*	DT
	Jack Johnson	DG
	Pete Johnson	DB

3 Building a Team from Scratch

Tex Schramm had many old ties with his former employer, the Los Angeles Rams, and he did not disdain using them to advantage in those hectic days when he was trying to build a team from scratch. He even went out there first in search of a coach. Sid Gillman had been head coach during the last few years that Schramm was the Rams' general manager. (Gillman had actually held the job since 1955.) Sid was a respected football strategist, and Schramm decided to feel him out about moving maybe a thousand miles east to help the Dallas Rangers get themselves started in the league.

At the same time, Schramm was well aware of a young assistant coach with the New York Giants. He had heard a lot about him and had seen the results of the man's work. While in New York and toiling during the week for CBS, he had watched the Giants play on a number of Sundays and had been impressed with the marvelous defense that was developed and guided by Tom Landry. Just the preceding year, in fact, the Giants had led the NFL in every category of defense except one, and for the past two years they had led the entire NFL in allowing the fewest points to be scored against them.

The word circulating in the league now was that Tom Landry had great potential for a head coaching job. His mentor with the Giants, head coach Jim Lee Howell, had already said that Landry "to my knowledge is the best defensive coach in the game today. He is an innovator who will make a big name for himself in the coaching ranks before he's through." And there was a steady stream of praise from those who had played with him, game greats like Frank Gifford, Kyle Rote, and Emlen Tunnell.

In his biography of Tom Landry, author Bob St. John quotes this laudatory message from Gifford: "Most of us in those days just played the game. Not Tom. He studied it, studied everything. When I was playing on the defensive unit with Tom in 1952, defense was just hit or miss with most everybody in those days. Not with Tom. He put the same kind of discipline in the defense that the offense had. He had begun to create pro defense as we play it today." And to put the Landry approach in its proper perspective, Gifford added this little vignette: "One time I remember I intercepted a pass. I'd just gone for the ball but I was out of position. Tom didn't say, 'nice play.' He just said, 'Frank, you know you were out of position on that play.'"

Jimmy Cannon, the well-known New York sports columnist, had written of the 1959 Giants' defense: "In 25 years of writing about football, this is the greatest defensive group I've seen. All of them, from Andy Robustelli to the newest kid . . . (but) congratulate one of them for having a good afternoon and they'll turn the interview away from themselves to the assistant coach (Tom Landry). Never in a lifetime of covering sports have I heard such compliments uttered by the guys who do the work." The credentials and the tributes were impressive, and on top of that, Tom Landry was a fellow alumnus of the University of Texas.

The two men sat down and talked in New York several times; finally, Tex Schramm and Tom Landry agreed that their interests were mutual, and the deal was cast—a five-year contract for Landry at $34,500 per annum and an honest promise that he would have total autonomy in running the team on the field. Now it was arranged to everyone's satisfaction: Clint Murchison would own it, Tex Schramm would operate the organization, and Tom Landry would coach the team. No one cared to encroach on the other's domain.

So New York City lost another resident as Tom Landry joined Schramm in moving back to Texas. Among the first things he did as the Dallas Ranger head coach was to hire three assistant coaches. For that closest to his heart, defense, Landry signed up Tom Dahms, who had been coaching at the University of Virginia and had spent seven years as a player in the NFL with the Los Angeles Rams, Green Bay Packers, Chicago Cardinals, and the San Francisco 49ers. For the offensive backfield, he wooed Boris "Babe" Dimancheff from the coaching staff of the Pittsburgh Steelers. Dimancheff had spent his 7-year pro-ball career with the Boston Yanks, Chicago Cardinals, and the Chicago Bears. Brad Ecklund, who was presently coaching high school football in Oregon, was lured to Texas to handle the Rangers offensive line. Ecklund had played one year in the old All-American Football Conference (AAFC) with the New York Yankees and four years in the NFL—two with the same Yankees, who were adopted into the league after the demise of the AAFC, one with the Dallas Texans, and one with the Baltimore Colts.

There was a lot to do in the early months of 1960. They were beginning from ground zero—absolutely nothing in an arena where all the others were firmly established and glistening with heritage. Tex Schramm set up the team headquarters and began hiring an office staff, among them Kay Lang to be ticket manager and box office treasurer, as the post was called back then. It was an innovation in those somewhat sexist days of professional sports. As Tex Schramm said at the time, "I don't believe there is any other woman holding such an important office in major league sports." It was just another one of those insightful choices that became part of the amazing story of longevity of key people in the Dallas organization; the Cowboys have never had another ticket manager.

In March 1960, Tex Schramm and Clint Murchison were troubled about the team name. Not that they were necessarily opposed to the "Rangers," but there was a problem; it seems there was also a Texas League baseball team in Dallas which went by the same name. There had been rumors that the minor-league club was about to go out of business or move out of the city, but when that did not occur by mid-May, Schramm and Murchison had to take a more serious look at the situation. It was agreed that the new NFL team ought not to take the chance of getting itself confused in any way with the baseball Rangers. After all, both Murchison and Schramm, even at that early stage, had hopes and plans for fielding a distinctly unique team in the NFL. So Tex Schramm came up with

Jungle Jamey

As the Cowboys convened that first summer out at Forest Grove, Oregon, one of the people to arrive was a barefoot place kicker, who, as it turned out, had a variety of other eccentricities as well. Sam Blair, in his book Dallas Cowboys, Pro or Con, tells the story best of the amusing anomaly who had nicknamed himself Jungle Jamey.

"Portland was the home of James Bacilerri, which meant it was only a short drive out to the Dallas camp in his battered 1949 Ford, which was covered with autographs and had a hunk of bear meat swinging from the radio aerial. Proximity meant nothing to Jungle Jamey, however. He had traveled the entire country in pursuit of his two greatest pleasures, visiting his favorite teams and gate-crashing. He was capable of turning up anywhere. . . .

"You knew right away that Jamey wasn't just another guy who dropped by to watch practice. A stocky man in his middle thirties, he wore a white hunter's hat with a snakeskin band, ragged short pants, a football jersey bearing number 22, and he was barefoot. Oh, yes, he had a large white rabbit on a leash. He called the rabbit 'Texas Freeloader.' Jungle Jamey and his rabbit soon were leading the players out of the locker room to the practice field, where he would try a few barefoot field goals and dispense a lot of advice. . . . But it was inevitable that Jamey soon would be at odds with Tex Schramm. Jamey claimed that Schramm shouldn't be there and was disturbed that Tex had so much authority and yet was neither coaching nor playing. Schramm had different ideas about who was out of place. . . .

"Intriguing character though he was, Jamey added nothing to the camp in Schramm's opinion. Several nights, Tex was ready to evict him, but couldn't find him. One night, Schramm got down on his hands and knees in the recreation room and looked under a grand piano, where Jamey sometimes slept. But that was one of the nights that Jamey went to the stadium and slept on the 50-yard line. . . .

"Landry had no objection to Jamey, and he talked Schramm into letting him stay. He was still there the first weekend in August, when the Cowboys flew to Seattle for their first exhibition game. Jamey was on the plane.

"Fritz Hawn had arrived earlier and decided there should be a band to meet the team at the airport. He hired some musicians and gave them a large sign 'Jungle Jamey's Jazz Band.' As the Cowboys left the plane, they played happily and nodded to Jamey."

The very first Dallas Cowboys team in training camp in Forest Grove, Oregon, in the summer of 1960. Included are (front row) Eddie LeBaron, 14, and Don Perkins, 43; (second row) Frank Clarke, 82, Don Meredith, 17; (third row) Jerry Tubbs, 50, and Tom Landry (coach).   (Pro Football Hall of Fame)

a new name—the Cowboys—and Murchison agreed to it. The Dallas Rangers officially became the Dallas Cowboys.

Training camp was scheduled to be held at Pacific University out in Forest Grove, Oregon, far from the stifling heat of the Dallas summer—at least the first phase of the camp. But before the hopefuls could invade that town to compete against each other for a place on the brand-new Dallas roster, Tex Schramm made his first significant trade. He and Tom Landry were only too aware that Don Meredith could not simply come into the NFL as a rookie and lead the Cowboys against the league's savvy and experienced defenses. The Cowboys had obtained Don Heinrich from the New York Giants in the expansion draft, but Heinrich had spent his six-year career up in Gotham playing second fiddle to one of the game's premier quarterbacks, Charlie Conerly. He was experienced in how the game of pro football was engineered from a quarterback's position, but he still was not a proven leader on the field. Schramm and Landry decided that to be on the safe side they needed a fully experienced quarterback. One who appeared to have become available was a newly accredited lawyer in Washington, D.C., who was thinking about getting out of the game altogether, Eddie LeBaron. LeBaron had quarterbacked the Washington Redskins every year since 1952, stepping in after the retirement of

the immortal Sammy Baugh. (Actually, LeBaron missed one of those years, 1954, when he jumped to the Canadian Football League.)

Eddie LeBaron was only 5 feet 7 inches, but he was a respected passer and ball handler and an experienced field general—with eight years as a front-line quarterback in pro football combat. Schramm went after him and got him, but it was an expensive proposition. He had to give Washington the Cowboys' first-round draft choice the following year, in the first college player pool that Dallas would be eligible for, as well as a sixth-round pick. But with LeBaron and Don Heinrich, it was hoped that the new Dallas franchise would pose a respectable offensive threat while Don Meredith was undergoing his NFL apprenticeship.

Forest Grove, about 20 miles west of Portland, was a gorgeous setting, with Oregon pine trees and a snow-capped Mount Hood standing majestically off in the distance. While little Pacific College was not totally prepared for the onslaught of such an army of football players, the Cowboys made do by appropriating both the men's locker room and the girls' physical education facilities. A prodigious and surely unprecedented total of 193 players would pass through the Cowboys' first training camp. As Eddie LeBaron remembers it, "It was like a Greyhound

Trivia

The first score to be posted in Dallas Cowboy history came from the toe of kicker Fred Cone, a 17-yard field goal in the Cowboys' first game, an exhibition against the San Francisco 49ers, August 6, 1960, in Seattle, Washington.

The first Cowboy touchdown came in the same game, scored by end Frank Clarke on a 56-yard pass play from Eddie LeBaron.

bus station . . . I was throwing passes to guys I had never seen before and never saw again."

Coach Tom Landry greeted the newcomers with what would become a Cowboy hallmark, the "Landry Mile." It would become a feature of the training camp routine for years to come. It does not sound like a real feat by the jogging society standards of the 1980s, but back in 1960 it loomed rather formidably. Backs and receivers were expected to complete the Landry mile in under six minutes; linemen were allowed an extra 30 seconds. That first year, no one qualified. The fastest time recorded was 6 minutes and 19 seconds by Greg Altenhofen, a 6 foot 3 inch, 195-pound rookie end from the University of Oregon. (Despite this relatively good start, he did not make the team.)

The slowest time was posted by Bob Griffin, a 30-year-old, 260-pound center and linebacker who had played for the Los Angeles Rams from 1953 to 1957 but had been out of football since then. As one sportswriter on the scene observed, "Griffin was the slowest, and it seemed for awhile he would have to be timed with a calendar." Actually, his clocking was 9:06. Griffin, like the more fleet Altenhofen, did not make the team.

Two players who ran the mile did not stay around for much else. They were Don Meredith and Don Perkins, both of whom had been selected to play for the College All-Stars. They left to report to that training camp at Northwestern University in Evanston, Illinois, where Coach Otto Graham would prepare a team of the college football elite to meet the NFL defending champions, the Baltimore Colts.

For the Cowboys, it was an unfortunate set of circumstances in that Don Perkins, for whom they had great expectations, broke his foot up there and was lost for the rest of the season. (The All-Stars went down to a decisive 32–7 defeat that year at Chicago's Soldier Field, but their single touchdown held a small ray of hope for the Cowboys. It was accomplished on a 60-yard pass play from their own Don Meredith to a halfback from the University

of Oklahoma, Prentice Gautt.)

Without the services of Don Meredith and Don Perkins, the Cowboys played their first game on August 6, 1960. They traveled north to Seattle for an exhibition game against the San Francisco 49ers. Under coach Red Hickey, the 49ers the year before had ended up in the middle of the NFL's Western Conference with a 7–5 record. They were still stocked with old and revered names like Tittle, McElhenny, J. D. Smith, and Nomellini, but they were toying with the idea of using a new quarterback named John Brodie, who had sat on the San Francisco bench for the previous three seasons.

Like most early preseason games, it was an exercise in

Eddie LeBaron, who had been quarterbacking with the Washington Redskins for most of the 1950s, was planning to retire after the 1959 season and devote his energies to the practice of law. The Cowboys, however, in need of an experienced quarterback, coaxed him into extending his playing days, and sent the Redskins their first- and sixth-round draft choices of 1961 for his services. LeBaron would guide the Cowboy offense for the first three years of the team's existence while Dandy Don Meredith was being groomed to take over those duties.   (Pro Football Hall of Fame)

experimentation. The sportswriters of the day took a certain demonic pleasure in describing the makeshift Cowboys who were being given their chance at playing professional football. They were referred to in the news as "a piano player from Contra Costa Junior College, fullback Ollie McClay" or "a rodeo cowboy at defensive back named Nyle McFarlane" or "an art teacher and Golden Gloves' boxer, running back Gene Babb."

The Cowboys' quarterbacking activities that first game were shared by Eddie LeBaron and Don Heinrich, and Don McIlhenny had a good night rushing with a total of 101 yards. And San Francisco, as it turned out, had its hands full with a team they perhaps had taken too lightly. But the team from the Golden Gate managed to deter a last-minute drive by Dallas which might have given them a win in their maiden NFL effort. The final score was San Francisco 16, the Cowboys 10.

From there, it was back to Texas, but the Cowboys' debut would not be in Dallas. They went to San Antonio for another exhibition, this one against the Cardinals, who, for the first time, were playing under the flag of the city of St. Louis after having resided in Chicago under one name or another since 1899. (The Cardinals have the longest history of any team in professional football.) The Cardinals had a premier running back in John David Crow, and Larry Wilson was a fine defensive back, but they had little else, and they were coming off a season in which they had won only two games and finished in the cellar of the NFL Eastern Conference. Nevertheless, they managed to beat the Cowboys 20–13 that August night in Texas, leaving the Cowboys with a winless record to take back with them to their home town.

Opening night in Dallas was the annual Salesmanship Club game, an event that had become one of the city's top sports attractions since its inception back in 1950. Each year, the Salesmanship Club had sponsored a preseason professional football game at the Cotton Bowl as a fund raiser for their pet charity, a camp for underprivileged children. The game had always featured the best of the NFL, bringing to Dallas such memorable teams as the Washington Redskins led by Sammy Baugh, the Detroit Lions and Bobby Layne, the New York Giants with Frank Gifford and Charlie Conerly (and, yes, Tom Landry), a Cleveland Brown team sparkling with the likes of Otto Graham, Lou Groza, and Dante Lavelli, and the Chicago Bears with Rick Casares and Willie Galimore.

The doomed Dallas Texans had been afforded the honor of playing the game back in 1952, but they went down to defeat 21–14 when a former resident hero, Doak Walker, led the Detroit Lions and clinched victory with a touchdown pass to end Bill Swiacki in the closing minutes of the game.

It was indeed an honor for the Cowboys to make their first home-town appearance at the Salesmanship Club game. More than 40,000 fans turned out on a hot August Saturday night to watch them. Many spectators wanted to see the neophyte Cowboys, who would represent them and the state of Texas now in the NFL, but many others simply wanted to see the reigning NFL champions, who had come down from Baltimore. The Colts were truly an awesome team. Led by quarterback Johnny Unitas and peopled with such other stars as Lenny Moore, Alan Ameche, Ray Berry, Jim Parker, Gino Marchetti, and Big Daddy Lipscomb, they had brutalized their way through the Western Conference with a 9–3 record the year before and then demolished the New York Giants for the NFL crown by a score of 31–16.

The Cowboys, however, did themselves proud that night. They were even leading in the fourth quarter 10–7. But the irrespressible Unitas came back with only a minute to play and on a fourth-down-and-10-yards-to-go situation fired a 62-yard pass to Lenny Moore to snatch a victory away from the Cowboys.

During this time, the Cowboys moved their training camp to Delafield, Wisconsin, to the campus of St. John's Military Academy. Sam Blair, in his book *Dallas Cowboys, Pro or Con* (Doubleday, 1970) noted the reactions of the players to this rather lusterless facility. "It was like a medieval castle," said (linebacker) Jerry Tubbs. "Big and dreary and remote. All it needed was a moat." And Sam Blair added, "The players soon learned it was a long walk to the only tavern in town. The nearest movie was seven miles away. Gil Brandt, who had arranged for the Cowboys to train there, was hanged in effigy twice."

The change of scenery perhaps helped. The Cowboys went to Louisville, Kentucky, to face their fourth preseason opponent, the New York Giants. And they won the game 14–3. It was Don Meredith's first appearance on the field of play in a Dallas Cowboy uniform, and he contributed a 74-yard touchdown pass to Frank Clarke. (His other stats that game left a bit to be desired; he only completed 4 of 19 passes.) But along with a 73-yard bomb from Eddie LeBaron to Clarke, it was enough to give the Cowboys their first victory.

The Cowboys were quickly derailed from their winning way, however, when, the following week, they went to Pendleton, Oregon, in the Blue Mountains, to face the Los Angeles Rams. There they were devastated 49–14. The last exhibition game of the 1960 season took place up in Minneapolis against the Green Bay Packers. Vince Lombardi, who had coached the New York Giant offense while Tom Landry was coaching that team's defense, unleashed Bart Starr, Paul Hornung, Jim Taylor, and the rest of that marvelous crew that was about to become the NFL dynasty of the 1960s. But they were barely able to sneak out a 28–23 win that day, salvaged in the last five

The Organization. Clint Murchison, Jr., principal club owner since the team's inception, hired Tex Schramm in 1959 as general manager before the official franchise was granted to Dallas by the NFL, who in turn hired Gil Brandt to search out talent for the organization. They have worked together, each in his own way, since the team was formally christened back in 1960. The theme of longevity in the Cowboy organization and coaching staff is unique in the NFL and, in the view of Clint Murchison, a key factor in the team's unequaled success story.   (Dallas Cowboys)

minutes of play. It prompted Lombardi to say to Tom Landry after the game: "We made you too strong."

They hadn't. And Vince Lombardi had not really been serious when he said it. He knew the Cowboys had not been allowed to participate in the college draft that year, and he was well aware of the NFL veterans they had been restricted to choose from. He probably knew, too, that what the Cowboys had gotten had come from their own ingenuity and relentless pursuit (Meredith and Perkins) and from a few propitious trades (Eddie LeBaron and, finally, as the regular season was about to get underway and other teams were paring their rosters, end Billy Howton, an eight-year NFL veteran and two-time All-Pro— 1956 and 1957). In 1960, no one had given the Cowboys anything, but then no one in the organization had really expected any gifts.

By Saturday September 24, the opening day of the Cowboys' regular season, Tom Landry and his coaching staff had held all the tryouts. They had finished their studies and assessments of the players; there was no longer any more time to experiment. They had whittled their roster to the NFL maximum of 42 players (only 38 could suit up for a given game, however, according to NFL rules), and now they were about to begin the one season that Cowboy fans everywhere would like to forget.

Question: *Going back to the beginning, the very beginning, what were some of the most difficult things for you to face in organizing a football team from scratch?*

Tex Schramm: *It was probably one of the most exciting periods of my life, probably more exciting than Super Bowls or any of that type of thing. We were starting from scratch, unbelievable in modern times. And every day was an adventure, and that's a lot of fun. When nobody expects a hell of a lot out of you, then everything is on the up side. Everything you do is a new experience, a new thrill. That's when you really have a lot of excitement and enthusiasm. It's a stark contrast to the time you've been a success and are trying to stay a success. That becomes, to me, a much more hard working arrangement. Let's face it, it's not pleasant to be a winner; it's fun to be a winner, but when you're trying to stay up, it becomes a very nerve-chafing experience.*

4 That First Awful Season

THE COWBOYS FACED THE 1960 regular season not merely with the worries of competing against established, polished NFL teams; they had an additional burden to fret about: vying for fans with Lamar Hunt's Texans of the AFL, who were scheduled to play their home games in the same city and the same stadium.

With the Chicago Cardinals' move that year to St. Louis, it was disconcertingly clear that a city, even a large one, might not be able to accommodate two professional football teams even if they were equally entrenched, much less equally brand-new. The Cardinals couldn't hack it and moved out, and a lot of eyes were on Dallas to see just how the two new entries would fare. It was not promising. After all, Chicago had a metropolitan-area population in 1960 of about 6.75 million, while the Dallas–Fort Worth metroplex was home to only about 2.25 million people. And there was the lingering memory of the Texans of 1952, whose contests drew less than many high school games in Dallas.

The Cowboys sent out a mailing of 200,000 letters soliciting season ticket holders. As it would turn out, they would eventually sell a relatively unimpressive total of 3,165 for the year 1960. The Cowboys were also at somewhat of a disadvantage in the quest for ticket buyers. As Tex Schramm explained it to sports columnist Dave Brady of the Washington *Post:* "We suffered at first because we were committed to established, long-range ticket and public relations policies while they (the AFL Texans) tried all kinds of propaganda and ticket-selling tricks. They tied in ticket promotions with the purchases of a carton of cigarettes, a bag of potato chips, gasoline, and

so forth. Finally, they were just giving away tickets."

But Tex Schramm maintained his confidence. He said, "We have a good hard core of fans who represent a pretty good cross-section of the city. We have the Salesmanship Club, most influential in town, behind us." And because of the support of that especially affluent group, he added with a smile, "We expect to have the biggest parking problem for privately owned planes in the league, similar to the congestion that occurs when Texas University plays Oklahoma here."

Confidence notwithstanding, the headline in the sports section of one Dallas newspaper the day of the Cowboys' opener against the Pittsburgh Steelers was not about the game but instead referred to the weekend: "The Battle of the Turnstiles." Who would draw more people into the Cotton Bowl—the Cowboys and Steelers on Saturday night or the Texans and the Los Angeles Chargers on Sunday afternoon?

The Cowboys had Roy Rogers and Trigger to help entertain their fans, but the Texans had a parade, an army of clowns, and floats, and they even gave away free balloons.

In their first head-to-head encounter, the Cowboys came out a loser on both levels. They were defeated by the Steelers 35–28, while the Texans won their season opener 17–0; and whereas the Cowboys drew 30,000 into the Cotton Bowl, the Texans boasted of a crowd of 42,000.

Coach Tom Landry left the worries of filling the stadium to Tex Schramm. His focus was the Cowboys' performance on the field. And it hadn't been too bad in that first effort against a solid Steeler team. Now what lay

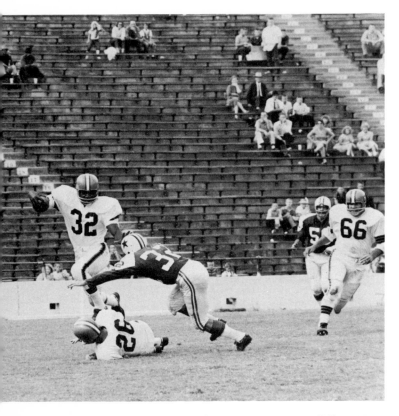

Even the Cleveland Browns' immortal Jim Brown (32) could not entice a large crowd to the Cotton Bowl in 1960. Here he vaults over teammate Ray Renfro (26) before an all but barren grandstand. Moving in for the tackle is Cowboy defensive back Tom Franckhauser (32). In the background is Cowboy linebacker Jerry Tubbs (50) and Brown Gene Hickerson (66). The Browns won, 48–7.   (Bradley Photographers)

in Sonny Jurgensen, a fine flanker named Tommy McDonald, who would one day play for the Cowboys, and an All-Pro defensive back, Tom Brookshier, who would become perhaps more nationally known later as a football TV broadcaster.

The Eagles had lost their first game of the season to the Cleveland Browns, and at that time no one was even remotely predicting that they would walk off with the NFL championship that year. No one was aware that the game in Dallas would be a kind of stepping-off stone for them, the launch of a nine-game winning streak. In fact, the Eagles would win 10 of their last 11 games and decisively seize the Eastern Conference title for 1960.

The Cowboys, however, were reluctant to let them get started. It was a game of errors. LeBaron threw five interceptions, while Van Brocklin managed only three. But the most costly for the Cowboys were the two second-half extra points that they allowed the Eagles to block because that turned out to be the winning margin. Eddie LeBaron threw two touchdown passes, one a 75 yarder to Frank Clarke and the other for 27 yards to Gene Babb, and carried 1 yard for another as the Cowboys lost 27–25.

The Cowboys' first road game of the season brought the team to Griffith Stadium in Washington, D.C., to face

ahead of them were the other 11 teams in the NFL. Because the Cowboys were an expansion team and made the Western Conference a bit lopsided with one extra team, they were to play a "swing schedule," which meant they would play each team in the NFL once rather than more of a concentration of games in their own conference.

Next to come to the Cotton Bowl were the Philadelphia Eagles, a rather tepid team the year before that had managed to end up in a tie for second place in the NFL East with a 7–5 record but well behind the 10–2 New York Giants. An aging Norm Van Brocklin was playing out his 12th and final season of pro ball at quarterback that year for the Eagles. Chuck Bednarik, the last of the great 60-minute men, was also in the twilight of his career. Both Van Brocklin and Bednarik had come up to the pros back in the same year, 1949, and had established reputations that would one day land them in the Pro Football Hall of Fame. The Eagles also had quite a back-up quarterback

---

Welcomings

After 10 straight losses in 1960, the Cowboys dueled the New York Giants to a 31–31 tie at Yankee Stadium in New York. The team flew back to Texas and was greeted at Dallas's Love Field by a party of two fans holding a sign that read: "Well Done, Cowboys."

As they walked into the airport, Tom Landry caught a glimpse of the two fans and turned to Tex Schramm, "Looks like we're making some progress," he said.

In the Dallas Morning News, Sam Blair noted two years later:

When the team plane was forced to land at Memphis with mechanical trouble following a big victory in Washington, there was a memorable moment.

It was a warm autumn evening in Dixie and once the pilot cut the engines at the far end of the ramp, there was only the sound of crickets when the door opened. Outside, sitting in a jeep, three maintenance men sat mutely.

Before the first player could deplane, however, owner Clint Murchison, Jr. rushed to the door.

"Look sharp, men!" he yelled. "This may be our biggest welcome yet."

That First Year

Here is an approximate accounting of the Dallas Cowboys' first year of operation. The total loss for the year, with all incidental and miscellaneous expenses added in, probably was close to $600,000.

Income

Ticket sales		$392,000
Television revenue		150,000
Radio rights		35,000
Program sales		3,000
	Total	$580,000

Outgo

Salaries*		$712,000
Travel		121,000
Office expenses		100,300
Communications		26,400
Training camp costs		29,000
Team equipment		27,400
	Total	$1,016,100

*Players, coaches, and scouts

The total gross income of the Dallas Cowboys in 1960—$580,000—according to Texas Business *magazine is roughly equal to the gross ticket receipts from a single game at Texas Stadium in 1980. (Revenue from TV alone in the 1980s exceeds $5 million a year.)*

Eddie LeBaron's alma mater, the Redskins. The Cowboys were 0–2, but they had comported themselves well in both games, and either one could have gone over to Dallas with a break or two. There were a lot of rough spots, especially in their pass defense, but there was still room for hope, although that began to subside that Sunday afternoon in the nation's capital.

Ralph Guglielmi, out of Notre Dame and LeBaron's back-up quarterback during the previous two seasons with the Redskins, threw for a total of 213 yards, including one touchdown. And the team rushed through the Cowboys' defense with, as one reporter put it, "impunity," to tack on another 149 yards. In addition, the Redskins' rookie place kicker, Bob Khayat, contributed four field goals.

Frank Clarke scored on a 32-yard pass from LeBaron, who also threw for the Cowboys' only other touchdown, certainly one of the shortest TD passes in NFL history. The line of scrimmage was the 2-inch line. Wide receiver Dick Bielski caught that quasi-historic toss. The final score was Washington 26, the Cowboys 14. It also would prove to be the Redskins only victory of the year.

The Cleveland Browns were a 13-point favorite when the Cowboys returned to the Cotton Bowl to host them. With Jim Brown and Bobby Mitchell running and Milt Plum passing, the Browns were an offensive powerhouse. The Cowboys and their fans discovered that quickly. At the half, the Browns led 28–0. By the end of the third quarter, it was 42–0. At the end of the game, 48–7. It was in this game that Don Meredith came off the bench to throw his first NFL regular-season pass. It was in the fourth quarter, and he actually threw six passes but completed only one of them for 6 yards.

The game with the Cleveland Browns was also the first in which a kind of shuttle quarterbacking system was used. Tom Landry had decided to use all three players—LeBaron, Heinrich, and Meredith—in an attempt to find one of them to truly take charge on the field or perhaps coerce one of them into it.

The following week, however, Eddie LeBaron stayed in for the entire game, and the Cowboys came as close to winning as any team could. They were leading the St. Louis Cardinals 10–9 with only 43 seconds left in the game, but then Cardinal place kicker Jerry Perry came on

Cowboy safety Bill Butler (22) clings to the leg of Cleveland Brown Prentice Gautt in this 1960 game at the sparsely filled Cotton Bowl. Other Cowboys moving in to finish the job are: defensive backs Gary Wisener (84) and Don Bishop (44) and linebacker Gene Cronin (85). The Cowboys lost that day to the Browns, 48–7.   (Bradley Photographers)

Running back Don McIlhenny moves out with a handoff from quarterback Don Meredith (17) against the Baltimore Colts in 1960. McIlhenny, who came to the Cowboys from the Green Bay Packers in the expansion draft, was the Cowboys' second leading rusher that year with a total of 321 yards. No. 89 on the Colts is defensive end and future Hall of Famer Gino Marchetti. (Bradley Photographers)

the field and booted an 18-yard field goal, and the Cardinals snuck off with a 2-point victory.

There was not an indulgence of hope in Dallas the following week when Weeb Ewbank brought his NFL defending champs, the Baltimore Colts, to town. The Cowboys had made a respectable showing against them in the preseason, but now the Colts, 3–2 for the season, were suddenly finding themselves in trouble in the NFL West, and everybody knew they were hungry for a win to keep their hopes for a repeat title alive.

And the Colts really did look like champs that day in the Cotton Bowl. Johnny Unitas threw only 16 passes, completing eight of them, but for a total of 270 yards, and four were for touchdowns; 68 yards to Ray Berry, 52 yards to Berry, 70 yards to Berry, and 20 yards to Lenny Moore. The final score was 45–7, the Cowboys lone score coming on a 5-yard pass from Don Heinrich to Billy Howton. The season was now half over, and the Cowboys' record was 0–6.

Now the quarterbacking shuttle went into full swing in Dallas. Don Meredith was chosen to start the next game against the Los Angeles Rams. But after a 38–13 loss there and Meredith's unhappy stats for the day (9 completions out of 28 attempts for 75 yards and three interceptions), it was decided that Don Heinrich would start the following week.

It didn't change things, however. The Cowboys went up to chilly Wisconsin to meet Vince Lombardi's Packers, who were 4–2 and very much in the race for the Western Conference title. Jim Taylor rushed for three touchdowns and a total of 121 yards that day, Bart Starr threw for another 149 yards, and Paul Hornung contributed 17 points with a touchdown, two field goals, and five extra points. The Pack won 41–7. The Cowboys' score came on Don Meredith's first NFL touchdown pass, a 14-yarder to Walt Kowalczyk in the waning moments of the game.

Two more losses followed, and the Cowboys continued to experiment with their quarterbacks as the San Fran-

1960

Preseason

Dallas	(1-5)	Opponents
10	San Francisco (22,000) @ Seattle	16
13	St. Louis (14,000) @ San Antonio	20
10	Baltimore (40,000) @ Dallas	14
14	New York (10,663) @ Louisville	3
14	Los Angeles (13,500) @ Pendleton	49
23	Green Bay (20,121) @ Minn.	28

Regular Season

		(0-11-1)	
L	28	Pittsburgh (30,000) (H)	35
L	25	Philadelphia (18,500) (H)	27
L	14	Washington (21,142)	26
L	7	Cleveland (28,500) (H)	48
L	10	St. Louis (23,128)	12
L	7	Baltimore (25,500) (H)	45
L	13	Los Angeles (16,000) (H)	38
L	7	Green Bay (32,294)	41
L	14	San Francisco (10,000) (H)	26
L	7	Chicago (39,951)	17
T	31	New York (55,033)	31
L	14	Detroit (43,272)	23
	177		369

cisco 49ers and the Chicago Bears added to their win columns. The Cowboys maintained full control of the NFL West's cellar with a record of 0–10.

Then came the season's high point. The Cowboys flew to New York to face Tom Landry's former employer, the Giants, at Yankee Stadium. Despite the Cowboys' abysmal record and the fact that the Giants, with a record of 5–3–1, were all but out of contention for their conference crown, more than 55,000 people showed up for the game, the largest crowd by far to come out to see the Cowboys play a game of football.

Eddie LeBaron started that afternoon, and he kept the Cowboys in the game during the first half. But when, in the third quarter, Pat Summerall, a place kicker in those days before his career in TV sportscasting, booted a field goal to increase the Giant lead to 24–17, most of the fans who had followed the Cowboys in the preceding weeks figured that this was undoubtedly the signal for the traditional spiral down to defeat. But they were treated to a different rendition this time.

In the fourth quarter, L. G. "Long Gone" Dupre, took a pass from LeBaron into the end zone, and with Fred Cone's extra point the Cowboys tied the score at 24 apiece. But then the Giants surged back. Lee Grosscup, who had replaced Charlie Conerly at quarterback, threw a 26-yard TD pass to end Bob Schnelker, and Pat Sum-

merall's extra point gave the Giants another 7-point lead with time running down.

The Cowboys, however, were undeterred. LeBaron mounted a steady drive down field and culminated it with an 11-yard pass into the hands of Billy Howton in the end zone. Cone converted, and the game ended in a 31–31 tie. As Dallas *Morning News* sportswriter Charles Burton observed: "The Cowboys didn't win, but they didn't lose either." It was one of the nicest things said about the Cowboys in weeks.

The following Sunday, the Cowboys played their last game of the 1960 season. It was up in Detroit where the Lions, behind the rushing of Nick Pietrosante (21 carries for 142 yards and two touchdowns) and the passing of Earl Morrall (12 of 14 for 145 yards and one touchdown) beat the Cowboys 23–14. And so ended for Dallas what

There was no Doomsday Defense in 1960, but on this play the Cowboy pass rush forces Hall of Famer Johnny Unitas to flee with the ball. Unfortunately, it was a rare moment that day; Unitas threw 4 touchdown passes to lead the Colts to a 45–7 win. No. 76 on the Cowboys is defensive end John Gonzaga, and awaiting Unitas is Tom Franckhauser (32).   (Bradley Photographers)

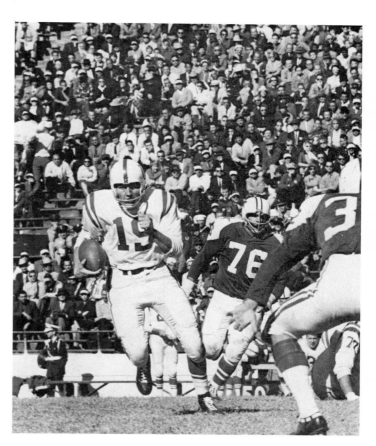

could rightfully be labeled "The Longest Season."

While all this was going on in the NFL, the Dallas Texans were struggling in the AFL. They ended up in second place in their division with a record of 8–6, and their premier running back, Abner Hayes, led the AFL in rushing with 875 yards (an average of 5.6 per carry). But the Texans were actually not any better off than the Cowboys. They, too, lost a good deal of money that year. Both Dallas teams had found that they could get people inside the stadium—maybe not throngs but at least something that could be called a crowd—but getting them to *pay* for the privilege was not nearly so easy. The Cowboys announced that their regular-season attendance was 128,500, an average of 21,417 per game. The Texans claimed a bigger turnout for their games, but it didn't really matter. At the bottom line, when the accountants were through analyzing everything, it still spelled loss in rich red ink.

Tex Schramm and Tom Landry and Clint Murchison certainly had not anticipated quite so bad a beginning; 0–11–1 was awful, the worst showing a team had made

Question: *What is the key to the Dallas success story? Why have they been able to maintain a place at the top for so many years?*

Tex Schramm: *Good people. I've got a regular spiel on this subject, but as far as our reason for continued success, there's several things—I think that you have to put professionals in the jobs. You must get the best people, put them in the jobs, and then let them do the job that they're best qualified to do. After you've got the people, if you have a problem, you try to correct the problem rather than change the people. By setting that up, the individuals— and I think this is probably one of the keys to your question—over a period of years, your people get the sense that they're there for the long run, a sense of permanency, and this enables them to make decisions not only for today but for tomorrow and on down the line.*

L. G. "Long Gone" Dupre churns out a few yards against the Baltimore Colts at the Cotton Bowl in 1960. It was one of the few positive moments that afternoon as the Cowboys were annihilated 45–7. The other Cowboys in the picture are end Fred Dugan (89) and fullback Gene Babb (33). No. 81 on the Colts is defensive end Ordell Braase. Dupre led the Cowboys in rushing that first year in the NFL with 362 yards, an average of 3.5 yards per carry.   (Bradley Photographers)

On the sidelines. Rookie quarterback Don Meredith and coach Tom Landry look grim as the Cowboys were going down to defeat at the hands of the Los Angeles Rams, 38–13, for their seventh consecutive loss of the 1960 season.   (Bradley Photographers)

Wide receiver Jim Doran was the first Dallas Cowboy to make an appearance in the Pro Bowl (for 1960). Doran led the team in pass receptions that year with 31, as well as total yardage receiving (554). He came to the Cowboys from the Detroit Lions, where he had played for the preceding nine years, via the expansion draft of 1960.   (Dallas Cowboys)

in the NFL since the war years when, in 1944, the Brooklyn Dodgers managed to go 0–10 in the Eastern Division and the wartime-caused consolidation of the Chicago Cardinals and Pittsburgh Steelers into a single team went 0–10 in the Western Division. Even the inept Dallas Texans of 1952 had at least one victory to their credit.

It had been an exciting year in the NFL, however, with Paul Hornung setting an all-time NFL scoring record of 176 points in a single season; Jim Brown of Cleveland, Jim Taylor of the Packers, and John David Crowe of the St. Louis Cardinals all rushing for more than 1,000 yards; and Ray Berry continuing to inscribe his name in the NFL record books by catching 74 passes for 1,298 yards. The age-worn Philadelphia Eagles managed to eke out a victory over the fast-rising Green Bay Packers in one of the more exciting NFL championships in some time. The final score was 17–13, with the Eagles stopping the Packers only 9 yards from the goal line as time ran out.

For the Cowboys, however, there were not a lot of superlatives to talk about. L. G. Dupre led the team in

rushing with a total of 362 yards (3.5 average per carry). The passing of LeBaron, Meredith, and Heinrich produced completion percentages of only 49, 43, and 38, respectively. Jim Doran caught the most passes (31) for a total of 554 yards, and became the first Cowboy to be invited to play in the Pro Bowl.

There were some players, however, whom Tom Landry was looking forward to seeing back in 1961. Jerry Tubbs, filling in after Jack Patera was injured, had proved to be a fine linebacker. Frank Clarke had shown promise as a clutch receiver, and Jim Doran and Billy Howton certainly had talent in that aspect of the game. Long Gone Dupre could run. The quarterback situation was still an enormous question mark. Don Perkins, however, would be well for the next season. And there was the college draft coming up. There were obviously going to be some changes in player personnel, but there would not be the uncertainty that came with never having played in the NFL before. And now they could enter the new season at least knowing that there was nowhere to go but up.

5 Building But Losing

As the year 1961 got underway, the city of Los Angeles was forced to admit that it could not support two professional football teams, and the AFL Chargers decided that they would move south to San Diego. That left only Dallas and New York with two teams within the same city limits, and there was a cloud of foreboding floating over both those cities.

In Dallas, the Texans challenged the Cowboys to face each other in a charity game at the Cotton Bowl. The idea garnered a lot of publicity but little else. For all practical purposes, the Cowboys ignored it and concerned themselves with other issues—like the roster, the building process.

The first draft that the Cowboys were eligible for had actually been held in late December 1960. The Cowboys had traded their first-round choice in that draft to the Redskins for Eddie LeBaron. But after the draft got started, Tex Schramm was able to do a little finagling on his own that would bring the Cowboys a pick in the first round. The Cleveland Browns, who had a choice down near the bottom of that round, discovered at the last minute that the player they wanted most they could not get; he had already signed with an AFL team. Schramm, on the other hand, was very much aware that the first choice he and Gil Brandt wanted was still available in the NFL and had not been signed by an AFL team. So he offered the Browns an on-the-spot deal. They could have a veteran tackle, Paul Dickson, and—more important—their first round draft choice the following year. Memories of the Cowboys' 0–11–1 record of 1960 and visions of how high up in the draft their first choice might be had

to dance in the minds of Cleveland officials. So they agreed. The Cowboys then made their first selection in the college draft and took a defensive end from Texas Christian by the name of Bob Lilly. It perhaps says something about the Cowboys' acumen in acquiring talent that their first choice would also become the first Dallas Cowboy to be enshrined in the Pro Football Hall of Fame.

The Cowboys had the first choice in the second round, picking a highly regarded linebacker from Texas Tech, E. J. Holub. But they would lose out here in the NFL-AFL signing war when Holub would choose the rival-league Texans.

Gil Brandt was at work on other fronts as well. He had found a free agent, Amos Marsh, who had played a little football and was a nationally ranked sprinter at Oregon State, and he recommended him to Tom Landry as a running back. Another free agent was defensive tackle Ken Frost from the University of Tennessee. There were a few trades, too, the most notable of which brought linebacker Chuck Howley from the Chicago Bears and defensive back Dicky Moegle from the Pittsburgh Steelers. Moegle had made national headlines when, as a defensive back for Rice, he was racing along the sideline for a touchdown in the waning minutes of the 1954 Cotton Bowl game against Alabama when a frustrated player raced from the Alabama bench on to the field to tackle him. (Moegle was awarded the TD, anyway, and Rice won the game 28–6.)

There was some rearranging in the NFL for the 1961 season. The Minnesota Vikings had formally joined the league now and were berthed in the Western Conference.

The Cowboys moved to the NFL East, joining the New York Giants, Philadelphia Eagles, Cleveland Browns, St. Louis Cardinals, Pittsburgh Steelers, and Washington Redskins. And the number of regular-season games was increased from 12 to 14. The age of NFL TV was also ready to break out of its embryonic state. NFL Commissioner Pete Rozelle persuaded the U.S. Congress to enact a piece of legislation that would exempt the NFL's package TV arrangement with CBS from antitrust laws.

The Cowboys of 1961 appeared to be a much more solid team than that of the preceding year, at least on paper. Don Perkins's foot seemed to have healed nicely, and Amos Marsh was looking awfully good as his tandem running back. Bill Howton, the second leading receiver at that time in NFL history behind the immortal Don Hutson, signed a three-year contract. Bob Lilly offered great hope for the defensive line. In the defensive backfield, there was a solid pair in Don Bishop and Tom Franckhauser, aided now by newcomers Moegle and Jimmy Harris. But the quarterback situation was still about as settled as dust in the Texas panhandle.

The remembrance of things past did not beleaguer those at Cowboy headquarters; in fact, there was a keen sense of anticipation. Owner Clint Murchison, known for an occasional practical joke, listed his predictions for the coming season. He felt the Cowboys would win eight to ten games, he told a group of reporters, and then ignored their arched eyebrows and the strange murmurs and went on to further prognosticate that there would be a crowd of 55,000 at the Cotton Bowl in December to see the Cleveland Browns play the Cowboys in a game that would decide the championship of the Eastern Conference.

The Cowboys chose a different site for their 1961 training camp, the campus of St. Olaf's College up in Northfield, Minnesota—the third summer locale in two years.

As the newcomers filtered in among the veterans, Eddie LeBaron was both surprised and delighted to discover that he was no longer the shortest man on the team. The 5 foot 7 inch LeBaron virtually towered over Cleveland "Pussyfoot" Jones, who stood 5 feet 4 inches in his football cleats. The "midget" wide receiver, as some sportswriters took to calling him, was a speedster with good hands and was there for a legitimate tryout. When Coach Tom Landry first saw him, he said, "I cringe to think what

Don Perkins (43) races wide for substantial yardage in the first battle between the two expansion teams of 1960–1961. The Cowboys beat the Minnesota Vikings, 21–7, their second consecutive victory of the 1961 season (as well as their second victory ever). It was only Perkins's second regular-season appearance in a Cowboy uniform but his first 100-plus–yard game. No. 75 on the Cowboys is tackle Bob Fry. Viking defenders are Don Joyce (83) and Ed Culpepper (71).   (Bradley Photographers)

might happen if a guy like Big Daddy Lipscomb barrels into that little fellow." (Pussyfoot made it all the way into the exhibition season but was a victim of the last roster cut.)

It was announced that there would be no price increase in tickets for 1961—still $4.60 for the best seat in the Cotton Bowl, although the season ticket would rise slightly because of the additional game.

The preseason for the Cowboys began at Sioux Falls, South Dakota, where 4,954 spectators paid to watch the Minnesota Vikings, under rookie head coach Norm Van Brocklin, play their first game ever. The Cowboys won it handily 38–13.

For the Cowboys, the preseason was a time for trial and error, experimentation, roster pruning, and the molding of a playing unit. The Cowboys lost their home exhibition opener to Green Bay, fell to the New York Giants out in Albuquerque, New Mexico, and then they surprised, or perhaps astonished, the always awesome Baltimore Colts by brutalizing them 35–24 at Norman, Oklahoma. They ended the preseason with a loss to the San Francisco 49ers.

For the Dallas Cowboys, the 1961 regular season would again begin with a visit from the Pittsburgh Steelers. Bobby Layne, 34 now, was still their quarterback, Ernie Stautner, 36, was still in the defensive line, and John Henry Johnson and Tom Tracy still handled most of the rushing chores.

The Cowboys took the lead early on a fancy third-down-and-one play where Don Meredith faked a handoff, then threw to Frank Clarke for a 44-yard touchdown. Allen Green, who had replaced the retired Fred Cone as place kicker, then booted his first point as a Dallas Cowboy.

Two second-quarter Steeler touchdowns, however, sent the Cowboys into their dressing room at the half trailing 14–10. (Green added a 15-yard field goal near the end of the half.)

Eddie LeBaron made his appearance early in the second half, and on his first play dazzled the 23,500 fans at the Cotton Bowl with a little flea flicker. He handed the ball to Amos Marsh, who lateraled it back to him, and LeBaron tossed a 45-yard touchdown pass to Billy Howton. Then Meredith returned, making it clear that the quarterback shuttle service was back in business. The Steelers came right back with a field goal and a touchdown (scored on the interception of a Meredith pass) and with less than one minute to play in the game, the Cowboys were trailing 24–17. It looked as if the previous year was happening all over again. But someone forgot to tell that to the Cowboys down on the field—they certainly forgot to inform Eddie LeBaron, who had now replaced Meredith at quarterback.

Sam Baker

Place kicker, punter, and fabled man about town, Loris Hoskins Baker, better known simply as Sam, spent only 2 of his 15 years in the NFL with the Dallas Cowboys, but while he was there, he kept all the members of the sports media in constant supply of anecdotes and the team's management and coaching staff, to put it delicately, off balance.

One day, he was explaining to a sportswriter how he had come to be traded by the Washington Redskins. "We had bad words [referring to team owner George Preston Marshall]. Only time in five years, a few bad words and the next day he traded me." What were the bad words, the newsman asked. "I asked him for more money."

In his first Cowboy training camp up on the Michigan peninsula in the summer of 1962, Baker was filling in during a scrimmage at fullback and had the assignment on one play to block tackle Bob Lilly. Baker, the kicker, surprised everyone with his ardor in carrying out the assignment, and the collision with the massive tackle could be heard all the way across the field. Those who turned saw Baker in a heap on the ground.

Players and coaches, including Bob Lilly, gathered around the motionless body. Slowly, Baker began to move. Looking up through a dense fog, he tried to focus on those staring down at him. The haze clearing, his eyes found Bob Lilly, and he forced a weak smile and said, "You'll be okay, Lilly, just shake it off."

Needless to say, the personalities of Sam Baker and Tom Landry were as diverse as their approaches to life. The Cowboys, even though they would be without an experienced kicker, traded Sam Baker to the Philadelphia Eagles before the '64 season for end Tommy McDonald.

In 1967, Tom Landry and his staff were pegged to coach the NFL East in the Pro Bowl game. As the squad was being put together, the story goes, Landry asked one of his assistants, "Who was the best kicker in the conference last year?" The assistant thumbed through his notes, then said, "Sam Baker of the Eagles." Landry looked up, studied the assistant for a moment, then asked, "Who was second best?"

For all his wit, antics, and hell raising off the field, however, Sam Baker was one of the game's finest kickers. In 15 years, he kicked 179 field goals and 428 extra points. That, along with two touchdowns he scored, gave him a total of 977 career points, to rank him among the top ten scorers in the history of the game. His punting average with the Cowboys (45.1 yds) is still a team record.

1961

Preseason

Dallas	(2-3)	Opponents
38	Minnesota (4,954) @ Sioux Falls	13
7	Green Bay (30,000) @ Dallas	30
10	N.Y. (21,500) @ Albuquerque	28
35	Baltimore (19,000) @ Norman	24
10	S. F. (22,130) @ Sacramento	24

Regular Season

		(4-9-1)	
W	27	Pittsburgh (23,500) (H)	24
W	21	Minnesota (20,500) (H)	7
L	7	Cleveland (43,638)	25
W	28	Minnesota (33,070)	0
L	10	New York (41,500) (H)	31
L	7	Philadelphia (25,000) (H)	43
W	17	New York (60,254)	16
L	17	St. Louis (20,500) (H)	31
L	7	Pittsburgh (17,519)	37
T	28	Washington (17,500) (H)	28
L	13	Philadelphia (60,127)	35
L	17	Cleveland (23,500) (H)	38
L	13	St. Louis (15,384)	31
L	24	Washington (21,451)	34
	236		380

From his own 25-yard line, LeBaron guided a drive down field, climaxing it with a 17-yard pass to end Dick Bielski for a touchdown. Green's extra point tied the game. Bobby Layne came right back, intent on leading the Steelers into field-goal range. But as the clock wound down to the final seconds, Cowboy linebacker Jerry Tubbs ended the Steelers' hopes by snatching a Layne pass at the Cowboy 38. There were only ten seconds left.

LeBaron came back and lofted a 41-yard bomb to Howton, who grabbed it and deftly stepped out of bounds with a mere second left on the clock. A nervous Allen Green trotted out. The ball was snapped to LeBaron, who put it down, and Green drilled a field goal through the goal posts as the gun went off. As Sam Blair wrote in the Dallas *Morning News* the next day: "Pittsburgh's salty Steelers stormed into the Cotton Bowl Sunday and silenced the Cowboy Cannon, Don Meredith, but they found out too late that they had no defense for a little pistol named Eddie LeBaron." And the Dallas Cowboys, entering their second year of life in the NFL, had posted the first regular-season victory in their history.

The Minnesota Vikings came to Dallas next. They were not the same team now that had faced the Cowboys early in the exhibition season. They were surprisingly well rounded for a team just beginning in the league. They had even begun the season with a startling win the week be-

fore over the Chicago Bears, 37–13. They had a 21-year-old rookie at quarterback, Fran Tarkenton, fresh from the University of Georgia, and a now somewhat aged but still threatening running back in Hugh McElhenny, a powerful fullback in Mel Triplett, and a defensive end playing the first of 20 seasons as a Viking, Jim Marshall.

The meeting of the two expansion teams drew only 20,500 people into the Cotton Bowl, who watched the Cowboys control the game and win easily, 21–7. Despite the theatrics of Eddie LeBaron the week before, Don Meredith played most of the game, and he had one of his finest days yet (12 of 22 for 163 yards and one touchdown). And Don Perkins proved clearly that his foot was as good as new by becoming the first Cowboy ever to rush for more than 100 yards in a game (108 on 17 carries). The winless Cowboys of 1960 were undefeated and tied with the Philadelphia Eagles, the reigning NFL champion, at the top of the Eastern Conference.

The following week, however, they lost to Cleveland 25–7. But the Eagles lost that week too, and the Cowboys stayed in a tie for the lead the next week by again stunning the Minnesota Vikings, this time by a score of 28–0. With a record of 3–1, they were in a four-way tie for first place in the NFL East (with Philadelphia, Cleveland, and New York). It was exhilarating.

The Cowboys came back to Dallas and a record-breaking crowd of 41,500 at the Cotton Bowl to play the New

Cowboy L. G. Dupre is tripped up by tackle Don Lawrence (78) of the Washington Redskins in a game that was played to a 28–28 tie at the Cotton Bowl in 1961. This was Long Gone Dupre's last year in the NFL.   (Bradley Photographers)

1962

Preseason

Dallas	(0–5)	Opponent
7	Green Bay (54,500) @ Dallas	31
24	Detroit (77,683) @ Cleveland	35
10	Baltimore (14,000) @ Roanoke	24
7	S. F. (20,000) @ Sacramento	26
26	Minnesota (12,500) @ Atlanta	45

Regular Season

		(5–8–1)	
T	35	Washington (15,730) (H)	35
L	28	Pittsburgh (19,478) (H)	30
W	27	Los Angeles (26,907)	17
L	10	Cleveland (44,040)	19
W	41	Philadelphia (18,645) (H)	19
W	42	Pittsburgh (23,106)	27
L	24	St. Louis (16,027) (H)	28
W	38	Washington (49,888)	10
L	10	New York (45,668) (H)	41
L	33	Chicago (12,692) (H)	34
L	14	Philadelphia (58,070)	28
W	45	Cleveland (24,226) (H)	21
L	20	St. Louis (14,102)	52
L	31	New York (62,694)	41
	398		402

The defense had allowed 380 points, the third worst in the NFL after Minnesota (407) and Washington (392).

There were some less than uplifting moments, at least from a Dallas rooter's point of view: Erich Barnes of the New York Giants picking off a LeBaron pass in the end zone and racing 102 yards with it for a touchdown and in the process tying the NFL record for longest interception return; Eddie LeBaron having had five passes intercepted in one game against the Cardinals; the series of injuries to plague Don Meredith (concussion, sore arm, shoulder); Sonny Jurgensen of the Eagles passing for 351 yards and five touchdowns one afternoon; Dick James of the Washington Redskins earning 146 of his full-season total of 374 rushing yards in one game against the Cowboys and scoring four TDs as well.

But there were some bright spots, too. Eddie LeBaron and Don Meredith both improved their passing performances, with completion percentages raised respectively

Bob Lilly was the Cowboys' first draft choice ever and would go on to become the first Cowboy to be enshrined in the Pro Football Hall of Fame. A unanimous-choice All-American from Texas Christian, he was elected to the NFL All-Rookie team in 1961 as a defensive end. But it would be at defensive tackle that he would prove to be one of the game's all-time greats. (Pro Football Hall of Fame)

York Giants. It was by far the largest crowd that the Cowboys had been able to attract to a home game (the biggest, in fact, since their very first game in 1960 when 30,000 showed). But the dream shattered before their collective eyes. The Giants, with a diversified and sustained offense, clobbered the Cowboys 31–10. The following week, the Eagles did the same thing before the same home-town fans, only they did it with a little more gusto; the final score was 43–7 this time.

The Cowboys were never in the title race again that year. They managed an impressive win over the Giants, 17–16, and played a lowly Washington Redskins team to a tie, but the remainder of their games were sheer disappointments. In the second half of the season, the Cowboys' record was a dismal 0–6–1.

When the 1961 season was over, the Cowboys found themselves in sixth place in the NFL East with a record of 4–9–1, ahead of the Washington Redskins, who managed to only win one and tie one of their 14 games that year, both of those highlights unhappily registered against the Dallas Cowboys.

The year 1961 was certainly an improvement over the one that had preceded it, but it was indeed a letdown after the exceptionally hopeful beginning. The Cowboys, as it turned out, scored a total of only 236 points, second lowest in the entire NFL behind the Redskins' woeful 174.

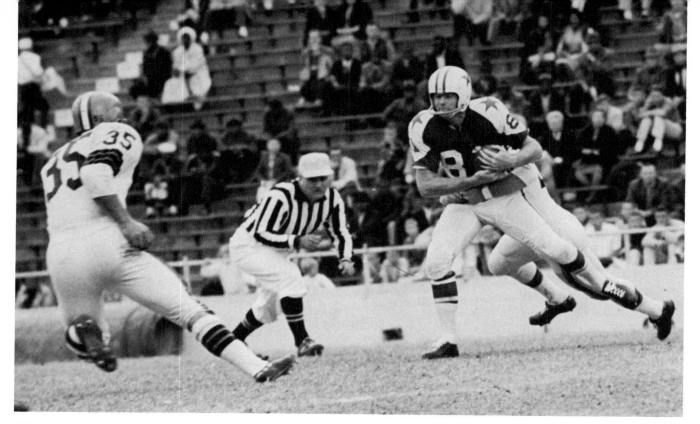

Billy Howton grabs one of his 56 catches for 1961 against the Cleveland Browns. Howton, one of the game's great receivers, came to the Cowboys in a trade that year and would lead the club in pass receptions for both 1961 and 1962. No. 35 on the Browns is Galen Fiss.   (Bradley Photographers)

to 51% and 52%. Between the two of them, they contributed a total passing yardage of 2,902 and 23 aerial touchdowns. Don Perkins had a sterling rookie year, rushing for 815 yards on 200 carries (4.1 average), and both Billy Howton and Frank Clarke had fine years receiving the passes thrown by LeBaron and Meredith. (Howton caught 56 for 785 yards and Clarke 41 for 919 yards, and Clarke's average gain of 22.2 yards was the NFL high for 1961.)

The year 1962 was historic in its own way in that it brought TV full swing to the NFL. Professional football would never be quite the same again. The league signed a two-year contract for more than $9 million with CBS to broadcast the games; as a result, each team would now receive an additional revenue of approximately $320,000 a year (nice then but paltry in terms of the $5 million plus per year that TV brings to each team in the 1980s). For Dallas, it was a special boon because they had lost money during the two previous years of their existence. As Commissioner Pete Rozelle put it: "The equal distribution of TV income will aid us appreciably in preserving a balanced league. It will enable teams like Dallas and Minnesota, both of which have made spectacular strides in their short existence, to compete on an even stronger level with the established clubs." It would take a few more years to illustrate just how correct the commissioner was, but

the frequent, future trips to the postseason playoffs and the Super Bowl for both the Cowboys and the Vikings would amply prove the veracity of his statement.

The NFL also introduced a new rule against grabbing another player's face mask. And a new five-year contract for Pete Rozelle was drawn up and signed (the same for the AFL's Joe Foss). The formal ground-breaking ceremony for the Pro Football Hall of Fame in Canton, Ohio, was held. And the NFL still felt comfortably secure against the competition mounted by the AFL even though there was growing concern about the talent the new league had lured away.

There were quite a few new faces with the Cowboys in 1962. The draft produced George Andrie, a huge defensive end from Marquette University (who had not played his senior year, however, when the school suddenly dropped intercollegiate football), and a future pick, an almost equally enormous player who happened to be a quarterback, Sonny Gibbs, who stood 6 feet 7 inches and weighed in excess of 225 as a junior at Texas Christian.

Gil Brandt was also at work, as usual, rounding up free agents, and it was in 1962 that he introduced what was to become a trademark of his—culling pro football players from other sports. He signed an All-American basketball player from Utah State, Cornell Green, and Mike Gaechter, a sprinter (9.5 in the 100-yard dash) from the University of Oregon. Brandt also located a tight end

Dickie Moegle played out his last year as a pro with the Cowboys in 1961. A running back and defensive back, Moegle had made the Pro Bowl once (1955) during his 6 years in the NFL (5 with the San Francisco 49ers and 1 with the Steelers). But he was perhaps better known as the Rice back racing down the sideline for a touchdown in the 1954 Cotton Bowl when Alabama's Tommy Lewis leaped from the bench, ran onto the field, and tackled him.   (Dallas Cowboys)

press: "In 1960, we had passing, but no running. In 1961, we got the runners—Don Perkins, Amos Marsh, and J. W. Lockett—but our offensive line lacked size and consistency. Now, with the right side of our offensive line entirely rebuilt, we have more balance." He was cautiously optimistic.

There was a shuffle in his coaching staff; perhaps house cleaning is a more accurate description. Ermal Allen, a one-time quarterback at the University of Kentucky and later an assistant coach at that school, first to Paul "Bear" Bryant (1948–1953) and then to Blanton Collier (1954–1961), was hired as offensive backfield coach. Dick Nolan, only 30 that year, who had played under Landry with the

George Andrie did not even play football his senior year in college because Marquette, the school he was attending, had dropped the sport that year. Still, he did not escape the Cowboys' eye for talent and was tabbed in the sixth round of the 1962 draft. Andrie quickly became a mainstay at defensive end, and during his 11-year Cowboy career went to the Pro Bowl four times.   (Dallas Cowboys)

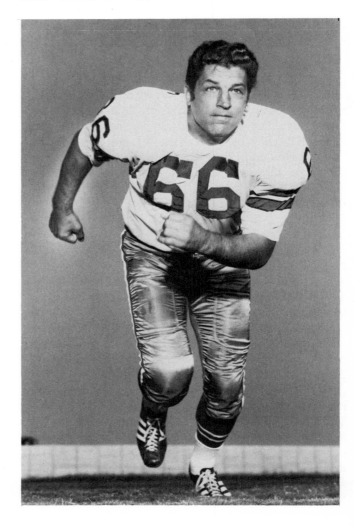

named Pettis Norman from a school called Johnson C. Smith University in Charlotte, North Carolina. Another new name on the roster was 30-year-old Sam Baker, who was acquired from the Cleveland Browns to handle the Cowboys' kicking chores (place kicking and punting). Baker had been around the league since 1953, first with the Washington Redskins, but had spent the last two years at Cleveland. His name and his reputation as a roisterer were also well known in the lore of off-the-field antics.

The Cowboys selected a new training camp for 1962, one about as far north as a person can get and still be within the continental United States. It was on the campus of gelid little Northern Michigan College, just below the shores of Lake Superior. Everyone who attended that camp, despite the fact that it was midsummer, truly believed they had been duped and were, in fact, working out somewhere well above the Arctic Circle.

As the season approached, Coach Tom Landry told the

The Cheerleaders, circa 1961–1962. (Bradley Photographers)

Giants and was in a way a protégé, retired from playing the game and was signed on to tutor the defensive backs. (He would later become head coach of the San Francisco 49ers and afterward the New Orleans Saints.) The offensive line would now come under the care of Jim Myers, who had been head coach at Iowa State and most recently at Texas A & M. Brad Ecklund switched over to coach the defensive line, but Babe Dimancheff quit, and Tom Dahms became a Cowboys scout.

If there were glimmers of hope in the early summer, the preseason did a lot to stanch those feelings. The Cowboys opened with the Salesmanship Club game on a broiling August evening before 54,500 fans, the Cowboys' biggest home crowd ever, entertaining the NFL defending champions, the Green Bay Packers. As Bud Shrake, columnist for the Dallas *Morning News* put it:

"In several ways that was really a remarkable crowd that staggered gasping into the Cotton Bowl . . . coats off and ties yanked askew as if the customers were walking in from a train that had broken down in the desert outside Needles, California . . . The press box was as comfortable and airy as a closet. The usual press box group, of which a few were actually working, fled outside into the comparative comfort of the announced 94 degrees. Of those who sat from start to finish in their glass tank, several were led

away babbling, eyes sunken, hair white, begging for refreshment."

No telling how hot it was down on the field, but it could be safely said that it was stifling for the Cowboys. The Packers, with that incredible cast, which included Bart Starr, Jim Taylor, Paul Hornung, Max McGee, Boyd Dowler, Herb Adderley, Ray Nitschke, Jerry Kramer, Jim Ringo, Willie Davis, and Forrest Gregg, among others, smothered the Cowboys 31–7.

It would not get any better. The Cowboys lost the four subsequent preseason games as well.

One of those preseason games was a rather unique trial, brainchild of the NFL schedulers. When the Cowboys played Detroit at Cleveland, it was one-half of an NFL double-header—the first ever—and it attracted a crowd of 77,683 into Cleveland Stadium. On the same bill was a game between the Cleveland Browns and the Pittsburgh Steelers.

The regular-season opener featured the Washington Redskins. The day was hot in Dallas, perhaps not as oppresive as the night of the Salesmanship Club game but enough so to induce a sluggishness in most human beings. Yet the Cowboys managed to unleash the highest scoring effort of their short history that day—35 points. Unfortunately, the Redskins matched them point for point, and when Sam Baker missed a field goal with only seconds remaining, they had to settle for a 35–35 tie. Still the Cowboys' offensive stats were impressive. Don Perkins rushed for 83 yards and Amos Marsh for 55. Eddie LeBaron threw 16 passes, 13 of which he completed for 176 yards, including one touchdown, and Don Meredith passed for another 175 yards and two TDs. Frank Clarke virtually rewrote the Cowboys record book for pass receptions, grabbing ten that day for 241 yards and three touchdowns (58, 11, and 55 yards, respectively).

The Cowboys also introduced a new version of their quarterback shuttle that day. It became what members of the press began calling the "quarterback messenger system." Instead of rotating linemen or an end to bring in a new play each down, Tom Landry decided to rotate his two shuttling quarterbacks, Eddie LeBaron and Don Meredith. "We didn't have two of anything but quarterbacks," he told Tex Maule, columnist for *Sports Illustrated.* "So we had to alternate LeBaron and Meredith. If we had an extra guard or end I probably would have used the same system as Paul Brown. But all we could spare

was an extra quarterback."

The Cowboys continued to show some offensive spunk the following week, scoring 28 points, but they could not contain the old pro Bobby Layne, and the Pittsburgh Steelers sent Dallas down to defeat 30–28.

When they went out to Los Angeles the next week to face the Rams, who were playing under the tutelage of their one-time legendary quarterback, Bob Waterfield, the Cowboys tallied their first win of 1962, 27–17. Then a loss to the Browns followed and a return to the Cotton Bowl. But it was not a quiet return; rather, it was a flash of glory, the most dazzling three hours perhaps in the brief Dallas history.

The Philadelphia Eagles were the team they faced—10 wins, 4 losses the year before and edged out of the NFL East title by only half a game by the 10–3–1 New York Giants. The Cowboys greeted the Eagles, however, as they had greeted few other teams in the past two and a half years. They virtually annihilated them, 41–19, setting a new record for most points scored in a game (the previous record having lasted only a month). And it was a day of

Second-year man Bob Lilly (74) moves in to tackle Redskin end Bill Anderson in the 1962 regular-season opener at the Cotton Bowl. Fewer than 16,000 fans were there that day to watch a wide-open game which finally ended in a 35–35 tie. Other Cowboys in the picture are linebacker Mike Dowdle (30) and end George Andrie (66).   (Pro Football Hall of Fame)

spectacular moments. Frank Clarke streaked for one TD on a 57-yard pass play from Don Meredith. Amos Marsh raced with a kickoff return 101 yards for another touchdown. Then rookie defensive back Mike Gaechter raced 100 yards with an interception for the final TD of the day. The Cowboys had never before scored on anything but a play from scrimmage.

Tom Landry, who had expressed sincere faith in his offense before the season, could now sit back and take some pleasure in knowing he had been right. At that point in the season, the Cowboys had racked up a total of 141 points (an average of 28.2 per game). In the preceding two seasons, 1960 and 1961, during the same period of time, they had scored only 84 points (a 16.8 average) and 93 (an 18.6 average), respectively. And the 354 yards that the Cowboys gained that Sunday brought their season total to 1,830 in five games, second in the NFL only to the mighty Packers, who had gained 1,876 yards.

Sportswriters around the country were now beginning to take a somewhat different view of the suddenly volatile Cowboys. Tex Maule, for example, in *Sports Illustrated*

Almost obscured by high-flying Cowboy George Andrie (66), Steeler quarterback Bobby Layne (22) looks toward receivers John Powers (88) and Dick Hoak (42) in this 1962 game at Dallas. Cowboy pass defenders are Don Bishop (44) and Chuck Howley (54). The Cowboys dropped a squeaker that day, 30–28, as Layne threw for two touchdowns. No. 51 on the Steelers is Buzz Nutter.   (Bradley Photographers)

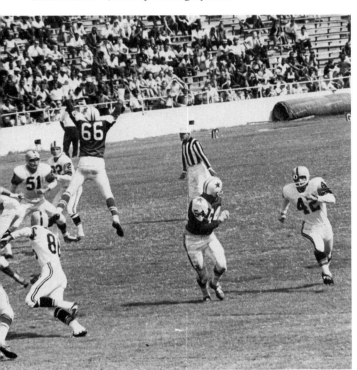

Dick Nolan came to the Cowboys as an assistant coach in 1962, but a rash of injuries forced him into a Cowboy uniform to fill a role in their defensive backfield. Earlier, he had played under Tom Landry's tutelage for four years at the New York Giants (1954–1957). Nolan would spend his coaching apprenticeship as an assistant with the Cowboys and would go on to become the head coach of the San Francisco 49ers (1968–1975) and the New Orleans Saints (1978–1980).   (Dallas Cowboys)

Question: *Who do you personally feel were your most exciting finds?*

Gil Brandt: *I think there are many that were very exciting. Roger Staubach, for example. Taking a chance on him as a red shirt, knowing that he had extra time to do after he graduated in the form of a military commitment, was a gamble, but it paid off. Then there was Calvin Hill from Yale, who only played in the Ivy League, and Cornell Green, who was signed as a free agent, and Drew Pearson, the same, who has since broken all kinds of Cowboy records. I could go on and on with that question. It's just that there are so many—great players from small schools like Jethro Pugh from Elizabeth City Teacher's College and Rayfield Wright from Fort Valley State, who was an All-Pro tackle for many years, and Cliff Harris from Ouachita Baptist. We found them from all over.*

Sam Baker boots a 36-yard field goal for the Cowboys against the Chicago Bears in 1962. Only 12,642 people showed up at the Cotton Bowl that day, the second smallest crowd in Cowboy history, and they were disillusioned watching the Bears snatch a last-minute win, 34–33. Baker, a notorious reveler as well as the Cowboys' all-time leading punter and one of the game's finest place-kickers, would remain under the Cowboy regimen for only two years.   (Bradley Photographers)

Amos Marsh explodes through a big hole in the Cleveland Brown line when the two teams met at the Cotton Bowl in 1962. In one of their most impressive showings of that season, the Cowboys won 45–21, and Marsh picked up 117 yards rushing, his best day ever as a Cowboy. In the background is Cowboy Eddie LeBaron (14). The Browns in the picture are Bernie Parrish (30), Vince Costello (50), and Bill Glass (80).   (Bradley Photographers)

wrote this way: "The extraordinary Dallas Cowboys, playing only their third season in the National Football League and depending largely on other teams' rejects, free agents, and a few draft choices, have suddenly developed into a potent NFL power." He referred to two factors for their success: "a radical departure from football custom (the quarterback messenger system) . . . and a scouting system that finds and utilizes talents in players others have long since given up on."

The following week, the Dallas offense went one point further to establish still another team scoring record as they romped over the Pittsburgh Steelers, 42–27. In that game, Eddie LeBaron set a Cowboy record, one that he still shares a part of today; he threw five touchdown passes (three to Frank Clarke, one to Billy Howton, and one to tight end Lee Folkins).

A loss the next week to the St. Louis Cardinals left the Cowboys at midseason with a record of 3–3–1. The explosive Cowboys were for the first time considered a threat in the conference, and the Giants, Browns, and Redskins, who had slightly better records at that point in the season, were not taking them lightly.

The second half of the 1962 season, however, could be termed a radical recession. The Cowboys won only two games, losing four others decisively (the Cardinals ran up a total of 52 points against them, the most any Cowboy defense had ever allowed) and dropping a squeaker to the Chicago Bears on a field goal with 31 seconds left in the game (Bears 34, Cowboys 33). When the season ended, the Cowboys were 5–8–1, in fifth place in the seven-team Eastern Conference.

Vince Lombardi's Green Bay Packers won the NFL championship that year for the second time in a row. Jim Taylor of the Pack finally dislodged Cleveland's Jim Brown from the rushing title, which he had claimed during the past five seasons. And some legendary names left the game when the season was over. Bobby Layne and Chuck Bednarik retired, and Coach Paul Brown was fired by Cleveland owner Art Modell.

For the Cowboys, the season was another, if short, step forward, and the potential for the next year was very real,

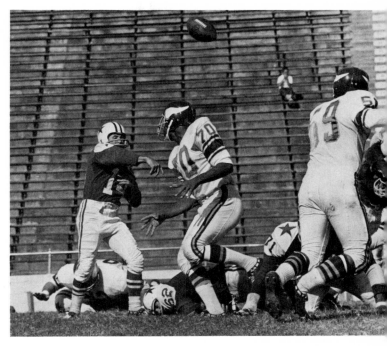

The solitary fan in the stands watching Eddie LeBaron unload this pass against the Minnesota Vikings testifies to the loneliness of the ticket-takers at the Cotton Bowl turnstiles in 1961. LeBaron handled the majority of quarterbacking chores that year, although Dandy Don Meredith would also register a good amount of playing time at that position. (Bradley Photographers)

almost everyone felt. Frank Clarke had turned into a league-wide respected flanker, leading the NFL in touchdown receptions (14) and in average yards gained per catch (22.4). He also became the first Cowboy to gain over 1,000 yards, receiving (1,043). Don Perkins rushed for 945 yards, fifth highest in the NFL, and became the first Cowboy to be named an All-Pro (and he represented the Cowboys in the Pro Bowl). Fullback Amos Marsh contributed another 802 yards rushing, and his average carry of 5.6 yards was the highest in the league. At the box office, it was not so encouraging. Attendance, now counted at the turnstiles, showed that about 20,000 less fans showed up at the Cotton Bowl in 1962 than had been estimated in 1961.

In the still-fledgling AFL, the Cowboys neighborhood rival, the Texans, under Coach Hank Stram, the expert quarterbacking of Len Dawson (189 of 310 for 2,759 yards and 29 touchdowns), and the brilliant running of Abner Haynes (1,049 yards rushing), took the AFL title. Even so, they still lost money and drew only a handful more spectators to the Cotton Bowl than the Cowboys. Even the glamour of a championship did not provide an edge to the Texans in the war for the city of Dallas.

And that war was just about to end.

6 Still Building, Still Losing

THE WORD LEAKED OUT EARLY IN 1963. The Texans were planning to move out of Dallas. Three years of financial woe and the fact that even an AFL championship couldn't bring them close to earning a profit prompted Lamar Hunt's sense of business acumen to take charge.

The town, as it might have been said in old-time Texas saloon talk, was not big enough for both of them. Hunt had talked it over with Clint Murchison and Tex Schramm, and he had come away convinced that the Cowboys were not ready to depart, so that left him really only one alternative. When the fans of the Texans got wind of Hunt's decision, they rose up in a show of both pique and support, the latter seemingly far more visible than it had been at the box office of the Cotton Bowl. The fans forced a city council meeting to discuss the pending move and try to come up with a way to keep the Texans in Dallas. Pleas were made directly to the mayor; petitions were circulated, signed, and presented to the city's legislative body; a march was held on city hall. The Texan fans even organized themselves and hired an attorney and a public relations man. It was to no avail, however.

On May 22, 1963, Hunt formally announced that the Dallas Texans would relocate in Kansas City, Missouri. And because the Kansas City Texans seemed a rather inappropriate name, they would henceforth be known as the Chiefs.

The Cowboys had sole claim now to the city of Dallas, and although that did not guarantee any larger crowds for their games at the Cotton Bowl, it seemed to the Cowboys' management a positive step in that direction.

In New York, there was NFL-AFL trouble, too, and the owner of the AFL Titans, Harry Wismer, declared bankruptcy. A five-man syndicate headed by Sonny Werblin, president of Music Corporation of America (MCA) and a director of Monmouth Park (N.J.) race track, bought the franchise for $1 million. He said the team would remain in New York and stay at the Polo Grounds but would change its name to the Jets.

Elsewhere in professional football, the year began with a number of sad notes. Big Daddy Lipscomb, the great defensive tackle for the Rams, Colts, and Steelers, died in Baltimore of a drug overdose. A week later, Ernie Davis, Heisman trophy award winner from Syracuse whom the Cleveland Browns had picked with the first-round draft choice of 1962 they had gotten from the Dallas Cowboys, died of leukemia without ever having played in an NFL game. On another level, Paul Hornung of the Green Bay Packers and Alex Karras, All-Pro defensive tackle for the Detroit Lions, were suspended for a year for having placed bets on games in which they had played. On still another level, Dandy Don Meredith had been reclassified by the Selective Service System, and, rumor had it, was about to be drafted into the U.S. Army.

New with the Cowboys for 1963 was a contract with a radio network to broadcast the Cowboys games not only in Texas but also in Oklahoma, Arkansas, and Louisiana, the first step in what would one day become by far the largest radio-network coverage of a team in professional football.

Another change would take the itinerant Cowboy training camp from the shores of Lake Superior to those of the Pacific Ocean, at least within a couple of miles of where those big waves broke. The fifth camp site in four years was to be on the campus of California Lutheran College in Thousand Oaks, California, about 45 miles north of Los Angeles. It apparently was not the southern California everyone envisions today. Pete Gent, Cowboys' flanker who later wrote the best-selling novel *North Dallas Forty,* described it in an article for *Esquire* magazine as ". . . in the southern California desert they called [it] Thousand Oaks, which would eventually contain thousands of people but had at the time only a bowling alley and an all-aluminum Lutheran college where we trained. The country was so desolate it served as location for *Gunsmoke.*"

The Cowboys' third venture into the NFL draft was another lucrative one. Their first-round choice was a small linebacker, Lee Roy Jordan, 6 feet 1 inches, 210 pounds, from the University of Alabama and a unanimous All-American, who was destined to become one of the NFL's best at that position.

The Cowboys also added two notable veterans. Jim Ray Smith, an offensive lineman who had played with the Cleveland Browns the past seven seasons and had been named All-Pro four times and a guest in the Pro Bowl five times; and well-regarded defensive back Jimmy Ridlon from the San Francisco 49ers, where he had spent the previous six seasons. The Cowboys also signed a rookie offensive tackle, Tony Liscio, from Tulsa University.

The Cowboys convened in California in July, and after weathering the annual Landry mile and enjoying the occasional salty breeze from the Pacific, they were ready to begin their fourth year in the National Football League. Don Meredith was there. Because of a combination of ailments, ranging from an ulcer and a bad foot to a variety of football-related injuries, he had failed his army physical and was now deferred from military service.

On other fronts, NFL observers had not forgotten the slick display of offense the Cowboys had displayed the year before. When they arrived in Los Angeles for their first preseason game against the Rams, Bob Oates, in the Los Angeles *Herald Examiner,* went so far as to suggest that their "clever offense could carry Dallas to first place (in the NFL Eastern Conference)." Whether it was the promise of a wide-open, high-scoring game that enticed 70,675 spectators to the Los Angeles Coliseum or that it was just a nice summer night for Californians to sit outside is perhaps arguable, but it was the largest crowd up to that time ever to show up for a Cowboy game. And it was in a way ironic because the Rams hardly seemed in a position to lure anyone out to the ballpark; the season before they had won only 1 game, lost 12, and tied another, and their offense put the least amount of points on the scoreboard in the entire NFL (220, an average of less than 16 points a game).

However, according to their new coach, Harland Svare,

the Rams were building. Their second-year quarterback, Roman Gabriel, was still unproven but well thought of. Running back Dick Bass had come along and in that dreadful season of 1962 had managed to rush for 1,033 yards (a 5.3 average carry), third best in the NFL. And anyone as defense conscious as Tom Landry had to look with envy at a front four that consisted of ends Deacon Jones and Lamar Lundy and tackles Merlin Olsen and Rosey Grier. Add to that a linebacker like Jack Pardee and defensive backs Ed Meador and Lindon Crow and the Rams were well equipped to face the offensive threat of the Cowboys. But Dallas prevailed that summer day in Los Angeles, 17–14.

That, along with two other wins (over the 49ers and Lions) and two losses (to the NFL Champion Green Bay Packers and to the Rams) was enough to give the Cowboys their first winning preseason (3–2).

Just before the season was to be formally launched, Tex Maule, in *Sports Illustrated,* picked them to win their conference, based on a splendid offense and a defense that he said was improving. It came perhaps as a surprise to those closest to the team that had won only 4 of 14 games the year before and had never won more than five in a single season. Tex Schramm shrugged it off; Clint

Almost, but not quite. Wide receiver Billy Howton (81) had this pass for a moment in the end zone, only to see it flutter away. It didn't matter; the Cowboys beat the Washington Redskins handily 35–20 that day in 1963. Cowboys in the picture are running back Jim Stiger (40) and flanker Frank Clarke (82). No. 40 on the Redskins is Lonnie Sanders. (Bradley Photographers)

Murchison felt it would be nice and appropriate and would make his Sunday afternoons that much more enjoyable; and Tom Landry was not thinking about anything other than their first regular-season game.

The St. Louis Cardinals were first on the agenda. They came to the Cotton Bowl to test the mettle of the Dallas offense and found it sadly wanting. They also discovered that the Dallas defense was still in a tissue-paper state. The Cardinals, who had finished behind the Cowboys the year before, demolished them in the 1963 season opener, 34–7.

Don Meredith had been given the starting call at quarterback, but he was unable to sustain any kind of an offense after the Cowboys had jumped to a 7–0 lead (a 17-yard pass to tight end Pettis Norman and a Sam Baker extra point).

It was unfortunate because it was a game they had hoped to win, had expected to win, one that would get the season off to a positive start. After all, coming up were the Cleveland Browns, always a serious threat with Jim Brown, whose great running was now complemented by some impressive quarterbacking from Frank Ryan. He had won full-time possession of that position by his performance the year before. Lou Groza, 39 now, in his 17th NFL season and at that moment the man who had scored the most points of anyone in the history of the NFL, was still kicking for the Browns; and flanker Gary Collins, in only his second year, was proving to be one of the best in the league.

Tom Landry said, "The key to this game will be in stopping Jim Brown." If they accomplished that, the effectiveness of Ryan's passing game would be curtailed, and Groza wouldn't get close enough to kick field goals. But they lost the key somewhere in the grass of the Cotton Bowl. Brown amassed a total of 232 yards rushing that day, including touchdown runs of 71 and 62 yards. Frank Ryan threw two TD passes to Gary Collins (17- and 4-yard plays, respectively) and ran 7 yards for another one. The final score was the Browns 41, the Cowboys 24.

The ill-starred Cowboys dropped their next two games in a row as well, to the Redskins and the Eagles. They were 0–4 and at the opposite end of the conference, which some thought they had been destined to win. The fans were discontent and far from reticent about it. Meredith, in particular, was the subject of their wrath and was often trumpeted on to the field with a herald of boos and assorted catcalls. A writer for the Dallas *Times-Herald,* Frank Boggs, described the fans' disillusionment with Dandy Don, using an analogy that perhaps illustrates how long ago 1963 really was: "Next time you're in a barbershop, odds are 8–5 you'll hear Don Meredith's name muddied quicker than the shine boy sticks out his hand for a tip." When asked about that statement later, Mere-

Question: *Were there any times during that first couple years that you thought the Cowboys might have to leave Dallas?*

Tex Schramm: *Never entered my mind. Never entered my mind. I came from an organization that had been very successful, the LA Rams, in the late 1940s and early 1950s. People have asked me that. Did you get worried after three or four years when you didn't win? I knew that we were improving, and I knew that we were getting a lot of things going within the organization that other clubs didn't have. I knew that we were doing well with the draft. I could see that we were getting our percent, what we considered, the better football players, which is the way it had been at the Rams. So I guess within myself, and within the organization, there was no question in my mind; I knew that we were aggressive. I knew I didn't have to worry about a coach because I knew that we had one who could do it. I couldn't care less what happened with the Texans. I had been through it before, having another team, a second team, in your own home town. It's a very disagreeable situation. You're constantly being compared. You wake up in the morning, and every time you look at the newspaper, you're reading about the other guy, and the town gets divided. You've got writers that like one and don't like the other. It wasn't a new experience to me. It was just aggravating. But it never had any affect as to what we did in our organization. We never tried to compete with them. They went very heavy into promotional fields. We didn't go into promotional fields. We spent our time and our money and our efforts in building up the team because we knew we were the* National Football League *team. I just knew that the success of the club would naturally follow. So other than from an aggravation standpoint, the presence of the Texans did not affect us.*

dith, who sported a flat-top crew cut in those days, just shrugged and said: "I may let it grow pretty long, bad as I hate to."

At midseason, the Cowboys cringed under a record of 1–6. Although Tom Landry and Tex Schramm had not entertained the same inflated enthusiasm as Tex Maule before the season, they had expected better than this.

Tex Maule noted in one of his *Sports Illustrated* columns: "One guy developed a story on what an idiot I am and he brought out my picking the Cowboys . . . You guess right and no one remembers, but pick one wrong and they're all over you."

The Cowboys went to Pittsburgh to begin the second half of the 1963 season, but before they got on the airplane, Coach Tom Landry announced that the quarterback situation would no longer be one of fluctuation. The shuttle and the messenger system was over now. Despite the critics in the stadium and some in the media, Don Meredith would be Landry's principal team leader on the field for the remainder of the season. Eddie LeBaron was 33 years old that year, and Landry knew he was about to retire. The future would have to be with a younger man, and if it was to be Don Meredith, he would have to show that he was truly capable of handling it.

The rest of the season was an erratic one. The Cowboys won three and lost four, but there were some brilliant moments, some real cause for hope in the future. Don Meredith had not suddenly arisen as a savior of the football team, but he did show just what he could do with a football. In a loss to the Steelers, he threw 18 completions out of 29 attempts for 290 yards and three touchdowns. The week after that, he tossed four touchdown passes to lead the Cowboys to a victory over the Washington Redskins. And the following week, he astounded the most skeptical of barbershop critics in Dallas when he passed for a total of 460 yards (30 of 48) against the San Francisco 49ers. Before that day, only five quarterbacks in the history of the game of professional football had thrown for more yardage in a single game—Norm Van Brocklin of the Los Angeles Rams in 1951, 554; Y. A. Tittle of the New York Giants in 1962, 505; Johnny Lujack of the Chicago Bears in 1949, 468; Billy Wade of the Chicago Bears in 1962, 466; and George Blanda of the Houston Oilers in 1961, 464. On that incredible day, Meredith tossed eight passes to Frank Clarke for 190 yards, seven to Lee Folkins for 112 yards, eight to Billy Howton for 107 yards, six to Jim Stiger for 32 yards, and one to Don Perkins for 19 yards. Despite all that, the Cowboys still lost that day to the 49ers, 31–24.

The week after that, Meredith led the Cowboys to a win over the Eagles at the Cotton Bowl by completing 25 of 33 passes for 302 yards and two touchdowns. Five days later, in the same city, one of the nation's darkest tragedies occurred when President John F. Kennedy was assassinated as he rode in a motorcade into Dallas. The day after, the Cowboys had to fly to Cleveland and, like all other NFL teams, play a football game while the nation mourned that dark November Sunday.

The Cowboys, with a record of 4–10, landed in fifth place again in the NFL East, this time ahead of the Redskins and the Eagles. Don Perkins had rushed for 331 yards less than he had the year before, but Don Meredith posted the best passing year of his pro career and certainly provided some electricity in the second half of the season. He completed 167 of 310 passes (54%) for 2,381 yards, by far the most in the Cowboys' four-year sojourn in the league. He threw 17 TDs but also 18 interceptions.

Rookie Mel Renfro hurtles Washington Redskin John Nisby (62) in the process of carrying an interception 39 yards for a Cowboy touchdown in this 1964 contest. It was one of three career touchdowns on interception returns for Renfro, who would eventually become the team's all-time leading interceptor with 52 aerial thefts. The Redskin lunging unsuccessfully for Renfro is Jim Carr (21). The Cowboys won that game at the Cotton Bowl, 24–18. (Bradley Photographers)

His NFL rating of 73.2 was tenth in the 14-team league.

The Cowboys' attendance did take a jump in 1963, fueled in part by the departure of the Texans, and the average crowd was up a little more than 5,000 for each home game (26,961 average). But two home-town favorites, Eddie LeBaron and Billy Howton, announced their retirement after the season, and the Cowboys' management knew they would have to scramble to fill the gaps.

A lot of changes would occur before the 1964 season got underway. There had been tremors of discontent among Dallas fans and some of the sportswriters about the so-far unimpressive NFL seasons that Cowboy fans had endured. Much of the rancor was heaped on Don Meredith, but there were also some rumblings in regard to head coach Tom Landry. But there were none in the Dallas front office. Tex Schramm and Clint Murchison got together to set the record straight on their feelings. Landry had one more year to go on his original contract; the two men offered him a new one, extending his employment for an additional *ten years,* an unprecedented move in the ever-fickle front offices of the NFL and the transient coaching ranks they manipulated.

With that out of the way, Schramm, Landry, and Gil Brandt got down to the job of beefing up the team. They would use the draft as a very effective tool that year, but the benefits would be deferred. The Cowboys made two excellent investments in the future. Their tenth-round draft choice was indeed the quite distant future; they claimed 1963 Heisman trophy winner Roger Staubach. After graduating from the U.S. Naval Academy, he would have a four-year commitment to the navy. If, after that, he wanted to play pro ball and was still able to, the Cowboys would take him. Three choices earlier in that draft, on the seventh round, they secured another future, Bob Hayes.

Olympic gold medal sprinter Bob Hayes was known as the "world's fastest human" when he was drafted by the Dallas Cowboys in 1964. Here, he is shown earning that title as he sets the world record of 9.1 seconds for the 100-yard dash at the AAU track and field championships of 1963. Cowboy talent scout Gil Brandt saw him as a wide receiver in a track uniform. (UPI)

He had one more year to go at Florida A&M and a command performance at the upcoming Olympic Games in Tokyo that summer. He did play football, but he was better known as the world's fastest human, holding the world's record of 9.1 seconds in the 100-yard dash and an odds-on favorite to win a gold medal at the Olympics. (He would win two that year—one for the 100-meter dash, the other as a member of the 400-meter relay team.)

Besides these investments, the Cowboys used their number-one choice to select All-American tackle Scott Appleton in a ploy they had arranged beforehand with the Pittsburgh Steelers. When they selected him, they promptly turned him over to the Steelers for flanker Buddy Dial, who had ranked fifth in pass receptions the year before with 60. The Cowboys, so often burned by Dial in the preceding seasons, had coveted him for some time, and now, with the departure of Billy Howton, it seemed the perfect time to bring him over to their side.

Gil Brandt used the first choice they had after that (second round) to obtain a fleet running back named Mel Renfro from the University of Oregon. He would be converted to a defensive back. As College All-Star Coach Otto Graham said of him: "Renfro can run faster backwards than most men can forward." The Cowboys, however, would let him use his frontal speed running back kickoffs and punts, which he would do with great virtuosity.

In trades, the Cowboys picked up a prime pass receiver from the Philadelphia Eagles, Tommy McDonald, one-time All-American and Maxwell Trophy winner from the University of Oklahoma and a receiver who had made trips to every one of the Pro Bowl games in the preceding six seasons. Now, with Buddy Dial and returnees Frank Clarke, Pettis Norman, and Lee Folkins, it prompted Tex Schramm to say, "I think we have the best group of ends in the league now." It cost them, however. Kicker Sam Baker was the price for McDonald, and although Coach Landry would not miss Baker's off-field antics, he would indeed miss his talented toe in 1964.

There was also a feeler from the New York Giants. They were thinking about trading their devastating middle line-backer, Sam Huff, who Gary Cartwright in the Dallas *Morning News* said was "to enemy quarterbacks what earthquakes are to small villages in Peru." But the asking price was too high. The Giants wanted Bob Lilly in return for Huff.

Two other new faces also joined the team. One was a basketball player from Michigan State who had come to the attention of Gil Brandt. His name was Pete Gent; he was given a tryout as a receiver, and he made the team. The other new face was hired to coach all the pass catchers. Red Hickey, who had quit as head coach of the San Francisco 49ers, signed on with the Cowboys.

The Cowboy roster by 1964 was beginning to take a

Pete Gent

Pete Gent was a member of the Dallas Cowboys from 1964 through 1968, a flanker, wide receiver, and sometime tight end, who, during his tenure with the team, provided Dallas sportswriters with a cornucopia of anecdotes and laughs.

When his good friend Don Meredith was having his highs and lows at quarterback, having three passes intercepted one week by Ross Fichtner of the Browns and then throwing four touchdowns the next, Gent slapped him on the shoulder after the latter game. "Don, you sure as hell made a terrific adjustment this week, not having Fichtner to throw to. It really surprises the hell out of me how you get your timing down, working with different receivers every week."

Bob St. John of the Dallas Morning News *remembered another incident in his biography of Tom Landry.*

Once (Bob) Hayes had been injured during a road game and on the return flight, Landry decided he'd move Gent from flanker to the other side, split end, where he'd start against Philadelphia, instead of the injured Hayes. Landry walked to the back of the plane, the players' section, and found Gent.

"Pete," said Landry, "you'll be moving to the other side this week. So get ready."

"You mean, coach," said Pete, "that I'm going to play for Philadelphia?"

Another time, when informed that he was going to be switched to tight end, Gent told newsmen: "Landry just wants me to sit on the bench at three positions instead of two."

Perhaps the biggest stir Pete Gent made around the Dallas front offices, however, was after he had departed the organization. His novel, North Dallas Forty, *a ribald romp behind the scenes of a professional football team, was also considered a* roman à clef *effort with transparent caricatures of Don Meredith, Tom Landry, and Tex Schramm, among others. It became a national best seller and was made into a successful motion picture.*

(Bradley Photographers)

somewhat solid shape. Don Meredith was the accepted choice at quarterback. He now had a bevy of experienced receivers. Don Perkins was a strong running back who promised still more.

The offensive line looked better than ever before, with Tony Liscio, Bob Fry, Jim Ray Smith, Joe Bob Isbell, and the center position a hotly contested one between Mike Connelly and newcomer Dave Manders.

The defense had been shuffled. Bob Lilly had been switched from end to tackle, a position where he would win All-Pro honors seven times in the coming years, and a new arrival, Jim Colvin (via a trade with the Colts), filled the other tackle slot; the defensive ends looked strong with George Andrie on one flank and Larry Stephens at the other. Lee Roy Jordan and Chuck Howley held down the outside linebacking positions, and Jerry Tubbs, one of the few holdovers from that very first season, worked out at middle linebacker. And there was comfort now in a defensive backfield where Tom Landry could pick and choose between six talented defenders—Don Bishop, Mike Gaechter, Cornell Green, Warren Livingston, Jimmy Ridlon, and Mel Renfro.

On paper, it didn't look bad at all.

One of the few beneficial finds in the 1960 expansion draft was Jerry Tubbs of the San Francisco 49ers. Tubbs became the Cowboys' starting middle linebacker for their very first game in 1960 and went to the Pro Bowl in a Cowboy uniform in 1962. He would serve as an important cog in the Dallas defense, both on the field and as tutor to such stalwart linebackers as Chuck Howley and Lee Roy Jordan. In 1966, he signed as an assistant coach but did not quit playing until the end of the 1967 season. (Dallas Cowboys)

During the preseason, however, it didn't look very good. The Cowboys lost four out of five games and were not really competitive in any one of the losses. On top of it, their only experienced quarterback, Dandy Don Meredith, was injured, tearing a cartilage in his knee that would haunt him off and on throughout the regular season. The Cowboys did some quick maneuvering to add a quasi-experienced quarterback to their roster and signed John Roach, who had played a couple of years with the old Chicago Cardinals and had been a back-up at Green Bay for the past four years.

The 1964 season was to be filled with some startling surprises. The defending champions of the NFL, the Chicago Bears, would sink to next to last place in the NFL West; at the same time, the team they beat for the cham-

pionship, the New York Giants, would drop to last place in the NFL East with a degrading record of 2–10–2. And a new type of kicker would enter professional football that year—Pete Gogolak of the AFL's Buffalo Bills—and he would introduce the soccer-style kick, which would forever influence the pro-football kicking game.

As for the Dallas Cowboys, the offense of which everyone spoke so highly and had such lofty hopes for would be nowhere to be found. The passing game that looked so good with all the tried-and-true receivers and a Don Meredith who was said to have come of age at the end of last season never would materialize. Their record at the end of the year would only equal their best effort so far (5–8–1).

It began on the proverbial wrong foot when the St. Louis Cardinals came to Dallas. Before the biggest regular-season home-town crowd that had yet come out to see the Cowboys and behind the three field goals of Jim Bakken, the Cards beat the Cowboys 16–6.

A win over the Redskins the following week added a

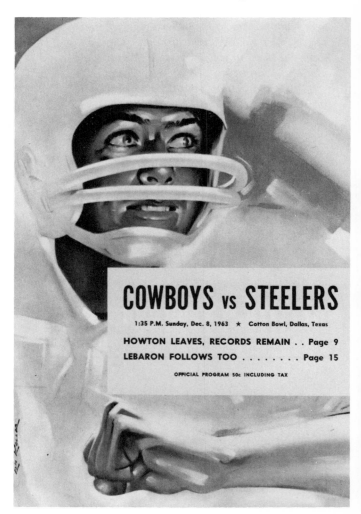

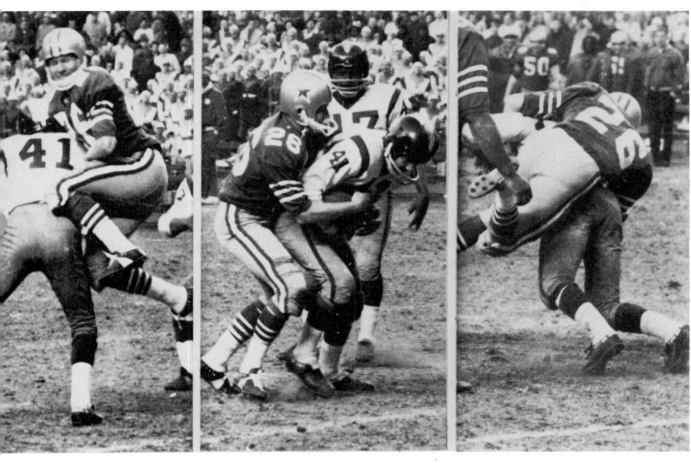

Cowboy flanker Buddy Dial (26) has his role reversed in this sequence, when a pass from Don Meredith is thrown into the arms of Redskin defensive back Jim Steffen (41), and Dial is suddenly forced to become the tackler. Dial held him to no gain after the interception but the Cowboys lost this 1964 game at Washington, 28–16. (Pro Football Hall of Fame)

touch of brightness, and their faith in turning Mel Renfro into a pass defender was rewarded when he picked off a Sonny Jurgensen pass and raced with it 39 yards for a touchdown. The Cowboys also offered several sustained drives that day, but Don Meredith was playing in a great deal of pain and had been forced to share the quarterbacking chores almost equally with John Roach.

Fans waiting for the honored Dallas offense to get going were not to be satisfied. Two straight losses to the Steelers and the Browns and the Cowboys were foundering again. They managed to hold the conference champs, the Giants, to a tie at the Cotton Bowl, but that was hardly an accomplishment in view of the situation—the Giants had lost three of their first four games that season and were clearly on a steady course of decline. The Browns came to Dallas the next week, and Jim Brown once again made shreds of the Dallas defense, racing through it for 188 yards. The Cowboy offense that day could only post 16 points, and that sadly was their third highest score of

the now six-game-old season.

The Cowboys then took their show on the road and surprised everybody by winning their next three games. The first win was an impressive one. The St. Louis Cardinals were in first place in the conference, but the Cowboys gave them a 31–13 drubbing. It was their first really decent offensive effort of the year. Meredith passed for 192 yards, including an 18-yard touchdown to Frank Clarke, and the Cowboys simply dominated the game from start to finish.

Then the Cowboys took on the defending NFL champs up in Chicago and picked the Bears apart 24–10. On to New York, and there the Cowboys embarrassed the Giants further, this time before a crowd of more than 63,000 fans. Meredith, still playing with injuries, managed three TD passes, two to Frank Clarke (14 and 8 yards) and one to Tommy McDonald (48 yards). Jimmy Ridlon brought everyone to their feet in Yankee Stadium when he snatched a Y. A. Tittle pass and raced with it 74 yards

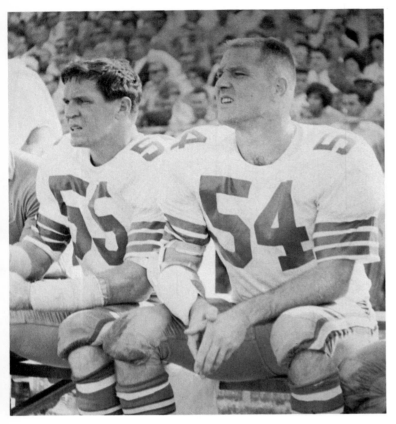

Linebackers Lee Roy Jordan (55) and Chuck Howley (54), here watching from the bench, would become two of the mainstays in the Cowboys' famous Doomsday Defense, only a few years down the NFL road.   (Bradley Photographers)

for another Dallas touchdown.

But just as everyone was getting excited again, the Cowboys' roller coaster apparently had peaked and now suddenly plunged. They lost their next four straight, to the Eagles and the Redskins, then a fearsome rout at the hands of the Green Bay Packers (45–21)—the most points by far the defense had given up all that year (28 was the most up to that game)—and once again to the Eagles.

The Cowboys edged the Steelers in the last game of the season, 17–14, but it was little consolation. Once again, the Cowboys languished in fifth place in the NFL East, this time ahead of the Steelers and the Giants.

The big surprise had been the disappearance of the Dallas offense. In 14 games, they had scored a lowly 250 points, the third lowest in the entire league—above only the 49ers (236) and the Giants (241). The defense, on the other hand, long the Cowboys' acute source of disappointment, allowed only 289 points, by far the least in the team's five-year history. That was almost 100 points less than they had given up the year before and 80 points less

than their previous best, which had been the 369 points scored against them in 1960 and that, incidentally, was in two fewer games.

If there was a highlight of the year, it had to be the performance of rookie Mel Renfro. He led the entire NFL in punt return yardage (418, an average of 13 yards per) and in kickoff return yardage (1,017, an average of 25 per). In addition, he led the team in interceptions with seven.

Don Perkins moved his rushing stats up a bit, gaining 768 yards, with a 4.6-yard average carry. Frank Clarke was named an All-Pro for the first time. He had led the Cowboys in pass receptions, grabbing 65 for a total of 973 yards (an average of 15 yards per catch) and scored five touchdowns. And from the defensive unit, Bob Lilly was a unanimous All-Pro selection, the first of seven such league-wide honors.

The season had been a disappointment, the only touch of encouragement was that 268,661 fans had paid to see the Cowboys play in Dallas, an average of 38,380 per game and a vast improvement over the preceding years, none of which even came close to averaging 30,000. But at the end of five years of play in the NFL, the Cowboys had a cumulative regular season record of only 18–46–4.

The truly important fact, the uplifting one, was, however, one that no one at that moment knew. The days of mediocrity and assorted on-the-field indignities were over; 1964 was the last year the Cowboys would have a losing season. The script was about to take on a new twist, a new direction, and the Cowboys and the city of Dallas and the football fans of Texas would never be the same again.

Lee Roy Jordan

Hall of Famer and Dallas Defensive Coordinator Ernie Stautner on Jordan: "If Jordan weighed as much as Dick Butkus, they'd have to outlaw him from football."

Jordan on Jordan: "I'm not a mean player. I like to think I'm aggressive. I try to hit as hard as I can because that's what this game is all about—hitting."

Billy Howton

Up to 1963, the most passes caught in the NFL and the most yardage gained in catching them were records held by the immortal Green Bay Packer, end Don Hutson. The records had stood for 18 years, ever since Hutson's retirement back in 1945.

Both records fell, however, in 1963 to Billy Howton, the end from Rice, who played seven seasons with the Packers, one with the Cleveland Browns, and the last four with the Dallas Cowboys. Hutson's lifetime record of 488 receptions was displaced by Howton's career total of 503, and the 7,991 yards Hutson gained was now second to the 8,459 toted up by Howton. It took Billy Howton one additional season to accomplish the records (12 seasons to Hutson's 11).

(Dallas Cowboys)

1963

Preseason

Dallas	(3-2)	Opponents
17	Los Angeles (70,675) @ L. A.	14
10	Green Bay (53,121) @ Dallas	31
17	Los Angeles (29,349) @ Portland	20
37	S. F. (9,927) @ Bakersfield	24
27	Detroit (51,218) @ New Orleans	17

Regular Season

	(4-10)	
L 7	St. Louis (36,432) (H)	34
L 24	Cleveland (28,710) (H)	41
L 17	Washington (40,101)	21
L 21	Philadelphia (60,671)	24
W 17	Detroit (27,264) (H)	14
L 21	New York (62,889)	37
L 21	Pittsburgh (19,047)	27
W 35	Washington (18,838) (H)	20
L 24	San Francisco (29,563)	31
W 27	Philadelphia (23,694) (H)	20
L 17	Cleveland (55,096)	27
L 27	New York (29,653) (H)	34
L 19	Pittsburgh (24,136) (H)	24
W 28	St. Louis (12,695)	24
305		378

1964

Preseason

Dallas	(1-4)	Opponents
6	Los Angeles (57,450) @ L. A.	17
34	S. F. (24,679) @ Portland	23
16	Los Angeles (30,565) @ Portland	25
3	Green Bay (60,057) @ Dallas	35
6	Chicago (35,000) @ New Orleans	21

Regular Season

	(5-8-1)	
L 6	St. Louis (36,605) (H)	16
W 24	Washington (25,158) (H)	18
L 17	Pittsburgh (35,594)	23
L 6	Cleveland (72,062)	27
T 13	New York (33,324) (H)	13
L 16	Cleveland (37,456) (H)	20
W 31	St. Louis (28,253)	13
W 24	Chicago (47,527)	10
W 31	New York (63,031)	21
L 14	Philadelphia (55,972) (H)	17
L 16	Washington (49,219)	28
L 21	Green Bay (44,975) (H)	45
L 14	Philadelphia (60,671)	24
W 17	Pittsburgh (35,271) (H)	14
250		289

7 The Tide Turns

IN THE ANNALS OF PROFESSIONAL FOOTBALL, 1965 should rightly be called "the year of the rookie." It was the year that the New York Jets of the AFL drafted Alabama quarterback Joe Namath and signed him to a contract which reportedly would give him an income of $400,000 a year. It was the same year in which the Chicago Bears drafted two future members of the Pro Football Hall of Fame, Gale Sayers and Dick Butkus, the Oakland Raiders landed receiver Fred Biletnikoff, the San Francisco 49ers signed fullback Ken Willard, and on and on.

In Dallas, it was also a fruitful year. The first round of the draft produced University of California quarterback Craig Morton. In the 11th round, Gil Brandt unveiled one of those serendipities he was becoming famous for; this time it was Jethro Pugh, a 6 foot 6 inch, 255-pound defensive end from an obscure little school in North Carolina called Elizabeth City State College. And it was the season to welcome their future choice from the year before, fresh from the Olympic Games, end Bob Hayes.

In addition, three others would make their NFL debuts in Cowboy uniforms that year: offensive guard Ralph Neely (Oklahoma University), running back Danny Reeves (South Carolina), and quarterback Jerry Rhome (Tulsa). Leaving was Tommy McDonald, traded to the Los Angeles Rams for veteran place kicker Danny Villanueva.

The team was being fleshed out in 1965; no one should have been more aware of it than Don Meredith, now the ranking quarterback, and he had noticed it. As Meredith told sportswriter Sam Blair: "That man (Tex Schramm) certainly has a knack for words. He told me that no player

on the Cowboy team was in a more secure position than me. But I checked our roster and counted nine or ten players with quarterbacking experience. Then I knew what he meant: The position is secure, but I'm not."

By 1965, it could be said, the people of Dallas and its environs had finally come around to something that could be recognized as valid team support. Attendance had been on the rise each year since the AFL Texans had abandoned the city, and all the signs were that it was to continue that way. In fact, when the Cowboys returned from Thousand Oaks for the annual Salesmanship Club game, 67,954 fans paid to watch them take on the Green Bay Packers at the Cotton Bowl, the largest crowd so far in home-game history for the Cowboys and almost 8,000 more than the crowd that showed for the same spectacle the year before. As it would turn out, attendance would take a dramatic leap upward that year for the Cowboys, and during the regular season they would play to their first sellout crowd in Dallas. The term of courting between the Cowboys and the football fans of Texas was coming to an end, the betrothal perhaps beginning, and the marriage was not too far down the road.

The turnout was especially impressive in view of the fact that the Cowboys had lost their previous two exhibition games that year: to the Rams, who had held them scoreless, and the 49ers, who had allowed them only one touchdown. But the Cowboys put on a show for the home-town crowd, winning handily 21–12 and leaving the fans with the feeling that they did have an offense, after all.

The following week, however, they found disaster in

The 1965 Dallas Cowboys. Front row: Danny Villanueva, Jerry Rhome, Craig Morton, Don Meredith, Mel Renfro, Bob Hayes, J. D. Smith, Obert Logan, Buddy Dial. Second row: Mike Gaechter, Dan Reeves, Russell Wayt, Cornell Green, Pete Gent, Perry Lee Dunn, Jim Stiger, Warren Livingston, Don Perkins. Third row: Don Bishop, Jerry Tubbs, Dave Manders, Dave Edwards, Mike Connelly, Chuck Howley, Lee Roy Jordan, Harold Hays, Leon Donohue. Fourth row: Mitch Jackson, George Andrie, Jake Kupp, Jim Boeke, Don Talbert, Ralph Neely, Bob Lilly, Jethro Pugh. Top row: Jim Colvin, Maury Youmans, Larry Stephens, Frank Clarke, Pettis Norman. (Pro Football Hall of Fame)

Birmingham, Alabama, where they faced their sibling expansion team, the Minnesota Vikings. The Cowboys were thunderstruck, the score 57–17. To this day, that total still stands as the highest number of points ever scored against a Dallas team in either the preseason, regular season, or postseason. A win over the Chicago Bears in the last exhibition game was a slight redemption and gave them a 2–3 record for the exhibition season.

The New York Giants, who had done such a dramatic flip-flop from a conference championship in 1963 to the cellar of their division in 1964, were the first visitors to Dallas for the 1965 regular season. The once-indomitable Giants defense was gone, and of the great names only Jim Katcavage remained. The offense was now guided by Earl Morrall, whom they had obtained from the Detroit Lions to replace the retired Y. A. Tittle. And Giant coach Allie Sherman was hoping their running game would be enhanced by rookie Tucker Frederickson from Auburn.

The fans came back out to welcome the Cowboys in their home opener, more than 59,000 of them, a record for a regular-season game, and the Cowboys entertained them by destroying the Giants 31–2. It was one of those days when just about everything went right. The defense

allowed the Giants to gain only 150 yards. On the other hand, the Cowboy running game was consistent and effective, and the passing of Dandy Don was accurate; the only dim moment came when Meredith had to fall on a bad snap in his own end zone to give the Giants their two points for the day. Speedster Bob Hayes took a 45-yard pass from Meredith into the end zone for his first NFL touchdown, and everyone who watched it hoped that it was just the promise of things to come.

Sonny Jurgensen, who always seemed to find the Cowboys' soft spot, brought his lethal arm and his teammates from Washington to the Cotton Bowl the next week, but the Redskins were controllable that day, and the Cowboys were able to hold Jurgensen to 13 completions out of 30 attempts for only 206 yards. At the same time, the Cowboy offense was showing a certain flair. They tallied 27 points, and Bob Hayes was part of two of the Dallas touchdowns, one on a pass from Meredith and the other on an 11-yard end-around play. The total of 61,577 who watched the suddenly interesting Cowboys that day set another record for regular-season, home-town attendance.

Unfortunately, during the next five weeks, the Cowboys

The Cowboys found Jethro Pugh at tiny Elizabeth City State College in North Carolina and signed him in 1965. Pugh, a charter member of the original Doomsday Defense, would hold down the tackle spot on the left side of the Dallas defense for most of his 14 years as a Cowboy. Playing under the shadow of the Cowboys' other tackle, Hall of Famer Bob Lilly, during many of those years, Pugh's accomplishments often were unheralded. (Dallas Cowboys)

returned to old times. Four losing road games plus another loss at home added up to a five-game losing streak, the longest since that fretful first season five years earlier. Everything seemed to be falling apart—the offense had stopped scoring, the passing was a mere trickle, the defense was suddenly paper-thin—and the Cowboys were 2–5 at midseason, in a four-way tie at the basement of the NFL East (with the Redskins, Eagles, and Steelers).

However, at this point, the unpredictable Cowboys came home and turned the season around. First they beat the 49ers 39–31, and then they laced the Steelers 24–17.

This sudden rebirth brought out the best in Texas football fans. The next week, the Cotton Bowl was virtually jammed and the Cowboys played before their very first sellout crowd in Dallas, an SRO audience of 76,251. Part of it might have had to do with the team that had come to play the Cowboys—the Cleveland Browns. They were in first place in the conference, boasting a record of 7–2.

They still had the game's premier running back, Jim Brown, and the passing combination of Frank Ryan to Gary Collins. Head coach Blanton Collier was deservedly pleased with both his offense and defense.

It would have been a nice win for the Cowboys, especially with all the people who showed up that day at the Cotton Bowl. And the Cowboys almost carried it off. In the first half, they had restrained Jim Brown (no one ever really stopped him), but they were losing 17–3, partly the result of a 67-yard punt return by second-year man Leroy Kelly. The Cowboys came back in the second half. Twice in the latter part of the fourth quarter they had a shot at tying the score, but on both occasions Don Meredith threw interceptions, and the Browns held on to win.

The following week, the Redskins, behind Sonny Jurgensen's three touchdown passes (two late in the fourth quarter) dealt the Cowboys their seventh loss of the year by the score 34–31.

Then, just to keep in character with the hills-and-valleys season, the Cowboys ascended, winning their last three games in a row. First, they took on the Eagles in Philadelphia, and with a solid day's rushing from J. D. Smith (90

1965

Preseason

Dallas	(2–3)	Opponents
0	Los Angeles (31,579) @ L. A.	9
7	S. F. (24,837) @ Portland	27
21	Green Bay (67,954) @ Dallas	12
17	Minn. (41,500) @ Birmingham	57
34	Chicago (33,525) @ Tulsa	21

Regular Season

		(7–7)	
W	31	New York (59,366) (H)	2
W	27	Washington (61,577) (H)	7
L	13	St. Louis (32,034)	20
L	24	Philadelphia (56,249) (H)	35
L	17	Cleveland (80,451)	23
L	3	Green Bay (48,311)	13
L	13	Pittsburgh (37,804)	22
W	39	San Francisco (39,677) (H)	31
W	24	Pittsburgh (57,293) (H)	17
L	17	Cleveland (76,251) (H)	24
L	31	Washington (50,205)	34
W	21	Philadelphia (54,714)	19
W	27	St. Louis (38,499) (H)	13
W	38	New York (62,871)	20
	325		280

Postseason

		Playoff Bowl Game *(Miami)*	
L	3	Baltimore (65,569)	35

yards) and Don Perkins (42) and 171 yards passing and two TDs from Don Meredith, they won a squeaker 21–19. The Cardinals, who had precipitated the Cowboys' worst losing streak earlier in the season, then came to Dallas, but the Cowboys wreaked their own kind of vengeance, obliterating them 27–13, with Don Meredith posting his best game of the year, throwing for 326 yards (16 of 30), including touchdown passes to Bob Hayes, Danny Reeves, and Pettis Norman.

Now, even with an uninspiring 6–7 record, the Cowboys still had a clear shot at a postseason game. While they had to face the Giants in New York, if they won, they would land in a tie with the Giants for second place in the NFL East. Dallas, however, would get the nod to go to the Playoff Bowl, the postseason game between the runners-up in each conference, because they would have beaten the Giants in their two encounters that season.

It was almost predictable at that point: as Meredith went, so went the Cowboys. That day, he had one of his better ones and threw for three touchdowns, including

two to Bob Hayes (one for 65 yards, the other for 33) and a 29 yarder to flanker Buddy Dial. And defensive back Obert Logan added a nice touch by racing with a blocked field goal 60 yards for another Cowboy touchdown. It all seemed very easy that afternoon, as the Cowboys won 38–20.

The regular season was over and the Cowboys had broken even: 7 wins, 7 losses, and, even better, they were going to Miami to represent their conference against the Baltimore Colts.

The famous Florida sun did not shine on the Cowboys the January day when they met the Colts. The consensus of observers thought it would because both Johnny Unitas and his back-up, Gary Cuozzo, had been injured and were not able to play. Halfback Tom Matte had been filling in at quarterback, a position he had not played since his collegiate days at Ohio State. On the other hand, Coach Don Shula had quite a roster, even if they were a little on the old side: there was end Ray Berry and flanker Lenny Moore, both 32, and guard Jim Parker, 31; but they also

No one in the league in 1965 could catch Bob Hayes, the world's fastest human, once he got into the open field. Chasing futilely here is Philadelphia Eagle linebacker Mike Morgan (89). As Hayes himself put it, "I never ran as fast as when I started seeing those linebackers coming at me." (Bradley Photographers)

Names

In March 1965, Clint Murchison entertained the idea of changing his team's name. So, via the Dallas newspapers, he put the question to the fans and suggested they call his office to tell what they thought of the idea. When sportswriter Steve Perkins inquired about the result, he got this letter from Murchison:

So far I have received only 1,148 telephone calls. These break down as follows:

Keep the name Cowboys 1,138
Change name to Texans 2
Murchison is stupid 8

The vote on this latter category is somewhat encouraging, since five years ago, when we originally changed the name, there were 16 such votes.

Under the circumstances, I think it is safe to say that sentiment is overwhelming that the team retain its present name.

Sincerely,
Clint

had an impressive young tight end in John Mackey, a mere 23.

It did not matter whether they were wounded or aged, however; the Colts totally dominated the day in the Orange Bowl, winning 35–3. After the game, a sportswriter asked Coach Tom Landry who should shoulder the blame: the offense? Defense? Meredith? Landry, expressionless as always, said simply, "It was a team effort."

The 1965 season, however, was the first one that could be termed a success. At the box office, it was a smash; the attendance had jumped to close to 400,000, and the average crowd at the Cotton Bowl was registered at 55,559, which exceeded the year before by more than 17,000 per game.

Both Bob Lilly and Mel Renfro were named All-Pro that year, and Bob Hayes would probably have been named Rookie of the Year if it had not been for a dazzling display of running up in Chicago by Gale Sayers.

Hayes could take some comfort in the fact that he led the NFL in touchdown receptions with 12 and in average gain per catch (21.8 yards). His total of 1,003 yards, gained on 46 catches, was the most ever in Cowboy history. Don Meredith's completion percentage was down to 46%, but he did pick up 2,415 yards and 22 touchdowns passing. And Danny Villanueva proved to be the answer to the Cowboys' kicking problems.

The new year had not even begun when the Cowboys' financial situation was given another surge of adrenaline. CBS announced that it had just signed a new contract with the NFL for broadcasting their games—a two-year package totaling $37.6 million, to be divided up among the teams in the league. Heralded as "the largest sports contract in television history," it was only for preseason and regular-season games. The postseason would bring additional TV riches.

For football fans, however, that was not the only major announcement in the months before the 1966 season. The real blockbuster came when Commissioner Pete Rozelle announced that the NFL and the AFL had decided to end their costly war and merge into one league. The formal announcement came June 6. Now there would be a common draft of players, preseason games between

Tony Liscio was the first of the masterful offensive linemen of the Cowboys. From the University of Tulsa, he joined the Cowboys in 1963 and became a starter the following year. After an injury sidelined him, Liscio came back in 1966 to become part of a great blocking tradition that would include the likes of Ralph Neely, John Niland, Rayfield Wright, and Blaine Nye. (Dallas Cowboys)

Danny Reeves (30) races untouched into the Pittsburgh Steeler end zone, as the Cowboys defeat the Steelers that afternoon in Dallas in 1965, 24–17. On the ground is Steeler Riley Gunnels (74), and looking on are John Campbell (53) and John Baker (78). Reeves would play 8 seasons with the Cowboys and serve as an assistant coach for 11 years before moving to Denver as head coach of the Broncos in 1981. (Bradley Photographers)

NFL and AFL teams, plans for league expansion into other cities, and playoffs culminated by a championship game between the winner of each league.

In the NFL expansion, the Atlanta Falcons were to join the Eastern Conference that year, with the New Orleans Saints scheduled to enter the NFL West the following year.

Pro football was entering a whole new era, and so were the Dallas Cowboys. It was in a way a new birth for the team because they would never again be looked upon as they had been. The longest sustained success story in the entire history of the game would begin with the Cowboys of 1966.

Once again, the draft was good to the Cowboys. They added guard John Niland from the University of Iowa in the first round; an immense defensive tackle from Tulsa, Willie Townes, came with the second round; and a few rounds down the line they picked up running back Walt Garrison from Oklahoma State, who was described in the press as a "rootin', tootin', real-life cowboy." He had been on Oklahoma State's rodeo team, and he announced, to

the chagrin of the Cowboy coaching staff and management, that he planned to continue: "Just a little bulldogging steers, roping calves, and bustin' broncs." He would forgo Brahma bull riding, adding, "Brahmas do try to stomp you and butt you sometimes." Instead of the automobile most sought-after players wished as a bonus for signing, Garrison asked for a two-horse trailer, and Tex Schramm gave it to him.

There was competition for most of the starting positions now, and the Cowboys knew there was a depth that had not been there before. As one writer put it, "Tom Landry has been collecting talent for years and now all the pieces fit together."

Tex Schramm had been moved up to president of the organization, with Clint Murchison claiming now only the title of chairman of the board. For the second year in a row, Jerry Tubbs announced his retirement as a player, then changed his mind with the approach of the season. And it was decided that Mel Renfro, who had been spending his time in the defensive secondary, would be given a shot at running back, the idea being that he would be able to run wide, providing a perfect complement to the rushing of fullback Don Perkins.

Tom Landry also hired a new assistant coach to handle the defensive line. Ernie Stautner, who as a Steeler had mauled many a Cowboy in their first few years of existence, had been an assistant with the Washington Redskins the year before after ending his 15-year career as a player.

There was a great deal of optimism when the Cowboys showed up that summer in Thousand Oaks. And just about everyone associated with the Dallas sports media was predicting that the home-town boys were going to win the Eastern Conference title. Steve Perkins of the *Times-Herald* went so far as to predict a 10-win, 4-loss record.

With two effortless wins on the road in the preseason, against the 49ers and the Rams, the Cowboys were riding high when they came to Dallas for the Salesmanship Club game of 1966. It had become a tradition now (since 1961) for the Green Bay Packers to come down to Texas each year for this game. It was especially nice, too, because the Packers were a tremendously exciting team during those years. In 1966, they were the defending NFL champions and a team that had won that title three times in the past five years.

The Cotton Bowl was packed for the game, a sellout crowd (75,504). And the Cowboys gave them something to cheer about. Green Bay's much-honored offense was held to a mere field goal, while the Cowboys reeled off three TDs, two on passes from Meredith to Bob Hayes and another on a little 1-yard lob from Craig Morton to Frank Clarke.

A quick trip to Tulsa followed to meet the Detroit Lions, who were handled with ease, and then a return engagement at the Cotton Bowl to play the Minnesota Vikings, who had embarrassed the Cowboys so badly the previous summer by running up a score of 57 points. This August, however, the Cowboys atoned for it, winning 28–24 and posting a perfect 5–0 record for the preseason, the first time they had ever done that (one of only two times in their entire history).

Tom Landry said simply: "I am looking forward to this season."

As the Cowboys lined up for the regular season, Don Meredith would be the quarterback, and Don Perkins and Danny Reeves would handle the running chores, Reeves taking over for Mel Renfro, who had been troubled by injuries during the preseason that were to carry through the early part of the season. When Renfro was finally ready, Reeves would have won the position, and Renfro would return to his old haunts in the defensive backfield. Pete Gent had had a fine preseason and replaced Buddy Dial at flanker; Bob Hayes was, of course, at wide receiver, and the other end position would be handled alternately

Flanker Buddy Dial came to Dallas in 1964 from the Pittsburgh Steelers in return for the Cowboys' first-round draft choice that year, tackle Scott Appleton, and would play through 1966. Since 1960, Dial and Steeler quarterback Bobby Layne had teamed to provide a consistent source of torture to the Cowboy pass defense. Dial, an All-American from Rice and a Pro-Bowler for 1961, had been the fifth leading receiver in the NFC in 1963 with 60 catches that garnered 1,295 yards. His average gain per reception of 21.6 was tops in the NFC that year. (Dallas Cowboys)

by Frank Clarke and Pettis Norman. The offensive line would consist of tackles Jim Boeke and Ralph Neely; guards Tony Liscio, Leon Donohue, and, occasionally, rookie John Niland; and center Dave Manders. The defensive line would have a front four of George Andrie, Bob Lilly, Jim Colvin, and Larry Stephens, who would lose the job later in the season to Willie Townes. The linebackers were Dave Edwards and Chuck Howley on the outside, with Lee Roy Jordan in the middle. Besides Renfro in the defensive backfield, there was also Cornell Green, Warren Livingston, and Mike Gaechter.

The New York Giants arrived for the regular-season opener, and many thought the boys from Manhattan would be a contender that year for the Eastern title. And everyone knew they were spoiling for revenge against the Cowboys, who had snatched the Playoff Bowl bid from them in the last game of 1965. At that time, no one would have predicted that the Giants were on the way to their worst season in 41 years in the NFL, one in which they would win only a single game. Nor would anyone have predicted the humiliation that would be heaped on them that opening day in the Cotton Bowl. The Cowboys, with an inspired offense and a stonewall defense, crushed the Giants 52–7. Since the Cowboys began in 1960, this was the most points the team had put on a football scoreboard. The headline the next morning in the Dallas *Morning News* was "Dandy Don Dazzles the Giants," and sportswriter Gary Cartwright referred to it as "Dallas in Wonderland." Meredith threw five touchdown passes that

Dandy Don Meredith gets some sideline suggestions from Coach Tom Landry. By 1965, when this picture was taken, Meredith was firmly entrenched as the Cowboys' front-line quarterback and on the way to his best season thus far as a Cowboy. (Pro Football Hall of Fame)

Bob Hayes

When Bob Hayes joined the Dallas Cowboys in 1965, he owned the world's records for the 100-yard dash (9.1), the indoor 60-yard dash (5.9), and the indoor 70-yard dash (6.9). In describing himself, he said, "I'm just the country boy going to the city with taps on my tennis shoes."

On his great speed, he said, "I may be quick but let me tell you I've never run as fast as when I started seeing those linebackers coming at me."

Bob Hayes, to this day, holds most of the Cowboys' all-time career receiving records. He gained more yardage receiving than anyone else (7,295), had the highest average gain per reception of anyone (20 yards), caught the most touchdown passes (71), and was the receiver on the longest single pass play in the team's history (95 yards). He also holds the club record for most yards receiving in a single game (246) and is tied with Danny Reeves, Calvin Hill, and Duane Thomas for the most touchdowns in a single game (4). His record of catching the most Cowboy passes (365) was surpassed in 1980 by Drew Pearson when he extended his career record to 378.

day, a Cowboy record, and gained 358 yards passing on 14 completions out of 24 attempts. Bob Hayes caught two of the Meredith TD strikes (one a 74-yarder), and Danny Reeves collected the other three. Two other club records were set that day, the most touchdowns and the most extra points in a game (seven, the previous record of six having been set back in 1962 against the Cleveland Browns).

The Vikings, two games into the season already, came down to Dallas next. They were smarting from a loss to the Baltimore Colts and a tie with the 49ers. For three quarters, it appeared they might post their first win of the season at the expense of an overconfident Dallas Cowboy team. In the fourth quarter, the Cowboys were losing 17–14, but Meredith engineered two sustained drives, capping the first with an 8-yard TD pass to Buddy Dial, while the second ended when Danny Reeves scampered 11 yards for a touchdown, and the Cowboys had their second win of the year.

The brand-new Atlanta Falcons hosted the Cowboys next and fell 47–14 in a game that produced what was now being called "the inevitable" TD pass from Meredith to Bob Hayes, this one a 49 yarder. There was also a spectacular 97-yard touchdown run by linebacker Chuck Howley, who grabbed the football after Jethro Pugh knocked it from the hands of Falcon running back Perry Lee Dunn.

Returning to the Cotton Bowl, the Cowboys prepared for the Eagles, who flew in to test the team the sportswriters were now calling "awesome" and "explosive"—and they quickly found out. It was another Dandy Don Meredith day. The young man who had absorbed so many boos in the past few years now was serenaded only with the oohs and ahs and cheers of the full houses that packed the Cotton Bowl. And the sounds were especially sweet that day because once again Meredith threw five touchdown passes, and this time the Cowboys set eight team records as they demolished the Eagles 56–7. During the game, as touchdown after touchdown was put on the board, the Philadelphia TV announcer said: "The Cowboys are not taking prisoners. They are shooting the wounded."

Entered into the legend of Cowboy records that day were: most points in a game (56); largest margin of victory (49 points); most touchdowns (8); most extra points (8); most first downs (32); most net yards passing (440); most yards total offense (652); fewest first downs allowed rushing (0).

Meredith's moments of glory that day consisted of three TD passes to Bob Hayes, one to Dan Reeves, and another to Frank Clarke. He also earned a total of 394 yards with his tosses; his completion ratio was 19 out of 26.

Now 4–0, the Cowboys were tied for first place in the NFL East with the St. Louis Cardinals. And at this stage of the season, Dandy Don was the NFL's leading quarterback, with 14 touchdown passes to his credit. (In 1964, he had only thrown nine in the entire 14-game season.) Leading the NFL in scoring was the young man who had come off the bench to replace a hobbled Mel Renfro, Danny Reeves, who had a total of 48 points, the result of eight touchdowns.

The Cowboys then traveled to St. Louis to determine who would be dislodged from the ranks of the undefeated. The Cardinals had a variety of threats, with the passing of Charley Johnson, the running skills of Johnny

By 1965, the Cowboy defense was coming into its own, as could easily be affirmed by St. Louis Cardinal running back Bill Triplett (38). Here, he feels the crunch and crush of tackles Bob Lilly (74) and Jim Colvin (77). Looking on are defensive back Mel Renfro (20) and linebacker Chuck Howley (54). The Cowboys drubbed the Cardinals that day in Dallas, 27–13.   (Bradley Photographers)

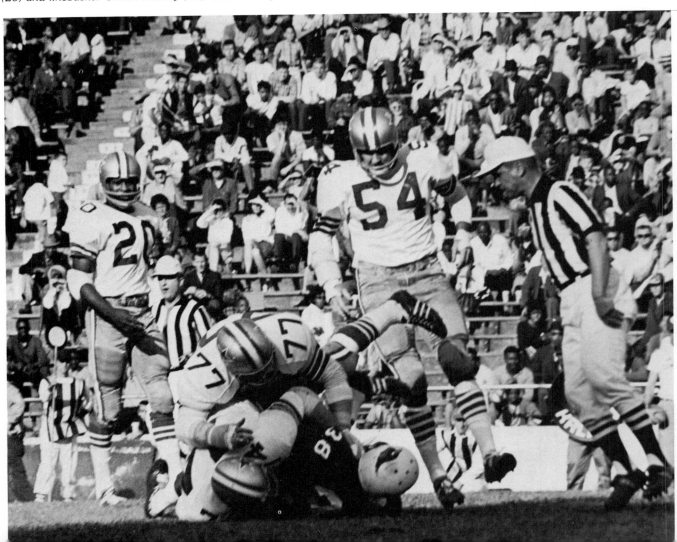

Roland, and the precision kicking of Jim Bakken. When the day was over, however, both teams were still undefeated. The Cowboys, winning in the fourth quarter 10–7 on the merits of a Danny Villanueva field goal and a touchdown pass from Meredith to Pete Gent, saw it all go for nothing when, with 3:57 on the clock, Jim Bakken kicked a 27-yard field goal. Afterward, Blackie Sherrod wrote in the Dallas *Times Herald*, "It was so quiet in both dressing rooms, you could hear a pennant drop." The Cowboys no doubt were reflecting on the three interceptions and one fumble they had turned over to the Cardinals that day.

The first loss for the Cowboys, however, was not long in coming. One week to be exact. The Cleveland Browns, still in contention in the conference race with a 3–2 record, handed it to them. But the Cowboys got back on track the following week, electrifying the fans in the Cotton Bowl with a 52-point effort against the Steelers, which included Mel Renfro's 87-yard kickoff return for a TD, Lee Roy Jordan's 49-yard romp for another with a pass interception, and four touchdown passes from Don Meredith (one an 84-yard play with flanker Pete Gent).

The Cowboys, however, fell from grace the next week when the Eagles beat them by a point, thereby dropping them to second place behind the Cardinals, who had only one loss. It was the specialty teams that let the Cowboys down that day, allowing Timmy Brown to return two kickoffs for touchdowns on runs of 93 and 90 yards and Aaron Martin to carry a punt return 67 yards for another

This brutal sack by Bob Lilly (74) and Jim Colvin (77) separates St. Louis Cardinal quarterback Charley Johnson (12) from the football on a cold December afternoon at the Cotton Bowl in 1965. The Cowboys won the game, 27–13; one of seven wins in 1965, their first .500 regular season. The other Cardinal in the picture is guard Ken Gray.   (Pro Football Hall of Fame)

Before a backdrop of palm trees at Miami's Orange Bowl, Dandy Don Meredith scrambles in the Cowboys' first postseason game. It was the Playoff Bowl for the 1965 NFL runners-up, and the Baltimore Colts annihilated them, 35–3. Chasing Meredith are Dennis Gaubatz (53) and Roy Hilton (85). The Cowboy in the background is tackle Jim Boeke.   (Bradley Photographers)

A rare glimpse of Mel Renfro as a running back is recorded here in the opening game of the 1966 regular season against the New York Giants. Renfro had been switched to an offensive back in the preseason but injuries would sideline him, and Danny Reeves would retrieve the starting position as tandem running back to Don Perkins. The Cowboy on the ground is tight end Pettis Norman; the Giant is Jeff Smith (57). (Bradley Photographers)

Flanker Buddy Dial makes this picture-perfect catch of a Don Meredith pass against the Philadelphia Eagles in 1966. It was one of 19 completions Meredith threw that afternoon for a total of 394 yards, as the Cowboys destroyed the Eagles, 56–7. Beaten on the play by Dial is Eagle defender Al Nelson (26). (Bradley Photographers)

score. Tom Landry also had the displeasure of watching his old bane Sam Baker boot a field goal to provide the necessary points for victory.

The Cowboys came back with two straight wins and on Thanksgiving Day were once again tied with the St. Louis Cardinals for the conference lead, both now with records of 7–2–1. The largest crowd in the history of the Cotton Bowl came out to watch the Cowboys play. They were taking on the Cleveland Browns, who, with a record of 7–3, could slip ahead of the Cowboys in the conference standings that day with a victory. At halftime they were halfway there, leading 14–13. A stingy Dallas defense, however, would not cede another point, and with two more field goals from Danny Villanueva (he had four that day) and a 10-yard touchdown run by Don Perkins, the Cowboys preserved their tie for first place in the NFL East.

The Cardinals were next. Both teams were 8–2–1, but the Cardinals were now playing without their fine quarterback, Charley Johnson, out for the season because of a knee injury. With his absence, the oddsmakers in Dallas made the Cowboys a 14-point favorite. And they were right on target. The Cowboys dominated the game from beginning to end and won it just as the bookmakers said they would, by 14 points, 31–17.

The deflated Cardinals lost the remaining two games of their season and ended up in fourth place. The Cowboys split, dropping a close one to the Washington Redskins on a day when Sonny Jurgensen again shone. When asked after the game why he always seemed to reach such brilliance against the Cowboys, he shrugged, "It's just cow-bustin', that's all." The Cowboys did not even need the win over the Giants the following week to earn the conference title, but they took it, anyway, and ended their first winning season with a record of 10–3–1, making sportswriter and prognosticator Steve Perkins look especially prescient. (You will remember he offered a preseason prediction of 10–4.)

In the NFL West, the Green Bay Packers cruised into the championship game on the calmest of seas, with a record of 12–2; the next closest team was the Colts, far back with a 9–5 record.

Green Bay was aging fast, some said, while the Cowboys were young and fresh, the new wave, but the Packers of old were also grizzled and tough and wily. Bart Starr had had one of the best of his many fine years in 1966, completing 156 of 251 passes for an amazing 62% completion record. His average yards gained per attempt of 9.0 was the highest in the NFL. Jim Taylor, 31, was still strong, but Paul Hornung, 29, had been bothered much of the season with injuries. The two affluent rookies, Donny Anderson and Jim Grabowski, earned their huge salaries largely on the specialty teams.

The game was scheduled for the Cotton Bowl New

Year's Day, and the winner would go to Los Angeles to play the AFL champ in Super Bowl I, although the classic would not be formally known as that for several years. The Cowboys knew they were to face a savage defense, but the Packers had to worry about the blazing speed of Bob Hayes and the patented bombs that Don Meredith had been lofting to him all year. Not just that; they would be facing the most volatile offense in the NFL, one that led the league with 445 total points, which was 110 more than the Packers were able to score.

The city of Dallas was in a state of virtual uproar as they anticipated hosting a championship game and having its own—now beloved—Cowboys as a participant. Tickets at $10 each were sold out the first morning they went on sale. It was a far cry from those lonely days at the beginning of the decade when there were usually two empty seats for every one that was occupied at a Cowboy game. In fact, the 1966 regular season attracted an average crowd of 67,625 to the Cowboy home games, 12,000 more than the previous year and the largest in the team's history.

They had barely finished sweeping out the stadium from the Cotton Bowl game the day before, when SMU played Georgia, before the Cowboys were on the field warming up. It was a clear, sharply cool day, although by

Question: *You came with the Cowboys in 1966. What was your first impression about the Dallas defense?*

Ernie Stautner: *The flex defense, Tom Landry's defense. It was very impressive. Take the layout of the playbook. Here a rookie could learn his keys right from it, where it took me five years as a player to learn keys by experience. It takes a rookie normally about three to five years to know what to do, to know what's happening, to know how to key. The first few years, you don't know what's happening. But Tom had it all worked out and down on paper. I had to bluff my way through the first year or two of coaching. It really takes a couple of years before you can teach Tom's flex defense with authority, with certainty. So I got through the first two years. After that, I probably added some different keys, some different moves, changed it a little bit, but not basically. I tried to implement the work that had already been done.*

Green Bay standards it could have been classified as almost warm.

The Packers won the coin toss and chose to receive.

The elusive Bob Hayes, all alone, streaks toward the end zone in this 1966 game against the Philadelphia Eagles. The ball, on its way from Don Meredith (17) who is on his way to the ground, landed in Hayes's hands at the 2 and he stepped into the end zone unmolested. It was one of five touchdown passes Meredith threw that afternoon as the Cowboys racked up the most points in their seven-year history, winning 56–7.   (Bradley Photographers)

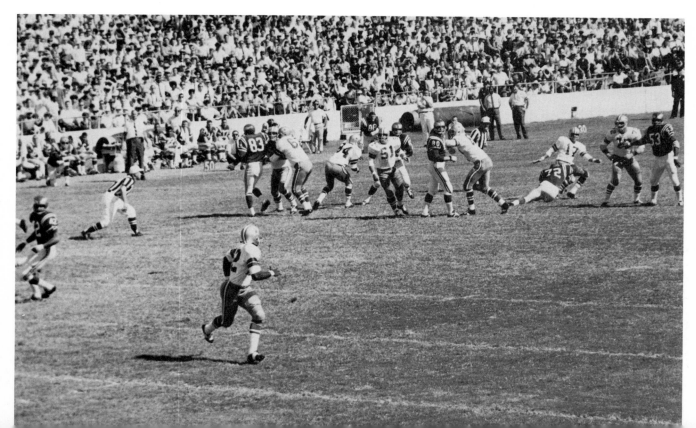

This is the way they lined up New Year's Day 1966 at the Cotton Bowl for the Dallas Cowboys' first NFL championship game.

Dallas Cowboys		Green Bay Packers
Offense		
Bob Hayes	WR	Carroll Dale
Pettis Norman	TE	Marv Fleming
Jim Boeke	T	Bob Skornonski
Ralph Neely	T	Forrest Gregg
Tony Liscio	G	Fuzzy Thurston
Leon Donohue	G	Jerry Kramer
Dave Manders	C	Bill Curry
Don Meredith	QB	Bart Starr
Pete Gent	FL	Boyd Dowler
Dan Reeves	HB	Elijah Pitts
Don Perkins	FB	Jim Taylor
Defense		
Willie Townes	E	Willie Davis
George Andrie	E	Lionel Aldridge
Jim Colvin	T	Ron Kostelnik
Bob Lilly	T	Henry Jordan
Chuck Howley	LLB	Dave Robinson
Lee Roy Jordan	MLB	Ray Nitschke
Dave Edwards	RLB	Lee Roy Caffey
Cornell Green	LHB	Herb Adderley
Warren Livingston	RHB	Bob Jeter
Mike Gaechter	S	Tom Brown
Mel Renfro	S	Willie Wood

Bart Starr marched the Pack down the field and climaxed the drive with a 17-yard pass to Elijah Pitts for the first touchdown of the day.

If that was an unhappy start, the next play was like a death in the family. The Packers kicked off, and Mel Renfro let loose of the ball at his own 18-yard line, only to see it gobbled up by Green Bay's Jim Grabowski, who took it straight into the end zone. Before they had a chance to execute their first offensive play, the Cowboys trailed 14–0. In another year, that might have signaled collapse, a blowout by the soaring Pack. But this was a different Cowboy team. This one was not only *not* used to losing, it was accustomed to perpetrating the blowout.

Ernie Stautner exhorted the defense on the sideline. Tom Landry made it clear to Meredith the offense had to produce, and quickly. And they did. A sustained drive brought the Cowboys all the way down the field, and finally Danny Reeves bucked in from the 3. The defense held, and the Cowboys began another march. This time,

Don Perkins burst into the clear and carried the ball 23 yards into the end zone, and before the first quarter was over, the score was tied.

Starr stung the Cowboys in the second quarter with a 51-yard pass to Carroll Dale for another Packer touchdown. The Cowboys responded with an 11-yard field goal from Danny Villanueva. At halftime, the Cowboys were behind by 4 points.

Another Villanueva field goal brought them within a point early in the third quarter. But Bart Starr's momentum that afternoon was irresistible. He came back with

Bob Hayes and Don Meredith were pegged the "Dynamic Duo" in 1966 because their exploits on the field were often as breathtaking as those of the camp TV heroes of the day, Batman and Robin. Meredith to Hayes was the most electrifying pass combination in the league that year, especially in the game they are taking a breather from here. That day Meredith led the Cowboys to a 56–7 victory over the Philadelphia Eagles, in a game where eight club records were broken. Leaving the game when the score was 42–0, Meredith had thrown five touchdown passes, three of them to Bob Hayes. (Pro Football Hall of Fame)

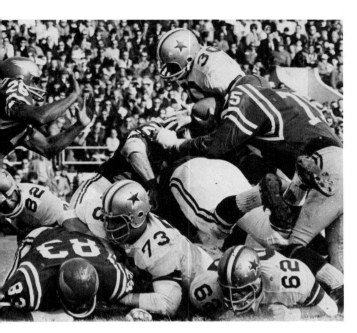

NATIONAL FOOTBALL LEAGUE CHAMPIONSHIP

COWBOYS PACKERS

COTTON BOWL · DALLAS, TEXAS · JAN. 1, 1967

$1.00 INCLUDING TAX

Danny Reeves finds it tough going up the middle in this 1966 game against the Philadelphia Eagles. Trying to gouge out a hole for him are blockers Frank Clarke (82), Ralph Neely (73), and Leon Donohue (62). On the way to their first appearance in an NFL championship game, the Cowboys split their two games with the Eagles that year. The Eagles in the picture are: Al Nelson (26), Don Hultz (83), and John Meyers (75).   (Pro Football Hall of Fame)

Frank Clarke, who switched from flanker to tight end in 1966, grabs a pass here against the Pittsburgh Steelers. Clarke came to Dallas from the Cleveland Browns in the 1960 expansion draft to launch a fine eight-year career with the Cowboys. He is the third-ranking receiver in Cowboy history. In the background is wide receiver Bob Hayes (22).   (Bradley Photographers)

two touchdown strikes, to Boyd Dowler and Max McGee, and the Packers had a commanding two-touchdown lead in the fourth quarter. It would have been a 15-point lead had it not been for a crucial play by Bob Lilly, who broke through to block the last extra point.

The fourth quarter was nothing but sheer excitement. The Cowboys would not give up. It was third down with a long 20 yards to go for a first down; Meredith whipped a bomb to a wide-open Frank Clarke, and a 68-yard touchdown was registered.

There was just a little over four minutes left when the Cowboys kicked off. It was now up to the Dallas defense to hold and get the ball back; a Cowboy touchdown and the extra point would send the game into a sudden-death overtime. They did hold, and Don Meredith and the rest of the Cowboy offense trotted back out onto the field with 2:19 left and the ball on the Green Bay 47-yard line. Frank Clarke made a move down the middle and grabbed Meredith's pass, bringing the ball to the Packers 26. Meredith

The First Postseason

Tex Schramm: *I can remember, probably one of the happiest, greatest thrills we've ever had—I've ever had. It was that 7–7 season, where we wound up finishing second and going to the Playoff Bowl in Miami (1965).*

It was after the last regular-season game. We played in New York, and when we got home, one of the girls in the office, Tom Landry's secretary, surprised us. Her husband worked for a downtown department store, and so, with her husband, she had gone down and gotten mannequins and palm trees and stuff like that they decorate their windows with, and when we came back to the office, they had all these mannequins with bikinis on, palm trees, that grass stuff on the floor, and the whole office was made up to look like Miami because we were going to the Playoff Bowl. That was as big to everybody then as going to any Super Bowl. We promptly went down and celebrated before the game. We got there and got the hell kicked out of us by Baltimore. They didn't have a quarterback. They used Tom Matte as their quarterback. But it was still a great experience, that first one.

Question: *Could you describe what the day of the draft is like?*

Gil Brandt: *The day of the draft is kind of like Christmas morning when you have a family of little children and everybody is opening presents. After the first two or three rounds go by and all the exciting players are drafted, you lose some interest in the draft.*

Question: *How is the final decision made as to who the Cowboys are going to draft and in what order?*

Gil Brandt: *We—Tom Landry and I—sit down with our scouts, and we use the computer list, and from that list we will talk about the players. We put them in order, and we will rearrange those players in terms of our needs. But the final list is usually very close to the computer list.*

Don Meredith (17) hands off to Don Perkins (43) during the Cowboys' first appearance in an NFL championship game. But Packer tackle Ron Kostelnik, eluding the block of guard Leon Donohue (62) here, zeroes in on Perkins. Although the Cowboys lost that New Year's Day 1967, Perkins led in rushing with 108 yards, an impressive average of 6.4 yards per carry.   (Vernon Biever)

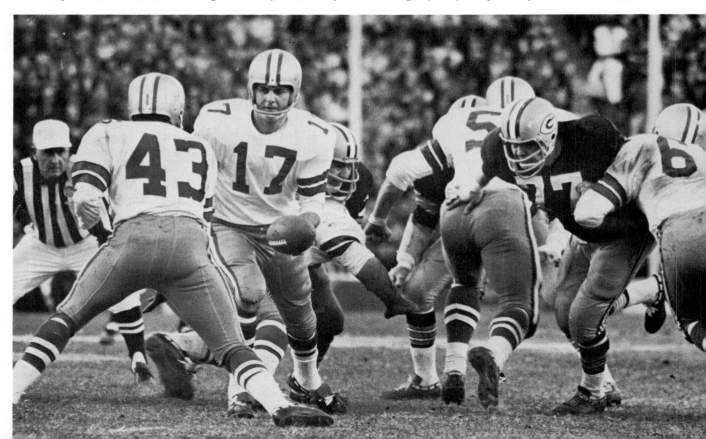

Tackles Bob Lilly (74) and Willie Townes converge on a hurried Bart Starr, as the Green Bay quarterback tries to unload the ball in the 1966 NFL conference championship game. Starr had a phenomenal afternoon at the Cotton Bowl, throwing 4 touchdown passes and completing 19 of 28 passes for 304 yards. The Packers won, 34–27, but the Cowboys were threatening all the way to the last 28 seconds of the game.   (Vernon Biever)

Cowboys vs 49ers
Cotton Bowl, 1:30 P.M.
Sunday, November 7, 1965
OFFICIAL PROGRAM 50¢ INCLUDING TAX

national football league
ILLUSTRATED

Rookie Bob Hayes, about to do what he would do so well during his 10-year career with the Cowboys—catch the football. Here, he does it against the San Francisco 49ers as defenders Kermit Alexander (39) and Wayne Swinford (23) chase after him. (Bradley Photographers)

decided to go to Clarke again. This time, Clarke did not catch the ball, but the referee's flag was on the ground at the 2-yard line—interference was the call on the Packers' Tom Brown. First down and goal to go at the two, and there was one minute and 52 seconds left in the game.

A slant off tackle by Danny Reeves picked up a yard. With the ball on the one, Meredith tried to go to his tight end Pettis Norman, who dropped the pass in the end zone. Worse, perhaps, was that tackle Jim Boeke of the Cowboys had jumped offsides and the 5-yard penalty moved the Cowboys back to the 6-yard line. A flare-out pass to Danny Reeves fell from his hands. On third down, Pettis Norman slanted out toward the end zone, but Meredith's pass was short, and he had to go down on his knees at the 2 to catch it.

1966

Preseason

Dallas	(5-0)	Opponents
24	San Francisco (28,899) @ S. F.	13
20	Los Angeles (44,217) @ L. A.	10
21	Green Bay (75,504) @ Dallas	3
20	Detroit (31,250) @ Tulsa	10
28	Minnesota (58,316) @ Dallas	24

Regular Season

(10-3-1)

W	52	New York (60,010) (H)	7
W	28	Minnesota (64,116) (H)	17
W	47	Atlanta (56,990)	14
W	56	Philadelphia (69,372) (H)	7
T	10	St. Louis (50,673)	10
L	21	Cleveland (84,721)	30
W	52	Pittsburgh (58,453) (H)	21
L	23	Philadelphia (60,658)	24
W	31	Washington (50,927)	30
W	20	Pittsburgh (42,185)	7
W	26	Cleveland (80,259) (H)	14
W	31	St. Louis (76,965) (H)	17
L	31	Washington (64,198) (H)	34
W	17	New York (62,735)	7
	445		239

Postseason

Championship Game
(Dallas)

L	27	Green Bay (75,504)	34

The Cowboys had one more down, one last play. It was listed in the playbook as "Fire 90 Quarterback Roll Right." In less esoteric language, it meant that Meredith would roll to his right with the option of passing or running. Meredith took the snap and headed out that way, but it was not the end zone his eyes beheld; all he really saw was the massive hulk of linebacker Dave Robinson looming down on him. As Dandy Don later described it: "He played it perfectly. He came in with his hands up high, screening off my receivers until he got close enough, and then he dropped his arms around me. I couldn't do anything but flip the ball into the end zone and hope someone in a white jersey would catch it." Instead, someone in a green jersey did, defensive back Tom Brown.

The ball was given to the Packers at their 20, and they ran the clock out to end what Tex Maule in *Sports Illustrated* described as "a flamboyant display of football histrionics," a game of "pure suspense and unremitting excitement." It was indeed all that, one of the very best in a long series of championship games.

When it was over, the Packers made plans to face the

Stautner, Landry, and a Bloody Nose

When Tom Landry was playing football for the New York Giants and Ernie Stautner was wearing a Pittsburgh Steeler uniform, their two teams played each other a number of times. Because both were defensive players, however, they were normally not on the field at the same time. Except once.

It was 1952 and the Giants were playing in Pittsburgh. Giants quarterback Charley Conerly was hurt during the game, then his back-up, Fred Benners, had to leave the game, so coach Steve Owen moved Landry to that position. It was the first time Landry had played quarterback since the days when Bobby Layne won that position from him back at the University of Texas, but it really didn't matter all that much because the Giants were losing to the Steelers at the time 63–7.

On one play, Landry dropped back to pass, and Stautner broke through, not only tackling him but popping him in the face at the same time with that great bludgeon of a hand he had. Landry was bleeding considerably from the nose and the mouth.

As Stautner remembers it, "I knew I shouldn't have done it, but it was just a spontaneous reaction. When I started to walk away, Tom started to pound me on the back and I just kept going because I knew I was wrong. He reminded me about it when I first came down here (to Dallas)."

It was more than a decade later, and the two men were talking about the possibility of Stautner's joining the Cowboy coaching staff. Stautner said suddenly: "Remember that time I hit you in the mouth, Tom? Well, I want to assure you it was an accident."

Landry nodded and said, "Bygones are bygones." Then, after Stautner left, he turned to one of his assistant coaches and added, "You know those linemen, they always tell you it was an accident."

Landry also enjoys telling his version of the incident: "As he helped me up, he said, 'Oh, gosh, I'm sure sorry. I shouldn't have hit you like that. You aren't a quarterback.' I still don't know just how he meant that."

Kansas City Chiefs in Super Bowl I, whom they would dispose of with facility (35–10). Bart Starr had had a wonderful day against the Cowboys—a pass-completion percentage of 67.9, a total 304 yards gained passing, and, of course, his four TDs. But the rugged Dallas defense had held Jim Taylor to a mere 37 yards that day, and the entire Packer running game only earned 102 yards. On the other hand, the esteemed Packer defense gave up 187 yards to the Cowboy rush, 108 of which were picked up by Don Perkins. It was a day of disappointment, but the Cowboys had nothing to be ashamed about. They had

played relentlessly, showed that they could come back, and proved to everyone they were a very definite force now in the NFL.

Before becoming an assistant coach with the Cowboys, Ernie Stautner played for 14 seasons with the Pittsburgh Steelers. One of the toughest defensive tackles ever to have played the game, Stautner was invited to nine Pro Bowl games. His jersey, No. 70, was retired when he left the Steelers, and he was elected to the Pro Football Hall of Fame in 1969. (Pro Football Hall of Fame)

Linebacker Dave Edwards surges after Green Bay Packer great Jim Taylor in the game for the 1966 NFL conference crown. The Cowboys held Hall of Famer Taylor to 37 yards that day, and the entire Green Bay rushing game to a mere 102 yards. But it was not quite enough, and the Packers earned the right to play in Super Bowl I. (Vernon Biever)

8 Journey to the Ice Bowl

THE WINTRY WINDS AND GRAY DAYS of January in Dallas did not seem quite so bad in 1967 as the Cowboy cadre settled into the season's aftermath. There was the warmth and gratification of their first winning season to take the sting out of nature's elements. The football-field events of the year were, in the words of Tex Schramm, "a pleasure to contemplate." And now there was a kind of current pulsing through the organization, one which stimulated the feelings that the Cowboys truly had accomplished something that year, had finally reached an aimed-for plateau, and were on the verge of ascending to the pinnacle.

In the season just past, the team had scored the most points it ever had—445—a record which stood until the 1980 season total of 454, which would be accomplished with the aid of two extra games. Their average of 31.8 points per game was far and away the best in the NFL that year and the highest in Cowboy history. And Dallas led the league with 24 touchdowns rushing, and in total passing yardage (3,331, an average of 238 yards per game), and the defense allowed the least yards rushing in the league (1,176).

Bob Hayes set a club record by gaining 1,232 yards on 64 pass receptions, and his 12 TD catches were the most a Cowboy had ever packed away up to that time. Danny Reeves set another team record by scoring a total of 16 touchdowns, and he also led the team in rushing, the first time since 1960 that anyone other than Don Perkins could claim that honor.

Kicker Danny Villanueva led the NFL in points after touchdown (56 of 56) and set an all-time Cowboy scoring record with 107 points.

The Cowboys placed four players on the All-Pro team of 1966: Bob Hayes, Bob Lilly, Chuck Howley, and Cornell Green. And Dandy Don Meredith received the Bert Bell Award as the Most Valuable Player in the NFL.

Clint Murchison announced that he was going to look into the possibility of finding a new stadium to showcase his new, now-winning Cowboys. The Cotton Bowl left much to be desired, he felt, in terms of its dated facilities; it did not fit with the chrome-modern image he wanted for the Cowboys. One site he had in mind was a little plot in Irving, a contiguous suburb, where Murchison owned or had options to buy some 90 acres. The seed that was to grow into Texas Stadium, it could be said, was planted there in the spring of 1967.

Everything was not on the upbeat, however. Don Perkins announced that he was planning to retire from the game. (He would change his mind and return for two more seasons.) And there was some disillusionment with the kicking game, despite Danny Villanueva's record-setting season in 1966, primarily in the area of punting—his were too short and did not hang in the atmosphere as long as they should, it was said—and his field goal range was a little less distant than what was desired. So Gil Brandt organized the "Kick Karavan," a committee composed of himself, former pro kicker Ben Agajanian, assistant coach Ermal Allen, and a few others, which would make a whirlwind tour of 28 cities across the United States to search for a kicker to fill their needs. It would garner a lot of publicity and a few laughs, but it would not produce a kicker, and Danny Villanueva would be back booting the ball for the Cowboys in 1967.

1967 Dallas Cowboys. Front row: Larry Gardner, Jim Myers, Danny Villanueva, Jerry Rhome, Craig Morton, Don Meredith, Lance Rentzel, Mel Renfro, Dick Daniels, Bob Hayes, Don Cochren. Second row: Dick Nolan, Mike Johnson, Les Shy, Mike Gaechter, Dan Reeves, Sims Stokes, Cornell Green, Pete Gent, Phil Clark, Don Perkins, Ernie Stautner. Third row: Leavie Davis, Craig Baynham, Jerry Tubbs, Dave Edwards, Mike Connelly, Chuck Howley, Lee Roy Jordan, Harold Hays, Malcolm Walker, Leon Donohue, Ermal Allen, Tom Landry (coach). Fourth row: Curtis Marker, John Wilbur, George Andrie, Jim Boeke, Willie Townes, Tony Liscio, Ralph Neely, Bob Lilly. Top row: Jethro Pugh, John Niland, Coy Bacon, Ron East, Frank Clarke, Harold Deters, Pettis Norman, Rayfield Wright.   (Pro Football Hall of Fame)

The draft was a lean one that year compared to the previous ones, and part of the reason was that the Cowboys had to cede their picks in the first and second rounds to Houston as part of the settlement over the Ralph Neely affair. In the seventh round, however, they tabbed Rayfield Wright, a 6 feet 7 inch, 235-pound tackle from Fort Valley State College, a school tucked away in the little town of Fort Valley, Georgia. And they added running backs Les Shy of Long Beach State College and Craig Baynham from Georgia Tech as well as defensive back Phil Clark from Northwestern.

The best deal of the year, however, was made with the Minnesota Vikings. The Cowboys acquired wide receiver Lance Rentzel for only a third-round draft choice.

After the Cowboys finished with the two traditional California exhibition games—losing to the Rams and defeating the 49ers—they came back to Texas for the Salesmanship Club classic with the Green Bay Packers. The game, played at the diametric opposite of the temperature scale from the one to take place in Green Bay at the end of the season, was attended by more than 78,000 people. They sweated through the 90-plus-degree heat and the

The New NFL

In 1967, the NFL split its two conferences into four divisions, which introduced an additional playoff game to the postseason agenda. The new lineup:

Eastern Conference	Western Conference
Capital Division	**Central Division**
Dallas Cowboys	Green Bay Packers
Philadelphia Eagles	Chicago Bears
Washington Redskins	Detroit Lions
New Orleans Saints	Minnesota Vikings
Century Division	**Coastal Division**
Cleveland Browns	Los Angeles Rams
New York Giants	Baltimore Colts
St. Louis Cardinals	San Francisco 49ers
Pittsburgh Steelers	Atlanta Falcons

soggy humidity and found it was hardly a replay of the exciting show the two teams had put on at the end of the 1966 season. Green Bay mauled the Cowboys that Au-

Lance Rentzel races across the frozen turf at Lambeau Field in Green Bay after catching a pass from halfback Danny Reeves on the first play of the fourth quarter. The result: a 50-yard touchdown that put the Cowboys ahead 17–14 in the 1967 NFL championship game, a lead they would maintain until the last 16 seconds, then lose. No. 84 on the Cowboys is tight end Pettis Norman. Chasing Rentzel is Packer defensive back Tom Brown (40). (AP)

gust night, 20–3.

Regardless of this setback, almost everyone was picking the Cowboys to win their division in 1967. The Eagles were perhaps the only team with a chance to snatch it from them, but it was a distant one, most felt, and the Redskins and the new expansion club in New Orleans were hardly considered threats.

The preseason play had exacted a toll from the Cowboys. Don Meredith, for one, had several ribs fractured in the last preseason game. It would not put him on the bench, but it would be the first of a variety of painful injuries which would trouble him throughout the season. Center Dave Manders was even less fortunate; he was out for the season with an injured knee.

More than 81,000 people were on hand at Cleveland's Municipal Stadium to watch the Cowboys and the Browns launch their seasons. The Browns were good even though Jim Brown was no longer around. Leroy Kelly had proved to be an admirable replacement and was the second leading rusher in the NFL the year before, a mere 90 yards behind the Bears' Gale Sayers, and Kelly's 15 touchdowns and his average of 5.5 yards per carry

were the highest in the league. Also, Frank Ryan now had two superb receivers since Paul Warfield had joined Gary Collins. Lou Groza, at 43, was still their place kicker.

The game, most sportswriters anticipated, would be repeated at the end of the regular season when both of the predicted division winners would play to see who would face the winner of the Western Conference for the NFL title.

That afternoon, the Cowboys had no trouble with the free-wheeling Browns. They dominated the game from the kickoff until the final gun and won it by a touchdown. For a young man with a shattered rib cage held together by adhesive tape, Don Meredith did surprisingly well, picking up 205 yards passing, including touchdown tosses to Bob Hayes and Danny Reeves.

Against the Giants the next week in Dallas, they quickly convinced the fans that the offense of the year before was still alive and well. Meredith threw four touchdown passes, completing 16 of 28 for 243 yards. Bob Hayes

1967

Preseason

Dallas	(2–3)	Opponents
6	Los Angeles (57,595) @ L. A.	20
30	San Francisco (31,212) @ S. F.	24
3	Green Bay (78,087) @ Dallas	20
30	Houston (53,125) @ Houston	17
7	Baltimore (58,492) @ Dallas	33

Regular Season

		(9–5)	
W	21	Cleveland (81,039)	14
W	38	New York (66,209) (H)	24
L	13	Los Angeles (75,229) (H)	35
W	17	Washington (50,566)	14
W	14	New Orleans (64,128) (H)	10
W	24	Pittsburgh (39,641)	21
L	14	Philadelphia (60,740)	21
W	37	Atlanta (54,751) (H)	7
W	27	New Orleans (83,437)	10
L	20	Washington (75,538) (H)	27
W	46	St. Louis (68,787) (H)	21
L	17	Baltimore (60,238)	23
W	38	Philadelphia (55,834) (H)	17
L	16	San Francisco (27,182)	24
	342		268

Postseason

		Eastern Championship Game (Dallas)	
W	52	Cleveland (70,786)	14
		Championship Game (Green Bay)	
L	17	Green Bay (50,861)	21

caught two of Meredith's touchdown tosses, Pete Gent another, and Danny Reeves the fourth on a little 2-yard floater into the end zone. The Cowboys gained 414 net yards and posted 38 points for the day. Newcomer Harold Deters from the Kick Karavan kicked his first (and only) Dallas Cowboys field goal, a 12 yarder.

The Cowboys had lost to the Rams in their first preseason game and had seen some of the electricity that Roman Gabriel had injected into the team's offense, a nice complement to George Allen's team's renowned defense. The front four of Lamar Lundy, Deacon Jones, Roger Brown, and Merlin Olsen, backed up by Jack Pardee, Maxie Baughan, and Myron Pottios, had allowed only a total of 16 points in their first two games, and the Rams had won both of them handily.

During the week before the game, charges were exchanged that scouting between the two teams had turned into spying. Tex Schramm told of a suspicious yellow Chevrolet parked near the Cowboys' practice field. He had gotten its license number, and after some sleuthing, it was traced to Hertz Rent-a-Car, and, lo and behold, if Hertz had not rented it to Johnny Sanders, who was the chief of the Los Angeles Rams' scouting system. Tex Schramm lodged a formal complaint with NFL commissioner Pete Rozelle.

George Allen came back with a countercharge. He said that the Rams coaching staff had observed a man sitting up in a eucalyptus tree with binoculars spying on their practice out in sunny California. They had chased the man but had not caught him. The man who got away, Allen said, looked an awful lot like Frank "Bucko" Kilroy, the former Philadelphia Eagle great who was now in the employ of the Cowboys as a scout.

The allegations of heinous espionage and peeping Tomism added a little flavor to the buildup to the game, but nothing ever came of the charges. The Rams and the Cowboys met in Dallas, and during the first half it was a game. But the Rams totally dominated the second half, scoring 14 points in each of the last two quarters and

ending the day with a 35–13 win.

The only encouraging note to come from the Rams game was the performance of Lance Rentzel, who caught nine passes for 102 yards, revealing a very real threat at the other side of the Dallas line from Bob Hayes. Rentzel reinforced that feeling the following week against the Redskins—eight catches for 104 yards, including a 25-yard TD pass. The Cowboys won that game, and Meredith had another fine day. But he reinjured his ribs, and that was compounded afterward with a case of pneumonia, and so Dandy Don went to the hospital instead of the practice field. Craig Morton took over the quarterbacking for the next three games, leading the Cowboys to wins over the Saints and the Steelers. In the game against Pittsburgh, Morton had a fine day, throwing 12 completions out of 16 passes for a total of 256 yards. Three of them were touchdowns, and seven of them were caught by Bob Hayes for 170 yards. He was not able to get the Cowboys past the Philadelphia Eagles, however, and that surprise loss left the Cowboys at midseason with a record of 5–2 but still in first place in their division, a game ahead of the Eagles.

For the second half of the season, a pained, wounded, and often wincing Don Meredith was back in uniform. He

Question: *About how many players do you seriously evaluate a year?*

Gil Brandt: *Well, we have files on probably three thousand seniors every year. In the spring of the year, we will come down to about two thousand players that we will write some type of report on. The spring of the year is the period where we eliminate a lot of candidates. Over the period of two years prior to the senior year, we acquire a lot of names, and we put all these names on a master list for the spring of the year that would be the start of that player's senior year. From that list of two thousand, we generally eliminate down to about six hundred. But during the course of the year we will probably have added to that original list of two thousand maybe another two hundred names, those we somehow missed or players that are late bloomers, players that have transferred, or whatever it may be.*

Question: *Do you have personal contact with all these people?*

Gil Brandt: *I see as many of the players as I possibly can. As far as personally contacting them, we do several things. We send them all a questionnaire. Whenever I'm on campus or a scout is, we try to meet as many as possible.*

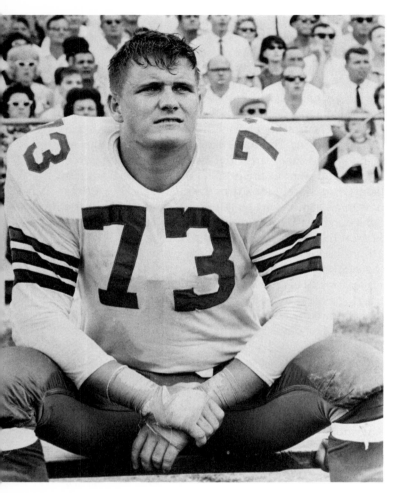

The Cowboys had acquired highly touted offensive lineman Ralph Neely in 1965, but he had also signed a contract with the AFL's Houston Oilers. For two years the courts would vacillate about who really owned his services, but during that time Neely played for the Cowboys, even if it was only on a tenuous, week-by-week basis. In 1967, however, he became a Cowboy for good, but the team had to give the Oilers in return their first- and second-round draft choices for that year.   (Bradley Photographers)

led the Cowboys to victories over the Atlanta Falcons and the New Orleans Saints. At the same time, the Eagles lost their first two games of the season's second half, which made the Cowboys a sure thing in the division race.

The rest of the season was a veritable seesaw. The Cowboys lost, won, lost, won, and lost, ending up with a record of 9–5, not as impressive as they might have hoped for, but the closest team to them in their division, the Eagles, had won only 6, lost 7, and tied 1.

Those who had predicted a Cowboy-Brown playoff game had been correct. And it had all the makings of a great game—potent offenses, both with the ever-present threat of a big play that could blow a game apart.

The Browns, like the Cowboys, had won their division with ease. When the last game of the regular season had ended, Leroy Kelly was the top rusher in the NFL. For the second straight season, he had carried the ball for more than 1,000 yards (1,205 in 1967, and he was the only NFL rusher to break the 1,000-yard barrier that year). Eleven touchdowns and 5.1 average per carry were also top stats in the league that year. Frank Ryan was well, having overcome the leg injuries which had hampered him during the season. And the Browns were surging, having won four of their last five regular-season games.

They were ready, head coach Blanton Collier told the media. "We are going to Dallas to collect our Christmas present a day early, the Eastern Conference title," he said. Only the Cowboys were not in a gift-giving mood.

The young men from Dallas ran up the biggest score of the season that Christmas eve. At halftime, it was 24–7; as the fourth quarter began, it was up to 45–7, and Tom Landry began to empty his bench to give the reserves a little taste of what it was like to romp in a postseason game. Meredith threw 13 passes; 11 of them were completions. One was a spectacular 86-yard TD to Bob Hayes. Don Perkins picked up 74 yards rushing, and

Cowboys v Eagle

COTTON BOWL / DEC. 10
FIFTY CE

NFL ILLUSTRATED

Craig Baynham, playing for an injured Danny Reeves, scored three touchdowns, two running and one on a pass from Meredith. Bob Hayes also entertained the hometown folks with two punt returns of over 60 yards each (neither for a touchdown, however).

The day belonged to the Cowboys. And Tom Landry hoped it had not sapped all their energies. They still had to face the Green Bay Packers, who had little trouble disposing of the Los Angeles Rams the day before, 28–7. It would be a repeat of the NFL championship game of 1966, only this time the Packers would host it.

It would come to be called the "Ice Bowl." And with good reason.

When the Cowboys boarded the plane out at Love Field, it had been pleasantly, if unseasonably, warm in Dallas on December 29—sport-coat weather, a kind of early October day that had somehow slipped down the calendar into the dead of winter. But they knew it was not going to be like that in Green Bay. Up there was a land where the December sports included slogging across glistening white fields in snowshoes or sliding across them on cross-country skis or sitting out on a lake above a hole axed through a foot of ice to spear a muskie or a northern who might pass in the water below; where people routinely went ice boating or tobogganing in those days before the proliferation of snowmobiles.

If anyone had chosen to gaze down through the clouds during the flight that day, they would have watched the gray and tan flatlands of northern Texas turn to hills and then erupt into the mountains of Arkansas and southern Missouri called the Ozarks, which would, in turn, give way to vast farm fields now blanketed with snow. They would have seen a radical change of seasons painted on the landscape.

The temperature was in the midteens when the airplane touched down at the tiny airport in Green Bay, but the wind made it feel even colder. The Cowboys had flown from sport-coat weather to parka weather in just a little more than two hours.

Jerry Izenberg observed in *Sport* magazine some years later: "On the day before the two clubs met to decide who would earn the right to face the Oakland Raiders in Super Bowl II, the name you kept hearing was Sy Ullsperger. Mr. Ullsperger never caught a pass, kicked a field goal or blitzed a quarterback. He was the National Weather Service's man in Green Bay and 24 hours before the title match he casually said, 'A cold air mass moving down from Canada will bring with it more fresh cold air.' "

On Saturday, the Cowboys worked out in the cold at Lambeau Field, the temperature remaining steady at about 15 degrees above zero. But Mr. Ullsperger had been correct; there was "more fresh cold air" on the way.

Cowboy flanker Pete Gent dives for a Don Meredith pass in this 1967 game against the Pittsburgh Steelers. He did not make the diving catch but the Cowboys went on to win, 24–21, that day at Pittsburgh. The Cowboy downfield is Bob Hayes (22); the Steeler defenders are Marv Woodson (47) and Brady Keys (26). (Pro Football Hall of Fame)

At eight o'clock the morning of the game, the temperature had sunk to 16 *below* zero.

It was New Year's Eve in the Northland, as Green Bayans liked to call the area they inhabited. Overnight, the snow outside the stadium had frozen on the ground and in drifts, its consistency something like crisp styrofoam now; stepping on it sounded like someone walking across a field of egg shells. The wind, when it would gust, hit a person in the face like a fusillade of needles. But still the fans came out to huddle in the icy, wind-swept arena named for Curley Lambeau—a sellout crowd of more than 50,000. They knew how to cope with the elements, those Wisconsinites, and they arrived wrapped in layers of clothing—thermal underwear and wool shirts and sweaters and furs and parkas and scarves, boots and battery-heated socks, ski masks, hats, earmuffs, and hand warmers, and most of them, anyway, were warmed inside by a variety of spirits designed to heat the innards and dull the senses.

Bubbles, a Fan

The Cowboys acquired a kind of special fan during the 1967 regular season. She was 19-year-old Theresa Cash, a freshman studying drama at Southern Methodist University. She appeared at the Cotton Bowl first that pleasant early November afternoon when the Cowboys played the Atlanta Falcons.

As John Crittenden, a sportswriter for the Miami News, *described it: "She upset the Cotton Bowl just by walking back to her seat from the concession stand . . . Through some coincidence of chemistry, suddenly men all around were pointing and grinning and cheering. The television cameras picked up the unrehearsed display of appreciation, and so did the newspaper photographers."*

Part of what caused that "coincidence of chemistry" was undoubtedly the fact that Miss Cash was endowed with measurements in a descending order of 40–23–35. The mini-skirt she wore probably had something to do with it, too. And her beaming smile showed she obviously enjoyed this sudden adulation.

Miss Cash was also used to that kind of thing because she held down a part-time job, presumably to help finance her education, at a local lounge in Dallas where she performed under the name of Bubbles Cash. As she described her work to another newsman: "I'm not an exotic dancer. And not exactly a stripper either. All I do is take my clothes off."

At any rate, her employer, thrilled with all the free publicity Miss Cash was getting as his star entertainer, procured a ticket for her for each of the remaining Cowboys games, at home and away. And she went to all of them, making frequent trips up and down the aisles to the concession stands, always to a symphony of hoots and howls, cheers, applause, eye rolling, and other gestures of appreciation.

Bubbles Cash did not, however, make the long trip north to the championship game in Green Bay. As her employer explained: "She wanted to go, but frostbite might have ruined her career."

By game time, the temperature had risen to 13 below zero, but the wind-chill factor was registering in the vicinity of 40 below. The field, frozen solid, was about as soft as a Wisconsin highway. Up in the open-air press booth, the television announcers watched in utter amazement as their steaming cups of coffee froze solid before their eyes.

The Packers were a single-touchdown favorite, but a lot of handicappers thought the weather was worth another 6 or 7 points on the spread for the Packers. In truth, however, the pros from Green Bay, although more accustomed than the Cowboys to playing football in a cold climate, were not going to reap any advantage from weather as extreme as this. The Cowboys won the coin toss at midfield, and as one sportswriter in the press box ad-libbed, "elected to play the game the following week in Dallas." As it turned out down on the field, the Cowboys chose to receive, lined up, and thought collectively that in three hours it would all be over and the world would be warm once again.

It was the second time in a calendar year that the two teams faced each other for the NFL title. On the very first day of 1967, they had gone at it in Dallas; now, on the last day of the year, they would do it again. Some of the names were gone, like Hornung and Taylor, but otherwise it was almost the very same cast.

The similarities did not end there, either. Just as they had a year ago, the Packers, on their first possession, marched down the field and scored, an 82-yard drive capped this time by an 8-yard pass from Bart Starr to flanker Boyd Dowler. The Cowboys could not get any kind of an offense going and were totally stopped in the first quarter. Then, in the first few minutes of the second quarter, Starr struck again. It was one of those third-down-and-short-yardage plays on which he so often in his career had stunned the opposition with an unexpected bomb. It was a play fake, and fullback Ben Wilson, in the game at the moment for Chuck Mercein, hit the line, but without the ball. Starr had it deep in his own backfield and threw to a streaking Boyd Dowler, who, a step or two ahead of Mel Renfro, caught the ball and went sliding across the frozen turf into the end zone. As they had 365 days earlier, the Cowboys trailed the Packers 14–0.

But just as they had then, they launched a comeback. This time, however, it was the defense that rose to the occasion. They even put some points on the board for the

Ice Bowl

A random observation on that day of the Ice Bowl, December 31, 1967.

"Before the kickoff, the first casualty emerged—the entire University of Wisconsin–LaCrosse marching band. Faced with the prospect of stepping smartly into the cold and going through the rest of their lives with their mouths frozen in a perpetual pucker around coronet mouthpieces, the band packed its instruments and fled for its buses."

—Jerry Izenberg, Sport *magazine*

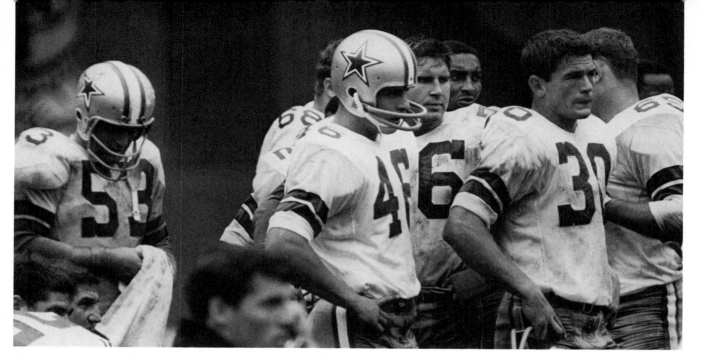

There were not a lot of grim moments in the Cowboys' 1967 regular season, although the faces on the sideline here reflect one of the more worrisome of them. Shown are center Mike Connelly (53), back Craig Baynham (46), guard John Niland (only the 6 of his number 76 showing), and back Dan Reeves (30). (Pro Football Hall of Fame)

How cold it was New Year's Eve 1967 in Green Bay, Wisconsin—at gametime, 13° below zero, with a wind-chill factor somewhere around 40° below. These Cowboys (left to right), Jethro Pugh, Pettis Norman, and Mike Gaechter, try to stay warm under a makeshift tent on the Cowboy bench, but there was little respite from the cold in Green Bay that day. (Vernon Biever)

Cowboys. It was well into the second quarter, and the Packers had the ball on their own 26-yard line. Bart Starr dropped back to pass, but Dallas put on a massive rush. Starr tried to scramble out of it and just about had, his arm going back to get rid of the ball, when Willie Townes hit him with the impact of a Mack truck. Starr and the ball were separated, both skittering across the ground in opposite directions. George Andrie, the other defensive end, snatched it and lurched 7 yards for a Cowboy touchdown. Danny Villanueva kicked the extra point, and the Cowboys were down by a mere 7 points.

The Cowboys kicked off and held the Packers. Still the Cowboy offense could not move the ball, and so they had to punt, too. But Willie Wood dropped the ball at the Green Bay 17-yard line, and Phil Clark of the Cowboys recovered the fumble. But three plays later the Dallas offense had moved the ball only 3 yards closer to the goal line, so Danny Villanueva came back on the field and kicked a 21-yard field goal. As the half ended, the score was 14–10.

The locker room respite from the cold did not help either team, and the third quarter was a simple exercise in handing the ball back and forth to each other. The Cowboy offense did, however, come to life momentarily, and Don Meredith led them on their only sustained drive of the game up to that point, moving all the way from their 11-yard line to the Packer 22. Then Meredith scrambled, picking up 9 more yards, only to lose the ball when he was tackled by Green Bay linebacker Lee Roy Caffey. Herb Adderley fell on it for the Pack. The Cowboys then got the ball back and were moving again, this time down to the Green Bay 30. A sack later, Danny Villanueva attempted a long field goal, but it fell short.

On the first play of the fourth quarter, the Cowboys turned to a little razzle-dazzle, and it worked. Meredith pitched the ball to running back Danny Reeves, who, behind a wedge of blockers, headed out around end, but instead of making the cut up the field, suddenly pulled back. Racing down field was flanker Lance Rentzel; the fake run had fooled both safety Willie Wood and right cornerback Bob Jeter. Reeves, the one-time college quarterback, lofted a floater to Rentzel, who came to an almost complete stop at the 20-yard line to catch it and then turned and raced in for the score. Villanueva's kick made it the Cowboys 17, the Packers 14.

Starr moved the Packers after the kickoff, but he could not get beyond the Cowboy 33. Don Chandler tried a field goal, but it was no good. The Cowboys now wanted to use up as much time as they could, ideally ending a long, time-consuming drive with a score of one sort or another. They were only able to accomplish the first part, however. They controlled the ball for nearly five minutes but then had to punt it away.

The Kick Karavan

It was dreamed up early in March 1967. To find a kicker, Gil Brandt, assistant coach Ermal Allen, and Ben Agajanian, the famous pro kicker of the 1950s and early 1960s (known as "The Toeless Wonder" because he had no toes on his kicking foot), would conduct a 10,000-mile, 23-city junket and hold tryouts for would-be kickers as they went.

The Kick Karavan, as Brandt formally dubbed it, took off in mid-March, traveling in a Twin Beach private airplane. For the next six weeks, they watched approximately 1,300 aspirants show what they could do by applying a foot to a football. When it was over, they had found 27 prospects, whom they brought back to Dallas for further tryouts. By June, it had been narrowed to 13 "finalists." In the last analysis, there would be only two. Harold Deters of North Carolina State was invited to the Cowboys' summer camp and made the final cut out in Thousand Oaks but would be let go before the season was over. The other survivor was Mac Percival from Texas Tech, whom the Cowboys signed and then traded to the Chicago Bears, where in seven seasons he would become their second all-time leading scorer.

But even if they didn't find a kicker, they had a lot of fun along the way. Moe Levine of Portland, Oregon, tried out, and although he kicked 15 consecutive field goals from the 20-yard line, was cut, most probably because he was 60 years old. (He was given an honorary contract, however, for his grit.) William Wallace wrote in the New York Times of some of the other memorable moments on the tour:

In Birmingham, Alabama, a bus with passengers aboard stopped outside the tryout field. The driver came out and kicked a few, with the change purse rattling around his waist. He missed one and drove on.

One fellow at Durham, N.C., showed up with a football stained black from water soakings. "He's been kicking it in the creek," his wife explained . . .

(Another wife explained) "He's been making me hold the ball, and my fingernails are all gone."

The most inept punter was found in Oklahoma City. On eight tries this youth hit the ball three times with his knee and five times with his shin . . .

And one young man who failed the tryout looked at the football shoes Ben Agajanian was wearing and said: "I guess I need one of those short shoes like you got. Where do you get them?"

"First you got to take your toes off," Agajanian told him.

There were 4 minutes and 50 seconds left in the game when the Packers took over, and the ball was at their own 32. From there began what has become one of the most famous drives in professional football history. First, there was a short pass to Donny Anderson from Starr, then a big hole for Chuck Mercein to carry the ball through, and Green Bay had their first first down of the drive. At their own 45, Starr went to Boyd Dowler, picking up another 13 yards. Inside Cowboy territory, the defense retrenched. Donny Anderson, on a halfback option to run or pass, was dumped 9 yards behind the line of scrimmage by Willie Townes. But Starr got 11 yards right back on a pass to Donny Anderson. Then he went to him again for 9 more and a first down. The Packers drive was alive again.

There was only 1:30 left in the game now, and there was a long 30 yards between the line of scrimmage and the goal line. Here the Packers' momentum and the ice-coated field proved to be too great an alliance.

Starr threw a short pass to Chuck Mercein out in the left flat, but as Cowboy linebacker Dave Edwards moved in for the tackle, he slipped, and Mercein raced by him down to the Cowboys' 11-yard line. Then a handoff to Mercein, charging off tackle. George Andrie moved in to plug the hole, but he slipped and fell. Mercein made it all the way to the 3-yard line. Donny Anderson carried it to the 1, and the Packers had a first down with less than a minute to play, with only a single yard to go for a touchdown.

Two plunges into the middle by Donny Anderson netted only a foot, however, and with 16 seconds left, the Packers took their last time-out. A field goal would send the game into a sudden-death overtime, and the Packers were in perfect field position to kick one. If they ran their third-down play and did not score or stop the clock with it, they would not have time to kick one. The field-goal team would never be able to get on the field, set up, and kick the ball.

Vince Lombardi and Bart Starr chatted on the sideline, and neither one even cast a glance in the direction of kicker Don Chandler. Starr came back out to the huddle and, as football fans everywhere know, scored on the next play. It was a quarterback sneak, the only one he had called that entire year, and he knifed into the line behind guard Jerry Kramer, who threw what may be the most famous block in the history of the game. Chandler's kick made it 21–17. The Packers were once again the champions of the NFL, and the Cowboys had to settle for another last-second disappointment.

After the game, Vince Lombardi explained, "I couldn't see going for a tie and making all those people in the stands suffer through a sudden death in this weather. That's why we gambled for the touchdown."

The Cowboys had lost, and their locker room under the stands of Lambeau Field was funereal. Some sat silently; some cried. They had played in one of the most dramatic games in the history of the sport under the worst conditions any football team had ever faced. They played with remarkable spirit that day. They had come back, and they had almost won the game, perhaps separated from the NFL crown by nothing more than just one of those slips on that ice-paved field. They were an honorable, saddened, bone-chilled group of athletes who glumly exchanged their uniforms for street clothes in that locker room. As Tom Landry said after the game. "You saw the real Cowboys today. They're the ones with the frostbitten fingers and the broken hearts."

In probably the most famous quarterback sneak in professional football history, Green Bay's Bart Starr (15) knifes in for the last-second touchdown to give the Packers a 21–17 win over the Cowboys for the NFL conference title of 1967. On the ground is Packer guard Jerry Kramer (64), who gouged out the hole for Starr. Cowboys in the picture are Chuck Howley (54) and Jethro Pugh (75). No. 30 on the Packers is Chuck Mercein. (Vernon Biever)

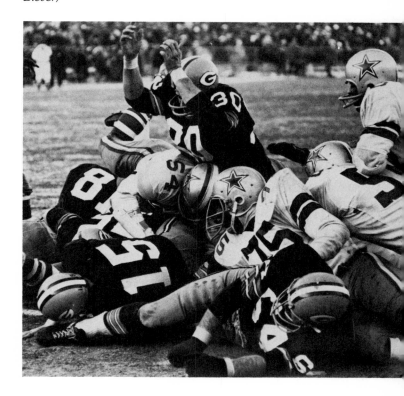

9 A Force in the League

IF A SOMEWHAT SKEPTICAL PRESS was often a bit rough on the Cowboys in the early part of the 1960s, they had turned full swing by the twilight of that decade. Now with the Cowboys a dominant factor in the NFL and a visitor two straight years to the game that decided the championship of that league, they had achieved status in a state whose natives had become accustomed to living with superlatives. Now the sportswriters were penning words about the Cowboys to a vastly different musical score. Now there was a rapture, a triumphant lilt to the stories. A typical example was this dispatch, which appeared in the *National Observer* in 1968·

"Here in Big D, opulence is ordering the Neiman-Marcus 'His and Hers' Christmas special, or cruising down to Austin in your Lear jet, or hosting a coming-out party draped in the latest shade of mink. But the newest display of success comes from the *nouveau riche* Dallas Cowboys, riding whip in hand toward their third straight National Football League championship game . . . And Texans can't peel off the bills fast enough to fight their way into the Cotton Bowl to cheer for the most successful expansion franchise in sports."

It was true. Texans were proud of their Cowboys by 1968. Average attendance at a home game was well up in the 60,000s, and it was about as easy to get a season ticket between the 30-yard lines as it was to acquire membership in Dallas's Petroleum Club.

The Cowboys themselves had recovered from the arctic cold of Green Bay and the disappointment of the last-second loss in that gelid town. The principal concern in

the front office and among the coaching staff now was how to channel the explosive force they had in uniform not just through the season but successfully through the postseason as well.

There were not a lot of weaknesses in the roster. The Cowboys were basically a young team, one that was, at least on paper, peaking. When the draft came around, there was no particular position that Gil Brandt and Tom Landry had a particular lust for; instead, they relied on their scouting apparatus and decided to merely take the best player at a position who was available when their pick came up. As it turned out, the first two choices were receivers, Dennis Homan from Alabama and David McDaniels of Eastern Mississippi. They were looked upon as back-ups because there was still Bob Hayes, Lance Rentzel, and Pete Gent to handle that aspect of the game on a regular basis. But deeper into the draft they selected three players who would contribute significantly to the Dallas fortunes in the coming years: Blaine Nye, a guard from Stanford came in the fifth round, followed by D. D. Lewis, the best linebacker in Mississippi State history, and down at the 16th round, Larry Cole, who had spent his college playing days at the Air Force Academy and the University of Hawaii.

The Cowboys were ready for 1968. Many in the organization felt the team they would field that year was the most promising ever—young but seasoned and certainly on the rise.

But the year 1968 was a bizarre one everywhere. The United States was heavily immersed in the Vietnam War, and the country was torn apart internally because of it.

Martin Luther King was gunned down in Memphis and Robert F. Kennedy slain in Los Angeles. The North Koreans seized the U.S.S. *Pueblo* and its crew on the high seas, and in Chicago police and demonstrators clashed violently on the streets at the Democratic National Convention. It was a strange and despairing time.

In the NFL, there was a different kind of turbulence. The Players Association presented a list of demands to management, and collective bargaining became a part of professional football. There were threats of a strike, even of cancellation of the 1968 NFL season, but the disagreement was eventually settled. Then there was "Heidi," the little girl who preempted the storybook ending of the New York Jets-Oakland Raiders game. With the Jets ahead 39–29 and only 1:05 remaining in the game, NBC switched to the children's show "Heidi," and the fans were deprived of watching Oakland come back and score two touchdowns to win the game. The reaction of fans was outrage, and the outcry to the media was perhaps the largest since Orson Welles on radio led everyone to believe the Martians were attacking planet earth. And lastly there were the New York Jets and Joe Namath and the

end to the NFL's cultivated sense of superiority over the AFL.

For the Dallas Cowboys, it would be a weird, surprising, and ultimately depressing year, too.

The season began early for the Cowboys that year—August 3, to be exact. They had been selected to play in an exhibition game at Canton, Ohio, a special one to benefit the Pro Football Hall of Fame, which had been established in that city back in 1963.

So the Cowboys flew from Thousand Oaks to the town where it all began in 1920 to face a team that had been around ever since that beginning, the Chicago Bears. Their coach for so many years, who had just retired from that position, George Halas, was a charter member of the Hall of Fame, and two of the Bears on the roster that day were future Hall of Famers, running back Gale Sayers and middle linebacker Dick Butkus.

As they lined up for the first exhibition of the 1968 season, a few familiar faces were gone from the Cowboys. Danny Villanueva had retired, and the Cowboys had had to add both a place kicker and a punter to replace him. For the place-kicking duties, they traded center Mike Con-

Craig Morton zeroes in on wide receiver Bob Hayes (22) in this game against the New Orleans Saints. Morton would lead the Cowboys in passing during the 1969 and 1970 seasons before relinquishing the starting role at quarterback to Roger Staubach. (Dallas Cowboys)

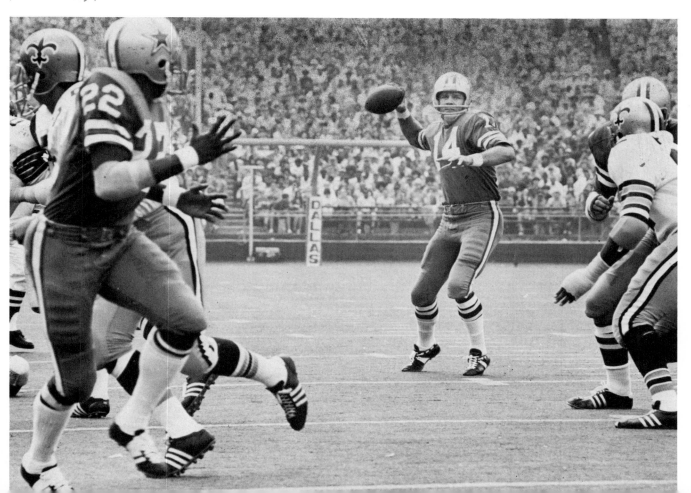

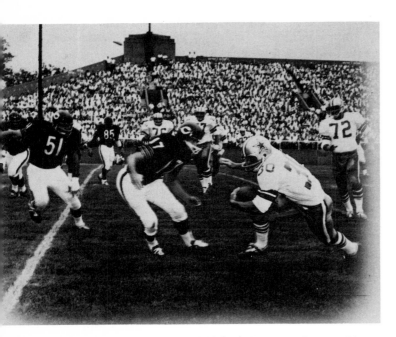

The Cowboys began the 1968 football year in Canton, Ohio at the Pro Football Hall of Fame. Dan Reeves (30) picks up a few yards during that game before being cut down by Chicago Bear defensive back Richie Pettibon (17). Other Cowboys are tackle Tony Liscio (72), center Malcolm Walker (57), and guard John Niland (76). The Chicago Bears shown are Hall of Famer Dick Butkus (51) and Willie Holman (85). The Cowboys lost on that hot summer day, 30–24. (Pro Football Hall of Fame)

nelly, an eight-year Cowboy veteran, to the Pittsburgh Steelers for Mike Clark, and they picked up punter Ron Widby as a free agent.

The Cowboys lost that sweltering August day to the Bears, 30–24. Back out in California, they bounced back to defeat both the 49ers and the Rams. They also beat Houston down in Houston but lost both the preseason games played in Dallas, to Green Bay and Baltimore. It could only be called a so-so exhibition season.

What counts, however, is the regular season, and the Cowboys were about to begin it with a pyrotechnical display that would entertain the most jaded fan. The Detroit Lions came to Dallas for the opener. They had been a mediocre team the year before (5–7–2), but they were a young team. Running back Mel Farr was a highly regarded second-year man, and now there were rookies Greg Landry to serve as back-up quarterback to the recently acquired Bill Munson, tight end Charlie Saunders, and wide receiver Earl McCullouch. And there were a few notable old-timers, too, such as lineman Alex Karras and linebacker Mike Lucci.

The Cowboys trailed the Lions in the first quarter 7–0 after Landry hit Mel Farr with a 45-yard pass, and there were some very definite rumblings of discontent coming from the stands, especially directed at quarterback Don Meredith. But he cut that emotion off as deftly as if he

were wielding a surgeon's knife when he drilled a bomb to Bob Hayes for a 50-yard touchdown. The boos turned to cheers, and it was only the beginning. The Cowboys went on to amass 59 points that day, the most they had ever scored and a record that would not be equaled until the 1980 season.

When it was all over, the Cowboys had gained 542 yards for the afternoon, 381 of them passing. Meredith was especially dandy that day, completing 16 of 19 passes for 228 yards, and Craig Morton got in the spirit of things as well, with 7 of 15 for 121 yards. And everybody was catching them—Hayes, Rentzel, Norman, Reeves, Gent, Homan, Baynham, and Perkins.

The next week presented more of a challenge, however. The Cleveland Browns were coming to town, and they had to be panting for revenge of the 52–14 embarrassment the Cowboys had dealt them in the conference championship game the year before. But if they were, it was a futile emotion. The Cowboys' defense was impenetrable that day. They held the league's top rusher of 1967, Leroy Kelly, to a mere 58 yards, and it took him 13 carries to gain that. The Browns could only gain 250 yards that day and were held to 12 first downs. The Cowboy defense added a little offense as well when the enormous Willie Townes lumbered 20 yards for a touchdown with a fumble. The Browns, never in the game, lost it by three touchdowns.

The Philadelphia Eagles, 0–2 when the Cowboys came to the City of Brotherly Love, were on their way to one of the worst seasons in the franchise's history. (They would only win 2 games and lose 12 in 1968.) And the

---

On Losing

There were a variety of observations on what happened to the favored Dallas Cowboys in the 1969 playoff game, the one in which the Cowboys lost to the Cleveland Browns 38–14. Here are a few of them.

"The wet field didn't bother us. We're used to that kind of weather. I don't think Dallas is a bad-weather team."
—Leroy Kelly, Brown running back

"We were playing on a wet field and they were playing on a dry field."
—Bob Hayes, Cowboy wide receiver

"The Dallas Cowboys are terrific in summer stock and tryouts in Bridgeport but despite their glitter and promise they can't cut it on Broadway."
—Larry Merchant, New York Post

Cowboys had no problem registering their third consecutive victory. The final score was 45–13, and Don Meredith accounted for five touchdowns with two passes to Lance Rentzel, one to Danny Reeves, one to Bob Hayes, and another to Don Perkins.

The St. Louis Cardinals proved to be another patsy the following week, but the Cowboys suffered a loss that day when Dan Reeves tore the ligaments in his knee and was out for the rest of the season. Wins over the Eagles and the Minnesota Vikings in the next two weeks brought the Cowboys back to Dallas undefeated after six games, the longest winning streak in their now 8½-year history, and they were accepted as the certified powerhouse of the Capital Division. The Giants, in second place with a record of 4–2, were clearly inferior to the Cowboys in just about every category.

The seventh game of the season was somewhat historic in that it was actually the first nationally televised Monday night football game. It was a trial on the part of the NFL and the TV industry to see if pro football might be popular at a time other than Sunday afternoon.

The game was nationally televised from the Cotton Bowl where a sellout crowd of 74,604 came to watch the agonies of a Green Bay Packer team without Vince Lombardi and said to be in a state of mortal decline. The Pack had won only two of their first six games that year and tied another. The dynasty was over, everyone was saying. Now here was the ideal opportunity for the Cowboys to wreak vengeance for those two heartbreaks the Packers had handed them in the 1966 and 1967 championship games.

But it was not to be. In fact, it was all too reminiscent of old times. Bart Starr, now 34, waited until the second quarter, with the Cowboys leading 10–0, before starting to do what he had always seemed to do so well against them—sustained drives, picking apart the defense, and, of course, throwing touchdown passes. The first one was to wide receiver Carroll Dale; then there were two in the third quarter to tight end Marv Fleming and a final one in the last period to Boyd Dowler. For the day, Starr had completed 17 of 25 passes for 219 yards. On the other side of the line of scrimmage, the NFL's leading passer at that point in the season, Don Meredith, had a most de-

Don Perkins explodes through an enormous hole in the Chicago Bear line during the preseason Hall of Fame game at Canton, Ohio in 1968. It was the beginning of Perkins's last year as a Cowboy, an eight-year career in which he led the team in rushing seven times. Perkins is still the Cowboys' all-time leading ball carrier, with a total of 6,217 yards on 1,500 carries, and he has also rushed for more TDs than any other Cowboy, 42. Other Cowboys in the picture are tackle Ralph Neely (73) and tight end Pettis Norman (84). The Chicago Bear is linebacker Doug Buffone (55).   (Pro Football Hall of Fame)

pressing day, completing only 13 of 30 and throwing three interceptions. To add injury to insult, Packer defensive end Willie Davis also managed to break Meredith's nose on one play. The Cowboys lost 28–17 that Monday night.

The second half of the season remained, and Coach Tom Landry said he wanted "a performance no less than the first half"; that meant a 6–1 record. And the Cowboys gave that to him. Their one loss was an upset at the hands of the New York Giants, but no one even came close to them in the other six games. The Cowboys ended their finest regular season ever with a record of 12–2; the Giants, in second place with a 7–7 record, never threatened.

The Cowboys had scored the most points of any team in the NFL in 1968 (431), racked up the most first downs in a season (297), which was then an all-time NFL record, even led the league in net passing yardage (3,026), and their defense gave up the least amount of yards rushing in the NFL, only 1,195. Meredith had one of his finest years in 1968, toting up the best completion percentage of his career (55.3), and his NFL quarterback rating of 88.3 was second in the league. Lance Rentzel caught 54 passes to break the 1,000-yard mark for receptions (1,009). Don Perkins rushed for 836 yards, the second-highest season total in his career. And Bob Hayes's average punt return of 20.8 led the league and was the highest in the NFL since Hall of Famer Jack Christiansen of the Detroit Lions averaged 21.5 yards back in 1952.

They were a heavy favorite, the Cowboys, when they went to Cleveland to face the winners of the Century Division. The Browns had taken that title on the last game of the season when they beat the St. Louis Cardinals 27–16. Their record of 10–4 was just a half game ahead of the Cardinals, who finished the season with 9 wins, 4 losses, and a tie. During the regular season, the Cowboys had manhandled both those teams, and they had a lot of confidence as they traveled to Cleveland.

The Browns were now under the guidance of a new quarterback, Bill Nelsen, who had replaced Frank Ryan, and had added some new life to the team's passing attack. The Browns could be explosive. Leroy Kelly had led the league in rushing for the second year in a row, this time with 1,239 yards, and his 16 rushing TDs were the best in the league. Wide receiver Paul Warfield's 12 TD receptions was also a league high.

The Cowboys were only a 3-point favorite, according to the nation's oddsmakers. Even though they were 12–2 and had demolished the Browns in their last four encounters, Cleveland was always tough at home. Still, one Cowboy put it, "If we win by only one touchdown, it will be a bad day."

It was bleak and cold in Cleveland on the afternoon of December 21, not nearly as frigid as it had been in Green Bay but still quite unpleasant under that leaden sky. The attendance at Municipal Stadium, however, was an impressive 81,497. The Browns' fans had been treated well over the years, and they were loyal and notoriously boisterous. They remembered the dynasty of the 1950s when the Browns were represented on the field by the likes of Otto Graham, Marion Motley, Dante Lavelli, Mac Speedie, Lou Groza, Dub Jones, and Bill Willis and on the sidelines by coach Paul Brown. And they remembered a more recent Brown, by the name of Jim.

The Cowboys played with a lackluster offense but managed to take the lead in the first quarter when linebacker Chuck Howley grabbed a fumble and ran it 44 yards for a touchdown. Mike Clark's extra point made it 7–3. A field goal in the second quarter by Clark widened

1968

Preseason

Dallas	(3–3)	Opponents
24	Chicago (14,578) @ Canton	30
16	San Francisco (27,530) @ S. F.	14
42	Los Angeles (64,978) @ L. A.	10
27	Green Bay (72,014) @ Dallas	31
33	Houston (52,289) @ Houston	19
10	Baltimore (69,520) @ Dallas	16

Regular Season

		(12–2)	
W	59	Detroit (61,382) (H)	13
W	28	Cleveland (68,733) (H)	7
W	45	Philadelphia (60,858)	13
W	27	St. Louis (48,296)	10
W	34	Philadelphia (72,083) (H)	14
W	20	Minnesota (47,644)	7
L	17	Green Bay (74,604) (H)	28
W	17	New Orleans (84,728)	3
L	21	New York (72,163) (H)	27
W	44	Washington (50,816)	24
W	34	Chicago (46,667)	3
W	29	Washington (66,076) (H)	20
W	28	Pittsburgh (55,069) (H)	7
W	28	New York (62,617)	10
	431		186

Postseason

		Eastern Championship Game *(Cleveland)*	
L	20	Cleveland (81,497)	31
		Playoff Bowl Game *(Miami)*	
W	17	Minnesota (22,961)	13

Some better-known Cowboys from some lesser-known places, or proof that Gil Brandt and the Cowboys do not rely wholly on major colleges for recruitment:

Margene Adkins	Henderson Junior College
Jim Boeke	Heidelberg (Ohio)
Doug Dennison	Kutztown State (Pennsylvania)
Toni Fritsch	Vienna, Austria
Cliff Harris	Ouachita Baptist (Arkansas)
Wendell Hayes	Humboldt State (California)
Thomas Henderson	Langston (Oklahoma)
Pettis Norman	Johnson C. Smith (North Carolina)
Jethro Pugh	Elizabeth City State (North Carolina)
Herbert Scott	Virginia Union (Virginia)
Rayfield Wright	Fort Valley State (Georgia)

the lead, but it did not last. Bill Nelsen found a wide-open Leroy Kelly down the field and lofted a pass good for a 45-yard touchdown, and the half ended in a 10–10 tie.

Disaster struck on the first play of the second half. Don Meredith went for Bob Hayes, only to see his pass picked off by linebacker Dale Lindsey, who carried it into the Cowboy end zone. In the same quarter, Leroy Kelly, on a sweep, broke free and raced 35 yards for another touchdown. Craig Morton replaced Don Meredith for the Cowboys, but it did no good. The Browns added another TD in the fourth quarter. The Cowboys simply were never in the game in the second half.

It was a shattering slice of reality. The Cowboys would not get to the NFL championship game that year, as so many of them had taken for granted. The idea of losing to Cleveland had been remote, if existent, and they now understood only too well the perils of overconfidence.

For the Cowboys, the 1968 season was over. They would make an appearance in the Playoff Bowl in Miami January 5, but that was merely anticlimax. They won that

Dallas safety Mel Renfro knocks a pass away from the waiting arms of Chicago Bear would-be receiver Charley Bivens (49) in this 1968 game in the Bears' old home at Wrigley Field. The Cowboys defeated the Chicagoans 34–3 that afternoon, in the process of running up their most impressive regular-season record ever (12–2). Cowboy No. 55 is Lee Roy Jordan.   (Pro Football Hall of Fame)

game, beating the Minnesota Vikings 17–13, but they thought that they should have been gearing up instead to meet the New York Jets in Super Bowl III. "Maybe next year" was becoming a familiar cry in Cowboys territory.

Although the Cowboys were destined eventually to play in the Super Bowl, Don Meredith, so much the focal point of the team since its inception back in 1960, was not so fated. He was only 31, but he decided it was time to get out of the game. He had grown weary of the boo birds in the Cotton Bowl, and he had other business interests to keep him occupied. Also, he had pains and scars to show for all the injuries he had sustained over the years; there were just all kinds of reasons for him to get out of the game.

He called a press conference at Cowboy headquarters, and everyone was there—Tex Schramm, Tom Landry, Gil Brandt, all the sportswriters and radio and TV broadcasters. Meredith had been making news for all of them one way or another for the preceding nine years. And now, as Sam Blair of the Dallas *Morning News* aptly described it: "The most controversial athlete in Dallas sports history, a man who played with tremendous pain and criticism and still took the Cowboys from nothing to almost the top, was finished."

He was followed into retirement by Don Perkins, who, by 1969, ranked as the fifth most productive rusher in NFL history. He had been there with Meredith from the very beginning back in 1960, although he had been sidelined that first season. They had both been signed to Tex Schramm's famous personal services contracts and had been the two key recruits before there ever was a team from Dallas in the NFL. They had suffered through the lean years, grew along with the team, and had lately tasted what it was like to play for a winner.

Craig Morton was the logical replacement for Meredith, but it was no cut-and-dried affair; he was going to get a run for the job from a 27-year-old rookie whose tour of duty with the U.S. Navy was now over. Roger Staubach had decided he would like a shot at playing professional football and said he would be coming out to Thousand Oaks in the summer.

Don Perkins would be replaced by bronco buster Walt Garrison. But the draft that year produced another running back, Calvin Hill, a superstar from Yale. It surprised many people when Hill was the Cowboys' first pick of 1969 because a first-round choice from an Ivy League school was indeed a rarity in modern-day professional football.

The second round of the draft brought wide receiver Richmond Flowers from Tennessee, and the Cowboys traded with the Pittsburgh Steelers to land tight end Mike Ditka, who had been an All-Pro with the Chicago Bears

In the spring of 1969, the Cowboys held a "quarterback camp" in Dallas where rookie Roger Staubach (center) joined veterans Don Meredith (right) and Craig Morton. Staubach was still in the U.S. Navy when this picture was taken, but had taken a two-week leave from his post at the Naval Air Station in Pensacola, Florida to attend the workout. He would leave the Navy in July that year and report to summer camp at Thousand Oaks, California to begin his Cowboy career.   (Pro Football Hall of Fame)

but had languished in Pittsburgh the past two years.

D. D. Lewis, lost to the military service, would not be around for the 1969 season. Neither would Willie Townes, who would be out for the season with a leg injury.

A new era was in a way beginning in Dallas with the 1969 season because there would be a totally new backfield—an offense inexperienced and untested.

It would also signify the end of an era because ground was broken over in Irving for a new stadium. It meant the end of the romanceless relationship between the Cowboys and the Cotton Bowl. They would play there for two more years while Texas Stadium was being built, but then the divorce would be final.

More than 87,000 people filled the Los Angeles Coliseum to see the exhibition opener between the Cowboys and the Rams, which said something about how the nation's sports fans were supporting professional football by 1969. The Rams, runner-up in their division to the NFL champion Baltimore Colts the year before, were one of the most highly regarded teams in the NFL. Their coach, George Allen, had been fired and then rehired after his players protested. He strongly emphasized defense, and he had all the old pros, who made the Rams the best in the league in that aspect of the game. Now their offense was coming into its own, and the Cowboys knew they would have their hands full. There would be a little feeling out, too, because the teams were scheduled to meet late in the regular season in a game that might be very important to either or both in their respective standings.

The Cowboys lost that game without showing much of an offense or a defense but then went on to win their next four. They dropped the last game of the preseason to the

When Mike Ditka joined the Cowboys in 1969, he came with a reputation as one of the league's great tight ends. An All-American at Pittsburgh, he had been named All-Pro four times and appeared in five Pro Bowls during six years with the Chicago Bears and two at the Pittsburgh Steelers. For the Cowboys, he would have the distinction in 1971 of catching the first touchdown pass of the preseason and the last of the postseason in Super Bowl VI. He became a Cowboy assistant coach in 1973. (Dallas Cowboys)

1969

Preseason

Dallas	(4-2)	Opponents
17	Los Angeles (87,381) @ L. A.	24
20	San Francisco (33,894) @ S. F.	17
31	Green Bay (73,764) @ Dallas	13
14	Houston (55,310) @ Houston	11
25	N. Y. Jets (74,771) @ Dallas	9
7	Baltimore (58,975) @ Dallas	23

Regular Season

		(11-2-1)	
W	24	St. Louis (62,134) (H)	3
W	21	New Orleans (79,567)	17
W	38	Philadelphia (60,658)	7
W	24	Atlanta (54,833)	17
W	49	Philadelphia (71,509) (H)	14
W	25	New York (58,964) (H)	3
L	10	Cleveland (84,850)	42
W	33	New Orleans (68,282) (H)	17
W	41	Washington (50,474)	28
L	23	Los Angeles (79,105)	24
T	24	San Francisco (62,348) (H)	24
W	10	Pittsburgh (24,990)	7
W	27	Baltimore (63,191) (H)	10
W	20	Washington (56,924) (H)	10
	369		223

Postseason

Eastern Championship Game
(Dallas)

L	14	Cleveland (69,321)	38

Playoff Bowl Game
(Miami)

L	0	Los Angeles (31,151)	31

previous year's Super Bowl contender, the Baltimore Colts. The preseason as a whole had been a rather innocuous one. Roger Staubach had gotten some playing time and had shown some promise. Mike Ditka and Pettis Norman fought hard to secure the full-time position at tight end. Craig Morton showed that he could fairly regularly get the ball into the hands of Bob Hayes and Lance Rentzel. Walt Garrison appeared to be a justifiable replacement for Don Perkins. But there was one exciting element, the running of rookie Calvin Hill. He had done extraordinarily well, and even though he had yet to play in an NFL regular-season game, there were a lot of people already comparing him to runners like Leroy Kelly and Gale Sayers.

When the regular season got underway, Roger Staubach gained the starting assignment at quarterback, the result of a dislocated finger on the hand of Craig Morton. And Staubach did a commendable job, leading the Cowboys to an easy 24–3 win over the St. Louis Cardinals. In the process, he threw 7 completions (of 15) for a total of 220 yards, including a 75-yard touchdown to Lance Rentzel.

The following week, however, Morton was back, but he was not very impressive. On the other hand, Calvin Hill, playing in the second game of his NFL career, rushed for 138 yards on 23 carries, which broke the club record of 137 yards set by Don Perkins back in 1962. The icing to Hill's performance was the sterling average of 6 yards per carry. The following week, against the Philadelphia Eagles, he was again explosive, picking up 91 yards in only 10 carries, one of which was a dazzling 53-yard touchdown run. But that wasn't all. He also caught three of Craig Morton's passes for a total of 71 yards and threw one himself to Lance Rentzel for a 44-yard gain. And all that was in the *first half.* Nursing a few minor pains, he sat the second half out on the bench as the Cowboys

slaughtered the Eagles 38–7. Craig Morton had a fine game, too, that afternoon, passing for a total of 261 yards (14 of 18) and three touchdowns.

The Cowboys dispatched the Atlanta Falcons the next week, then gave it to the Eagles again, this time 49–14. Craig Morton threw five touchdown passes in the latter to tie the team record. (Meredith had done it three times and Eddie LeBaron once.) His 13 completions for the day on 19 attempts netted 247 yards. Lance Rentzel caught three of the touchdown passes, also tying a Cowboy record that day. Even tackle Bob Lilly scored a touchdown, carrying an Eagle fumble 9 yards into the end zone.

An easy win the following week over the Giants, and just like the year before, the Cowboys were 6–0, comfortably ahead of the second-place Washington Redskins, who had lost one and tied one of their six games. The Cowboys had outscored their opponents 181–61, a statistic that could enthrall lovers of offensive or defensive football.

Running back Craig Baynham follows tackle John Wilbur (65) into Green Bay Packer land in this 1969 preseason game at Dallas. The Cowboys tasted a little of the sweetness of revenge for the NFL championships they had barely lost to the Packers a few years earlier by drubbing the Packers 31–13 that evening in the Cotton Bowl. On the ground is Cowboy tackle Ralph Neely (73).   (Pro Football Hall of Fame)

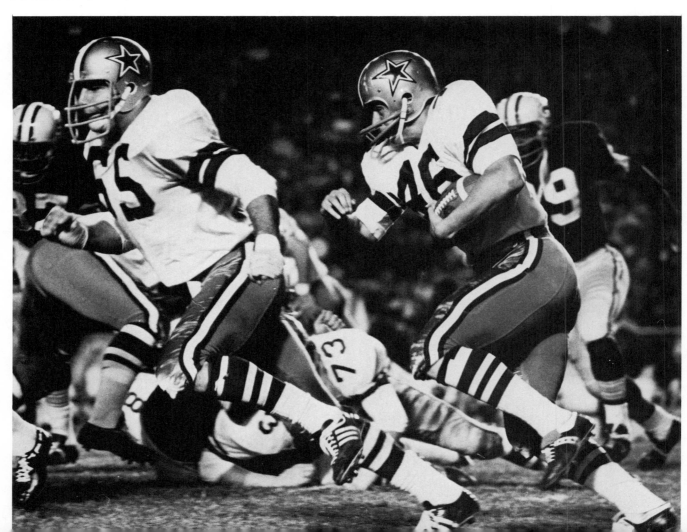

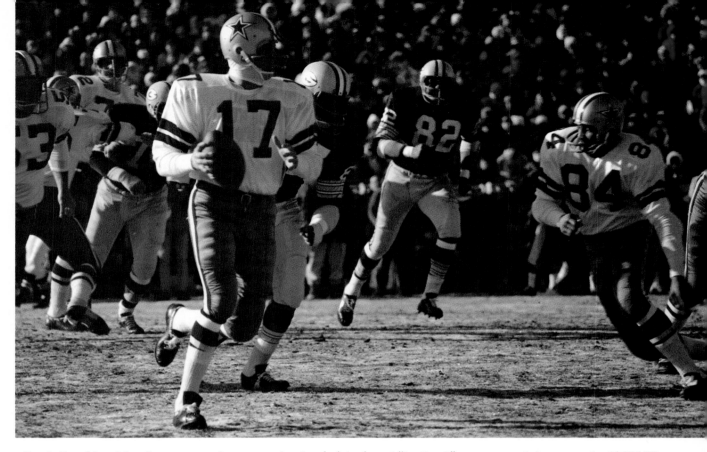

Dandy Don Meredith rolls out across the concrete-hard turf of the famed "Ice Bowl," more precisely known as the 1967 NFL championship game. No. 84 on the Cowboys is Pettis Norman.   (Vernon Biever)

About to unleash a pass in a historic game of 1968, a record 59–13 rout of the Detroit Lions, is Craig Morton. Other Cowboys in the picture are offensive linemen Malcolm Walker (57) and John Wilbur (65).   (Bradley Photographers)

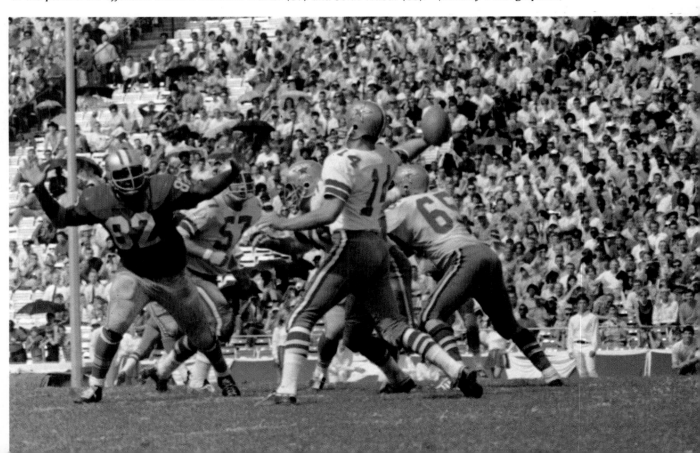

Cowboy corner back Benny Barnes leaps high to break up a pass intended for Ram receiver Harold Jackson (29) in this 1975 game. The Cowboy with the chorus-line kick is rookie defensive back Randy Hughes (42). (Ron Scribner)

All-Pro safety Cliff Harris soars in from the left to knock away a pass intended for St. Louis Cardinal receiver J. V. Cain in a 1976 game at Texas Stadium. Coming in at the right is tandem safety Charlie Waters. Corner back Mel Renfro (20) is on the ground. (Ron Scribner)

Terry Bradshaw of the Steelers makes the acquaintance of Ed "Too Tall" Jones on this pass rush during Super Bowl X. (Vernon Biever)

Golden Richards leaps for a Roger Staubach pass against the St. Louis Cardinals in 1977, but All-Pro defender Roger Wehrli (22) manages to bat it away. The other St. Louis player is Mike Sensibaugh (20). (Ron Scribner)

Roger Staubach scrambles against the Minnesota Vikings in the 1977 season opener, their first overtime game, a 16–10 victory, at Bloomington, Minnesota. Behind Staubach is center John Fitzgerald.   (John Biever)

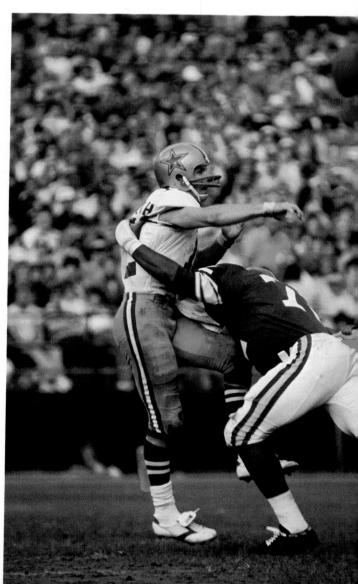

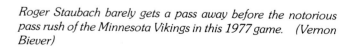

Roger Staubach barely gets a pass away before the notorious pass rush of the Minnesota Vikings in this 1977 game.   (Vernon Biever)

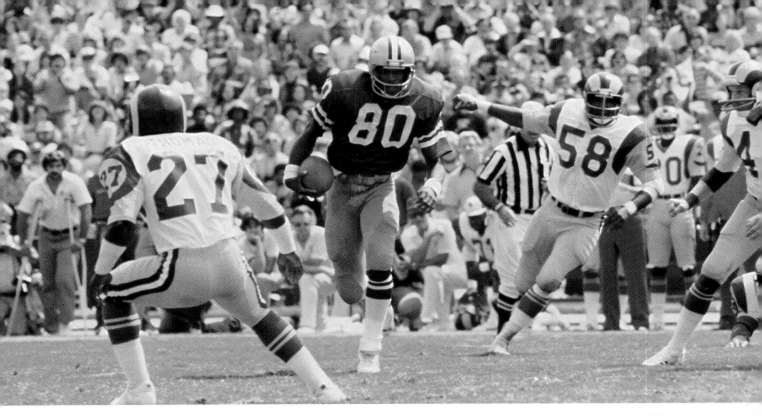

Tony Hill gains a few yards here after grabbing a pass from Roger Staubach in this early regular-season game of 1978 against the Rams at the Los Angeles Coliseum. (Ron Scribner)

It is brutal in the proverbial pro football trenches, as the blood on Bob Lilly's jersey attests. The other Cowboy here is linebacker D. D. Lewis. (Ron Scribner)

Free-agent, All-Pro wide receiver Drew Pearson does some fancy stepping here after catching a Roger Staubach pass in this 1976 divisional playoff game against the Los Angeles Rams.   (Pro Football Hall of Fame)

Drew Pearson raises the football in triumph after catching the 365th pass of his Cowboy career to tie the all-time club record set by Bob Hayes. Congratulating Pearson is fellow wide receiver Tony Hill.   (Ron Scribner)

Every Cowboy fan wishes that this was the scene the day after Super Bowl XIII. Unfortunately, it was taken as part of the publicity hype the day before that game for the NFL title. And the day after, the Super Bowl XIII trophy went to the Steelers. (Vernon Biever)

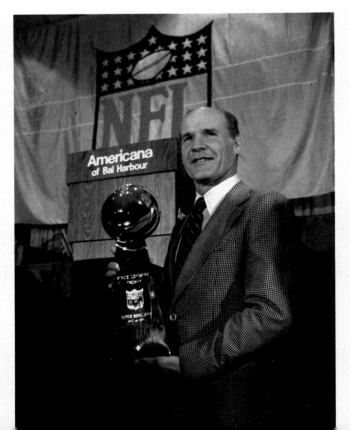

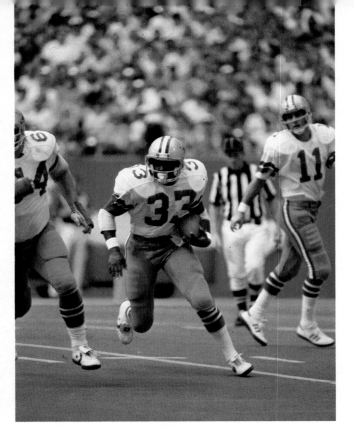

Randy "Manster" White drives one-time Cowboy Craig Morton to the artificial turf in Super Bowl XII. The Dallas defense sparkled that Sunday in the New Orleans Superdome. (John Biever)

Tony Dorsett brought some needed excitement to the Cowboy running game after being acquired in the first round of the 1977 draft. Here, he has taken a handoff from Danny White and is about to chalk up a few of the 1,185 yards he gained in the 1980 regular season. (Dallas Cowboys)

Tony Dorsett sweeps right against the Denver Broncos in Super Bowl XII. The Cowboy on the ground is wide receiver Butch Johnson. (Vernon Biever)

Joy. A moment after Tony Hill grabbed Roger Staubach's "semi-Alley-Oop" pass to defeat the Washington Redskins and win the Eastern Division championship of 1979, an ecstatic Staubach leaps into the arms of fullback Ron Springs. (David Woo)

"It takes a very special young lady."—Suzanne Mitchell, Director, Dallas Cowboys Cheerleaders (Dallas Cowboys)

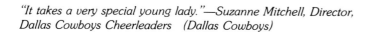

It was the Cleveland Browns, instead of the Green Bay Packers, in 1969 who would break the Cowboys' six-game winning streak, and they would do it before a crowd of 84,850 at Municipal Stadium up in Cleveland. The Cowboys' hearts still ached at the sight of the Browns, who had so decisively removed them from the playoffs the year before. The momentum, it would seem, should have been with the Cowboys that day. They were surging and revengeful. But it wasn't meant to be. The mighty fortification that had been the Cowboys' defense crumbled that day. There was no pass rush to speak of, and the defensive secondary could not have been more riddled with holes if the Browns' Bill Nelsen took a machine gun to it. As it turned out, Nelsen threw for five touchdown passes and a total of 255 yards (18 of 25). Paul Warfield caught two of the TD bombs, and Gary Collins caught another two. The Cowboys could never get anything going on offense. The score was 28–3 at half-time and 42–10 at the final gun, a most depressing afternoon for the Cowboys.

The Cowboys got back into the swing of things with two wins over the next two weeks, bringing their record to 8–1, before they fell by a single point to the Rams, who maintained a perfect record (10–0) with that victory.

Calvin Hill had started the second half of the season with the same explosiveness he had the first. In the first two games, he rushed for 109 yards and 150 yards, respectively, the latter a club record that replaced the one he had set earlier in the year. A foot injury, however, kept him out of the game at Los Angeles and, for all practical purposes, from the one the following week against San Francisco. (He got minus 2 yards on four carries.) The Cowboys were held to a tie with the 49ers and were lucky to escape with that on a fourth-quarter TD pass from Morton to Rentzel. Then they won their last two games handily, beating the NFL title holder, the Baltimore Colts, 27–10 and the Washington Redskins, who by that time were out of the running for the Capital Division crown.

The season record of 11–2–1 was the second best the Cowboys had recorded up to that time. The offensive unit was second in total scoring in the NFL that year with 369 points, 10 behind the Minnesota Vikings, who had just finished the best season in their history. The defense gave up the least amount of rushing yardage (1,050) for the second year in a row and allowed the least number of rushing TDs (52).

The Cowboys had a host of All-Pros that year, with the different selectors naming Ralph Neely, Chuck Howley, John Niland, Calvin Hill, Cornell Green, Mel Renfro, and the omnipresent figure on that honor roll, Bob Lilly.

Craig Morton had had a respectable year: a 54% completion average, a total 2,619 yards passing, and 21 TDs. Lance Rentzel led the NFL in touchdown catches with 12 and in average yards per reception (22). Mel Renfro

Craig Morton just barely gets this pass away before suffering the embrace of Baltimore Colt linebacker Ted Hendricks in the last preseason game of 1969. The Colts, who had lost the preceding Super Bowl to the New York Jets and Joe Namath, were playing their final year in the NFC, and would move to the AFC in 1970. They clobbered the Cowboys in the Cotton Bowl that September afternoon, 23–7. No. 51 on the Cowboys is center Dave Manders. (Pro Football Hall of Fame)

grabbed the most interceptions in the league (10). And Calvin Hill was the league's second most productive rusher with 942 yards, 90 less than Gale Sayers of the Chicago Bears.

The Cowboys were now making the trip to the playoffs for the fifth consecutive year (if one includes the 1965 Playoff Bowl for runners-up).

As they had been the year before, the Cleveland Browns were the Century Division champs, this time winning it with ease. Their record of 10–3–1 was by far the best in a division where all three of the other teams posted losing records. (The Giants were second, 6–8.)

This year, however, the Browns would have to come to Dallas to face the Cowboys and would not have the home-field advantage. And once again the Cowboys were the favorites, this time by 6 or 7 points, depending on which bookmaker a person talked to.

D. D. (or Dwight Douglas) Lewis signed with Dallas in 1968 to begin a long and varied career with the Cowboys. A devastating special team player who developed into a premier linebacker, Lewis bears one of the most familiar names associated with the Cowboy fabled defense. He has also centered on punts and served as a back-up punter.   (Dallas Cowboys)

It had rained heavily before the game, and the field was a muddy mess at kickoff time. It had all the makings of a defensive battle in the muck. But the Browns began with a big break. Don Cockcroft punted to Bob Hayes, who decided not to field the ball, which took a wacky bounce and caromed off the leg of Cowboy Rayfield Wright, who was back to block for Hayes. A Cleveland player fell on the ball deep in Dallas territory. Bill Nelsen took advantage of the break and led a swift drive that ended with a 2-yard touchdown run by Bo Scott.

The Cowboys had great difficulty moving the ball that afternoon, the offense as lethargic as an old sow in the slop of the Cotton Bowl. In the second quarter, the Browns widened the lead to 14 points with a short TD pass from Nelsen to tight end Milt Morin. A 29-yard field goal by Don Cockcroft made it 17–0 at the half.

In the third quarter, it went to 24–0 before the Cowboys finally registered a score (a 2-yard run by Craig Morton).

But the home-town boys were being totally dominated, and everyone sitting in the damp cold of the Cotton Bowl that day knew it. The outcome was already decided when the Browns' defensive back Walt Sumner snatched a Morton pass and, amid groans and other obscene sounds, raced with it 88 yards for a touchdown.

For the Cowboys, Roger Staubach came off the bench in the fourth quarter, but the game was nowhere within reach. When it was all over, the Cowboys had again allowed Cleveland access to the NFL championship game. This year the score was 38–14. And an amazed, befud-

---

Question: *Everybody assumes that the football season is run from training camp to the Super Bowl or the Pro Bowl, if you're lucky. But is that the length of your season? Is that the busiest time?*

Gil Brandt: *It's an all-year affair. The last full game—I think this year's is the Japan Bowl, which is played January 18—goes almost into spring practices, which start about the first of February. Most schools in the South will start that first week in February. The only time there isn't something actively going on is usually the month of June because the draft takes place in May, the end of spring practice is in May, the signing of players is usually over by sometime in early June, so that is the only time I really have free time—just prior to the time we go to our training camp.*

Question: *Is there a kind of chronological list of refinements or innovations you have instituted over the years in the selection of players?*

Gil Brandt: *I think the first thing we did was to come up with that form (player rating form). It helped us cover all the various phases of what we were looking for. Once you have a form like that, then it's just improving on methods of grading it. Then the methods were to get everybody thinking together. How did you get people thinking together? You had to draw categories so that they had to place a player in the category to give them that grade. We improved on that every year. Now we've written our own manual on how to evaluate a football player. We used to measure players because we wanted to get the tallest player in all cases and because a lot of times we found out that players who were supposed to be 6 feet 3 inches were really 6 feet 1 inch. The thing is—it's very easy to distinguish who the top people are and who the bottom people are. But there's a massive group in the middle, and the key to being successful is to find the best of that group.*

Rookie running back Calvin Hill (35), the Cowboy first-round draft choice from Yale in 1969, introduces Dallas fans to his dazzling running style in this preseason game against the New York Jets at the Cotton Bowl. The Cowboys lost the game, but Hill soon established himself as Dallas's premier running back and led the team in rushing that year with 942 yards, only three less than Don Perkins's club record at that time. Cowboy No. 76 is guard John Niland. The Jets are defensive end Verlon Biggs (86) and linebacker Larry Grantham (60).   (Dallas Cowboys)

dled, frustrated, and disheartened group of Cowboys would have to trudge on down to Miami and make one more appearance in the "Also-Ran game," which was more formally known as the Playoff Bowl. No one cared very much about the game, and it turned out to be not much more than a showcase for Rams quarterback Roman Gabriel, who threw four touchdowns as the Rams shut the Cowboys out, 31–0.

It had been a wonderful regular season with a monumental disappointment to tarnish it as the end. The Cowboy fans were beginning to think their life was one of *déjà vû,* that history does indeed repeat itself, that their team could not surmount a postseason jinx. And some were thinking a lot worse things.

But although Super Bowl IV would not be theirs, there would be Super Bowl V. And things would change for the better because the Cowboys were about to enter the fabulous 1970s. They would play in five Super Bowls and would be the only team from the National Football Conference to win the Super Bowl during that decade, and they would do it twice. If the Cowboys and their coaches and the front-office people only knew all that as the 1969 season formally ended, they might have felt a little better than they did at the time.

10 Finally, the Super Bowl

THE FILM BEGINS WITH A FOCUS on one empty football stadium, then fades to another. Organ music in the background summons the appropriate reverential mood. Then the deep, resonant voice of John Facenda intones slowly, dramatically, as if from the heavens: "America's football palaces . . . Sunday's cathedrals . . ." On the screen, the scene shifts to people, crowds of them, filing toward the stadium, then fades to the inside of it, jammed full now with cheering, pennant-waving fans. And Facenda continues. "During the seventies, more than one hundred million weekend worshippers turned out to hear their favorite gridiron gospel." It was the same John Facenda whose flair for the melodramatic and penchant for mellifluous description once prompted a press-box denizen to observe, "If they ever announce the Last Judgment, he's got to get the job."

In truth, professional football did grow considerably in the 1970s, rising from its obscurity in the 1920s, the indifference and eventual acceptance in the intervening years, finally to attain the stature of a national pastime. As a tribute and as an entertainment, the NFL decided to make a movie of that most recent chapter in the story of professional football—the 1970s—to highlight the great performances, the dramatic games, the unforgettable moments (which include such things, in the words of John Facenda, as "Hail Mary passes" and "immaculate receptions").

Perhaps the metaphors emotionalized by Facenda are in reality hyperboles, and perhaps the drama on the football field is somewhat less in the overall scheme of human things than, say, world wars or reformations, but the game did, in fact, become a prime source of entertainment for tens of millions of people and a very big business during the 1970s.

In the structure of the NFL and in the game itself, there would be many changes which would occur during that decade.

A new realignment in 1970 would forever meld the two leagues into one, with a National Football Conference and an American Football Conference, and create a new and more exciting system of playoffs. TV would become an even more significant factor in the game—"ABC's Monday Night Football" would be introduced in 1970 and become a standard prime-time event. Compensation from TV for each of the 26 NFL teams would be upped to $1.7 million that same year, and by the end of the decade, each team would be reaping about $5 million from the video vaults. The rules of the game would change significantly; a new challenger, the World Football League, would rise, send a fleeting scare through some NFL hearts, then fizzle out; two new teams would join the league, the Seattle Seahawks and the Tampa Bay Buccaneers; and the players and the team owners would become accustomed to confronting each other across the figurative bargaining table as if they were teamsters and trucking company owners.

No team was more visible, however, or more an integral and imperishable part of the 1970s than the Dallas Cowboys. There was, of course, the imposing presence of the Miami Dolphins in the first half of the decade and the awesome reality of the Pittsburgh Steelers in the latter half, but it was the Cowboys who maintained a brilliance of the first magnitude throughout the entire ten-year pe-

1970 Dallas Cowboys. Front row: Ron Widby, Bob Belden, Roger Staubach, Craig Morton, Lance Rentzel, Mel Renfro, Bob Hayes, Margene Adkins, Dennis Homan, Herb Adderley. Second row: Dan Reeves, Walt Garrison, Duane Thomas, Cornell Green, Calvin Hill, Joe Williams, Charlie Waters, Cliff Harris, Richmond Flowers, Mark Washington. Third row: D. D. Lewis, Dave Manders, Dave Edwards, Chuck Howley, Lee Roy Jordan, Tom Stincic, Steve Kiner, Blaine Nye, John Fitzgerald, Larry Cole. Fourth row: Halvor Hagen, Doug Mooers, George Andrie, Pat Toomay, Rayfield Wright, Tony Liscio, Ralph Neely, Bob Lilly, Jethro Pugh. Fifth row: John Niland, Ron East, Bob Asher, Mike Clark, Pettis Norman, Reggie Rucker, Mike Ditka. Top row: Jack Eskridge, Ray Renfro, Jerry Tubbs, Ernie Stautner, Bobby Franklin, Jim Myers, Tom Landry (coach), Larry Gardner, Don Cochren. (Dallas Cowboys)

riod. John Facenda made special note of it: There were, he said, "the teams that set the standards for all the rest . . . Throughout the decade, the Dallas Cowboys star was a symbol of football excellence . . . the man behind it, Tom Landry, the game's most creative strategist . . . and transforming Landry's ideas into action, Roger Staubach, the focal point of professional football's most sophisticated attack."

No one would have dreamed such a thing after watching the Cowboys muddle through the first preseason of that decade. They managed to beat a meek and faltering San Diego Charger team in the first preseason game and then lost the next five in a row, two to weak-sister teams in the AFC and one to the now debilitated Green Bay Packers, who would drop to the cellar of the NFC Central Division that year. It was the Cowboys' worst exhibition season since they had lost four of five games back in 1964.

There was mild astonishment and a lot of soul searching in the organization when the preseason ended. After all, the Cowboys of 1970 were again a unanimous pick to

sweep their division. Just about everyone was back from the fine team of 1969, and some who had been nonstarters, like Blaine Nye and Rayfield Wright, were truly coming into their own. But besides that, the Cowboys had had one of the most lucrative drafts in their history, or anyone else's for that matter. They had picked up running back Duane Thomas from West Texas State in the first round, followed by tackle Bob Asher (Vanderbilt), wide receiver Margene Adkins (Henderson Junior College), cornerback Charlie Waters (Clemson), linebacker Steve Kiner (Tennessee), center John Fitzgerald (Boston College), defensive end Pat Toomay (Vanderbilt), defensive back Pete Athas (Dade Junior College), and cornerback Mark Washington (Morgan State). In addition, they picked up cornerback Cliff Harris as a free agent and traded with Green Bay for All-Pro defensive back and future Hall of Famer Herb Adderley.

Dan Reeves, because of his knee problems, would never return to top form as a runner, although he would play for a few more years. But in 1970 he had the distinction of becoming the youngest assistant coach in the NFL.

The Cowboys hired him to help coach the offensive backfield, the one he was still a part of.

Before the opening curtain of the regular season, Tom Landry announced that he was not at all happy with the way things were going and there would be some major changes. And if *they* didn't work, there would be still more.

Craig Morton's wounded shoulder had been bothering him most of the preseason, and his performance at best had been disappointing. The Landry ax fell on him first, and Roger Staubach was slated to start the 1970 regular season, as he had the 1969 season. Bob Hayes and Ralph Neely were the next to get the word. They, too, would sit out the opener against the Eagles up in Philadelphia, replaced, respectively, by Dennis Homan and Blaine Nye.

Roger Staubach once again proved to be a good choice to pitch the opening day game, throwing 11 completions out of 15 passes and steering the Cowboys to an easy win over the Eagles, 17–7. Perhaps his finest moment came on a 31-yard TD toss to Lance Rentzel in the third quarter which broke the game's tie. Calvin Hill picked up 117 yards rushing that day, and the Dallas offense looked solid. There was another relatively easy win the following week over the Giants for Staubach and the Cowboys, but

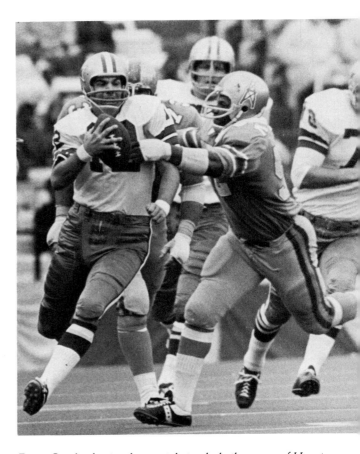

Roger Staubach tries desperately to elude the grasp of Houston Oiler linebacker Garland Boyette in this 1970 preseason encounter at the Astrodome. No. 78 on the Cowboys is tackle Bob Asher. Houston decimated the Cowboys that day, 37–21, in what was the worst Cowboy preseason since they had lost all five exhibition games back in 1962. The preseason debacle, however, would be more than atoned for in the regular season by a division championship and in the postseason by a trip to the Super Bowl. (Pro Football Hall of Fame)

Monday Night

The Dallas Cowboys made their debut on "ABC's Monday Night Football" on November 16, 1970, against the St. Louis Cardinals, and allowed a national TV audience to witness the only regular or postseason game in their history in which they were shut out. The final score was: the Cardinals 38, the Cowboys 0.

Announcing that game were the Monday night threesome of Howard Cosell, Dandy Don Meredith, and Keith Jackson. (Frank Gifford would not appear until the following year.) During the second half, with the Cowboys offense going nowhere, the home-town fans at the Cotton Bowl let Cowboy quarterback Craig Morton know how they felt about it. When things got worse in the fourth quarter, the boos turned to a chant: "We want Meredith." Up in the press booth, Dandy Dan, who so often had heard the boos directed at him on the field in that same stadium, shook his head and said: "No way!" Then he smiled, even laughed at the irony of it all.

Morton did have an especially poor game that evening, completing only 8 of 26 passes and throwing three interceptions. Later, he said of it, "Following that loss to St. Louis, the only thing that gave me any kind of a lift was when Ralph Neely gave me a Spiro Agnew watch."

then they had to face the team which many felt was their biggest threat in the division that year, the St. Louis Cardinals.

Staubach started for the third week in a row, but when he threw two interceptions in the first quarter, Landry yanked him and brought in Craig Morton. But Morton caused little in the way of excitement that day, and the Cowboys suffered their first loss. In fact, they didn't put a point on the scoreboard until late in the fourth quarter when they were already down 20–0.

But that was only a mild rebuke compared to the bloodbath they were subjected to several weeks later. It occurred up in Bloomington, Minnesota, at the hands of the Vikings, who were the reigning conference champions and were a favorite in the game, but no one expected them to do to the Cowboys what they did that October afternoon.

The Viking defense was the pride of the league by 1970, having displaced the Rams from that honor. The front four of Carl Eller, Alan Page, Gary Larsen, and Jim Marshall were called the "Purple People Eaters," referring to their jersey color and not the hue of the people they allegedly consumed. But it was both their offense and defense which combined that day to annihilate the Cowboys. At the half, the Cowboys trailed 34–6; by the end of the third quarter, the score had grown to 51–6; then, finally, it was 54–13. That infamous day, the largest number of points ever were scored against the Cowboys. It also stands as the largest margin of defeat in the team's history (along with the 48–7 drubbing the Cleveland Browns handed them back in 1960).

Both Craig Morton and Roger Staubach had the misfortune to take part in that debacle, but Morton got the call to go it alone the next week in Kansas City against the Super Bowl champion Chiefs, known still in Cowboy territory as the one-time Dallas Texans. The Chiefs, at that

Dave Manders would have a 10-year career at center for the Cowboys, a position that was always hotly contested during those years. Manders, who went to the Pro Bowl in 1966, was one of the hardest-working Cowboys. As assistant coach Ermal Allen once observed, "When we're trying to tell if a player is really putting out, we compare him with Manders." (Dallas Cowboys)

1970

Preseason

Dallas	(1-5)	Opponents
20	San Diego (39,392) @ San Diego	10
10	Los Angeles (64,646) @ L. A.	17
34	Green Bay (72,389) @ Dallas	35
21	Houston (46,548) @ Houston	37
0	Kansas City (69,055) @ Dallas	13
21	New York Jets (55,297) @ Dallas	29

Regular Season

		(10-4)	
W	17	Philadelphia (59,728)	7
W	28	N.Y. Giants (57,239) (H)	10
L	7	St. Louis (50,780)	20
W	13	Atlanta (53,611) (H)	0
L	13	Minnesota (47,900)	54
W	27	Kansas City (51,158)	16
W	21	Philadelphia (55,736) (H)	17
L	20	N.Y. Giants (62,928)	23
L	0	St. Louis (69,323) (H)	38
W	45	Washington (50,415)	21
W	16	Green Bay (67,182) (H)	3
W	34	Washington (57,936) (H)	0
W	6	Cleveland (75,458)	2
W	52	Houston (50,504) (H)	10
	299		221

Postseason

		Divisional Playoff (Dallas)	
W	5	Detroit (73,167)	0
		NFC Championship Game (San Francisco)	
W	17	San Francisco (59,625)	10
		Super Bowl V (Miami)	
L	13	Baltimore (80,055)	16

point in the season, were not doing any better than the Cowboys. Both teams had 3–2 records and were in second place in their respective divisions, and both had much higher expectations.

The Cowboys came off their embarrassment at Minnesota to win the game largely on the running of rookie Duane Thomas, who got most of the rushing calls after Calvin Hill left the game with an injured back. Thomas gained 134 yards that day on just 20 carries (6.7 yard average), including a 47-yard TD that had everybody in Kansas City's Arrowhead Stadium on their feet. Another gemstone that afternoon was an 89-yard bomb from Morton to Bob Hayes for the Cowboys' last touchdown, enabling them to win by 9 points.

By November 16, when the Cowboys would play in

"ABC's Monday Night Football" game, against the Cardinals in Dallas, their first, the team had a creditable 5–3 record, but the division race was a tossup at this point, with the Cardinals ahead (6–2) and the New York Giants dead even with the Cowboys in second place.

Presented with a chance to move into a tie for first place, the Cowboys instead suffered through the first— and only—regular-season shutout in their history. The final score was a denigrating 38–0, and the chance for a division title was suddenly remote indeed. Now, with a record of 5–4, they would have to win all five of their remaining games, while the Cardinals would, minimally, have to lose at least three and tie one of their five games.

Fortunately, the Cardinals were accommodating. After their mortification of the Cowboys, they came up with a tie the next week, a win the week after, and then dropped their last three games. The Giants stayed in the race until the last game of the regular season, too. Going into that final weekend, the Cardinals were 8–4–1, and the Cowboys and the Giants were a nose ahead with records of 9–4. But the Giants were decimated by the Rams 31–3, and the Cardinals dropped a real squeaker to the Redskins 28–27, while the Cowboys savaged the Houston Oilers 52–10 to gain the undisputed crown of the NFC East on what should have been named "Craig Morton Day." He threw 13 of 17 for 349 yards and tied the Cowboy touchdown passing record of five, with four of them going to Bob Hayes (also a Cowboy all-time record) and the other to rookie Reggie Rucker, a free agent who had been brought up from the Cowboy taxi squad. The youngster Rucker had taken over from Lance Rentzel, who, a few weeks earlier, had been arrested in Dallas for the felony of indecent exposure to a minor child and as a result asked to be removed from the team's roster. The unfortunate result of a variety of personal and emotional problems, it would end Rentzel's career as a Cowboy. He

Before the 1970 NFC championship game against the San Francisco 49ers, Cowboy assistant coach Ernie Stautner talks tactics with Larry Cole. Looking on are end George Andrie (68) and tackle Ron East (73). It must have paid off, because the Cowboys held the 49ers to a mere 10 points while scoring 17 and qualifying themselves for Super Bowl V.   (Pro Football Hall of Fame)

would be traded the next year to the Los Angeles Rams.

The "Doomsday Defense," a nickname bestowed upon the Cowboys' defensive unit by Dallas *Morning News* sportswriter Gary Cartwright, allowed only 15 points in the last four games of 1970 and only one touchdown in the last 17 quarters of the season. But despite the notoriety of Dallas's prominent defense, only Chuck Howley was named to the All-Pro team that year, and for the first time in seven years, Bob Lilly's name was omitted from that prestigious list.

Duane Thomas had had a splendid rookie year and led the Cowboys in rushing with 803 yards; his average rush of 5.3 was the best in the entire NFL that year. Craig Morton's passing percentage of only 49% was substandard, and the quarterbacking situation was still a disturbing issue. And once again the questions loomed. How would the Cowboys fare in the playoffs this year? Would they once again deny themselves the ultimate honors of their sport, or would fate deal them another cruel blow?

The first team they were to face was the wild-card Detroit Lions, but they would have the advantage of playing at the Cotton Bowl. More than 73,000 hopeful but skeptical fans turned out, accustomed to having been tantalized, coaxed into optimism, then rudely dumped into the playoff pit reserved for also-rans.

The Dallas defense was again superb that day, giving up a combined passing/rushing total of only 136 yards to the Lions. And Dallas won by the baseball score of 5–0. It was, in fact, the first NFL playoff game without a touchdown since 1950 when the Cleveland Browns, with two field goals and a safety, beat the New York Giants 8–3. The Cowboy scoring that day came on a first-quarter field goal by Mike Clark (26 yards) and a fourth-quarter safety when George Andrie and Jethro Pugh dumped Lions quarterback Greg Landry in his own end zone. The Lions had made a desperate bid for a touchdown in the waning moments of the game and had reached the Cowboys' 29-yard line, but the last-ditch drive was stifled when Mel Renfro intercepted a pass.

Now there was one more game before the Super Bowl. The Cowboys would meet the recently recharged San Francisco 49ers, who, the day after Dallas's win, upset the Minnesota Vikings 17–14 when John Brodie snuck the ball in for a touchdown with 1:20 left in the game.

The game was scheduled for January 3 at Kezar Stadium out in San Francisco. Coaching the 49ers was an old teammate of Tom Landry's and a former employee of the Cowboys, Dick Nolan, who had been a Cowboy assistant coach from 1962 through 1964. The 49ers were an offensive Gatling gun, guided by John Brodie, who had led the entire NFL in passing yardage (2,941), completions (223), passing touchdowns (24), and the lowest percentage of interceptions (2.7). His chief receiver, Gene Washington,

An inflated Dallas Cowboy is part of the pregame hype at Super Bowl V. Looking on are a very early version of the Dallas Cowboy Cheerleaders.   (Vernon Biever)

Before Super Bowl V

Some random quotes before Super Bowl V:

Herb Adderley: *Being in the Super Bowl for a third time is really beautiful. I can't describe the feeling . . . I've been telling the guys to stay loose, have fun, and grab the $25,000 winners' swag."*

Lee Roy Jordan: *"We're back in Miami, and this time it ain't for the Toilet Bowl." (referring to their three previous trips to the Playoff Bowl in Miami)*

Craig Morton *(asked about his shoulder separation, which had been surgically repaired by transplanting a tendon from his ankle): "I'm the only quarterback with a foot for an arm."*

Johnny Unitas *(when asked about his age, 37): "Well, my hair is longer now, and my passes are shorter. But I can always cut my hair."*

The starting lineups for Super Bowl V:

Dallas Cowboys		Baltimore Colts
Offense		
Bob Hayes	WR	Eddie Hinton
Reggie Rucker	WR	Roy Jefferson
Pettis Norman	TE	John Mackey
Ralph Neely	T	Bob Vogel
Rayfield Wright	T	Dan Sullivan
John Niland	G	Glenn Ressler
Blaine Nye	G	John Williams
Dave Manders	C	Bill Curry
Craig Morton	QB	Johnny Unitas
Duane Thomas	RB	Norm Bulaich
Walt Garrison	RB	Tom Nowatzke
Defense		
Larry Cole	E	Bubba Smith
George Andrie	E	Roy Hilton
Jethro Pugh	T	Billy Ray Smith
Bob Lilly	T	Fred Miller
Dave Edwards	LLB	Ray May
Lee Roy Jordan	MLB	Mike Curtis
Chuck Howley	RLB	Ted Hendricks
Herb Adderley	LCB	Charlie Stukes
Mel Renfro	RCB	Jim Duncan
Cornell Green	S	Jerry Logan
Charlie Waters	S	Rick Volk

yards, and Walt Garrison had added another 71 on the ground. Brodie completed only 19 of 40 passes, and so the Cowboys' rushing game clearly won the duel with the 49ers' passing attack. The Dallas Cowboys had ended four years of frustration and failure, defeating the San Francisco 49ers, 17–10, to win the National Football League championship. The Cowboys had finally done it; they were going to the Super Bowl.

Miami's Orange Bowl was the setting for Super Bowl V. This was incidentally the first year that the term *Super Bowl* was used; the four previous games had been known

At Super Bowl V, Herb Adderley trots onto the field for his third appearance in a Super Bowl. The former Green Bay defensive back, here in the uniform of the Dallas Cowboys, would appear again the following year, for a record four appearances in the six years of Super Bowls. Adderley was inducted into the Pro Football Hall of Fame in 1980. (John Biever)

also was a league leader with 1,100 total yards. Ken Willard was still a powerhouse rusher who had churned out 789 yards that season. And the 49ers had scored the most points in the NFL that year, 352.

One newsman wrote: "The game is expected to be a duel between the passing of John Brodie and the running of Duane Thomas and his tandem back Walt Garrison." At first, the duel was hardly noticeable. The defense of both teams prevailed, and by halftime the score stood at 3–3. As they trudged off to the locker room, the Cowboys had now gone 23 consecutive quarters without giving up a touchdown.

Dallas at last got its offense moving in the second half. Two well-executed drives resulted in a pair of touchdowns, and they were ahead 17–3. Duane Thomas had run the ball in from 13 yards out for one, and Walt Garrison had grabbed a little 5-yard pass from Morton for the other TD. John Brodie threw for a touchdown during the same period, but that was the end of the scoring. For the day, Duane Thomas had been superb, rushing for 143

The Dallas Doomsday Defense awaits the Baltimore Colts at the goal line in Super Bowl V. From the left: Mel Renfro (20) George Andrie (66), Bob Lilly (74), Jethro Pugh (75), Dave Edwards (52), Tom Stincic (56), and Larry Cole (63). The mighty Doomsday defenders faltered here, however, and the Colts scored a fourth-quarter touchdown on a 2-yard run by Tom Nowatzke which, along with the ensuing extra point, tied the score at 13–13.   (Pro Football Hall of Fame)

simply as the "AFL-NFL World Championship Game." The Cowboys' opponents would be the Baltimore Colts, a team that had crossed over to the AFC that year and one that held the unwanted distinction of having lost in Super Bowl III to Joe Namath and the New York Jets in that same stadium in Miami.

The Colts had had an impressive season, 11–2–1, taking the AFC East from a powerful Miami Dolphin team that was just a year away from asserting itself as an AFC champion. An aged Johnny Unitas, 37, was still at quarterback, backed up by almost-as-elderly Earl Morrall, 36. And there were a number of other respected names on the Colts' roster, like defensive end Bubba Smith, defensive tackle Billy Ray Smith, offensive tackle Bob Vogel, linebacker Mike Curtis, safety Rick Volk, and tight end John Mackey.

The Cowboys were quartered at the Galt Ocean Mile Hotel up in Fort Lauderdale. They arrived a week before the game and held workouts at a nearby stadium during that week and then ran through drills at the Orange Bowl on the Saturday before the game.

There had been no hoopla on the other postseason treks they had made to Miami. No one had really cared much about the game between the consolation teams in the Playoff Bowls. Now they were in for a new experience altogether. The NFL had virtually moved their offices from New York City down to Miami Beach's Americana Hotel. Almost 80,000 tickets had been sold at $15 per. More than 800 press credentials had been issued. Buses were chartered to take the writers and broadcasters back and forth between the team headquarters and the NFL command post. People by the thousands were pouring

A Media Bonanza

Super Bowl V, featuring the Dallas Cowboys and the Baltimore Colts, became the most widely broadcast sporting event up to that time in TV history. An estimated 62 million people watched it on 510 different TV stations. The special NBC Network colorcast was carried live on 225 stations in the United States, including those in Alaska, Hawaii, Puerto Rico, and the Virgin Islands. In Canada, 265 stations offered the telecast, and it was broadcast in Spanish on 20 stations in Mexico. Even a delayed telecast was beamed to the United Kingdom to a populace much more accustomed to watching rugby.

To handle the play by play, NBC lined up Curt Gowdy, Kyle Rote, and Bill Enis. They would also employ 11 color TV cameras and a production crew of 58.

NBC-Radio signed Al DeRogatis and Jay Randolph to broadcast the game to 320 network stations in the United States. The radio broadcast was also picked up by the American Forces Radio and Television Service and sent by worldwide short wave to 400 radio outlets in the Far East, Europe, and Latin America.

When the game was over, the NBC crew had to pack up:

150 tons of assorted gear
3½ miles of audio cable
2½ miles of camera cable

into the city, filling all the hotels in Miami and Miami Beach, Coral Gables and Fort Lauderdale, all over the area.

It was a first-rate pageant. Press conferences were going on constantly. Western Union was transmitting more than a million words about the spectacle from the hordes of writers attending the spectacle. Parties popped up in practically every hotel in town. Members of the media were given free passes to Hialeah, if they wanted to watch the thoroughbreds run, and to all the dog tracks and jai alai frontons in the area. Of a more formal nature there was: on Thursday, the Super Bowl V Golf Tournament at Doral Country Club; on Friday, the Calypso Countdown (cocktails, a buffet dinner in the Grand Ballroom of the Americana, and a musical extravaganza billed as a salute to the AFC and NFC champions); a Super Bowl heavyweight boxing match later the same night between former champion Floyd Patterson and someone known as Levi Forte at the Miami Beach Convention Hall; on Saturday, there was the Super Bowl V Parade; and on Sunday morning, the Super Bowl V Pre-Game Brunch, also in the Grand Ballroom of the Americana. There would be some

pregame festivities in the Orange Bowl itself, nothing perhaps as gross as Super Bowl I when down on the sidelines, just before the start of the game, 4,000 pigeons were let loose at the Los Angeles Coliseum to flutter frantically above the 62,000 fans, who almost simultaneously raised their souvenir programs to serve as umbrellas.

Kickoff was set for two o'clock Eastern Standard Time, and it was a clear, sunny, 70 degrees when that hour finally arrived. For a little while, it looked as if the famous Florida sun was set to shine all day on just the Cowboys. They sustained a drive in the first quarter, 47 yards in eight plays, but had to settle for a 14-yard field goal from Mike Clark. Things were going very badly for the Colts. Unitas had thrown an interception to Cowboy linebacker Chuck Howley, and punt returner Ron Gardin had fumbled the ball over to the Cowboys. And the Dallas Doomsday defense was thwarting the Colts at every turn.

As the quarter was nearing an end, Craig Morton arched a bomb to Bob Hayes, which brought the Cowboys all the way to the Colts' 12-yard line. The first quarter ended, and the team moved to the other end of the field. There, however, the Cowboys began moving *away* from the goal line instead of toward it, and finally Mike Clark

An exhausted, disconsolate Larry Cole reflects the Cowboy frustrations at Super Bowl V. The Cowboys lost 16–13 on a Baltimore Colt field goal with only 5 seconds left in the game. Cole would go on to play in four more Super Bowls in his long and distinguished career as a Cowboy defensive lineman.   (Vernon Biever)

was called on again. This time he contributed a 30-yard field goal and Dallas led 6–0.

A short time later, the Colts had the ball on a third and 10 situation. Unitas dropped back to pass and rifled the ball to Eddie Hinton, who managed to get a hand on it, sending the football careening through the air. Cowboy defenders Mel Renfro and Cornell Green made stabs at grabbing it, but the ball ended up in the hands of John Mackey at the Cowboy 45, and he raced with it all the way in for a touchdown. The referee ruled that it was legal because Mel Renfro had touched the ball. Renfro claimed he did not, but that was of little consequence on a judgment call. "I was never so upset about a call in my life," Renfro said afterward. No matter, it was officially registered as a 75-yard touchdown play. The extra point, however, was blocked by the Cowboys' Mark Washington, and the score was tied at 6 apiece.

The Colts, however, seemed destined to continue their efforts to hand the game to the Cowboys. Unitas fumbled, and Dallas had the ball at the Colt 28-yard line. A short pass to Dan Reeves, then one to Duane Thomas, who took it into the end zone, and with Mike Clark's extra point, the Cowboys had the lead again, 13–7.

Unitas then faded back to throw his last interception of the day because he was hit just as he released the ball so hard that one of his ribs was cracked. Earl Morrall replaced him for the rest of the game.

After Super Bowl V

Some random quotes from after Super Bowl V:

Tom Landry: *"We beat ourselves. The fumbles and interceptions killed us . . . This hurts pretty bad. We fought uphill for eight weeks. You don't measure disappointment."* And when asked what he said to the team in the locker room after the game, *"You can't say anything. I tried, but you can't say anything."*

Jim O'Brien: *"I had a dream about this last week. I dreamed of this long field goal going through to end it all . . . Another funny thing. My mom called me and said we couldn't lose. She's big on astrology and she figured it all out . . . This is the Age of Aquarius, isn't it? And I'm an Aquarius."*

Clint Murchison *(remembering the Ice Bowl championship game with Green Bay in 1967):* *"At least we're closing in. We got it down to five seconds from thirteen."*

Duane Thomas: *"It isn't the ultimate game. If it was, they wouldn't be playing it next year."*

Johnny Unitas: *"Thank God I've got six months to rest."*

The fatal field goal that extinguished all hopes of the Cowboys in Super Bowl V. With only 5 seconds left in the game, Baltimore rookie Jim O'Brien kicks a 32-yarder to give the Colts a 16–13 win. Racing in from the side to try to block the kick is Mark Washington (46). (Pro Football Hall of Fame)

MVP

Even though the Cowboys lost Super Bowl V, Sport mag-azine's award for the Most Valuable Player in the game went to Cowboy All-Pro linebacker, Chuck Howley.

The Colts managed to get all the way down to the Cowboy 2-yard line as the half was running out. But three plunges by rookie Norm Bulaich gained only about a foot. There were only 21 seconds left when the Colts decided to disdain the field goal and try for the touchdown. Morrall threw to tight end Tom Mitchell, but it was incomplete, and the half came to a rather inglorious end for the Colts.

The Cowboys kicked off to start the second half and got the ball back within seconds when Jim Duncan fumbled at his 31 and Richmond Flowers fell on it for Dallas. The Cowboys drove down to the Colts' 2-yard line, where Landry called for a handoff to Duane Thomas, but all visions of the score going to 19–6 were shattered when on a highly controversial call the referee ruled that Thomas fumbled the ball and the Colts recovered it.

Neither team managed to score during the third quarter. In the fourth period, the sun that had in its own erratic way been shining on the Cowboys must have slipped behind a very dense cloud. Morton threw a pass intended for Walt Garrison, but Colt safety Rick Volk got it instead and raced with it 30 yards to the Cowboy 3-yard line.

Fullback Tom Nowatzke bulled it in for a touchdown, the extra point was good, and the score was again tied.

As time was running down, the Cowboys had the ball, but they were deep in their own territory, and most of the people in the Orange Bowl were thinking that this strange game was going to go into overtime. But the show was not over. On third down, with only a little more than one minute to play, Morton threw to Dan Reeves. But the pass went through his outstretched hands and into those of Colt linebacker Mike Curtis, who charged with it to the Dallas 28-yard line. A couple of running plays picked up another 3 yards. The clock had run down to a mere five seconds, and the Colts took a time-out to stop it. Jim O'Brien, the Colts' rookie place kicker, who was called "Lassie" by his teammates because of his fashionably long hair, came out onto the field. The snap and the hold were perfect, and so was the 32-yard field goal. The final score was 16–13.

The game had been a sloppy one, a comedy of errors, as some described it. Tex Maule, in *Sports Illustrated,* called it the "Blunder Bowl." In that respect, the two teams split: the Colts led in turnovers (interceptions and fumbles) 7–4, but the Cowboys won decisively in penalties 9–4 (or 133 yards to 31). Tex Maule observed: "And to think television was worried that situation comedy was dead." Perhaps he summed it up best when he wrote, "Both teams bumbled through a laugher of a Super Bowl, but in the end the joke was on the Cowboys, who made the biggest mistake of all—losing."

11 Winning It All

TEXAS STADIUM, THE EDIFICE Clint Murchison was building out of 2,600 tons of steel, 50,000 cubic yards of concrete, and 91,000 square feet of Tartan Turf over in the town of Irving, would not be completed by the start of the 1971 season, as had been hoped. In fact, it would not be ready until the sixth game of the regular season. That, according to one sportswriter looking at it in retrospect, "put it a game or two ahead of the Cowboys of '71."

On paper, the Cowboys had everything going for them. They were the reigning NFC champions, and they had fully deserved the title. They had lost the Super Bowl in a chaotic game that was not at all characteristic of the inbred quality of the team. The fates that day had simply played another cruel prank on the Cowboys; that was all. That setback did not deter the forecasters; coming into the 1971 season, the Cowboys were deemed the NFC's premier team. The trouble was they just would not realize that themselves until the season was half over.

There were a lot of things gnawing away at the team, however, and life at the top, they found, was often far from paradise. Everyone, players and management alike, had been moved by the predicament of an emotionally troubled Lance Rentzel, and his status and future as a professional football player were still unresolved in the early months of 1971. There were others with assorted problems. During the previous season, Steve Kiner, at a rock concert, had hit an off-duty policeman with a folding chair and was awaiting the outcome of some charges pending there. Craig Morton had had a run-in with the police in the wee hours one morning when he was observed relieving his bladder on a Dallas street behind his

automobile, and on top of that he had financial problems that sent him into personal bankruptcy.

The most publicized dilemma, however, was the relationship between running back Duane Thomas, the NFC's rookie of the year, and just about everybody else. He wanted his old contract torn up and a new, more lucrative one drawn up. His three-year contract called for a salary of $18,000 the first year, which would increase $2,000 in each of the next two years. With incentives, however, and playoff revenues, he took home about $74,000 the first year. Tex Schramm refused to issue a new contract, and the breach between Thomas and the organization became canyonlike.

Bob Hayes also had contract problems. He was a holdout, having played out his option in 1970. He was adamant, he had the Players Association behind him, and he had a lawyer, but everybody was trying to work something out so he could play in 1971. It was living proof of how the relationship between players and management had changed as the business of the game got more sophisticated. The internal workings of the teams of the 1970s had become as appropriate to the pages of the *Wall Street Journal* as they were to the sports pages of a local newspaper.

All-Pro linebacker Chuck Howley announced that he would not be in attendance at the Cowboys' training camp that year, either, although his reason was simply that he planned to retire. But there were a number of other players who arrived at Thousand Oaks without signed contracts, and they included Craig Morton, Mel Renfro, Blaine Nye, and Jethro Pugh.

As sportswriter Steve Perkins of the Dallas *Times-Herald* aptly quipped: "Unless you wanted to accompany Staubach to a church meeting, there seemed to be few happy stories on the Cowboys' beat."

The draft was less prolific than it had traditionally been for the Cowboys. Their first-round pick was Tody Smith, a defensive end from Southern Cal who, although he was 6 feet 5 inches and 250 pounds, was still referred to as the little brother of Bubba Smith of the Colts. There was also Ike Thomas, a cornerback and kick-return specialist from Bishop College in Dallas; Bill Gregory, a defensive end from the University of Wisconsin; and Ron Jessie, a wide receiver from Kansas, who would show a lot of promise but would be traded to the Detroit Lions because of the healthy abundance of veteran receivers in the Cowboy camp.

For once, the Cowboys went with verve to the bartering board. They found a home for Lance Rentzel with the Rams, and got tight end Billy Truax in exchange. Then they sent their own tight end Pettis Norman, along with tackles Tony Liscio and Ron East, to the San Diego Chargers for All-Pro flanker Lance Alworth. They also acquired a fine wide receiver from the Kansas City Chiefs, Gloster Richardson, a four-year veteran of the AFL, and the Cowboys coaxed former Green Bay Packer All-Pro and future Hall of Famer Forrest Gregg out of his announced retirement. He would be 38 that season, but the Cowboys felt his vast experience in the offensive line would benefit the team and the younger linemen as well.

Another major trade turned out to be one of the shortest on record. The malcontent Duane Thomas and offensive lineman Halvor Hagen were sent to the New England Patriots for running back Carl Garrett and the Patriots' first-round draft choice the following year. As it happened, two uncomfortable situations came out of it. On his ar-

Duane Thomas

The most famous, or infamous, press conference ever held involving the Cowboys was the one called by Duane Thomas in July 1971. Discontent with his contract and the way he felt he was being treated, he went to Dallas and set up his own press conference while the team was out in Thousand Oaks, California. At it, he called:

Tom Landry "a plastic man, no man at all";

Gil Brandt "a liar";

Tex Schramm "sick, demented, and completely dishonest." When told of Thomas's description of him, Schramm shrugged, then laughed. "That's not bad," he said. "He got two out of three."

Lights Out

In his first start as quarterback in the 1971 regular season, Roger Staubach was knocked unconscious after throwing one pass and was led from the field. He never knew what hit him until he watched the game films the next day. There he saw Philadelphia Eagles defensive end Mel Tom whack him from the blind side with a savage forearm to the head.

No penalty had been called for the flagrant violation, and Roger explained his reaction to it in his autobiography Time Enough to Win:

A bunch of players were sitting around our locker room discussing the incident and I said, Boy, I'd like to catch that guy some dark night and use some of my hand-to-hand combat on him. That was a joke. Tom was about as big as a freight train, around 6 feet 7 inches, 260 pounds.

Steve Perkins, a local reporter, heard me say that and wrote a story about it. Only Steve wrote it straight, as if I were serious and wanted to go one-on-one with Tom in an alley . . .

So the next time I saw Perkins I said, "Steve, if I really were serious about taking on Tom, why do you think I went out the next morning and bought 100,000 papers with your story in it?"

"I dunno," he said. "Tell me."

"So Mel Tom wouldn't read one."

rival, Carl Garrett told Dallas newsmen how delighted he was to be a Cowboy, that he was glad to be away from the Patriots and especially the offensive line. "This year I'll have someone blocking in front of me," he said. Garrett no doubt wished he had never said that when, within days, the trade was dissolved and he was on his way back to New England. It seems Duane Thomas did not quite last through one full practice session with the Patriots. He walked out of camp after a rather heated run-in with one of the assistant coaches. Thomas said it was clear the Patriots didn't want him and therefore he certainly didn't want them. It was agreed to call off the trade, and Thomas once again was a property of the Cowboys.

There were two late additions to the squad. One was Toni Fritsch, the Cowboys' first soccer-style kicker. To recruit him, Gil Brandt had had to go all the way to Vienna, Austria. The other was defensive end Don Talbert.

When the Cowboys settled in Thousand Oaks for their traditional summer sojourn, Chuck Howley came back out of his premature retirement. At 35, he decided he still had another year in him, and neither he nor the Cowboys

1971 Dallas Cowboys. Front row: Ron Widby, Roger Staubach, Craig Morton, Toni Fritsch, Mel Renfro, Bob Hayes, Margene Adkins, Herb Adderley, Dan Reeves, Gloster Richardson. Second row: Duane Thomas, Cornell Green, Calvin Hill, Joe Williams, Ike Thomas, Charlie Waters, Claxton Welch, Cliff Harris, Mark Washington. Third row: D. D. Lewis, Dave Manders, Dave Edwards, Chuck Howley, Lee Roy Jordan, Tom Stincic, Steve Kiner, Blaine Nye, John Fitzgerald. Fourth row: Larry Cole, Halvor Hagen, George Andrie, Pat Toomay, Rayfield Wright, Rodney Wallace, Don Talbert, Bob Lilly, Jethro Pugh. Fifth row: John Niland, Bill Gregory, Bob Asher, Forrest Gregg, Mike Clark, Tody Smith, Billy Truax, Mike Ditka. Top row: Don Cochren, Jim Myers, Tom Landry, Ernie Stautner, Jerry Tubbs.   (Dallas Cowboys)

would regret his decision.

Despite the turmoil and uncertainty in the months before the 1971 season, the Cowboys got right down to business once they put the tape and pads and jerseys on. They went out and won all six of their exhibition games that year, including a 27–14 triumph over the same Baltimore Colts who had snatched the NFL crown from them in the Super Bowl seven months earlier.

Newcomer Lance Alworth was a casualty of the Browns game, however, coming out of it with three cracked ribs, which would keep him out of action for a while, but other than that, the preseason casualties were mostly just aches and annoyances.

But the quarterback issue remained undecided. Both Craig Morton and Roger Staubach were pitted in a duel for the starting position, which Landry said was to be contested in camp and the exhibition games. Each would get a fair chance at it. Staubach's preseason stats turned out to be better. In the six-game period, he had a 53% completion ratio to Morton's 50.6%, threw for 714 yards

to Morton's 618, and had six TD passes to his credit while Morton only had two. But then, Tom Landry said, there was the question of Morton's overall regular season experience—that was a factor which also had to be taken into consideration.

Then, just before the regular-season opener against the Bills up in Buffalo, Landry announced that he had reached his decision—but to many it was considered a nondecision. He said he had "two number-one quarterbacks" and he was going to use them alternately, like the shuttle system he had initially employed with Eddie LeBaron and Don Meredith (not the messenger system which brought a new quarterback in for each play but an interchange of starters as well as the use of a "relief" quarterback during a game.) When he made the announcement to the media, Landry could undoubtedly have used a flak jacket himself. The most vociferous critic was Dandy Don Meredith, now a TV celebrity. As a Cowboy quarterback, he had been through all that, and he said on national TV: "It's Landry's responsibility as head coach to pick a quarterback. After all this time, if he still has no idea which one is best, then get another coach."

Flak, however, never bothered Landry. He was well aware that if you put yourself in the public eye, before its scrutiny, you would surely attract criticism from one corner or another no matter what you did. Meredith, of course, knew that, too; he could not help but remember the boo birds whose droning notes were so often directed like daggers at him in the Cotton Bowl.

Craig Morton was selected to start in Buffalo, and Roger Staubach was told he would have the assignment the following week in Philadelphia. Calvin Hill and Walt Garrison would be the running backs. Duane Thomas had, surprisingly, come back the week before the opening game still surly but now ready to play. That would not be possible, however, because he had been listed as "retired" and the NFL office of the commissioner would have to approve his return. Also, he had not worked out at all with the team, and no one at the Cowboys knew if he was in shape to play, so he would not be in uniform until all that was resolved. Reggie Rucker would fill in for the damaged Lance Alworth, and Mike Ditka would start at tight end. Bob Hayes, now contentedly signed to a new contract, would line up at wide receiver.

The offensive line, which many felt was the best now in the entire NFL, would consist of tackles Ralph Neely and Rayfield Wright, guards John Niland and Blaine Nye, and center Dave Manders. On defense, the front four would be ends George Andrie and Larry Cole and tackles Bob Lilly and Jethro Pugh. The linebackers were the same

---

Question: *How do the Cowboys use the computer?*

Gil Brandt: *We use the computer as a method of taking the human faults out of the evaluation of football players. We found out that if you put good information into the computer, of course, you're going to get a very good final reading out of the computer. Whereas sometimes people —individuals—let their feelings take a better part of their judgment, the computer doesn't. Sometimes you'll go to a school, and if a player is very polite to you and pleads he always wanted to play with the Cowboys, that sticks out in your mind. Whereas you go to another school and another player's answer is, all I want to do is play where the most money is. When you make a final decision based on those kinds of statements, it's easy to go with the one who has told you he loves the Cowboys and always wanted to play in Dallas. But that is not a very good reason for picking a player. The computer doesn't judge that way.*

The Cowboy quarterback messenger system was reinstituted at Soldier Field in Chicago in 1971, this time with Roger Staubach and Craig Morton bringing in the plays on alternating downs. Eight years earlier it had been Don Meredith and Eddie LeBaron who shared equally the quarterbacking chores. After the Cowboys posted one of their three regular season losses of 1971 to the Bears, 23–19, Coach Tom Landry ended the quarterback shuttling and awarded the job to Staubach, as he had to Meredith back in 1963.   (Pro Football Hall of Fame)

familiar sight: Dave Edwards, Lee Roy Jordan, and Chuck Howley; and the secondary would consist of cornerbacks Mel Renfro and Herb Adderley and safeties Charlie Waters and Cliff Harris. Mike Clark was still the place kicker, and Toni Fritsch would languish on the taxi squad.

The opener was like an offensive free-for-all, and the Cowboys ended up winning it 49 to 37. Surprisingly, the only one who did not have a knockout day moving the ball was the Bills' superstar, O. J. Simpson; he gained a mere 25 yards on 14 carries. From the other side of the line, Calvin Hill picked up 84 yards and scored four touchdowns, while Walt Garrison rushed for 78 yards.

The Bills' quarterback, Dennis Shaw, on the other hand, threw 18 completions for 353 yards and four touchdowns. Craig Morton had 10 of 14 for 221 yards, including a 76-yard TD pass to Bob Hayes and a 19 yarder to

A new home. With seats for 65,101 fans, elegant circle suites, Tartan turf, and a sun roof, Texas Stadium was much more in line with the Cowboys' modern image than the timeworn Cotton Bowl where they had played out their first 11 seasons.   (Dallas Cowboys)

The dance of the Dallas defense. Pirouetting to the right is Cornell Green (34); stepping out at the left is Cliff Harris (43). Leaping between them is New York Giant wide receiver Don Hermann in vain search of a pass thrown by Fran Tarkenton. It was incomplete, and the Cowboys defeated the Giants that 1971 day in New York, 42–14.   (Pro Football Hall of Fame)

Reggie Rucker. It was a fanciful and frenetic beginning to what would become the Cowboys' most illustrious season up to that time in their history.

Roger Staubach led the Cowboys on to the field the next week but threw only four passes before being helped to the sidelines. He had, in the vernacular of the game, been "cold-cocked" by the Eagles' defensive end Mel Tom. Morton came on and threw 22 passes, completing 15 of them for 188 yards. Gloster Richardson posted his first Cowboy touchdown with one of Morton's passes. The Cowboys had no trouble whatsoever that day in Philadelphia, beating the Eagles 42–7, a shutout prevented only by a fourth-quarter, 101-yard run by Al Nelson, who caught a field-goal attempt and ran it back for a touchdown.

George Allen was now coaching the Washington Redskins, the Cowboys' next opponent, and he had gathered together an eclectic group of veterans from all over the league to carry out his football philosophy that "the future is now." His potpourri of talent was definitely experienced, but the players' ages prompted the nickname of the Redskins to be changed by the ever-critical media to the "Over the Hill Gang." They were far from over the hill, however, when they met the Cowboys and dealt them their first loss of the 1971 season. Morton played the first three quarters that day, and with the Cowboys down 17–9, Staubach was brought in to replace him, but it was too late, and he could not turn it around. The final was 20–16.

It was Staubach to start the next week against the Giants, and he built a 13–6 lead but then was replaced by Morton. In that game, Calvin Hill injured his knee, and in spite of having missed training, Duane Thomas came off the bench to gain 60 yards in nine carries.

The next week it was back to Morton as quarterback—for the first half, anyway, and then he was relieved by Staubach. The Cowboys trailed the New Orleans Saints 17–0 when Staubach came in, and even his seven of ten passing (for 117 yards), which included the only two scores the Cowboys could post that day—a 41-yard TD to Gloster Richardson and one for 16 yards to Bob Hayes —was not enough. It was the Cowboys' second loss of the season, their record a distressing 3–2 and their standing a somewhat distant second in the division behind the undefeated "Over the Hill Gang." So the mood was not all that gala when the Cowboys came back to Dallas to christen the newborn Texas Stadium.

Clint Murchison had a double Circle Suite, seating 24, and had as his guests that day former President Lyndon B. Johnson and two former first ladies, Lady Bird Johnson and Mamie Eisenhower. The rest of the seats in the lower level and the upper level and in the other Circle Suites were filled that day, a soldout crowd to properly welcome the Cowboys to their new home.

The Cowboys were apparently inspired by their handsome new stadium because at halftime they were ahead of the New England Patriots 34–7 and wound up the day with a 44–21 win. Roger Staubach had a fine game, throwing for two touchdowns, both to Bob Hayes, and running another in himself. For the day, he was 13 of 21

1971

Preseason

Dallas	(6-0)	Opponents
45	Los Angeles (87,187) @ L.A.	21
36	New Orleans (73,560) @ Dallas	21
16	Cleveland (69,099) @ Dallas	15
28	Houston (49,078) @ Houston	20
27	Baltimore (22,291) @ Baltimore	14
24	Kansas City (74,035) @ Dallas	17

Regular Season

		(11-3)	
W	49	Buffalo (46,206)	37
W	42	Philadelphia (65,358)	7
L	16	Washington (72,000) (H)	20
W	20	N. Y. Giants (68,378) (H)	13
L	14	New Orleans (83,088)	24
W	44	New England (65,708) (H)	21
L	19	Chicago (55,049)	23
W	16	St. Louis (50,486)	13
W	20	Philadelphia (60,178) (H)	7
W	13	Washington (53,041)	0
W	28	Los Angeles (66,595) (H)	21
W	52	N. Y. Jets (66,689) (H)	10
W	42	N. Y. Giants (62,815)	14
W	31	St. Louis (66,672) (H)	12
	406		222

Postseason

		Divisional Playoff *(Minnesota)*	
W	20	Minnesota (49,100)	12
		1971 NFC Championship Game *(Dallas)*	
W	14	San Francisco (66,311)	3
		Super Bowl VI *(New Orleans)*	
W	24	Miami (81,035)	3

Duane Thomas (33) slogs for a few yards in the slop of the 1971 divisional playoff game in Minnesota. Blocking for him is Rayfield Wright (70). Viking No. 36 is linebacker Carl Winfrey. Thomas was the game's leading rusher, slipping and sliding for 66 yards on 21 carries, as the Cowboys took their first postseason step toward Super Bowl VI. (Vernon Biever)

for 197 yards. When the game was over, LBJ dropped by the locker room, smiled at Staubach, and said, "You sure know how to break in a new stadium."

Another cause for celebration that weekend was word that the Redskins had lost, bringing the Cowboys within one game of a tie for the division lead.

The shuttle system, Coach Landry announced during the next week, would be replaced by the messenger system, just as it eventually was in the LeBaron/Meredith era. But it was not effective at all, and a lackluster Chicago Bears doled the Cowboys their third loss of the season. On the brighter side, to many minds, anyway, it brought about the end of the quarterback messenger system as well as the quarterback shuttle. Coach Landry, as he had done nine years earlier, made a midseason decision to go with *one* quarterback. Don Meredith had gotten the call back then, and in 1971 it was Roger Staubach.

With the season half over, the Cowboys had slipped two games behind the Redskins. Lance Alworth was back now, playing with a little pain but otherwise unhampered. Toni Fritsch was brought in to replace Mike Clark in an effort to upgrade the Cowboys' kicking game. The word was that Calvin Hill was recovering nicely and would probably be back in uniform in a game or two. Duane Thomas was doing a fine job running with the ball on the football field, but he was not speaking to anyone, the press or his teammates, off it. He wore a stocking cap pulled deeply down over his forehead most of the time, and when told he would be fined if he did not wear a suit coat and tie when he traveled with the team, wore them, but without a shirt. Another time, he wore simply a sport shirt with an untied tie draped around his neck. Steve Perkins described him as "a riddle wrapped in a mystery inside an enigma."

With the aid of Roger Staubach's passing, scrambling, and running, the Cowboys won all seven games in the

There were some memorable events during the other games in the latter half of the season: Roger Staubach carrying the ball six times for 90 yards against the Eagles; Toni Fritsch booting three field goals against the Cardinals, including the game winner in the last two minutes of play; Ike Thomas running back the opening kickoff against the Rams for 89 yards and a touchdown and topping that against the Jets by running one back 101 yards (which tied a Cowboy record set by Amos Marsh back in 1962). Calvin Hill also came back and clearly proved that his running was as good as it had ever been.

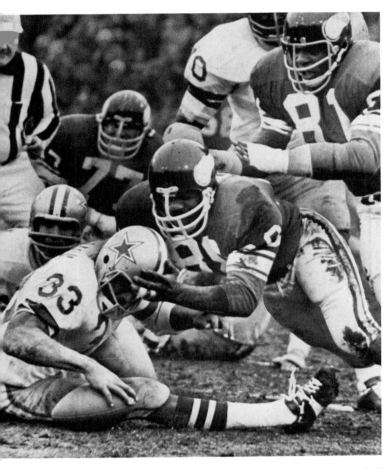

In the mud of Minnesota, running back Duane Thomas (33) finds himself sitting next to a Roger Staubach fumble in the 1971 divisional playoff game against the Vikings. All-Pro tackle Alan Page (88) of the Vikings dives desperately at the loose ball, followed by All-Pro end Carl Eller (81). Looming behind him is Cowboy four-time All-Pro tackle Rayfield Wright. Thomas recovered the fumble and the Cowboys won the game, 20–12. (Pro Football Hall of Fame)

second half of the 1971 season, the longest regular-season win streak up to that time and a record that would stand until 1977 when the Cowboys would win their first eight in a row. In compiling the 1971 win streak, the Cowboys outscored their opponents 202–77.

The pivotal game that year was played in Washington on November 21. The Cowboys were 6–3, with the Redskins a half game ahead at 6–2–1. The winner would have sole possession of first place in the NFC East. And the Cowboys rose to the occasion; they shut the Redskins out 13–0. Roger Staubach's 20-yard TD run in the first quarter was all that was needed, but Mike Clark, who had been recalled to fill in for a lame Toni Fritsch, added two field goals to enrich the victory. The Redskins were never in the running for the division title after that.

The Presidents Speak

Don Shula, head coach of the Miami Dolphins, was at home watching a film of his team's victory over the Baltimore Colts for the 1971 AFC championship. It was 1:30 in the morning, and he was surprised when the telephone rang.

"Mr. Shula, please," the voice at the other end said when he answered it.

"Yeah, speaking."

"The president is calling."

And suddenly there was the familiar voice of Richard Nixon. After they exchanged pleasantries, the president said: "Now you understand that I'm a Washington Redskin fan, but I'm a part-time resident of Miami [referring to his winter home at Key Biscayne], and I've been following the Dolphins real close, Don. Now the Cowboys are a good football team, but I still think you can hit Warfield on that down-and-in pattern against them. You know the one."

A few days later, Tom Landry received a telegram from Austin, Texas. It was from former President Lyndon B. Johnson.

"Tom, my prayers and my presence will be with you in New Orleans, although I have no plans to send in any plays.—Lyndon B. Johnson"

After the game, Tom Landry was handed a telephone in the winners' locker room. It was a call from President Nixon. When the brief conversation was over, Landry showed the trace of a smile: "He complimented us on playing almost perfect football," he said to the writers and broadcasters flocked around him, "especially our offensive line." One sportswriter asked quickly, "Did he mention anything about the down-and-in to Warfield?" The flicker of a smile again crossed Landry's face. "No, that never came up."

The team of Hill, Thomas, and Garrison now posed one of the league's most threatening backfields. Roger Staubach could also take pride in the fact that he threw nine touchdown passes in the last four of those games.

No team came close to the Cowboys in the number of points scored during the 1971 season. Dallas had racked up 406 (an average of 29 points per game), while the next nearest was the Oakland Raiders in the AFC with 344. The Cowboy offense also led the entire league in first downs (288) and touchdowns rushing (25) and their conference in touchdowns passing (22). The Dallas Doomsday Defense allowed the least amount of yards rushing in the league (1,144) and caused the most opponent fumbles (40, 25 of which the Cowboys recovered).

Four Cowboys were named All-Pro that year—from the offense, tackle Rayfield Wright and guard John Niland, and from the defensive unit, tackle Bob Lilly and cornerback Mel Renfro.

Roger Staubach had the highest ranking of any quarterback in the NFL that year, and his 59.7% completion ratio was the top in Cowboy history. Bob Hayes's eight touchdown receptions were the most in the NFC, while his

Walt Garrison (32) looks for a couple of Cowboy yards as he moves out behind guard John Niland (76) in the NFC championship game of 1971 against the San Francisco 49ers. The Cowboys won handily, 14–3, and the tobacco-chewing Garrison picked up 52 yards on 14 carries that day in Texas Stadium. (Vernon Biever)

Cowboy middle linebacker Lee Roy Jordan proved to be a mudder as the Cowboys battled the Vikings in the 1971 divisional playoff game. Here, he carries an interception back 5 yards, the fourth pass that afternoon from Viking quarterback Bob Lee to be picked off by the Cowboys. Making the tackle is Viking wide receiver Bob Grim. No. 52 is linebacker Dave Edwards. (Vernon Biever)

average gain per catch of 24 yards was the best in the league. Duane Thomas rushed for 11 TDs, another league high that year. And Mike Clark, despite a brief demotion to the taxi squad, led the league in extra points, kicking 46 of 46.

The Washington Redskins, runner-up to the Cowboys, had gotten into the playoffs as the NFC wild-card team, and it was the first time they had reached the playoffs since 1945. They were pitted against the winner of the NFC West, the San Francisco 49ers, who had snuck by the Rams again, their 9–5 record just a half game better than Los Angeles's 8–5–1.

The Cowboys would face the Minnesota Vikings up in the cold north country on Christmas Day. The Vikes had produced a record identical to that of the Cowboys (11–3), and the two teams were the winningest in the entire NFL. Minnesota clearly had the best defense in the league, having allowed a paltry 139 points in their 14 regular-season games (an average of less than 10 points a game). Many sportswriters were saying that the Cowboy-Viking game would really determine the NFC championship, the game for the winner the following week merely an afterthought.

Surprisingly, it was not very cold up in Bloomington, Minnesota, that Christmas afternoon; in fact, it was not even below freezing, an unseasonal phenomenon in that climate.

The Cowboys struck first. Jethro Pugh had recovered a Viking fumble, and Roger Staubach worked the ball downfield. When he could go no farther, Mike Clark came out and kicked a 26-yard field goal. In the second quarter, Fred Cox booted a 27 yarder to tie the score. But then another turnover on Minnesota's part—Chuck Howley intercepted a Viking pass—enabled Mike Clark to add his second field goal of the day, a long 44 yarder.

The Cowboys really came to life in the third quarter. Cliff Harris stole another of Bob Lee's passes and raced with it to the Viking 13. It took one play for Duane Thomas to carry it into the end zone. On their next possession, the Cowboys moved fluidly down the field, and Staubach, scrambling, finally found Bob Hayes all alone in the end zone. The touchdown and ensuing extra point made the score 20–3. The Vikings were able to add 9 points in the last quarter, but they were never really a threat.

George Allen's "the future is now" suddenly became past history when the 49ers dumped them from the playoffs with a 24–20 defeat. So, as in 1970, Dallas and San Francisco would square off for the conference crown.

The 49ers were unpredictable, and they could be exceptionally explosive. With John Brodie throwing and people like Gene Washington and Ted Kwalick receiving, anything could happen. The passing game was also augmented in 1971 by an intimidating running game; Ken Willard and Vic Washington had combined to run for 1,666 yards during the regular season.

When they took the field the day after New Year's, however, the 49ers were no match for an inspired Doomsday Defense, which asserted itself early, holding the 49ers scoreless during the first quarter and then, when it seemed the Cowboy offense couldn't get anything started, giving an offensive hand. John Brodie, deep in his own territory, fired off a pass, but Cowboy defensive end George Andrie threw his great hulk of a body in front of it, wrapped his arms around the ball, and then, like an incensed rhinoceros, lurched to the 2-yard line. Calvin Hill carried it in for the only score of the half. The Dallas defense gave up only one first down during those first two periods of play.

In the second half, 49er Bruce Gossett drilled a 20-yard field goal, but that was the extent of the scoring in the

Before Super Bowl VI. In New Orleans, Landry says his team is prepared; Staubach, that he is primed. (Pro Football Hall of Fame)

These were the starting lineups for Super Bowl VI:

Dallas Cowboys		**Miami Dolphins**
Offense		
Bob Hayes	WR	Paul Warfield
Lance Alworth	WR	Howard Twilley
Mike Ditka	TE	Marv Fleming
Tony Liscio	T	Doug Crusan
Rayfield Wright	T	Norm Evans
John Niland	G	Bob Kuechenberg
Blaine Nye	G	Larry Little
Dave Manders	C	Bob DeMarco
Roger Staubach	QB	Bob Griese
Duane Thomas	RB	Jim Kiick
Walt Garrison	RB	Larry Csonka
Defense		
Larry Cole	E	Jim Riley
George Andrie	E	Bill Stanfill
Jethro Pugh	T	Manny Fernandez
Bob Lilly	T	Bob Heinz
Dave Edwards	LLB	Doug Swift
Lee Roy Jordan	MLB	Nick Buoniconti
Chuck Howley	RLB	Mike Kolen
Herb Adderley	LCB	Tim Foley
Mel Renfro	RCB	Curtis Johnson
Cornell Green	S	Dick Anderson
Cliff Harris	S	Jake Scott

third quarter. In the final period, the Dallas offense dominated. Roger Staubach directed a beautifully sustained drive, 80 yards on 14 plays, that took up close to 7½ minutes. The climax came when Duane Thomas bucked in from the two. Mike Clark's extra point made it 14–3, and that was the way it stayed until the final gun.

It had been a yawner of a game. Still no one in Dallas was complaining; it qualified the Cowboys for their second consecutive appearance in the Super Bowl.

While all those nice things were happening with the Cowboys in the NFC, there were some fireworks going off in the AFC as well. The Miami Dolphins won their divisional playoff game against the Kansas City Chiefs in a sudden-death overtime, a game which turned out to be the longest ever played in the NFL. The overtime lasted 22 minutes and 40 seconds before Garo Yepremian kicked a 37-yard field goal to give the Dolphins a hard-fought 27–24 victory. The wild-card Baltimore Colts, in the other AFC playoff, handled the Cleveland Browns easily, 20–3. The showdown between the Colts and Dolphins for the other Super Bowl spot was rated a tossup; each had beaten the other during the regular season. But it turned out to be no match at all; the Colts were shut out 21–0.

The Dolphins were a young team, but their record of 10–3–1 was impressive. Their quarterback, Bob Griese, had the highest ranking in the AFC, having completed 55% of his passes and with 19 passing touchdowns to his credit. Larry Csonka was the second leading rusher in the AFC in 1971, his 1,051 yards representing a fine 5.4-yard average per carry. He trailed Denver Bronco Floyd Little by only 82 yards, but it had taken Little 89 more carries to get those additional yards.

The Cowboys set up camp at the Hilton Inn out by the New Orleans airport for Super Bowl VI. They were scheduled to use the Saints' practice field for their daily workouts. It was an exciting week, but it was not novel as it had been in Miami the year before. All that was going on around them now had a certain routineness about it, many of the players remarked. Apparently, it was easier the second time around.

There were, of course, all the parties, buffets, press conferences, parades, celebrity visitors, and ancillary entertainments, and this year there was the added lure of the French Quarter. The game would be played in Tulane Stadium (the Louisiana Superdome was still four years away), and more than 81,000 spectators, along with about a thousand members of the press, radio, and television, would jam into it.

CBS-TV would handle the telecast that year, and it was estimated that more than 65 million people would view the game. That was approximately 3 million more than the audience for Super Bowl V, the top-rated sports event of all time at that point. There would be 15 cameras to

---

Some new Super Bowl records set in game VI:

Most yards rushing by a team	*Cowboys, 252*
Most first downs by one team	*Cowboys, 23*
Most first downs rushing, one team	*Cowboys, 15*
Fewest total yards allowed	*Cowboys, 185*
Fewest touchdowns allowed	*Cowboys, 0*
Most appearances by a player	*Herb Adderley, 4*

The rush—the chase—the crush. Miami's quarterback Bob Griese flees the pass rush of the Cowboy Doomsday Defense on the last play in the first quarter of Super Bowl VI. Bob Lilly (74) and Larry Cole (63) chase Griese 29 yards behind his line of scrimmage and then drop him in a sack of monumental proportions. After that, the Dolphins were never again in the game, and the Cowboys carried out a 24–3 Super Bowl slaughter at Tulane Stadium in New Orleans.   (UPI)

capture the action, one of them situated in the Goodyear blimp, which would hover above the stadium. There would also be 40 microphones, about six miles of cable, 84 television monitors, and a crew of about 100.

It was a clear, sunny morning that Sunday of Super Bowl VI, but it was crisply cool, with a bladed wintry wind, more typical of a day in a city about 10 degrees latitude farther north. But by kickoff time, the temperature had risen almost to 40, and it turned out to be a really perfect day for a football game.

The Cowboys lost the coin toss and kicked off to the Dolphins. In the early going, not much happened. Then, with the game just over six minutes old, Larry Csonka hit the line and dropped the ball. Cowboy linebacker Chuck

After Super Bowl VI

Some random quotes from after Super Bowl VI:

Don Shula: *"My biggest disappointment was that we never challenged. They completely dominated. They had the ball more than forty minutes, and we had it less than twenty."*

Tex Schramm: *"This is just the beginning. We have a young team. I can see the Cowboys becoming a dynasty . . . We have many championships in front of us."*

Bob Lilly: *"I knew how it was going to be, but I didn't really believe it. Oh, goddam. Isn't it great. You know when I really started believing it? When the offense crammed the ball down their throats in the third quarter. On their butts. They just knocked everybody on their butts."*

Tom Landry: *"This certainly is my biggest thrill. It is the ultimate goal of all teams."*

Bob Hayes: *"Which would I rather have, the Super Bowl or the Olympic medal? Both."*

Mike Ditka *(on an end-around where he was stopped at the 2-yard line):* *"Well, there's two reasons why I didn't go all the way in for a touchdown. First, my blockers got in the way, and secondly, I thought the five yard line was the goal line."*

Herb Adderley: *"In the first Super Bowl with Green Bay, I was nervous. In the second, I was relaxed. Last year, I was totally relaxed. This year, I was afraid I was too relaxed. I went to sleep on the bus coming out."*

Clint Murchison: *"This is a successful end to our twelve-year plan."*

Howley fell on it, and Csonka stood there stunned, not from any bodily contact but because it was the first time he had fumbled the football all season. The Cowboys then

---

Trivia

The first points scored in Texas Stadium were put on the board when Duane Thomas raced 56 yards for a touchdown in the first quarter of the Cowboys' maiden appearance there against the New England Patriots, October 24, 1971.

Staubach

Going into Super Bowl VI, Roger Staubach's record as a starting quarterback was 13–0 for the 1971 season and 16–1 for his career. And he had thrown only one interception in his last 192 passes. (In the Super Bowl, he would extend his won-loss record to 17–1 and add another 19 passes to his interceptionless record.)

moved the football down field but could not get it into the end zone. So they settled for a 9-yard Mike Clark field goal.

In the second quarter, Staubach got the Cowboys moving. He used his running attack primarily and moved all the way to the Miami 7-yard line. Then—a little variance —he dropped back and hit Lance Alworth with an angular pass right at the juncture of the goal line and the sideline. With the extra point, the Cowboys led by 10. The Dolphins came back and were able to get on the scoreboard just before the half with a 31-yard field goal from Garo Yepremian.

The second half, however, was all Dallas Cowboys. The Doomsday Defense simply demolished the Dolphin offense. They could not run, nor could they move the ball aerially. In the meantime, the Cowboys marched once in each quarter, adding a touchdown in the third on a 3-yard run by Duane Thomas and another in the fourth quarter on a 7-yard pass from Staubach to tight end Mike Ditka. The final score was 24–3; the young Dolphins had never really been in the game.

Roger Staubach completed 12 of 19 passes that Super Sunday for 119 yards, and he guided the team with mastery. Duane Thomas rushed for 95 yards on 19 carries and

Cowboy running back Calvin Hill cannot avoid the clutches of Miami safety Dick Anderson (40) in Super Bowl VI. But that was one of the few times that day the Miami Dolphins were able to contain the Cowboys, who totally dominated the game for the NFL crown. With Hill, Duane Thomas, Walt Garrison, and a carry or two from Roger Staubach, Dan Reeves, Mike Ditka, and Bob Hayes, the Cowboys outrushed the Dolphins 252 yards to 80. (Dallas Cowboys)

Cowboy cornerback Herb Adderley breaks up a pass here intended for Dolphin Jim Kiick (21) in Super Bowl VI. The Cowboy defense was invincible that afternoon in New Orleans, allowing the Dolphins a paltry 3 points and a total of only 185 net yards all day. (Vernon Biever)

caught three passes for another 17 yards. The spectacular Dallas defense that day held Larry Csonka to a mere 40 yards and Jim Kiick to 40, and that was the entire rushing yardage for the Dolphins all afternoon.

In the locker room after the game, there was great jubilation. President Nixon called Tom Landry to congratulate him, Duane Thomas with mentor Jim Brown at his side even said a few words to the press, Bob Lilly puffed on a cigar, Clint Murchison and Tex Schramm were pushed into the teeming showers. It was bedlam; everyone was smiling and shouting and shoving and expressing deep-down rejoicing that they could no longer be called

MVP

The Sport *magazine award for the Most Valuable Player in Super Bowl VI was won by Cowboy quarterback Roger Staubach.*

"Next Year's Team." They were celebrating the fact that they were "This Year's Team," and they were enjoying every moment of it.

Disproving forever the statement that Tom Landry never smiles, he shows here the jubilation that comes with winning a Super Bowl —with John Niland (76) and Rayfield Wright (70). The photos were taken only moments after the Cowboy victory in Super Bowl VI, bringing Dallas its first pro football world championship.   (Vernon Biever)

Former President Lyndon B. Johnson congratulates Dallas running back Calvin Hill after the Cowboys' smashing victory in Super Bowl VI.   (Vernon Biever)

12 Always So Close

THE COWBOYS RETURNED TO DALLAS TRIUMPHANT. In six years of Super Bowls, they—an expansion team with a mere twelve-year heritage—had been in two of them and won the most recent one. They had had six straight winning seasons, with seven consecutive trips to postseason games. In the preceding six years, they had played for the NFC championship four times and won it twice.

By 1972, the team that had once been looked upon as a perennial loser, was now *the* team to beat in the NFL. Their running attack was punishing; they could pass; the offensive line could gouge out holes like a bulldozer or fend off pass rushes like the wall of a medieval castle; the name Doomsday Defense spoke for itself. But the Cowboys would soon learn that might and power are vulnerable and glory is never a permanent state.

In the NFL, the year 1972 was one where a variety of changes would take place. There were some highly publicized trades. Fran Tarkenton went from the Giants to the Vikings. The Cowboys sent Duane Thomas to the San Diego Chargers, although he would become a holdout there and not play during the 1972 season. The Denver Broncos finally landed a first-rate quarterback when they acquired the veteran Charley Johnson. There was even some trading around in the ownership ranks. The estate of the late Los Angeles Rams owner Dan Reeves (no relation to the Cowboys' player/coach) sold the team to Robert Irsay, who then turned around and traded the franchise to Carroll Rosenbloom for the team he owned, the Baltimore Colts.

The bomb and the other aerial pyrotechnics which had become such an exciting part of the game would diminish

drastically in 1972. It would turn out to be the year that the zone pass defense would become so effective that teams throughout the league would have to alter their offensive attacks accordingly. As a result, 1972 would become the year of the runner. Ten rushers would gain more than 1,000 yards that year. (From the AFC, there was O. J. Simpson of the Bills, Franco Harris of the Steelers, Marv Hubbard of the Raiders, Mike Garrett of the Chargers, and two from the Dolphins backfield—Larry Csonka and Mercury Morris; in the NFC, there was Larry Brown of the Redskins, Ron Johnson of the Giants, John Brockington of the Packers, and the Cowboys' own Calvin Hill.) And a quarterback, the Chicago Bears' Bobby Douglas, almost joined that elite crew of ground gainers when he picked up 968 yards rushing. A year earlier, there had been only five players to rush for 1,000 yards, and prior to that more than one or two was a rarity.

The Cowboys added some new names to the roster in 1972, picking up Billy Parks, a wide receiver, from the San Diego Chargers and Ron Sellers, another pass catcher, from the New England Patriots. Ron Widby went to the Green Bay Packers after the Cowboys drafted punter Marv Bateman from Utah. The draft also produced running back Robert Newhouse (University of Houston), Bill Thomas, another running back (actually their first-round selection that year, from Boston College), and tight end Jean Fugett from Amherst. Gil Brandt also found a defensive back in free agent Benny Barnes of Stanford.

For the first time, the Dallas Cowboys received the dubious honor of traveling to Chicago in late July to open

Defensive end Harvey Martin, who would become an All-Pro and NFL defensive player of the year in 1977 and a four-time veteran of the Pro Bowl, was the Cowboys' third-round draft choice in 1973. An All-American from East Texas State, he would develop into one of the most effective and feared pass rushers in the game.   (Dallas Cowboys)

their preseason against the College All-Stars. The game, a tradition since 1934 and once looked upon as a top sports event which often played to crowds of 100,000, was by 1972 viewed by the pro coaches and owners as nothing more than a potential source of injury for promising rookies who additionally had to miss most of their initial training camp to participate in the game.

Equally traditional was for the game to be won by the pros, and the Cowboys ran true to form. They beat the All-Stars 20–7 in a game in which all touchdowns were scored by Dallas players. The lone All-Star TD came on a one-yard plunge by Cowboy draftee Robert Newhouse.

The Cowboys' quarterback situation, which seemingly had been resolved in the latter half of the 1971 season, was suddenly altered in the second preseason game out at the Los Angeles Coliseum. A scrambling Roger Staubach met a charging Marlin McKeever, the Rams linebacker, and what gave were the bones in Staubach's

shoulder. The separation would keep him out of action for most of the season, so Craig Morton became the number-one quarterback.

When the regular season was about to begin, the Cowboys could boast that they had never lost a game in their new home stadium. They had won five regular-season games there in 1971 and the NFC championship against the 49ers, and now they had added three preseason victories.

The Cowboys hosted the Philadelphia Eagles in the opener of the 1972 season. The Eagles were considered the soft spot of the division, and they would indeed live up to that reputation, winning only two games in 1972. The Cowboys were a little slow getting started against them, however, and held only a 1-point lead at the half. But they quickly changed all that in the third quarter with two touchdowns. They added another in the fourth quarter, scored by rookie Robert Newhouse, whose squat build (5 feet 10 inches, 215 pounds) had every sportswriter referring to him as either a fire hydrant or a pit bulldog. The Cowboys won handily 28–6.

Question: *Could you trace how a player might come to the Cowboys?*

Gil Brandt: *The way one would come would be by one or two methods. First, it would be either a recommendation from his college coach, or his name had been submitted by a scout when he was an underclassman. When a scout visits the school, he's asked to turn in a list of sophomores who would be pro prospects two years from now, and juniors would be a prospect a year from now. We chart these and keep the list. In February, or prior to a player's senior year, we draw all the names out of that list, and the scout that covers that school is asked to report on all those. Some of those players that were turned in as sophomores are no longer at that school; some of them had not developed as expected, but that's what we have to find out. No player is ever rejected before he is seen personally. With those that remain, a complete report will be written on each in the spring of his senior year. With a top player like Mark Hermann, the quarterback at Purdue in 1980, we would probably have three scouts see him sometime during the course of the fall. Usually, one will see him early, during the two days prior to the season, then once during the middle part of the season, and once at the end of the season. Plus we have the opportunity to look at most of the top players in bowl games. The others we evaluate additionally through films, scouting reports, things like that.*

Except for the absence of Staubach and Duane Thomas, the Cowboys were fielding the same team that had started the year before. But they could not be referred to as youngsters anymore. Chuck Howley was 36; Bob Lilly and Herb Adderley, 33; George Andrie, Dave Edwards, Cornell Green, Lance Alworth, and Mike Ditka were 32.

But if the Cowboys were aging, the Redskins were clearly the league's senior citizens. Sonny Jurgensen was 38, and anybody else found in their locker room under the age of 28 was probably one of the players' sons. But that was George Allen's philosophy for building a team—play for today with long-experienced warriors—and it was considerably different from that espoused by the people who guided the Cowboys.

The first half of the season had never really been the most constructive era for the Cowboys. As one writer put it, "They usually dug themselves a hole in the early going and spent the second half digging themselves out of it." The year 1972, therefore, was a typical one. Even though they posted a respectable record of 5–2 at the midway point, they had lost to the Redskins, who were astounding everyone and leading the division with a record of 6–1. There were, of course, still seven games to go, and the Cowboys' confidence was far from flagging. Certainly the "Over the Hill" gang would not be able to maintain such a pace through the remainder of the season. And the Cowboys were known for their late-season redemptive powers—plus the Cowboys would have another shot at the Redskins in Texas Stadium in early December.

But there were to be no seven-game or five-game win streaks in the second half of the 1972 season for the Cowboys. It was going to be a veritable street fight all the way through, with the Cowboys coming out on top five times and taking a licking twice.

The Redskins would fade, but not as the Cowboys had hoped, and when they would do it, it would not be until the last two games of the season. The two losses would simply reduce their record to 11–3, still a full game ahead of Dallas. It was the first time since 1965 that the Cowboys had not won the NFL East. Fortunately for Dallas, their record of 10–4 was enough to qualify them for the playoffs as the NFC wild card.

Craig Morton had directed the offensive attack all season, although Roger Staubach got back into a uniform in the second half and served as a sometime reliever. He was far from 100%, however. Calvin Hill became the first runner in Cowboy history to gain more than 1,000 yards rushing (1,036, a 4.2-yard average per carry). Rayfield Wright and John Niland made the All-Pro team again. The Dallas defense was still up there, third stingiest in the league in giving up points, and they ceded the least amount of yards rushing of any team in the NFL. At the

On Staubach

"We're going to have to do something about this guy. He's going to ruin the image of an NFL quarterback if he doesn't start smoking, drinking, cussing, or something."

　　　　　　　　　　　　　—Don Meredith

"There's no question in my mind that when he finished playing he was the number one sports hero in the United States. I think he crossed all age barriers, he crossed everything. He was what people wanted to see when they thought of an authentic American hero. That's who they wanted to see—Roger Staubach. That rubs off a helluva lot on the organization."

　　　　　　　　　　　　　—Tex Schramm

"His idea of breaking training is putting whipped cream on his pie."

　　　　—Bob St. John, Dallas Morning News

"He can play until he's 40 because he doesn't know what a hang-over is."

　　　　　　　　　　　　　—Sonny Jurgensen

"I'm not happy with the way the press treats me . . . It's gotten to the point where I can't say something in jest without it being taken seriously. I once went to pick up my kid's dog at the vet and it wound up in print like it was my favorite pastime. Hell, I didn't even like the dog."

　　　　—Roger Staubach, in Sport magazine

same time, the Cowboys led the league in penalties (90) and the number of yards assessed against them for those violations (841).

Dallas drew San Francisco for their first game in the conference playoffs. They had beaten the 49ers twice in the preceding two years of playoff action, and San Francisco coach Dick Nolan wanted nothing better than to cull some retribution from his friend and one-time mentor Tom Landry. The 49ers had had a respectable season and despite a rather uninspiring record (8–5–1) had had little trouble winning the NFC West. They were quarterbacked that year by Steve Spurrier, who filled in for an injured John Brodie. But Brodie was back in shape for the playoffs and would take over.

On Thanksgiving Day in the regular season, the 49ers had mauled the Cowboys unmercifully, 31–10, the largest margin of defeat they had suffered the entire year. So the Cowboys had a little avenging of their own in mind.

San Francisco would have an advantage in that the game was being played out at Candlestick Park, where the 49ers had relocated the year before, moving from old, decaying Kezar Stadium. The Cowboys, however, were still the Super Bowl champions, and wild card or not, they were a team to be reckoned with. Most observers felt it would be a close game, but no one was prepared for just how strikingly dramatic it would turn out to be.

It did not seem at all like the Cowboys' day when the game got underway. Toni Fritsch boomed the opening kickoff down to the 3-yard line where 49er Vic Washington caught it, headed straight up field, then sliced to the sideline, and sprinted along it all the way into the end zone for a touchdown. The Cowboys were able to salvage a field goal in the first quarter, but just inside the next period, Morton was sacked and fumbled on his own 15. A

few plays later, 49er Larry Schreiber plunged in for the score. Before the half was over, he repeated that act. Another Toni Fritsch field goal and a 28-yard TD pass from Morton to Lance Alworth kept the Cowboys within a beggar's hope of being in the game. The score was 21–13 at the half.

In the third quarter, however, Calvin Hill fumbled the ball on his own 5-yard line, and the 49ers recovered. A few moments later, Larry Schreiber scored his third 1-yard touchdown of the day.

Just before the third quarter had ended, Tom Landry decided to yank Morton and bring in Roger Staubach. Some new fuel was needed, or maybe a spark, something

Like every other back in the NFL, Roger Staubach would always find it tough to run against the Minnesota Viking defense. Here, he feels the crunch from some of the infamous Purple Gang, linebacker Jeff Siemon (50) and corner back Bobby Bryant (20). (Dallas Cowboys)

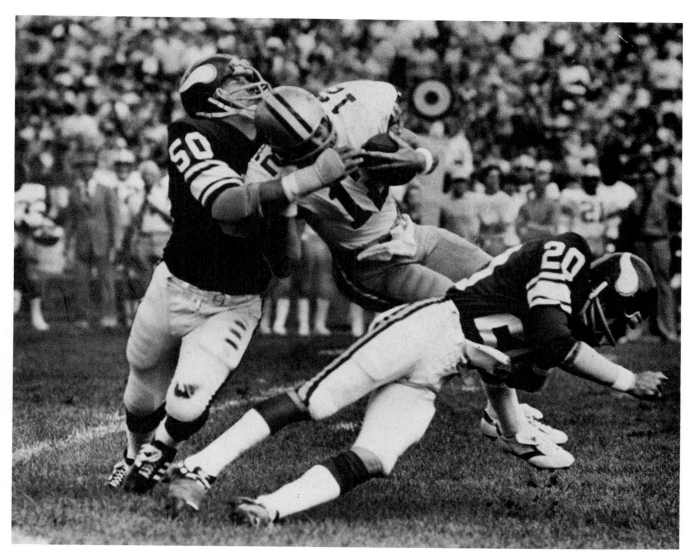

to fire the offensive furnaces. But it didn't seem to help. Between pass incompletions, Staubach was sacked several times, and on one of those occasions he fumbled the ball over to the 49ers. The 49ers got within field-goal range, but Bruce Gossett missed it. It was Calvin Hill who finally got the Cowboys out of the hole. It seemed as if they were stalled again in their own territory when he burst through a hole and raced for 45 yards. The Cowboys got a field goal out of it, which brought them within 12 points of the 49ers.

Time was running out quickly now, however. The 49ers felt sure they had the game won. There was only a little less than two minutes to go, and many San Francisco fans were already filing out of the stadium to beat the rush. There were smiles and backslapping and talk of going all the way this year. On the field, linebacker Dave Wilcox, gloating, yelled across the line at what he felt was the Cowboys' vanquished offense, "How does it feel to lose a game like this."

The Cowboys would not know, at least that day. Staubach completed two straight passes to Walt Garrison, and the Cowboys were moving in their hurry-up offense. Billy Parks ran a post pattern, and Staubach hit him for a touchdown. It was 28–23 when the Cowboys lined up to kick off, but there was only 1:30 left in the game.

Everyone knew they would try an on-side kick. The 49ers had backs and receivers—all their surest hands—up on the line to field the ball. Fritsch sliced it off the tee, and the ball went bouncing crazily on a sharp diagonal course across the field. Preston Riley, a wide receiver on the 49ers, grabbed it, but he didn't fully have possession of it when Cowboy rookie Ralph Coleman hit him. The ball flew from his hands. Mel Renfro dove on it, and an incredulous crowd, or what was left of them, realized that the Cowboys were not yet buried, as they had thought not too many moments earlier.

Staubach dropped back to pass on first down, but his receivers were covered. He saw a large hole and took off through it, racing down field 21 yards to the 49ers' 29-yard line. Then a 19-yard pass to Parks and the Cowboys were on the 10, and the 49ers fans were dumbstruck. On the next play, the 49ers threw an all-out blitz at Staubach, and he was just barely able to get a pass away. It floated over the blitzing 49ers' heads and landed in the hands of Cowboy receiver Ron Sellers in the end zone. He turned around and around, holding the ball in one hand high above his head, his legs moving, and then suddenly he was engulfed in a wave of jubilant Cowboy players. With the extra point, the final score was 30–28.

A disconsolate Dick Nolan accepted Landry's condolences and for the third year in a row walked dejectedly from the field, having surrendered his championship

The classic tandem safety, Charlie Waters (41) and Cliff Harris (43). During the Cowboy summer camp at Thousand Oaks, California, they team for a novel football field assault. They fared much better in their more normal encounters with would-be pass receivers and enemy running backs.   (Dallas Cowboys)

dreams to the Cowboys.

It had been an incredible finish—two touchdowns within 38 seconds. Everyone got carried away. One writer described Staubach as "Thor hurling thunderbolts from the blue." Tom Landry shook his head and actually smiled. "This is unreal," he said. "I think it was the best comeback we ever made. It was one of the greatest moments in our history."

Besides Staubach's magical manipulations, there were other noteworthy performances that day. Calvin Hill had run for 125 yards, and Billy Parks had caught seven passes for a total of 136 yards.

Meanwhile, George Allen's "Over the Hill" gang had eliminated the Green Bay Packers, winners of the NFC Central, from the playoffs. So they would face each other for the third time that year, and the outcome this time would determine who would go to Super Bowl VII.

The fans and the press in Dallas had from time to time despaired of the Cowboys during the season. A repeat performance in the Super Bowl, they felt, was unlikely. The team just did not seem to have the polish, the precision, and the awesome power that the Cowboys of 1971 exhibited. But after the miracle at San Francisco, the blood was pumping, the fever rising. Suddenly, Dallas travel agents were besieged with requests for reservations on flights to Los Angeles and hotel-room bookings in that city, which was to be the site of Super Bowl VII. Calls for Super Bowl tickets rained down on the switchboard at the Cowboys' offices. In the Dallas–Fort Worth metroplex, a lot of people had forgotten that there was still another game to go before qualifying for the Super spectacle.

In Washington, however, they had not forgotten. Billy Kilmer, the Redskin quarterback, was being quoted more often around the nation's capital that week than President Nixon. George Allen, it seemed, was talking to every journalist in town except possibly Jack Anderson. The Redskins were psyching themselves up. Like any other team, they wanted to go to the Super Bowl, but it would be an added treat to earn it by defeating the Cowboys. The rivalry between Dallas and the Redskins had grown white hot over the past decade and now rivaled in intensity some of the old-line NFL rivalries like the Packers and the Bears or the Rams and the 49ers.

The game was played on New Year's Eve, a chilly, damp, overcast day. The game itself was a dull one and as gloomy as the weather for those cheering for Dallas. Roger Staubach had been given the starting assignment at quarterback, but the wizardry he had summoned the week before was nowhere in evidence in RFK Stadium. The Cowboys' running game was totally shut down, with Calvin Hill eking out only 22 yards and Walt Garrison gaining just 15. It was Washington's day, that last one of

1972

Preseason

Dallas	(6-1)	Opponents
20	College All-Stars (54,162) @ Chi.	7
26	Houston (65,405) @ Dallas	24
27	Los Angeles (66,051) @ L. A.	13
30	New Orleans (81,070) @ N. O.	7
34	N. Y. Jets (65,386) @ Dallas	27
10	Kansas City (79,592) @ K. C.	20
16	Oakland (62,607) @ Dallas	10

Regular Season

		(10-4)	
W	28	Philadelphia (55,850) (H)	6
W	23	N. Y. Giants (62,725)	14
L	13	Green Bay (47,103)	16
W	17	Pittsburgh (65,682) (H)	13
W	21	Baltimore (58,992)	0
L	20	Washington (53,039)	24
W	28	Detroit (65,378) (H)	24
W	34	San Diego (54,476)	28
W	33	St. Louis (65,218) (H)	24
W	28	Philadelphia (65,720)	7
L	10	San Francisco (65,124) (H)	31
W	27	St. Louis (49,797)	6
W	34	Washington (65,136) (H)	24
L	3	N. Y. Giants (64,602) (H)	23
	319		240

Postseason

Divisional Playoff
(San Francisco)

W	30	San Francisco (61,214)	28

NFC Championship Game
(Washington)

L	3	Washington (53,129)	26

1972, as they dominated Dallas 26–3. They would have to play the Super Bowl without the Cowboys that year.

Commissioner Pete Rozelle was kept a rather busy man after the 1972 season ended. A lot of things were happening in his league. For one, it was to be challenged again. Announcement was made that the World Football League was being formed and would start operating in 1974. WFL officials said they would award franchises for 12 cities (or areas): Birmingham (Alabama), Chicago, Detroit, Florida, Hawaii, Houston, New York, Philadelphia, Portland (Oregon), Southern California, Toronto, and Washington. A raid on players in the NFL was sure to follow, no doubt accompanied by offers of high-rolling salaries and bonuses. The NFL, as it so often did when the threat of competition menaced it, began to study further expansion of its own league.

Then, the shimmering TV light brightened, at least for the pleasure of the pro football fan. Traditionally, home games had been blacked out in the NFL. Now Congress

On the Team Plane

With the Dallas Cowboys, sportswriters and various media people have the pleasure, or sometimes displeasure, of traveling on the team plane. Steve Perkins of the Dallas Times-Herald described how it was back in the early 1970s:

The team plane, a Braniff 727, splits the coaches and the press and the club officials into the first-class section and the players into the tourist. The middle seats in the rows of three back there are kept vacant so the big men can spread out. At the top of the boarding ramp a steward-ess hands out two cans of cold beer apiece. That's sup-posed to be it for the players, and it usually is. Very few of them bootleg any whiskey in the attache cases they use for luggage. When the plane gets airborne, a curtain is pulled between the sections and a stewardess wheels out a folding cart to set up a bar in the forward entryway. The rule is, you can roam into the players' section with a can of beer in your hand, but you don't tote any kind of hard stuff back there.

Once airborne, the players break into the same groups every trip. They have a way of smashing the chairbacks forward to open up two pairs of seats for a card game. There's no poker, only gin, whist, pitch, cribbage, hearts, and a game called Tonk, which is a mystery to me though I have been trying to kibbutz it for eight years. Green and Hayes are always in the same seats on the port side, facing Pugh and Wright in what must be the longest-running Tonk game in history. Wright is the come-lately, filling out the fourth when Don Perkins retired several years ago. Further aft and on the opposite side of the aisle, Morton and Edwards and Ditka and Alworth or Garrison are in another one. At training camp these games are played for stakes that would make a sportswriter blanch, but I have never seen any money change hands on a plane. Finally, on the stewardesses' low bench seat between the rear johns sits Ralph Neely. I think Neely got in the habit of sitting there when he and Meredith used to sip Scotch on the long rides from losing games. It was a vantage point that provided maximum alert when Landry started his tour of the section. Now Meredith is gone, so is the Scotch, and Neely likes the bench because it allows him to stretch his legs down the aisle. *

*From Winning the Big One by Steve Perkins, Grosset & Dunlap, 1972.

passed a law which forbade such blackouts if the game was a sellout at least 48 hours before the kickoff. A new word would come into the jargon of professional football, the "No-show"—the person who bought a ticket but pre-sumably stayed home to watch the game on TV. It obvi-ously would not hurt ticket sales but would probably cut into the profits from the sale of all that beer and all those hot dogs and programs and pennants.

It was also a year in which some gold-plated records would be engraved in the NFL Manual.

In the first month of 1973, the Miami Dolphins, when they won the Super Bowl (for the 1972 season), became the first team ever to go undefeated and untied through both the regular season and the playoffs, posting an amaz-ing record of 17–0. The Chicago Bears back in their hey-day were undefeated and untied in the 1934 and 1942 regular seasons but each time managed to lose the NFL championship game. Then, in the upcoming season, O. J. Simpson of the Buffalo Bills would not only break Jim Brown's seasonal rushing record of 1,863 yards, set back in 1963, but would become the first runner ever to rush for more than 2,000 yards (2,003).

In Dallas, Bob Lilly, by this time a Cowboy legend, said that he was now going to cash it all in. His back, which had troubled him the season before, wasn't a lot better, and he was unhappy with the squabbling he sensed among other team members, so he was talking retirement. Craig Morton was discontent, too, over both the amount of money he was earning and the amount of playing time he could foresee on the field. Staubach was back, and he had been moved ahead of Morton in the previous post-season.

Bob Lilly would not retire, talked out of it by Tex Schramm. But a number of others would, including Lilly's sidekick on the defensive line, George Andrie, and such other stalwarts as Lance Alworth, Herb Adderley, and Mike Ditka. Actually, Ditka traded his pads and helmet for a whistle and a clipboard, becoming a full-time assistant coach for the Cowboys.

In the draft, the Cowboys found several players who would become mainstays in the years to come. The first round produced tight end Billy Joe DuPree from Michi-gan State and in the second round tabbed Golden Rich-ards, a wide receiver from the University of Hawaii, who would become their front-line punt returner that year. Then there was defensive tackle Harvey Martin from East Texas State; Jim Arneson of Arizona, an offensive guard who could also play center; and running back Les Stray-horn of East Carolina.

To round out the list of newcomers, there was also a free-agent plum that year, a fleet wide receiver from the University of Tulsa with a journalistically famous name, Drew Pearson.

1973

Preseason

Dallas	(4-2)	Opponents
24	Los Angeles (75,461) @ L. A.	7
26	Oakland (53,723) @ Oakland	27
24	New Orleans (61,022) @ Dallas	14
24	Houston (46,942) @ Houston	27
27	Kansas City (57,468) @ Dallas	16
26	Miami (61,378) @ Dallas	23

Regular Season

		(10-4)	
W	20	Chicago (55,701)	17
W	40	New Orleans (53,972) (H)	3
W	45	St. Louis (64,815) (H)	10
L	7	Washington (54,314)	14
L	31	Los Angeles (81,428)	37
W	45	N. Y. Giants (64,898) (H)	28
L	16	Philadelphia (65,954)	30
W	38	Cincinnati (58,802) (H)	10
W	23	N. Y. Giants (70,128)	10
W	31	Philadelphia (61,985) (H)	10
L	7	Miami (64,100) (H)	14
W	22	Denver (51,706)	10
W	27	Washington (64,458) (H)	7
W	30	St. Louis (43,946)	3
	382		203

Postseason

Divisional Playoff
(Dallas)

W	27	Los Angeles (64,291)	16

NFC Championship Game
(Dallas)

L	10	Minnesota (64,524)	27

The Cowboys lost two preseason games to AFL teams in 1973, the Oakland Raiders and the Houston Oilers, but they won the other four. The last game of the exhibition season was especially gratifying. The Miami Dolphins, with their perfect record from the season before and their images still reflected in the silver Super Bowl trophy, came to Texas Stadium, and before more than 61,000 highly partisan Dallas fans, they lost.

The Cowboys faced a relatively tough schedule in 1973. Their division featured a very strong Redskin team, whom they would meet twice, and then outside the division they had to play the Dolphins again as well as the Los Angeles Rams, Denver Broncos, and Cincinnati Bengals, all well-regarded contenders in their respective divisions.

Roger Staubach, as everyone, including Craig Morton, anticipated, was the selected starter for the regular season. His shoulder was fully mended now, and Tom Landry was hoping for a season from him like that blissful one of 1971.

The Cowboys got off to a fine start, winning their first three games, the second of which, over the New Orleans Saints, marked the Cowboys' 100th regular-season victory. It was, however, the easiest stretch of the season, and only the Chicago Bears in the opener gave them anything to fret about. The Cowboys had to pull that game out in the fourth quarter with a Toni Fritsch field goal, but neither the Saints nor the St. Louis Cardinals came within 35 points of them in the other two games.

Then came the Washington Redskins, who dislocated their championship hopes the year before. The Cowboys led 7–0 all the way into the fourth quarter, but then a

Calvin Hill ran over everything in his path in 1973—including referees—on the way to setting a Cowboy rushing record of 1,142 yards, one which stood until Tony Dorsett gained 1,325 in 1978 (but Dorsett had the help of two extra games in the regular-season schedule). Hill was the second leading rusher in the NFC in 1973 and was also named to the All-Pro team. (Al Panzera, Fort Worth Star-Telegram)

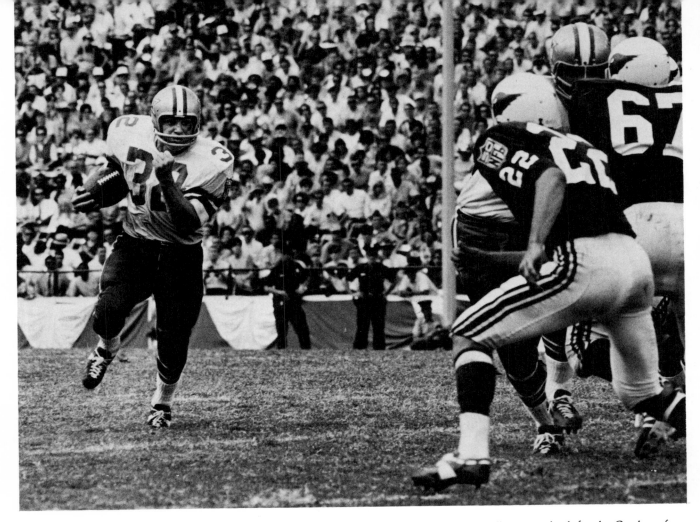

Walt Garrison (32), running the ball here at long-time rivals, the St. Louis Cardinals, was an all-purpose back for the Cowboys from 1966 to 1974. He is the fifth leading rusher in Dallas history and led the team in 1971 in pass receptions, 40 for 396 yards. (Dallas Cowboys)

39-year-old Sonny Jurgensen, long-time torturer of the Cowboys, went to work on them. He marched the Redskins down the field with a calculated display of precision passing and topped it with a little 1-yard pass to his favorite receiver, Charlie Taylor, to tie the score.

Craig Morton, who had replaced Staubach in the third quarter when Roger was injured, tried to get something going. He threw to tight end Billy Joe Dupree on a third-down play but put the ball in the hands of Redskin safety Brig Owens who carried it in for another Redskin score. With the score 14–7 and little time remaining, Morton led a last-ditch assault, which came close but not close enough. The final gun went off with Walt Garrison at the Redskin one trying desperately to lunge with the ball into the end zone but unable to get free of the clutches of safety Ken Houston, who wrestled him to the ground.

The Cowboys lost two of their next three games. In one of them, against the Rams, John Hadl, who had replaced Roman Gabriel that year as quarterback, consumated a marvelous union with his wide receiver Harold Jackson, who caught 7 of Hadl's 12 completions for 238 yards of

Hadl's total of 279. And four of Jackson's catches were for touchdowns. The other loss was a complete surprise, administered by the Philadelphia Eagles. They were 1–4–1 when the Cowboys visited them at Veterans Stadium. Roman Gabriel was now their quarterback, and he was having a good season even if the Eagles weren't. In the first half, Gabriel threw two touchdown passes to his 6 foot 7 inch wide receiver Harold Carmichael and ran another in himself. When the day was over, the Eagles had a 30–16 win for their efforts.

At midseason, the Cowboys had a record of 4–3. Their arch-rival Redskins were out in front of the division with a 5–2 record. Again, the Cowboys were in a hole and would have to try to extricate themselves from it. They started the second half of the season positively by winning three games in a row with ease. (The closest anyone came to them were the Giants, who lost 23–10.)

The Miami Dolphins arrived then for a nationally televised game on Thanksgiving Day at Texas Stadium. In the first quarter, the Dolphins ripped off two quick touchdowns, one after a Jake Scott interception of a Staubach pass, followed by a 1-yard plunge by Larry Csonka, and the other on a 45-yard bomb from Bob Griese to Paul Warfield. Then the game became nothing more than a defensive brawl. The Cowboys squeezed out a lone TD in the fourth quarter when Walt Garrison lunged in from the one, but that was all, and the Dolphins won 14–7.

A win over the Denver Broncos the following week and suddenly the Cowboys were faced with what would be the most important game of their season. The Redskins, a game ahead of them in the NFC East, came to Dallas seeking to clinch the crown. As they trotted out on to the Tartan Turf, one of the many banners that graced Texas Stadium that day, Biblically referenced, prognosticated what was to come: "They shall not pass over Jordan." And

they did not pass over Lee Roy that afternoon, nor over anyone else. Nor did they run over a Cowboy or past one that day. The Redskins were held to a lone touchdown, and it came late in the fourth quarter when they were hopelessly trailing the Cowboys 27–0.

The Cowboys won the last game of the 1973 season on a bone-chillingly cold day up in St. Louis. Drew Pearson, the rookie free agent, caught five of Staubach's passes that afternoon for 140 yards; two of them were for touchdowns. After a 3–3 tie in the first quarter, the game was all Dallas Cowboys, the final score 30–3. The Redskins won, too, and both teams ended the season with records of 10–4.

In the division, both teams had identical 6–2 records,

San Francisco Giant fullback Larry Schreiber goes over the top for a yard and a touchdown in the 1972 divisional playoff game. One of three 1-yard touchdown plunges by Schreiber that afternoon, it was not enough to stop the wild-card Cowboys. Down 28–13 at the end of the third quarter, the Cowboys rallied with a 17-point fourth quarter, including two TD passes from Roger Staubach in the last two minutes of the game, to take out a 30–28 win and a trip to Washington to face the Redskins for the NFC crown. Identifiable Cowboys here are linebacker John Babinecz (53) and defensive back Cornell Green (behind Schreiber).   (Russ Russell)

but as a result of the NFL's tie-breaking procedures, the Cowboys were the winner of the NFL East because the point differential in the two games the teams played was in Dallas's favor. They had beaten the Redskins by 20 points and in the other encounter had only lost by 7. The Redskins would go to the playoffs as the wild-card team, as the Cowboys had the year before. The advantage to Dallas would be simply that they would get to play their divisional playoff game at home, and the Redskins would have to journey to Bloomington, Minnesota.

During the regular season, there had been some particularly pleasing moments: Lee Roy Jordan intercepting three passes in the first quarter against the Cincinnati Bengals; Billy Joe DuPree, a rookie, catching three touchdown passes against the St. Louis Cardinals; Craig Morton coming off the bench to throw three passes against the Cardinals, two of them for TDs; Drew Pearson becoming a starter and a premier receiver midway through the season; Robert Newhouse rushing for his first 100-plus-yard game against the Cardinals (124); Roger Staubach passing for more than 200 yards in six separate games.

With the season's statistical wrap-up, Staubach received the highest ranking in the NFL. His 62.6 completion percentage was also the best in the league, and so was his total of 23 touchdown passes.

Calvin Hill set a Cowboy rushing record that year with a total of 1,142 yards (an average carry of 4.2 yards), and he was second in the NFC that year, a scant 2 yards less than Green Bay's John Brockington.

Four Cowboys received All-Pro honors that year: tackle Rayfield Wright and running back Calvin Hill from the offense and linebacker Lee Roy Jordan and cornerback Mel Renfro from the defensive unit.

The Rams had won the NFC West easily with a 12-2 record, and they had handled the Cowboys successfully during the regular season. Tom Landry spoke openly about the hazards of getting behind, especially against a team like the Rams. They had done that earlier in the season, and they had put on a spirited comeback, but they still had lost. It was imperative, Landry said, to move against the Rams quickly and force them to play catch-up football.

The Cowboys heeded Landry's words, but the Rams helped quite a bit, too, in enabling Dallas to accomplish Landry's directive. On the Rams' first possession, John Hadl threw a pass right into the hands of Lee Roy Jordan. The Cowboys turned the turnover into a touchdown, Calvin Hill slicing in from the 3-yard line. When Los Angeles had the ball again, they handed it right back over to the Cowboys, this time on a fumble which Mel Renfro recovered. Roger Staubach moved the Cowboys to the four and then hit Drew Pearson with a little pass for the second touchdown of the first quarter. They added a field goal before the quarter ended and luxuriated in a 17–0 lead.

The Rams were not intimidated, however. They charged back in the second quarter and capped two sepa-

Lance Alworth (19), known to his contemporaries as "Bambi," steps out here after getting the ball from Roger Staubach (12). Alworth came to the Cowboys in 1971 to fill the void caused by Lance Rentzel's departure, and he brought with him a reputation as one of the game's all-time great receivers. As a flanker and later a wide receiver, he was named to the AFL All-Pro team seven times during his career with the San Diego Chargers. (Dallas Cowboys)

Chuck Howley

"There's a real irony in my life. When I look back on all the really big plays I've made in my career, I realize I've always been out of position when I made them."

rate drives with field goals by David Ray.

Neither team could get anything going in the third quarter, and the Cowboys suffered a crucial loss when Calvin Hill, going after his own fumble, emerged from the pileup with a season-ending broken elbow. Robert Newhouse chugged out on to the field to replace him.

In the fourth quarter, Ray kicked another field goal for the Rams. They came within a point a short while later when Tony Baker scored the Rams' first touchdown of the afternoon. Suddenly, the luxury had flowed out of the Cowboys' lead like water down a bathtub drain.

When the Cowboys had the ball, they found themselves logjammed at their own 17-yard line on third down, a distant 14 yards to go for a first down. Staubach dropped back to his own goal line and then let fly with a great arcing pass. At the 50-yard line, Drew Pearson went up between two defenders, grabbed the ball, then raced from between their falling bodies all the way in for a touchdown. The play went for 83 yards and destroyed the Rams just as a dart would a balloon. The Cowboys even had time to pad the lead with a field goal in the closing minutes. The final score was 27–16. The Cowboys, as a result, would make their sixth appearance in eight years of NFC championship games.

The Vikings had beaten the Washington Redskins the day before, so they would come to Dallas. And they were flying high, the octane provided by the league's most scrambling quarterback, Fran Tarkenton. Now they also had a superb running back in Chuck Foreman, who as a rookie that year led the Vikings' rush with 801 yards. The other running slot was filled alternately by Oscar Reed, Ed Marinaro, and Dave Osborn, all very strong runners. And, of course, there was the magnificent Viking defense, which led the entire NFL in 1973 in giving up the fewest

amount of points (allowing only 168, or an average of 12 per game).

It would be a conservative game, the sportswriters were predicting. Defense would be the critical factor, they said.

The Vikings, at least in the first half, were winning the battle of the defenses. They kept the Cowboys off the scoreboard and managed a field goal and a touchdown themselves (the latter on a 5-yard burst by Foreman).

The third quarter was still more of the same grind-it-out football with a regular exchange of punts to punctuate the ennui. That is, until rookie returner Golden Richards took one, found a hole, then the sideline, and sped 63 yards to put the Cowboys back in the ballgame, only a field goal behind. Unfortunately, a minute later, Fran Tarkenton scrambled out of the pocket, eyed wide receiver John Gilliam in the open, and tossed him a 54-yard touchdown pass.

From that point on, it was hard to believe that this was the NFC championship game and the two teams on the field were the best the conference had to offer. It turned into a gaudy display of ineptitude as each team tried desperately to give the game to the other. As Tex Maule described the debacle in *Sports Illustrated:*

"First, the Cowboys were given the ball on a fumble by Foreman, which they recovered on the Minnesota 37. Roger Staubach gave it back by throwing a pass that bounced off tight end Billy Joe DuPree and wound up in the hands of middle linebacker Jeff Siemon. Next, Tarkenton forced a sideline pass to Gilliam, and cornerback Charlie Waters stepped in front of him for an easy interception, carrying the ball to the Minnesota 24.

"Staubach fumbled a few plays later, Minnesota recovering on its 45. Foreman fumbled the ball back, Dallas recovering on the Minnesota 47. Staubach threw a bad pass to Bob Hayes, which was picked off by cornerback Bobby Bryant and returned 63 yards for the score that wrapped up the game for the Vikings."

Two years in a row now the Cowboys had fallen at the last hurdle to the Super Bowl. "We had a good year with a lot of young players," Tom Landry said once it was all over. "But you aren't really successful unless you get to the Super Bowl. We'll be back a lot stronger next season."

13 A Rocky Road to Super Bowl X

THE YEAR 1974 WOULD BE to professional football a little like what 1968 had been to the realm of politics and government in the United States. It would be a time of turmoil, challenge, and change.

The National Football League braced for the assault on its ranks from the wolfish World Football League, whose rapacious franchises made it clear they were on the prowl for proven pro-football talent. The NFL owners and officials, secure somewhat in their solidarity and seniority, were not unwary, but they were astounded when the list of defecting players grew to alarming proportions. The biggest shocker was the multiple signing of Larry Csonka, Jim Kiick, and Paul Warfield, an enormous chunk of the offensive unit of the two-time NFL champion Miami Dolphins. But there were many other big names looking to the WFL as well: Quarterbacks Daryle Lamonica and Kenny Stabler (Raiders), back Charlie Harraway (Redskins), tight end Ted Kwalik (49ers), linebacker Bill Bergey (Bengals), wide receivers Ron Jessie (Lions) and George Sauer (Jets), were just a few among them.

The Cowboys were especially hard hit. Calvin Hill, their premier running back, signed with the WFL franchise in Hawaii, and Craig Morton did the same with the Houston Texans. None of the players, however, were scheduled to switch to the WFL until their NFL contracts ran out, so Hill and Morton would be in Cowboy uniforms for the 1974 season. But Morton would be traded to the New York Giants after the first regular-season game.

If the WFL's plundering didn't unduly strain the league structure, the relationship between owners and players certainly moved it toward the threshold of disaster. For the first time in NFL history, the players went on strike. They had presented their demands, but collective bargaining had not brought them what they wanted, so, like other forms of labor, they walked off the job. How that is done by pro-football players is that they simply do not show up for training camp and threaten to hold out through the regular season if the situation is not resolved. In 1974, the unionized players did just that, and there were fears the entire season would have to be canceled, but agreement was reached, and the only effects were that veterans did not train at summer camp—only the rookies did—and the College All-Star game was called off (to no one's regret except perhaps the Chicago *Tribune* Charities, the beneficiary of the annual affair).

The most sweeping set of rules changes were also invoked that year. Not since 1933, when the NFL decided to allow forward passing from anywhere behind the line of scrimmage and moved the goal posts to the goal line, had the game been so altered. Now the league moved the goal posts back to the end line, set kickoffs back from the 40- to the 35-yard line, and adjusted rules that would give receivers more freedom and open up the punt-return game. All tie games would now be decided by a sudden-death overtime period. The intention clearly was to liven up the game, which was fast becoming a rather dogged, dull contest among runners.

Despite all the unrest, the 1974 regular season got underway as usual, and if all the clouds hovering above the NFL did not roll by, no one paid a lot of attention to those that remained once the pros were back on the playing fields.

1975 Dallas Cowboys. Front row: Mitch Hoopes, Roger Staubach, Toni Fritsch, Clint Longley, Mel Renfro, Doug Dennison, Preston Pearson, Charles Young, Benny Barnes. Second row: Scott Laidlaw, Charlie Waters, Randy Hughes, Cliff Harris, Robert Newhouse, Roland Woolsey, Mark Washington, D. D. Lewis, Dave Edwards. Third row: Bob Breunig, Randy White, Lee Roy Jordan, Thomas Henderson, Kyle Davis, Calvin Peterson, Blaine Nye, John Fitzgerald, Larry Cole. Fourth row: Burton Lawless, Pat Donovan, Herbert Scott, Rayfield Wright, Ed Jones, Ralph Neely, Jethro Pugh, Bill Gregory, Bruce Walton. Fifth row: Harvey Martin, Percy Howard, Golden Richards, Jean Fugett, Ron Howard, Drew Pearson, Billy Joe DuPree, Ken Locker, Buck Buchanan, Don Cochren. Top row: Tom Landry, Jim Myers, Ernie Stautner, Ermal Allen, Dan Reeves, Jerry Tubbs, Mike Ditka, Alvin Roy, Gene Stallings, Jim Hughes. (Dallas Cowboys)

Dallas, which had sent wide receiver Billy Parks and defensive end Tody Smith to the Houston Oilers the year before, had gotten in return the Oilers' first- and third-round draft choices for 1974. The Oilers then were gracious enough to finish with the worst record in the league in 1973, 1–13, thus giving the Cowboys the very first selection in the draft. With it, the Cowboys drafted a mountainous defensive end, Ed "Too Tall" Jones from Tennessee State, who stood at 6 feet 8 inches and weighed 260 pounds. With the third-round choice from Houston, they chose what would turn out to be an investment for the future, Arizona State quarterback Danny

White, who would play his first two years in the ill-fated WFL and not come to the Cowboys until 1976.

The Cowboys also signed another quarterback, Clint Longley, from Abilene Christian, who acquired the nickname "Mad Bomber" because of some rather erratic passes he threw in training camp; one, it was said, was almost caught by Tom Landry in the coaching tower, which he ascended daily to survey his troops.

Six-time All-Pro linebacker Chuck Howley finally retired, however, and kicker Toni Fritsch would sit the season out with a bad knee. The Cowboys signed rookie Efren Herrera to handle Fritsch's place-kicking duties, but

The Great Draft

The incredible draft of 1975. These 12 draftees, an unprecedented number of rookies to earn their way directly from college to an NFL team, made the team that year.

	Draft Choice	Position	College
Randy White	1 (a)	DE	Maryland
Thomas Henderson	1 (b)	LB	Langston
Burton Lawless	2	OG	Florida
Bob Breunig	3	LB	Arizona State
Pat Donovan	4 (a)	DE	Stanford
Randy Hughes	4 (b)	S	Oklahoma
Kyle Davis	5 (a)	C	Oklahoma
Rolly Woolsey	6	CB	Boise State
Mike Hegman	7	LB	Tennessee State
Mitch Hoopes	8	P	Arizona
Herbert Scott	13	OG	Virginia Union
Scott Laidlaw	14	RB	Stanford

not before Mac Percival of the Cowboys' famous Kick Karavan, who had gone up to Chicago and made a name for himself, finally donned a Dallas uniform for a cameo appearance in his last year as a pro. The only successful toe to emerge from the Kick Karavan, Percival kicked two of eight field goals and four of five extra points in the beginning of the 1974 season but then stepped aside for Herrera.

The Cowboys muddled through a 3–3 exhibition season, which served mostly as a testing ground for the rookies who had attended training camp. There was not the most ebullient sense of anticipation as the regular season approached, especially from the press.

The feeling of dissatisfaction increased considerably when the Cowboys got off to their worst start since the early 1960s, a time when they routinely would lose a majority of early (and later) games. After an impressive 24–0 win over the Atlanta Falcons, the Cowboys dropped the next four games in a row, two to the weakest links in their division, the Eagles and the Giants. After five games, they were cohabiting with the Giants in the cellar of the NFC East.

Roger Staubach had thrown for more than 200 yards in four of those five games, and the rushing attack, alternately spearheaded by Calvin Hill, Walt Garrison, and Robert Newhouse had been consistent. But the Cowboys just couldn't put enough points on the scoreboard. The games they lost were close ones, but that, of course, meant absolutely nothing in the division standings.

The Cowboys, however, turned it around against the Eagles and the Giants in the two ensuing weeks. Calvin Hill had his best afternoon of the season in the first of those games, rushing for 140 yards and three touchdowns. But at the halfway mark of the season, the Cowboys still had a disappointing record of 3–4. The surprise of the year was the St. Louis Cardinals. All the preseason prognosticators had foreseen another Cowboy-Redskin battle for the division. But here was St. Louis with a record of 7–0, having beaten both the Cowboys and the Redskins. They had accomplished it behind the superb passing of Jim Hart, the receptions of Mel Gray, and the often breathtaking running of Terry Metcalf. There was now another very major presence in the NFC East.

And it was the Cardinals whom the Cowboys had to open the second half of the season against. It turned out to be a remarkable game, and like so many of the Cardinals' earlier contests that year, it was a true cliff hanger. (Of their seven wins, the Cardinals had won five in the last minute of play). This time, however, the roles were reversed. The Cardinals led 14–7 going into the fourth quarter of a game marked by defense on both sides, but then the Cowboys came back to tie the game. And they came back still another time. With four seconds left on the clock, Efren Herrera came on to the field to kick the game-winning 20-yard field goal.

With a victory over the 49ers the following week, which added up to a win streak of four, matching the preceding losing streak, the Cowboys still were alive in terms of the playoffs, but it would take a full-fledged miracle.

The Cowboys, when they hosted the Redskins on Thanksgiving Day, had improved their record to 6–5, but they would have to beat the Redskins, and they would have to win the two games after that, and the Redskins would have to lose their last two. It was mathematically possible but realistically improbable.

The Cowboys took the first step in the right direction before a sellout crowd in Texas Stadium on Thanksgiving Day afternoon. And they did it in a way no one would ever have predicted.

The first half was a profile of tedium. The only interest seemed to be in watching the once-recalcitrant Cowboy Duane Thomas try to gain a few yards for the Redskins, who had adopted him, but he was not doing very well, much to the Dallas crowd's glee. At the same time, the Cowboys weren't doing any better. The first half ended as nothing more than a battle of field goals, with Washington's Mark Moseley getting the nod over Efren Herrera 3–1, leaving a score of 9–3 in favor of the Redskins.

The second half, however, stimulated a medley of groans from Cowboy fans as loud and as mournful as those at the stockyard pens of a Texas ranch when Duane Thomas took a 9-yard pass from Billy Kilmer to score the game's first touchdown. The atmosphere became almost

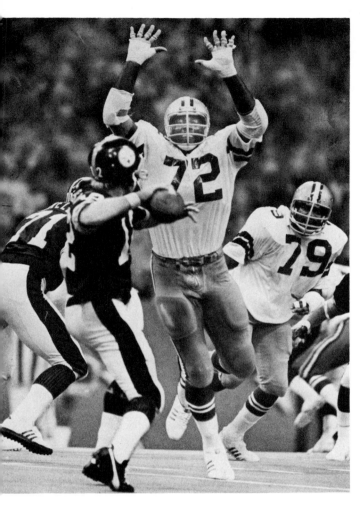

Ed "Too Tall" Jones demonstrates the reason for his nickname here to Pittsburgh Steeler quarterback Terry Bradshaw. A rookie in 1974, the 6'9" defensive end from Tennessee State quickly established himself as not only the tallest but also one of the most awesome pass rushers in the NFL. He would also become known as one of the most dependable and effective playoff players in the game. No. 79 is Harvey Martin. (Dallas Cowboys)

funereal when a dazed Roger Staubach was led off the field and the unknown rookie Clint Longley jogged out to replace him. Longley had not spent a solitary moment on the field during an NFL regular-season game, and he faced not only a 9-point deficit but a hungry Redskin defense that perceived in him what a lion does in a tender baby gazelle.

Life on the football field, however, is never predictable. The marauding Redskins were unable to beat and claw and terrorize the rookie, as their instincts told them to. Instead, Longley moved the Cowboys down the field. Then he threw a 35-yard touchdown pass to Billy Joe

DuPree—fluke perhaps, one of football's myriad of fleeting ironies. The Redskins, however, could not counter and turned the football back to the Cowboys and its young quarterback.

Again he moved the team, this time a concerted drive. At the 1-yard line, he handed the ball to Walt Garrison, who crashed through, and suddenly the Cowboys were ahead in the game. The fourth quarter brought back the bad dream to Cowboy fans. Once again, Duane Thomas was there, this time carrying the ball 19 yards for a touchdown and returning the lead to Washington. The Cowboys got the ball, a sliver of momentum left, but they fumbled it away. There were five minutes to go when the Redskins tried a field goal, but it was blocked by "Too Tall" Jones. Then the Cowboys fumbled and lost the ball again. Thoughts of Cowboy supporters, even the most ardent, quickly began to be rerouted to turkey and dressing and mashed potatoes.

The Cowboys, however, got the ball back one last time. There was only a minute and 45 seconds left. They moved the ball to mid-field, where they had a first down with 35 seconds left but no timeouts. Tom Landry sent the play in, and the Redskins went immediately to a prevent defense with no less than *seven* defensive backs in the game.

1974

Preseason

Dallas	(3-3)	Opponents
7	Oakland (41,049) @ Oakland	27
13	Los Angeles (46,468) @ L. A.	6
19	Houston (53,148) @ Dallas (OT)	13
7	N. Orleans (56,563) @ N. Orleans	16
25	Kansas City (43,492) @ Dallas	16
15	Pittsburgh (43,900) @ Dallas	41

Regular Season

		(8-6)	
W	24	Atlanta (52,322)	0
L	10	Philadelphia (64,088)	13
L	6	N. Y. Giants (45,841) (H)	14
L	21	Minnesota (57,847) (H)	23
L	28	St. Louis (49,885)	31
W	31	Philadelphia (43,586) (H)	24
W	21	N. Y. Giants (61,918)	7
W	17	St. Louis (64,146) (H)	14
W	20	San Francisco (50,018) (H)	14
L	21	Washington (54,395)	28
W	10	Houston (49,775)	0
W	24	Washington (63,243) (H)	23
W	41	Cleveland (48,754) (H)	17
L	23	Oakland (45,850)	27
	297		235

Nevertheless, Longley dropped back and fired for the deep sideline. Drew Pearson, streaking in the same direction, looked up at the 4-yard line and leaped to grab the ball. He danced into the end zone to tie the score, 23–23. Efren Herrera kicked the extra point and the 1974 season's most extraordinary game was inscribed in the record book.

The next week, the Cowboys slaughtered the Cleveland Browns, 41–17, with Roger Staubach throwing for 230 yards and three touchdowns—two bombs to Golden Richards and one to Billy Joe DuPree. But the Redskins also won that day, stifling the Cowboys' remote chance for a place in the playoffs.

The final record, 8–6, was the Cowboys' poorest since 1965, and 1974 was the first year the Cowboys would not play in a postseason game since 1964.

Drew Pearson dances into the end zone after a 29-yard pass from Roger Staubach in the first quarter of Super Bowl X. It was the first score of the game, and it looked like the Cowboys were on their way to a second Super Bowl championship until the Steelers found redemption with a safety, two field goals, and a touchdown in the fourth quarter. (Dallas Cowboys)

The performers, like the performances, had been respectable but not the same quality of recent years. Roger Staubach had his least effective year thus far, completing only 52.8% of his passes and dropping from the highest ranking in the league the year before to 14th in 1974. For the first time in three seasons, Calvin Hill had not rushed for 1,000 yards. And the team's overall defensive and offensive statistics were nothing more than mediocre.

On the brighter side, Drew Pearson had blossomed beautifully and led the NFL in pass-reception yardage (1,087), the second highest in Dallas history, outgained only by Bob Hayes's 1,232 in 1966. And Pearson was the only Cowboy to be named an All-Pro that year.

It was headlined a "year of rebuilding." The Cowboys were in the process of transition—one team on the way out, newcomers settling in. Before the 1975 season, Bob Lilly, Walt Garrison, and Cornell Green had announced their retirements. Besides them, a roster of other big names from the Cowboys' Super Bowl teams of 1970 and 1971 had left the game—Howley, Andrie, Manders, Alworth, Liscio, Adderley, and Ditka.

And others would depart—Calvin Hill who would play in the WFL; wide receiver Bob Hayes was sent to the 49ers; guard John Niland, traded to the Eagles; and defensive end Pat Toomay, dealt away to the Buffalo Bills. Efren Herrera would miss the season because of injury, and the recovered Toni Fritsch would be back to do the kicking.

Never in a history of great drafts, however, would there be one richer than that in which Dallas reveled in 1975. Fully 12 rookies from that draft would earn a place on the Cowboys' squad that year, including such soon-to-be household names around Dallas as Randy White, Thomas Henderson, Bob Breunig, Randy Hughes, Scott Laidlaw, Mike Hegman, and Pat Donovan. Beyond that, the Cowboys would pick up Preston Pearson as a free agent after the Pittsburgh Steelers put him on waivers.

The running attack of the Cowboys was obviously depleted with the departure of Hill and Garrison, so to offset that Coach Tom Landry introduced the shotgun formation, which would initially surprise NFL teams that year and then stay around to beleaguer them in years to come.

The preseason was an especially ineffectual one, the first loser in fact since 1970. The Cowboys won only two of six games, and they were badly thrashed by the Los Angeles Rams, the same team against whom they would open the regular season at Texas Stadium.

The Rams were a strong favorite to win the NFC West. None of the other three teams was even considered in their league. They had a ripening James Harris at quarterback, backed up by Ron Jaworski, and such excellent receivers as Harold Jackson and Ron Jessie. There was

1975

Preseason

Dallas	(2-4)	Opponents
7	Los Angeles (62,843) @ L. A.	35
20	Kansas City (35,630) @ K. C.	26
13	Minnesota (45,395) @ Dallas	16
17	Houston (46,951) @ Houston	14
20	Oakland (39,562) @ Dallas	31
17	Pittsburgh (43,186) @ Dallas	16

Regular Season

		(10-4)	
W	18	Los Angeles (49,091) (H)	7
W	37	St. Louis (52,417) (OT) (H)	31
W	36	Detroit (79,784)	10
W	13	N. Y. Giants (56,511)	7
L	17	Green Bay (64,934) (H)	19
W	20	Philadelphia (64,889)	17
L	24	Washington (55,004) (OT)	30
L	31	Kansas City (63,539) (H)	34
W	34	New England (60,905)	31
W	27	Philadelphia (57,893) (H)	17
W	14	N. Y. Giants (53,329) (H)	3
L	17	St. Louis (49,701)	31
W	31	Washington (61,091) (H)	10
W	31	N. Y. Jets (37,279)	21
	350		268

Postseason

		Divisional Playoff (Minnesota)	
W	17	Minnesota (48,341)	14
		NFC Championship Game (Los Angeles)	
W	37	Los Angeles (84,483)	7
		Super Bowl X (Miami)	
L	17	Pittsburgh (80,187)	21

also the running prowess of Larry McCutcheon and Cullen Bryant.

Beaten by 28 points in the exhibition season, the Cowboys were a decided underdog opening day. But whatever it was the Rams had earlier, it was not present that September afternoon. The Cowboys shut the Rams out until late in the fourth quarter and came out with a surprising 18–7 win. The following week, their own division champs, the Cardinals, came to Texas Stadium. The game was an exciting one, especially the second half. The Cowboys extended a touchdown lead in the third quarter to 14–3. But the Cardinals came right back with a touchdown. Then they scored again, this time on a spectacular 80-yard pass from Jim Hart to Earl Thomas.

The Cardinals sent the kickoff hurtling down to the 3-yard line where rookie Thomas Henderson gathered it

in and ran 97 yards for a touchdown—the fifth scored in that period of play. And it was the fifth longest kickoff return in Cowboy history.

In the fourth quarter, the Cardinals came up with two nifty touchdowns on passes from Hart to Jackie Smith (35 yards) and Mel Gray (37 yards). The last one tied the score at 31–31 and sent the game into sudden-death overtime. Roger Staubach then marched the Cowboys down field and ended the game with a little 3-yard pass to Billy Joe DuPree.

Having prevailed in the toughest games of the early sector of the season, the Cowboys coasted through the next two and claimed a record of 4–0, a full game on top of the NFC East.

Three losses in the next four games, however, brought the Cowboys back to earth and dumped them into third place in the division. Tom Landry called it "a midseason slump" and he said they would pull out of it. And the Cowboys did, with a three-game win streak. They lost a

Rayfield Wright, four times All-Pro, was one of the most widely respected offensive linemen in the game during his 13-year Cowboy career. Here, he moves out with purpose against a Detroit Lion defensive lineman.   (Dallas Cowboys)

game up at St. Louis and then triumphed in their last two games to finish with a record of 10–4.

Other than the overtime loss to the Cowboys, the Cardinals had lost only two other games. They took the division crown with an 11–3 record. The old-timers on the Redskins had wearied, and they ended up two full games behind the Cowboys.

The season had been a hilly one but not bad for a team rebuilding. The Cowboys had done a lot better than many people thought they would in that year of renovation and experiment; 10–4 was certainly a respectable record, and it had been good enough to land them back in the playoffs after their one-year hiatus. As the NFC wild card, they would meet the Vikings up in Minnesota in the first round of the NFC eliminations.

There were some moments from the regular season that Cowboy fans could savor. The game at Texas Stadium against the Eagles was played on "Bob Lilly Day,"

Cliff Harris (43) snags Washington Redskin running back Mike Thomas in the Cowboy secondary as rookie safety Randy Hughes (42) moves in to help. Harris, or "Captain Crash" as he was dubbed by teammates, in his 10-year career in the Cowboy defensive backfield was a four-time All-Pro and was invited to the Pro Bowl six times. (Dallas Cowboys)

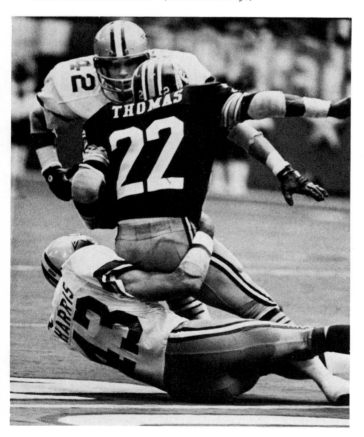

a special recognition for his incomparable performances as a Dallas Cowboy. He became the premier member of the Cowboys' "Ring of Honor" that day. As the Cowboys' *Media Guide* pointed out, Bob Lilly "never missed a game in 14 years with the Cowboys," and he earned All-Pro honors seven times and would on his first year of eligibility be inducted into the Pro Football Hall of Fame.

Roger Staubach also came up with the two most productive games of his career to that point, throwing for 307 yards against the Cardinals and then topping it with a 314-yard performance against the Eagles. And Drew Pearson had his best day as a Cowboy against the Lions, catching six passes for 188 yards, including two touchdowns.

Preston Pearson racked up his first 100-yard rushing day as a Cowboy when he gained 101 against the Packers. And Robert Newhouse threw a 46-yard TD pass to Drew Pearson in a little bit of razzle-dazzle against the Lions.

All of that, however, was merely an overture to the surprises and excitement that the Cowboys were about to pull off in the postseason.

First, they had to face the heavily favored Minnesota Vikings in that upturned igloo known as Metropolitan Stadium. Some had Minnesota an 8-point favorite. The Vikes had monopolized the NFC Central, losing only two games and ending up five games ahead of their nearest competitor. Fran Tarkenton had led the league in passing with a 64% completion average and 2,994 yards on 273 completions. His 25 TD tosses were also a league high. Chuck Foreman gained over 1,000 yards rushing (1,070), and the Vikings' fabled defense led the league in a majority of categories.

The game was played, as one writer put it, "in frozen gloom," but that was the typical climate in the late season up in Bloomington, Minnesota. It was also a dull slugfest, with a lot of line plunges and massive tackling and punting back and forth, about as colorful a game as the slate-gray afternoon on which it was played. Late in the fourth quarter, the Vikings led 14–10. The Cowboys were back near their own goal line with just a few minutes left. It was their last chance, and everyone on the field and in the grandstands knew it. Staubach managed to move the Cowboys out of the hole, but then the Vikings' defense stiffened. There were 44 seconds left, and the Cowboys were faced with a fourth down and 16. There was good protection for Staubach as he stood back in the pocket, and suddenly he saw the man he was looking for. Drew Pearson had angled in, then made his move toward the right sideline, and Staubach threw a perfect strike to him just before he stutter-stepped out of bounds at the 50-yard line.

Staubach was now in the shotgun formation. The ball was still on the 50, but now there were only 24 seconds

Clint "Mad Bomber" Longley, out of Abilene Christian, lasted with the Cowboys only two years. His feud with Roger Staubach, to whom he was back-up, was a heated one and culminated in the locker room at Thousand Oaks on the last day of the 1976 training camp when he threw a surprise punch that sent Staubach to the hospital for stitches and Longley to the San Diego Chargers. He did have one spectacular game as a Cowboy, however, when he came off the bench in 1974 to replace an injured Staubach in a "must" game. The Cowboys were losing at the time by 9 points, but Longley engineered 3 second-half touchdowns (2 on passes) and pulled out a last-second victory. (Dallas Cowboys)

left. Drew Pearson was lined up wide to the right and, when the ball was snapped, took off toward the defender, Nate Wright. He made a move to the inside and then dashed for the sideline. Staubach lofted a towering pass, known in the vernacular as a "Hail Mary" pass because it is usually thrown up as a prayer. Nate Wright was running right alongside Pearson as the ball hurtled toward them, but somehow they collided, and suddenly Wright was tumbling toward the ground. The ball landed in Pearson's hands, then bobbled at his hip and down his leg, but it never got below the knee before he had it secure again for the last few steps into the end zone. The referee signaled a touchdown, and an ecstatic Pearson wheeled and tossed the ball into the stands. As Roger Staubach later

recalled in his autobiography, "I never had a more eerie sensation on a football field than during the aftermath of our touchdown. The crowd was so shocked there wasn't a sound from the stands. It was as though all of a sudden we were playing in an empty stadium. The silence, as they say, was deafening."

The Hail Mary pass had turned into a divine ending for the Cowboys. They upset the Vikings 17–14 and earned the right to leave the wintry north and travel to sunny southern California for the NFC championship game.

When the Cowboys arrived in Los Angeles, the odds-makers were giving the Rams a 6-point advantage. It was, after all, their home field, and they would be surrounded by their own raucous fans. The powerhouse from L.A. had easily swept through their division, winning 12 and losing only 2, while the closest team to them, the 49ers, could manage a paltry 5 wins while suffering 9 losses.

The Cowboys were responsible for one of the Rams' two losses in 1975, which they had levied in the season

Cowboy Drew Pearson cradles the football on his hip and steps into the end zone after the famous "Hail Mary" pass from Roger Staubach which beat the Minnesota Vikings in the 1975 conference playoff game. With 24 seconds left and the Cowboys trailing by 4 points, Staubach threw a desperation bomb, 50 yards, which Drew Pearson picked out of a crowd and somehow managed to hold on to for the game-winning touchdown. The Vikings in the picture are: Paul Krause (22), Nate Wright (43), and Terry Brown (24).   (Dallas Cowboys)

Thomas "Hollywood" Henderson arrived at the Cowboy camp in 1975 with great promise, an irrepressible volatility, and an obsession with showmanship. A publicity magnet, Henderson would often find himself far outside the team pattern that Tom Landry had established. One of the fastest linebackers in the league, he would win a starting position in 1977 and go to the Pro Bowl the following year. But his uncontrollability and side-line antics would bring his Cowboy career to an abrupt end midway through the 1979 season.   (Dallas Cowboys)

opener. The youngsters from Dallas remembered that, and despite the dismal predictions of the bookmakers, they were confident.

Positive mental attitude, momentum, youthful extravagance, the heady warmth of sunny California, whatever it was, the Cowboys had it, and they were simply magnificent that January afternoon at the Los Angeles Coliseum. Before 84,483 astonished fans, they virtually demolished the mighty Rams. It was never even a contest. The Cowboys amassed 37 points before they finally allowed the Rams a single score, and it came in the fourth quarter, the result of a pass-interference call. Dallas's defense was so impregnable that day it gave up only 22 yards rushing in the entire game, a mere 96 yards passing, and only nine first downs.

Roger Staubach had found another Pearson to bestow his passes on that afternoon. Instead of Drew, this time it

was Preston. Staubach found him three times for touchdowns, and Preston Pearson had a total of 123 yards in seven receptions for the day. Staubach also found Golden Richards for his fourth TD pass of the game, and Toni Fritsch contributed three field goals to complete the mortification of the Rams.

So the team rebuilding became the team going to the Super Bowl. It would be their third appearance in the championship classic, and it would be the first time a wild-card team ever made it that far in the playoffs. (The Kansas City Chiefs were not divisional winners when they won Super Bowl IV; they had come in second, which qualified them for the playoffs in those days when the AFL had only two divisions and ten teams).

Facing the Cowboys in Super Bowl X, would be the winners of Super Bowl IX, the Pittsburgh Steelers. They had decimated the Baltimore Colts in the divisional playoff game and then barely snuck by a fired-up Oakland Raiders for the AFC title. But the Steelers were the mammoths of the National Football League. They had posted the best record (12–2) in an extraordinarily potent conference. (In their own division, the third-place team, the Houston Oilers, had a record of 10–4.) The Steelers were in the process of building their own little dynasty.

The Pittsburgh defense was fully accepted as one of the most intimidating and effective ever to prowl a pro-football field. Linemen like Mean Joe Greene, L. C. Greenwood, Ernie Holmes, and Dwight White were among the most punishing in the league. The linebacking corps, all three of them, were named to the All-Pro team in 1975: Jack Ham, Jack Lambert, and Andy Russell, an unprece-

Jimmy the Greek Predicts

Jimmy the Greek came to Dallas to assess the situation before moving on to Miami for Super Bowl X. While in town, he wrote in his syndicated column: "The view of the Super Bowl from Dallas is that champion Pittsburgh will be going in with an inflated ego and that the Cowboys will kick their tails in next week as they did Minnesota and Los Angeles." He talked then about the Cowboys' being underrated and of the impressive talents of Roger Staubach and of the sturdy Dallas defense. On the other hand, he noted that "if Bradshaw has a big day, as Jim Hart of the Cardinals had against them, it's curtains." He wished the Cowboys luck but concluded, "Personally, I think Franco Harris can be held in check only so long. A big man wears down the defense the longer the game goes on. Franco's still the big man, and it's still Pittsburgh by 7."

The starting lineups for Super Bowl X:

Dallas Cowboys		Pittsburgh Steelers
Offense		
Golden Richards	WR	John Stallworth
Drew Pearson	WR	Lynn Swann
Jean Fugett	TE	Larry Brown
Ralph Neely	T	Jon Kolb
Rayfield Wright	T	Gordon Gravelle
Burton Lawless	G	Jim Clack
Blaine Nye	G	Gerry Mullins
John Fitzgerald	C	Ray Mansfield
Roger Staubach	QB	Terry Bradshaw
Preston Pearson	RB	Rocky Bleier
Robert Newhouse	RB	Franco Harris
Defense		
"Too Tall" Jones	E	L. C. Greenwood
Harvey Martin	E	Dwight White
Jethro Pugh	T	Mean Joe Greene
Larry Cole	T	Ernie Holmes
Dave Edwards	LLB	Jack Ham
Lee Roy Jordan	MLB	Jack Lambert
D. D. Lewis	RLB	Andy Russell
Mark Washington	LCB	J. T. Thomas
Mel Renfro	RCB	Mel Blount
Charlie Waters	S	Mike Wagner
Cliff Harris	S	Glen Edwards

dented honor. Lambert, the most ferocious of them all, was described by Pete Axthelm in *Newsweek* as "the successor to former Chicago star Dick Butkus as the most feared and fearsome defender of all. Not only do opponents hesitate to invade his area of the field, but teammates stay away from Lambert on the bench, where he can usually be observed twitching, scratching, and generally psyching himself toward new levels of lonely rage."

The offensive unit had Franco Harris to carry the ball (1,246 yards rushing in 1975), ably complemented by Rocky Bleier. And for the passing game there was Terry Bradshaw, ranked fourth in the NFL, with such sure-handed receivers as Lynn Swann, John Stallworth, and Randy Grossman. Chuck Noll said it himself. "I have one helluva team."

In Dallas, the mood was something akin to Times Square on VE Day. When the Cowboys returned from L.A., they were welcomed at the airport by a crowd that was as excited as it was large. On the following day, an announcement was made that tickets for Super Bowl X would go on sale at seven the next morning over at Moody Coliseum on the SMU campus. That blustery cold night, as it was described in an Associated Press dispatch, the ticket-sale site was populated by about 2,000 hopefuls, and it "looked like something out of the 1930 depression. There were makeshift tents, smudge pots, kerosene lamps, three or four people huddled in one sleeping bag, and a shelter made of cardboard boxes . . . Dallas, Big D, the cultural center of the Southwest, had lost its cool over the Cowboys."

The Cowboys flew to Miami the week before the game and set up residence once again at the Galt Ocean Mile Motel in Fort Lauderdale where they had stayed during their first Super Bowl visit. Thirteen of the Cowboys of 1975 had been there back in 1970 and at New Orleans in 1971 and were now about to engage in their third Super Bowl: Larry Cole, Dave Edwards, Cliff Harris, Lee Roy Jordan, D. D. Lewis, Ralph Neely, Blaine Nye, Jethro Pugh, Mel Renfro, Roger Staubach, Mark Washington, Charlie Waters, and Rayfield Wright.

Once again the spectacle would be held in the Orange Bowl, with more than 80,000 spectators in attendance and a record 75 million expected to watch it on the tube. Tickets were priced at $20, but already scalpers were getting as much as $75 to $100 each. A record of 1,735 press credentials were also issued for the game.

Before Super Bowl X

Some random quotes before Super Bowl X:

"Let's have a Super Bowl the pre-game show can be proud of."

—Larry L. King, Sport *Magazine*

"I'm told the Steelers are so sure about winning they are savoring the thought of becoming the first team to win three straight championships next year. That's the kind of overconfidence that cost the Vikes and the Rams before them."

—Jimmy the Greek, oddsmaker/columnist

"I read that stuff [Cliff] Harris said. He was trying to intimidate me. He said that because I had a concussion I would be afraid out there. Well, he doesn't know Lynn Swann . . . He can't scare me or this team."

—Lynn Swann, Pittsburgh Steelers

"Even if we win, you people [the sportswriters] are still going to say I'm a dumb quarterback."

—Terry Bradshaw, Pittsburgh Steelers

Now, in 1975, one minute of commercial time on TV would set an advertiser back $230,000, and the NFL, as a result of its radio-TV arrangement, would receive gross revenues of $3.8 million.

Extra flights by the airlines would bring an estimated 120,000 people from Texas, Pennsylvania, and a variety of other places. All those football fans and media types would spend an estimated $130 million in the Miami area during the weekend of the game. As a spokesman for the Miami Tourist Bureau, with a strange choice of metaphor, put it: "Super Bowl fever is the greatest single epidemic any community can hope to have."

To add to the hype, both teams bared fangs and went at each other before the game. Charges were bandied concerning on-field brutalities, cheap shots, dirty players, and questionable ethics. Cowboy safety Cliff Harris suggested Steeler wide receiver Lynn Swann would no doubt be wary when he ran his pass patterns, the implication

being, of course, that he had intentions of pulverizing him on one of them. It fueled the inherent savagery in people like Jack Lambert and Mean Joe Greene, not to mention Lynn Swann, and they had a few nasty retorts. It was all part of the build up, something to remind all those people who came to Miami that besides all the parties and pageantry there was also going to be a football game.

When the day of that contest dawned, the famous Florida sun was in full burst, and the temperature began a rise that would peak at game time in the upper 50s, most pleasant football weather for everyone inside the Orange Bowl that day. The pregame coin toss had an air of conspicuous consumption to it; the coin was a solid-gold national bicentennial medal, 3 inches thick, weighing almost a pound, and worth about $4,000 in 1975 money.

Dallas took the lead early in the first quarter. When Steeler punter Bobby Walden lost the ball on his own 29-yard line, the Cowboys took over. They capitalized on

Roger Staubach (12) decides to mix things up a little in Super Bowl X and run with the ball. Forming a wedge for him are Blaine Nye (61), Burton Lawless (66), and Rayfield Wright (70). Staubach ran for 22 yards at the Orange Bowl in Miami that day and gained another 204 passing, but it was not enough as the Steelers edged the Cowboys, 21–17, and took possession of the Super Bowl trophy. (Vernon Biever)

the very first play. Staubach sent Drew Pearson on a pattern over the middle and rifled the ball to him at the 15. Pearson carried it in for the touchdown.

The Steelers tied it up in the same quarter as Terry Bradshaw guided a sustained running attack, interrupted once with a 32-yard pass to Lynn Swann. The score came on a 7-yard pass to tight end Randy Grossman.

In the second quarter, Toni Fritsch put the Cowboys back in the lead with a 36-yard field goal. And the half ended with the Steelers in the hole, 10–7.

The third quarter was as quiet as the cloisters of a monastery as both defenses tightened and nerves grew taut. At one point, Steeler kicker Ron Gerella missed a field goal, and Cowboy safety Cliff Harris gave him a pat on the head to let him know how pleased he was with the failure. Gerella did not take as much offense to the gesture as did Steeler linebacker Jack Lambert, who immediately whacked Harris and sent him sprawling. The referees moved in, but no penalty was called. When the third quarter ended, the score had not changed, and the tempera-

ments of both teams were still strained.

Then the fourth quarter erupted. Three and a half minutes into that final period, Cowboy rookie punter Mitch Hoopes, standing at his own goal line, got his foot into the ball, only to see it soar into the outstretched paw of on-rushing Steeler Reggie Harrison. The ball went in the direction opposite which Hoopes had intended, bouncing

---

After Super Bowl X

Some random quotes after Super Bowl X:

"If there's any consolation in losing, I sure don't feel any now."

—*Randy White, Dallas Cowboys*

"This is a team in love with themselves . . . I just don't think they respected us. They didn't even expect us to get to the Super Bowl. My thoughts right now are that the wine of success has apparently intoxicated the Steelers. There were a lot of incredible cheap shots taken out there today."

—*Jean Fugett, Dallas Cowboys*

"[I knew] that Landry would start planning his next year's winner on the walk across the field to the locker room."
—*Pete Gent, Esquire Mazagine*

(On the Lambert/Harris altercation): "When I see injustice, I do something about it . . . I try to hit before I get hit. If the other guy plays clean, I play clean. If he plays dirty, I play dirty . . . I was stirred up before the game and then what Harris did got me more stirred up."
—*Jack Lambert, Pittsburgh Steelers*

"Lambert really popped me, but I wasn't about to hit back. I saw an official looking straight at us and I would have been the guy kicked out of the game."
—*Cliff Harris, Dallas Cowboys*

(After the sack by Cliff Harris in the 4th quarter): "I was in the locker when I finally figured out what happened . . . I'm still a little hazy about things. I got hit from the blind side and I heard bells ringing. I never saw the pass, the catch, anything."
—*Terry Bradshaw, Pittsburgh Steelers*

"We got beat by a good team. We are not going to alibi . . . Pittsburgh made the plays when they had to, you have to give them credit. There will be a next season. We'll come back. We're still young and looking for better things."

—*Roger Staubach, Dallas Cowboys*

In Super Bowl X, Cowboy linebacker D. D. Lewis lunges desperately at a poised Terry Bradshaw. This blitz didn't work, but late in the game a sledgehammer tackle by Cowboy safety Cliff Harris knocked Bradshaw unconscious and forced him to spend the last few minutes of the game on the Steeler bench. (Vernon Biever)

crazily until it skittered out the back of the end zone—an automatic safety and two points for the Steelers. The Cowboys had to kick from their own 20-yard line, and the Steelers ended up with good field position and then worked their way into field-goal range. Gerella kicked a 36 yarder, and the Cowboys for the first time that afternoon

SUPER BOWL X

AFC versus NFC for the NFL Championship and the Vince Lombardi Trophy
Sunday, January 18, 1976   2:00 P.M.
Orange Bowl Stadium   Miami, Florida $2.00

were on the low end of the score, 12–10.

The Cowboys ran headlong into another disaster on their first set of downs. Staubach threw an interception to Mike Wagner, who ran the ball tot he Cowboy 7-yard line. The defense held and forced the Steelers to settle for another field goal.

There was now just a little over 6½ minutes remaining in the game. The Cowboys were far from out of it; no one was forgetting the climactic comeback against the Vikings two playoff games earlier. Still the Cowboys were unable to penetrate the Steelers defense.

With 3 minutes left, the Steelers had the ball. It was third and four. Bradshaw dropped back to pass and the Cowboy blitz exploded; only the first man in, linebacker D. D. Lewis, went thundering over him as Bradshaw did a neat ducking act. When he straightened up, he glimpsed Lynn Swann streaking far down the field. He just barely got the long, looping bomb off before he was blasted into Palookaville by blitzing safety Cliff Harris. Bradshaw was on the ground, unconscious, when the ball fell in Swann's hands, and he never did see him race with it across the goal line for a 64-yard touchdown.

But it was not over. It was now Roger Staubach's turn. In five plays, he moved the Cowboys from their 20 to the Steelers' end zone, culminating the drive with a 34-yard touchdown pass to wide receiver Percy Howard with 1:48 left in the game.

An on-side kick did not work, but the Dallas defense did. They held the Steelers on four downs, although they had to use up all their timeouts in the process, and took over the ball at their own 39-yard line. Staubach moved the Cowboys as precious seconds ticked away. They got to the Steeler 38-yard line. There were only seconds remaining, and 80,000 people were on their feet. Staubach went for his sometime partner in miracle making, Drew Pearson, looking for that touch of magic, but this time it didn't work. Instead, the ball was grabbed by Steeler safety Glen Edwards, and the most exciting game in the ten-year history of the Super Bowl came to an end with the Steelers a 21–17 victor.

14 On to Super Bowl XII

As the Dallas Cowboys moved into the second half of the decade of the 1970s, they could take a certain pride in the fact that they had established themselves as one of the most successful franchises in the league. They had played in three Super Bowls, an achievement at that time equaled only by the Miami Dolphins. And the Dolphins' dynasty appeared now to be in a state of decline. The rugged brawlers from Pittsburgh were on the rise, but then so were the Cowboys. Tex Schramm had said repeatedly that his deepest wish was for the Cowboys to become *the* team of the 1970s, the one that would be remembered as the ultimate class of the league when people would later speak of that segment of the pro-football story.

The Cowboys certainly had a shot at attaining that stature. The team had been a major factor in the first half of the 1970s and were looking better all the time. Tom Landry was regarded as a masterful leader and one of the finest football minds in the game. The organization was solid, positive, and enthusiastic from the front office to the playing field. "We have several more Super Bowls in our plans for the next five years," Tex Schramm had said. "You will be hearing a lot more from the Cowboys. We've gotten to like the habit of winning."

Elsewhere on the pro football scene, there were still some unsettled and unsettling situations. The World Football League had ceased to be a concern to anyone by 1976, having gone out of business late in the preceding season, but a total of 380 players lost their livelihoods as a result. The best of them would reemerge in the NFL in 1976, but the others would have to look for a new profession. In the NFL, there was still friction between the team

owners and the players' union, and there was still no formal agreement between the two groups on various arbitrary issues. Two new franchises, however, were welcomed into the league, the Tampa Bay Buccaneers, joining the AFC West (they would move to the NFC Central the following year), and the Seattle Seahawks, entering the NFC West.

The Cowboys finally signed their wayward draftee of 1974, Danny White, who was one of the WFL unemployed, and he would quickly become their first-line punter and senior apprentice to Roger Staubach at quarterback. Their most illustrious defector to the WFL, Calvin Hill, signed with the arch-rival Washington Redskins and would use his talents against the Cowboys in the future.

Place kicker Efren Herrera was well again, so the Cowboys sent Toni Fritsch off to the San Diego Chargers to make room for him on the roster. The draft was a tame one after the preceding year's treasure trove. But the Cowboys did cull from it defensive back Aaron Kyle (Wyoming), wide receiver Butch Johnson (University of California/Riverside), and offensive guard Tom Rafferty (Penn State). As a free agent, tight end Jay Saldi of South Carolina was also signed to a Cowboy contract.

Emotions were running very high when the Cowboys moved into the dorms at California Lutheran out in Thousand Oaks the summer of 1976; the veterans, anyway, were still glorying in last year's unanticipated appearance at the Super Bowl. The team was, in the words of Tom Landry, "a nice blend of experienced players and young men moving into their own, two groups who meld together especially well." Lee Roy Jordan, at 35, and about

1976 COWBOYS

1976 Dallas Cowboys. Front row: Efren Herrera, Danny White, Roger Staubach, Mel Renfro, Doug Dennison, Aaron Kyle, Preston Pearson, Charles Young, Benny Barnes. Second row: Scott Laidlaw, Jim Jensen, Charlie Waters, Randy Hughes, Cliff Harris, Robert Newhouse, Mark Washington, D. D. Lewis, Jim Eidson. Third row: Bob Breunig, Randy White, Lee Roy Jordan, Thomas Henderson, Mike Hegman, Blaine Nye, John Fitzgerald, Larry Cole, Tom Rafferty. Fourth row: Burton Lawless, Pat Donovan, Herbert Scott, Rayfield Wright, Ed Jones, Ralph Neely, Jethro Pugh, Bill Gregory, Greg Schaum. Fifth row: Harvey Martin, Beasley Reece, Golden Richards, Butch Johnson, Jay Saldi, Drew Pearson, Billy Joe DuPree, Ken Locker, Buck Buchanan. Top row: Tom Landry, Jim Myers, Ernie Stautner, Ermal Allen, Jerry Tubbs, Dan Reeves, Mike Ditka, Gene Stallings, Ed Hughes, Don Cochren. (Dallas Cowboys)

to play his 14th and last season with the Cowboys, was the patriarch. Roger Staubach was just a year younger than he, and Ralph Neely, Rayfield Wright, Jethro Pugh, Mel Renfro, and Preston Pearson also qualified for the over-30 club.

For the most part, the preseason was uneventful, with the Cowboys losing their first three games and then winning the remaining three. There was a high point, however, and that occurred when the villainous Pittsburgh Steelers paid a visit to Texas Stadium. It was enough of an event to bring out a crowd of more than 64,000, the first time a preseason turnout of that size was registered since the Houston Oilers came up to Dallas with busloads

of their fans back in 1972. The Cowboys took particular delight in drawing a little of the blood of vengeance as they beat the Steelers 20–10.

When the regular season got underway, no one was talking any longer of the Cowboys as a team being rebuilt or one going through some kind of professional football metamorphosis. They were simply looked upon as the defending conference champions who were also an odds-on favorite to win at least their division in 1976 and probably much more.

The Cowboys shocked the Eagles in the season opener 27–7. Scott Laidlaw, in his first Cowboy start, gained 104 yards rushing on 19 carries. Roger Staubach also illus-

1976

Preseason

Dallas	(3-3)	Opponents
14	Oakland (52,391) @ Oakland	17
14	Los Angeles (60,158) @ L. A.	26
9	Denver (54,567) @ Dallas	13
36	Detroit (30,340) @ Memphis	16
20	Pittsburgh (64,264) @ Dallas	10
26	Houston (58,844) @ Dallas (OT)	20

Regular Season

		(11-3)	
W	27	Philadelphia (54,052) (H)	7
W	24	New Orleans (61,413)	6
W	30	Baltimore (64,237) (H)	27
W	28	Seattle (62,027)	13
W	24	N. Y. Giants (76,042)	14
L	17	St. Louis (50,317)	21
W	31	Chicago (61,346) (H)	21
W	20	Washington (55,004)	7
W	9	N. Y. Giants (58,870) (H)	3
W	17	Buffalo (51,779) (H)	10
L	10	Atlanta (54,992)	17
W	19	St. Louis (62,498) (H)	14
W	26	Philadelphia (55,072)	7
L	14	Washington (59,916) (H)	27
	296		194

Postseason

		Divisional Playoff	
		(Dallas)	
L	12	Los Angeles (62,436)	14

They were unable to produce a strong running game. For the most part, the team's rushing had been divided up among Doug Dennison, Robert Newhouse, Scott Laidlaw, and Preston Pearson, but none of them were a breakaway threat, nor would any one of them even remotely approach the 1,000-yard rushing standard. In fact, the Cowboys' two top rushers that year combined would not total a thousand yards, and if ever there was a year of the runner, the Cowboys notwithstanding, it was 1976. A total of 12 NFL rushers would gain more than 1,000 yards that year. In the NFC, there would be Walter Payton (Bears), Delvin Williams (49ers), Lawrence McCutcheon (Rams), Chuck Foreman (Vikings), and Mike Thomas (Redskins); in the AFC: O. J. Simpson (Bills), Lydell Mitchell (Colts), Franco Harris (Steelers), Rocky Bleier (Steelers), Mark Van Eeghen (Raiders), Otis Armstrong (Broncos), and Greg Pruitt (Browns).

But the Cowboys managed to overcome their weaknesses, or at least make up for them in other ways, and

Thomas "Hollywood" Henderson adds a new dimension to the obligatory spike by introducing the crossbar slam-dunk. Here he stuffs the ball, à la Dr. J, over the Tampa Bay Buccaneer goal post after returning an interception 79 yards for a touchdown. The Cowboys defeated the Bucs, 23–7, at Texas Stadium that afternoon. (Dallas Cowboys)

trated that he was in the best of form, throwing for 242 yards and two touchdowns.

With exceptional passing, the Cowboys glided through the first five games of 1976, never really threatened in any one of them. At that point in the season, Staubach was high atop the ranking of NFL quarterbacks with a phenomenal 73.5% completion average. In one of those games, against the Colts, he had what would prove to be the most productive day passing in his entire career. That afternoon at Texas Stadium, he completed 22 of 28 passes for 339 yards.

By midseason, the Cowboys had lost only one game, and that had been a close one to the St. Louis Cardinals. They were a full game ahead of the Cardinals and the Washington Redskins, who were tied for second place in the NFC East with records of 5–2.

The Cowboys, however, now had two serious problems. Against the Chicago Bears, Roger Staubach had broken a finger, and it was hampering his passing. And the effect of an inhibited passing attack took on definite significance in light of the Cowboys' second problem.

continued their victorious course, thrashing in succession the Redskins, Giants, and Bills. Following that, the Cowboys were set back in two of their last four games, by the Falcons and the Redskins, but it didn't matter. When the regular season was over, their record of 11–3 was one game good enough to earn the NFC Eastern crown. The Redskins and Cardinals both trailed with records of 10–4.

Wide receiver Drew Pearson and safety Cliff Harris were named All-Pros after the 1976 season. Pearson had led the NFC in pass receptions that year (58). Efren Herrera made a fine comeback and ended up in a tie with Rick Szaro, New Orleans Saints' kicker, for the best field-goal percentage in the league (18 of 23 for 78%). Butch John-

son set a club record for yardage on punt returns (489), second only in Cowboy history to James Jones's 548 in 1980. And a raft of Cowboys were honored with invitations to the Pro Bowl: Billy Joe DuPree, Cliff Harris, Harvey Martin, Blaine Nye, Drew Pearson, Roger Staubach, Charlie Waters, and Randy White.

During the season, two more retired Cowboys were added to the Ring of Honor, Don Meredith and Don Perkins. The ceremony was held at Texas Stadium at halftime of the Cowboys-Giants game, and their names were now emblazoned on the stadium wall along with that of Bob Lilly. Of course, neither Meredith nor Perkins had ever had the pleasure of playing in the stadium where

Rookie Tony Dorsett shows some gymnastic prowess as he vaults over the St. Louis Cardinals for a Cowboy touchdown. By this, the ninth game of the 1977 season, Dorsett had secured the starting position at running back. The Cowboys needed more than his TD here, however, and ended up losing, 24–17, one of only two defeats the year of Super Bowl XII. Other identifiable Cowboys are tight end Billy Joe DuPree (89), tackle Ralph Neely (73), tight end Jay Saldi (87), and back Preston Pearson (26).   (Dallas Cowboys)

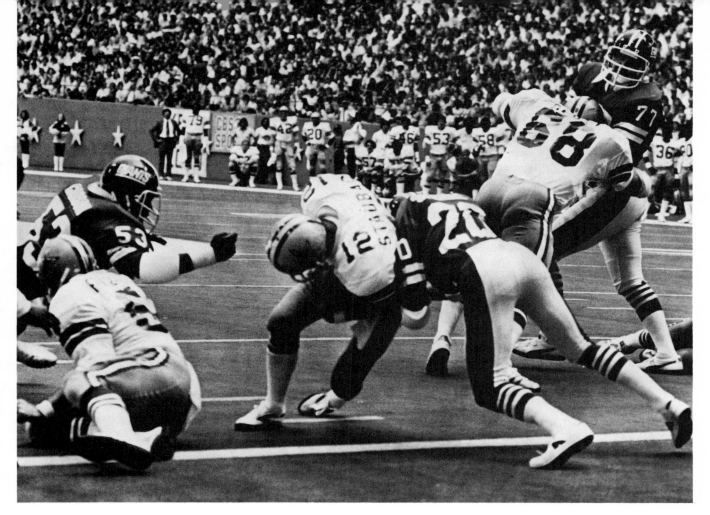

Roger Staubach knifes in for six points to launch a parade of touchdowns against the Giants in the 1977 Cowboy home opener. When it ended, Dallas had a 41–21 victory, their second in what was to become an 8-game win streak, the longest in the club's history. The Cowboy on the ground is center John Fitzgerald; No. 68 is guard Herb Scott. The Giants are Harry Carson (53), Jim Stienke (20), and Troy Archer (77).   (Dallas Cowboys)

their names were honored; both had played only in the antiquated Cotton Bowl.

The divisional playoff game for Dallas was set for December 19 on the Cowboys' home field against the NFC West champs, the Los Angeles Rams. The runner-up in the NFC East, the Washington Redskins, qualified as the wild card, and they would go to Minnesota to play the Vikings.

Pat Haden, who had come from the defunct WFL, had taken over the Rams' quarterbacking chores in the latter part of the season, replacing James Harris. The Rams' passing game had been excellent, and that, along with outstanding rushing efforts from Lawrence McCutcheon and John Cappelletti, was enough to give them the highest scoring offense in the NFC that year. Their defense ranked second in allowing the fewest points; the game was rated a tossup.

The Cowboys scored on an Efren Herrera field goal in the first quarter, a 44 yarder which was just two yards short of his season's longest. The Rams' Pat Haden then ran the ball in from the 4-yard line for the game's first touchdown. The Cowboys countered with a 1-yard plunge from Scott Laidlaw to take a 10–7 lead into the locker room at halftime.

No one scored in the third quarter. The Rams were trying very hard to give the game to the Cowboys. But for some strange reason, the Cowboys would not accept it. When the day would finally end, the Rams would have to remember the two punts that were blocked by Charlie Waters, his interception, and the other two passes stolen by cornerback Benny Barnes. But despite this largess, the Cowboys were unable to take advantage of it that day. The offense could not dredge up a score of any kind in the fourth quarter. The lone touchdown the Rams came up with when Larry McCutcheon bucked in from the 1 was all that was needed. As time ran out, the Rams' punter Rusty Jackson did not bother to punt the ball from his own end zone, and so the Cowboys were awarded their only 2 points of the second half on a safety. The final score was 14–12, and the Cowboys' hopes for another Super Bowl appearance came to a frustrating end.

The following week, it was the Rams' turn to be disappointed when the Vikings, behind Fran Tarkenton and Chuck Foreman, totally dominated the NFC championship game, 24–13. The Vikes, an expansion team one year younger than the Cowboys, became the first NFL team to appear in four Super Bowls. But for all Minnesota had going for it, they could not break the AFC's almost total monopoly of the NFL championship and fell to the Oakland Raiders, 32–14. With the end of the 1976 season, only once since the Green Bay Packers of 1967 had an NFC team walked off with the Super Bowl trophy. And that team, of course, had been the Cowboys of 1971.

1977

Preseason

Dallas	(3-3)	Opponents
34	San Diego (59,504) @ Dallas	14
17	Seattle (58,789) @ Seattle (OT)	23
14	Miami (56,820) @ Dallas	20
23	Baltimore (54,835) @ Dallas	21
14	Houston (49,777) @ Houston	23
30	Pittsburgh (49,824) @ Dallas	0

Regular Season

		(12-2)	
W	16	Minnesota (47,678) OT	10
W	41	N.Y. Giants (64,215) (H)	21
W	23	Tampa Bay (55,316) (H)	7
W	30	St. Louis (50,129)	24
W	34	Washington (62,115) (H)	16
W	16	Philadelphia (65,507)	10
W	37	Detroit (63,160) (H)	0
W	24	N.Y. Giants (74,532)	10
L	17	St. Louis (64,038) (H)	24
L	13	Pittsburgh (49,761)	28
W	14	Washington (55,031)	7
W	24	Philadelphia (60,289) (H)	14
W	42	San Francisco (55,848)	35
W	14	Denver (63,752) (H)	6
	345		212

Postseason

		Divisional Playoff	
		(Dallas)	
W	37	Chicago (62,920)	7
		NFC Championship Game	
		(Dallas)	
W	23	Minnesota (61,968)	6
		Super Bowl XII (New Orleans)	
W	27	Denver (76,400)	10

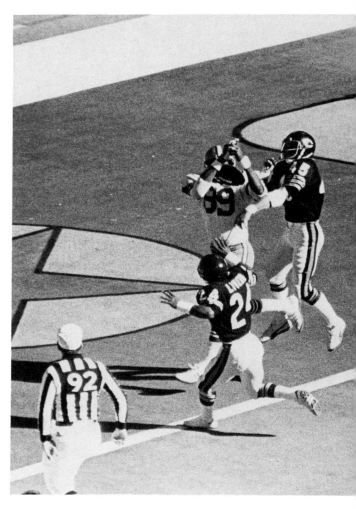

Tight end Billy Joe DuPree (89) goes up between two Chicago Bear defenders to snag this TD pass in the second quarter of the 1977 divisional playoff game in Dallas. It was one of four touchdowns that day for the Cowboys but DuPree's only reception. The Bears are Virgil Livers (24) and Gary Fencik (45). (Dallas Cowboys)

The lackadaisical running game of the Dallas Cowboys in 1976 would be remedied the next season, it was hoped, by the draft of Tony Dorsett, a unanimous All-American from the University of Pittsburgh and the winner of the 1976 Heisman Award trophy. To get Dorsett, the Cowboys wheeled and dealed a little with the Seattle Seahawks, who, as a result of their awful 1976 season (2–12), had a much higher first-round draft choice. In exchange for their first pick, the Seahawks received the Cowboys' first-round choice as well as three second-round selections, which they had accumulated from other trades. Dorsett, everyone around the Dallas headquarters felt, had the potential for the really big running play. He was a breakaway runner, one who would keep opposing defenses honest at all times, one who would provide the needed complement to Roger Staubach's passing game.

The Cowboys also acquired another speedster in the 1977 draft, Tony Hill, a wide receiver from Stanford. Less fleet perhaps but still important products of the draft were defensive tackle Dave Stalls (Northern Colorado), offensive tackle Andy Frederick (New Mexico), quarterback Glenn Carano (Nevada/Las Vegas), and linebacker Guy Brown (Houston). The Cowboys also signed as free agents running back Larry Brinson (Florida) and linebacker Bruce Huther (New Hampshire).

Once again, the Cowboys moved through their preseason with a split record, 3–3. The highlight was the return visit of the Steelers to Texas Stadium for the last exhibition game, which proved to be heavenly rapture for the Cowboys and their 50,000 rooters as the Cowboys shut out the supposedly dynastic Steelers 30–0.

It was, apparently, inspirational because the Cowboys charged into the regular season with the same kind of ferocity. They seemed obsessed with asserting themselves, and they did it in grand fashion, forging for themselves the longest winning streak in their history, eight straight games.

It began with the closest game, which also was the Cowboys' very first overtime game. The NFC defending champions, the Minnesota Vikings, were the host on a hot, humid Sunday afternoon in mid-September. The Cowboys took the field without Lee Roy Jordan and Blaine Nye, both of whom had retired, and Rayfield Wright, who was about to undergo knee surgery. Eleven-year veteran Preston Pearson had gotten the call to start ahead of rookie Tony Dorsett.

The Cowboys were losing to the Vikings in the fourth quarter, but they came from behind to take a 10–7 lead when Roger Staubach hit Preston Pearson with a 7-yard TD toss. But with 1:35 left in the game, the Vikes ever-reliable Fred Cox kicked a 35-yard field goal to tie it. The Cowboys had one last chance to win the game in regulation time. Butch Johnson ran the kickoff back 48 yards, and Staubach passed the Cowboys all the way down to the Vikings' 15-yard line. With six seconds on the clock, Efren Herrera tried for the field goal but missed. It was actually the first time in his three years with the Cowboys that he had missed a field goal inside the 30-yard line.

The Vikings won the toss of the coin and would receive the overtime kickoff. Fran Tarkenton moved them to their 45, but then the Dallas defense rose to the occasion. Harvey Martin, now sporting the nickname "Too Mean," charged Tarkenton and forced him to throw the ball away, flagrantly enough to incur a 15-yard penalty for grounding. On the next play, it was Larry Cole. He sacked Tarkenton for a loss of 9 yards. The Vikings, nowhere near a first down, were forced to punt, but Neil Clabo shanked

Ernie Stautner on:

Bob Lilly: *"Bob Lilly is the number one defensive player that we've had. And anytime you have a man like that on your team, you get him to play your defense, but still you do not take away his natural freedom. Bob has such great quickness. He had excellent strength. He had good size. He was 6 feet 5 inches, 259, and he was extremely quick. He could go around a block and make the play where another lineman with the normal type of professional ability, who is damn good, couldn't make those type of plays. Bob disciplined himself, and his experience told him to do things with his ability; he had an uncanny sense to be where the action was."*

George Andrie: *"George Andrie is another who did an excellent job for us. George probably was one of the best technique men I've had at the end spot. Tremendous. We have a technique that we call a 'crash,' where our end makes a very strong move with the snap of the ball, and George probably did that better than any of them I've had yet."*

Larry Cole: *"Hell, I taught him how to make touchdowns. No, really, the first year he came with us he scored two touchdowns against the Redskins, one in each game and the second year he scored another touchdown against them. [In 1980, Larry Cole scored his fourth touchdown, and again it was against the Redskins, on an interception he returned 43 yards.] When I first saw Larry at a rookie workout, I thought, my God, what an awkward guy. But Larry wasn't and he would always make the big play. When we played the Rams in the playoffs a couple of years ago, he's the one who made the big plays out there. Larry's not the fastest guy in the world, the quickest movement, but damned if he doesn't know how to make the big play."*

Jethro Pugh: *"Jethro was one of the best tackle technique men we've ever had. Jethro probably would have been an All-Pro with us several years, had it not been for [Bob] Lilly. Lilly was known to be so great he overshadowed Jethro. Jethro was a very solid, stabilizing factor in our defenses."*

All alone, Golden Richards waits for this 32-yard pass from Roger Staubach. It fell into his arms and he turned and stepped into the end zone for the Cowboys' first touchdown in their 23–6 romp over the Vikings in the 1977 NFC championship game. Chasing in vain are Minnesota defensive backs Bobby Bryant (20) and Paul Krause (22). (Dallas Cowboys)

it, and Minnesota only gained 26 yards.

Roger Staubach then took over, and the Cowboys moved. Two passes to Drew Pearson, another to Golden Richards, and the Cowboys were at the Minnesota 15. Robert Newhouse bulled his way into the line and moved the ball to the 9. Efren Herrera was dancing around, warming himself up on the sideline, hoping to be able to atone for his still-paining gaffe at the end of the fourth quarter. Preston Pearson carried the ball to the 4, and the Cowboys had a first down and goal. Then Staubach rolled to his left and found a hole big enough to send a posse through, let alone a single Cowboy, and he stepped untouched into the end zone. The touchdown made the score 16–10, and the Cowboys' chores for the day were over.

Only one of the next seven wins was even close. That was the game against the Cardinals up at St. Louis. In the fourth quarter, Dallas was losing 24–16 and had to stage a dramatic comeback. Two touchdowns, a 1-yard plunge by Dorsett, and a 17-yard pass from Staubach to Golden Richards did turn the game around for the Cowboys and

kept intact their perfect record. After the eight wins, the Cowboys had outscored their opponents 221–98, and they were far out in front in the NFC East. The Cardinals were in second place, but they had already suffered three losses.

The Cowboys ran into some sticky going in the next two games and lost to the Cardinals and the Steelers. But they rebounded and surged through the last four games with ease, defeating the Denver Broncos in the last game of the season, a training ground perhaps for the Super Bowl to come in a month or so.

Five Cowboys won All-Pro honors in 1977: safeties Cliff Harris and Charlie Waters, defensive end Harvey Martin, wide receiver Drew Pearson, and place kicker Efren Herrera. Former linebacker Chuck Howley became the fourth Cowboy to be named to the Ring of Honor; the ceremony was held at halftime of their game with the Detroit Lions. To add to the festivity of it all, the Cowboys at that intermission were basking in a 23-point lead and were on their way to a 37–0 shutout.

Roger Staubach led the NFC in practically every area

of passing that year. He was ranked first in the conference, threw for the most yards (2,620), the most TDs (18, actually tied with Ron Jaworsky of the Eagles), the most completions (210), the most yards per attempt (7.3), and the lowest percentage of interceptions (2.5).

Tony Dorsett, who did not become a full-time starter until the tenth game of the season, was named Rookie of the Year and became the first Cowboy ever to rush for more than 1,000 yards in his premier season (1,007). He was the ninth most productive rusher in the NFL that year, and Drew Pearson led the league in the number of yards gained on pass receptions (870).

The Chicago Bears managed to slip into the playoffs in 1977 as a wild-card entry, the first time they had made a postseason appearance since they had won the NFL crown back in 1963. They would come down to Texas Stadium to become the first visitor of what later was

Before Super Bowl XII

Some random quotes from before Super Bowl XII:

"We bent the Steel, We crushed the Snake. Dallas is going to be a piece of cake." (referring to the Steelers and to Raider quarterback Kenny "Snake" Stabler)
—An unidentified Bronco fan

"I predict the Broncos will win this one."
—Howard Cosell

"Orange Crush is soda water, baby, you drink it. It don't win football games."
—Harvey "Too Mean" Martin, Dallas Cowboys

Roger Staubach finds little pressure as he lofts a pass in the first round of the 1977 playoffs against the wild-card Chicago Bears. The rest of the afternoon was just as easy, and the Cowboys breezed to a 37–7 win. The other identifiable Cowboys in the picture are center John Fitzgerald (on the ground), Ralph Neely (73), and Tony Dorsett (33). The Bears are Mike Hartenstine (73), Jim Osborne (68), Ron Rydalch (76), and Billy Newsome (87). (Dallas Cowboys)

Fullback Robert Newhouse slashes through the Washington Redskin defense on his way to a touchdown in this 1977 game. Newhouse, who ranks third in all-time rushing yardage for the Cowboys, had a fine game that afternoon at Texas Stadium, scoring two touchdowns, as the Cowboys clobbered the Redskins 34–16. The unsuccessful Redskin tackler is Diron Talbert (72). (Dallas Cowboys)

described as "the Cowboys postseason slaughterhouse."

The Bears' quarterback, Bob Avellini, threw four interceptions that afternoon, three to Cowboy safety Charlie Waters (an NFL playoff record), while the Cowboy offense sustained a steady and decimating assault. Going into the fourth quarter, the Cowboys led 34–0, and they ended the day with a definitive win, 37–7.

The Minnesota Vikings won their divisional playoff game by edging the Rams 14–7. It would be their fourth trip to the National Football Conference championship in five years, and it would be the second time they would face the Cowboys in that classic. At the same time, it was the Cowboys' sixth appearance in the NFC championship in eight years.

Dallas not only had the home-field advantage, but the Vikings would have to play without the services of their ace quarterback Fran Tarkenton. After coming up with the best completion percentage in the league that year (60.1%), he had been injured. Back-up Bob Lee would have to direct the Viking attack.

The bone-crushing Dallas defense allowed the "Purple Gang," as they were now being called, only two field goals all day, while Roger Staubach and his gang ran up 23 points for another easy victory. The slaughterhouse was working at full capacity, and now it would be relocated in New Orleans for Super Bowl XII.

That game, scheduled for January 15, would be the first Super Bowl to be played indoors but not the first NFL championship to have that dubious honor. Back in 1932, a game that was to decide the title between the Chicago Bears, with their star backs Red Grange and Bronko Nagurski, and the Portsmouth (Ohio) Spartans was played in the Chicago Stadium, an arena more accustomed to basketball or hockey games or the circus. Because of the size of the arena, that game was played on a field only 80 yards long, and it was the first game where

---

Going in Style

With Super Bowl XII marking the Cowboys' fourth visit to that classic, they knew how to do it now with style. Their act was described this way in Sports Illustrated.

"For its part, the Cowboys organization had learned from past experience . . . that too much time can be squandered unless someone is there to take care of every little detail. Things like getting a car for a player or a plane reservation for his wife, or a dinner reservation for a distant cousin at Moran's or Antoine's. Thus, Dallas had a special squad of people assigned to do nothing but conquer the French Quarter. The organization set up an elaborate office with seven secretaries who were there to do nothing more than handle player requests, and those of Cowboy owner Clint Murchison, General Manager Tex Schramm, Landry, and their pals. If Harvey Martin wanted to go to the King Tut exhibition to see what a real mummy looked like, as opposed to those in Pat O'Brien's or Galatoire's, a special secretary handled it. The Cowboys were also prepared to get tickets, sometimes in huge quantity, for any friend of the Texans'. They even had a team acupuncturist in town."

hashmarks were used (because the walls of the arena were only a foot or two from the sideline).

The Louisiana Superdome was certainly a world apart from the strange indoor arena of 1932. More than 76,000 people would pay $30 each for a seat and jam into it to watch the Cowboys face the Denver Broncos on Super Sunday. (Only 11,000 watched the Bears-Spartans match back in 1932.) It would also be viewed by the largest TV audience in the history of the tube, at least up to that time. More than 85 million viewers were expected to sit before TV screens and stare at the game which would decide the NFL champ for 1977.

The Super Bowl was truly a multimillion-dollar affair by 1977. The league would get $4.5 million from CBS for the telecast, and CBS would charge its sponsors as much as $325,000 a minute for commercials. Each member of

the winning team would get a total playoff bonus of $32,-000, and each member of the losing team would be consoled with $23,000. They would also get rings; $42,000 was set aside for the fingers of the winners, while the losers would have to settle for rings that could be fashioned for $21,000.

Super Bowl week attracted celebrities and fans alike to New Orleans. And TV was at the center of it all. As one sportswriter put it, "CBS has everyone down here, except William Paley, Walter Cronkite, and Carroll O'Connor." There was a huge pregame television extravaganza, a 90-minute special featuring everybody from Joe Namath to Billy Carter. And there was a TV guided tour into the French Quarter hosted by former players and well-known bon vivants Paul Hornung, Nick Buoniconti, and Sonny Jurgensen. And finally there would be the game with the

Such a familiar sight: Drew Pearson outracing a defender into the end zone to gather in another touchdown pass. Pearson has caught more passes for the Cowboys than any other player in the team's history. Here, he is beating Buffalo Bill defensive back Doug Jones, in a 1976 regular-season game the Cowboys won 17–10.   (Dallas Cowboys)

voices of Pat Summerall and Tom Brookshier, with intermediary comments by Phyllis George, Jimmy the Greek, and Brent Musburger.

The Denver Broncos were truly a Cinderella team, and there was the constant comparison with the famous New York Jets of 1968, who surprised everyone by wrenching the NFL title from the NFC for the first time. The Broncos were even likened to another New York team from another sport when they were dubbed "the Mets of the Mountains." The team had also cultivated one of the most boisterous and enthusiastic groups of fans ever, and they were so fervid that the whole scene gained the name "Broncomania," and the term became a part of the pro-football lexicon.

The Broncos had had a fine season (12–2), edging out the ever-explosive Oakland Raiders to win the AFC West. They went to the playoffs for the first time in their history and did away with the mighty Pittsburgh Steelers, while people in Denver went literally mad with the color of orange, which signified winner to everyone. Then they

The starting lineups for Super Bowl XII:

Dallas Cowboys		Denver Broncos
Offense		
Golden Richards	WR	Jack Dolbin
Drew Pearson	WR	Haven Moses
Billy Joe DuPree	TE	Riley Odoms
Ralph Neely	T	Andy Maurer
Pat Donovan	T	Claudie Minor
Herbert Scott	G	Tom Glassic
Tom Rafferty	G	Paul Howard
John Fitzgerald	C	Mike Montler
Roger Staubach	QB	Craig Morton
Tony Dorsett	RB	Otis Armstrong
Robert Newhouse	RB	Jon Keyworth
Defense		
"Too Tall" Jones	E	Barney Chevous
Harvey Martin	E	Bob Swenson
Jethro Pugh	T	Ruben Carter
Randy White	T	Lyle Alzado
Thomas Henderson	LLB	Joe Rizzo
Bob Breunig	MLB	Randy Grandishar
D. D. Lewis	RLB	Tom Jackson
Benny Barnes	LCB	Louie Wright
Aaron Kyle	RCB	Steve Foley
Charlie Waters	S	Bill Thompson
Cliff Harris	S	Bernie Jackson

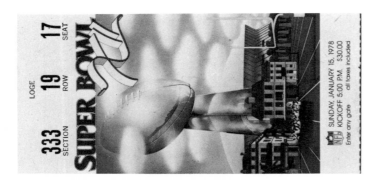

Preston Pearson became a free agent in 1975 after 9 years in the NFL. The Cowboys picked him up and found to their great pleasure one of the most reliable clutch players ever to don a Dallas uniform. Both as a running back and as a receiver he would be part of some of the Cowboys' most crucial plays during his 6-year tenure with the team. Pearson holds the club record for pass receptions for a running back (47 in one season) and is the fifth-ranking pass receiver in Cowboy history. He is the only player in the NFL ever to appear in Super Bowls with three different teams (Colts, Steelers, Cowboys). (Dallas Cowboys)

It is third down and 10 for the Cowboys in Super Bowl XII when Roger Staubach decides to go for broke and unleashes a 45-yard bomb. Wide receiver Butch Johnson makes a spectacular diving catch and falls into the end zone for the touchdown. It was Staubach's only TD pass of the day during a game in which the Cowboys could do no wrong. The final score was 27–10, bringing the Cowboys their second Super Bowl crown.   (Vernon Biever)

sank the Oakland Raiders and won the AFC title.

The Broncos had the best defense in the entire AFC, allowing only 148 points to be scored on them (an average of just a little over 10.5 points a game). They were called the "Orange Crush," and they gave up the fewest yards rushing in the league; the Cowboys, incidentally, were runner-up in that same category.

Former Dallas Cowboy Craig Morton was the Bronco's quarterback, and he ranked second that year in the AFC behind only Bob Griese of the Miami Dolphins. His favorite receivers were tight end Riley Odoms and wide receiver Haven Moses. The running game was divided up among Otis Armstrong, Lonnie Perrin, and Rob Lytle. None of them, however, had gained over 500 yards for the year.

The game was billed, at least by *Time* magazine, as "Broncomania vs. Cowboy Cool." Dallas was a 6-point

MVPs

The award for Most Valuable Player in Super Bowl XII was shared by Randy "Manster" White and Harvey "Too Mean" Martin. Presented by Sport *magazine, the award included a Ford automobile of the player's choice. This was the first time two players were so honored, and each got a Ford.*

favorite, and most serious handicappers were saying that the experience of Dallas and their wonderfully balanced attack would be just too much for the colorful, high-flying Cinderella team from Denver.

The Denver partisans arrived in New Orleans with everything orange—orange clothes, orange pennants and banners; one fan even had painted his skin that shocking hue. It was all a message and a well-orchestrated one; only the Broncos on the field never quite heard the symphony.

The Cowboys received the opening kickoff but were unable to gain and had to punt the ball away. Denver may have been instilled with Broncomania, but they quickly found out that the Cowboys much-praised defense had only one thing in mind—broncobusting. The front four would beat and batter the hapless Bronco offense all afternoon, and the fiery emotion that was so much a part of the Denver fans would fizzle and die like an old ember.

The Cowboys scored first. Tony Dorsett sliced in from the 3-yard line for a touchdown in the first quarter. Not long after that, Efren Herrera booted a 35-yard field goal for a 10-point lead.

For the Broncos, Craig Morton, who had had such a fine regular season, was having one of the worst after-noons of his football life. In the first half alone, he threw four interceptions, a Super Bowl record. At the same time, the Broncos could not run with the ball. At halftime, their entire rushing output was only 44 yards. Nor could they hold on to the ball; besides Morton's four interceptions, they had turned three fumbles over to the Cowboys—seven turnovers in one half, another disenchanting Super Bowl benchmark.

The score was only 13–0 at the half, however—the Broncos eminently fortunate it wasn't something like 35–0 after all the gifts they had laid at the Cowboys' feet. In the third quarter, Morton was no better and eventually was taken out of the game by Bronco coach Red Miller. He had had such a fine year, but this January day he could not get anything going, his stats a disappointing 4 comple-tions of 15 passes for a meager 39 yards and, of course, his four interceptions. Back-up quarterback Norris Weese replaced him.

Nothing really went right for Denver Bronco quarterback and former Cowboy, Craig Morton, during Super Bowl XII. Here, he finds his face being rearranged by the massive hand of Too Tall Jones (72). Morton threw 4 interceptions that afternoon before being replaced by back-up quarterback Norris Weese. The Dallas defense gave up only 156 net yards in their fourth appearance in the 12 years of Super Bowls. (Vernon Biever)

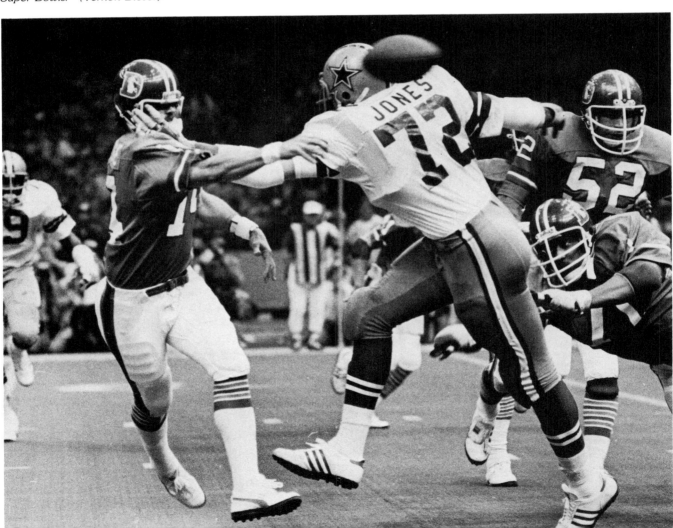

The spoils of victory. Tex Schramm triumphantly holds aloft the Vince Lombardi Trophy, awarded for the Cowboys' success in Super Bowl XII. (Dallas Cowboys)

The Broncos had managed a field goal before Morton exited the game, a 47 yarder by Jim Turner. But the Cowboys countered with a score of their own. On third and ten at the Bronco 45, Roger Staubach opted for the bomb and unleashed a long pass which Butch Johnson dove for and caught in the end zone on his fingertips. It was one of the most spectacular touchdown plays in Super Bowl history.

Norris Weese brought a little better fortune to the Broncos. After Rich Upchurch returned a Dallas kickoff all the way back to the Cowboys' 26-yard line, he moved the Broncos to the one, where rookie Rob Lytle smashed in for the score. With Turner's extra point, the Broncos trailed by 10. But that was all they could muster. The Dallas defense remained ornery and niggardly and totally denied the Broncos any offensive life whatsoever. Then, with the last period about half over, the Broncos gave up their fourth fumble of the day, this one recovered by cornerback Aaron Kyle on the Denver 29-yard line. It was time for a little Cowboy razzle-dazzle. On the first play, Staubach handed off to Robert Newhouse on what ap-

The pleasures of winning a Super Bowl are reflected here in the expressions of two young men who contributed substantially to that outcome in XII: the right side of the Cowboy defensive line, tackle Randy White (54) and end Harvey Martin (79). (Vernon Biever)

peared to be a sweep left. Following his blockers, New-house suddenly pulled up, cocked his arm, and let fly with a pass to Golden Richards, who was streaking down the sideline. It landed in his outstretched hands, and he went in for the final touchdown of the day. The score was Cowboys 27, Broncos 10.

For the Denver Broncos, it had been a day of forgetta-ble records: most fumbles, most interceptions, fewest yards gained, fewest first downs, and other similarly un-happy stats. But for the Cowboys the game was some-thing else altogether. It was their second world champion-ship—at that point in NFL history no team had won more Super Bowls. The Packers, the Dolphins, and the Steelers each had two Super Bowl victories, and now Dallas was a part of that illustrious union.

It had been one of their most magnificent seasons. They had been awesome in the regular season and savage in the playoffs, and now they had another handsome silver trophy to take back to Tex Schramm's office in Dallas.

After Super Bowl XII

Some random quotes from after Bowl XII:

"And so it was in Super Bowl XII . . . Dallas's superior resources struck midnight on Denver's Cinderella sea-son."

— *John Facenda, narrator*

"This is the greatest Cowboy team ever."
— *Mel Renfro, Dallas Cowboys*

"This is really exciting. The Super Bowl is one of the greatest things in sports. This team has worked hard all year and they paid the price. They deserved it."
— *Tom Landry*

"They were a little better than we were today . . . The turnovers hurt."

— *Red Miller, Bronco Coach and master of understatement*

"I've played some bad games. I certainly played one today . . . Now we'll start preparing to get back in this thing next year."

— *Craig Morton, Denver Broncos*

"I'm going to give this [the Vince Lombardi trophy for winning the Super Bowl] to Tom Landry, who is not only the coach of the year, but the coach of the century."
— *Clint Murchison, owner, Dallas Cowboys*

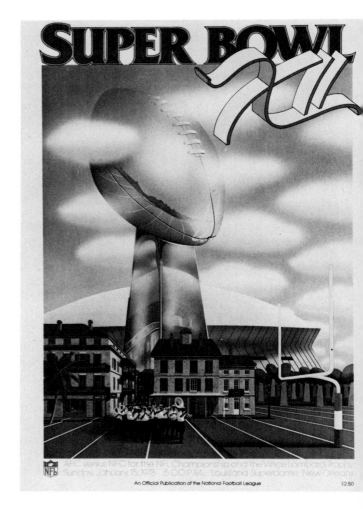

AFC versus NFC for the NFL Championship and the Vince Lombardi Trophy. Sunday, January 15, 1978 · 5:00 P.M. · Louisiana Superdome, New Orleans

An Official Publication of the National Football League $2.50

15 The Battle for the 1970s

THE COWBOYS OF 1978, it was said, were a team for all seasons, a perfect blend of high-scoring, yardage-gobbling offense and punitive defense. A thunderstorm in an otherwise placid conference, they were expected to deluge all opponents even though they were playing one of the most difficult schedules in the league. As Joe Marshall in *Sports Illustrated* wrote: "This was the season the Dallas Cowboys were supposed to be undefeated, untied, unscored upon, and under orders from NFL headquarters to hold the score down."

It would be a longer regular season, with 16 games now instead of 14 and a shorter exhibition period, cut back to four games. Ralph Neely had retired after a distinguished 13-year career in a Cowboy uniform. And youth seemed to be the order of the day. Only seven players could trace their Cowboy heritage back to that first Dallas Super Bowl in 1971, while 28 had joined the club within the last four years.

It had been an especially lean draft that year, at least according to what Dallas had become accustomed to. They did, however, sign defensive end Larry Bethea from Michigan State, their first-round choice, and defensive back Dennis Thurman, an alumnus of Southern Cal. And a new place kicker joined the Cowboys, free agent Rafael Septien, whose release from the Los Angeles Rams was as timely as it was essential to the Cowboys' well-being. Efren Herrera and the Dallas front office had not been able to agree on contract terms, and so Herrera had been traded to the Seattle Seahawks.

Tony Hill managed to take the starting job at wide receiver away from Golden Richards, who would move

from the bench to the Chicago Bears before the season would end. And 38-year-old tight end Jackie Smith would be enticed out of retirement after Jay Saldi was injured. Smith, during a 15-year career with the St. Louis Cardinals, had been one of the best tight ends in the game, right up there along with the likes of John Mackey and Charlie Sanders.

As the football year got underway, it certainly looked like the kind of Cowboy season everyone was predicting. In exhibitions, the Cowboys doused the lights on the Steelers for the fourth preseason in a row, this time 16–13, and did away handily with their foes from the preceding year's Super Bowl, the Broncos, 21–14. They lost only one game due to a little staleness on an afternoon the Houston Oilers came up to Texas Stadium.

The Cowboys opened the regular season before a national TV audience and clearly indicated to them that they were watching the legitimately crowned NFL champions. They virtually obliterated the Baltimore Colts on a Monday night in early September when even Howard Cosell was pressed to find enough superlatives in his overworked thesaurus to describe the 38–0 massacre. The Cowboys gained a total of 583 yards that evening while their omniverous defense allowed only 181. Roger Staubach threw four touchdown passes, including a 91 yarder to Tony Dorsett and another for 38 yards to Drew Pearson. Dorsett also picked up 147 yards on 15 rushes and another 107 yards with his three receptions.

The next week, it was the New York Giants, and the Cowboys picked them apart at Giants Stadium up in East Rutherford, New Jersey, 34–24. Tony Dorsett had an-

1978 COWBOYS

1978 Dallas Cowboys. Front row: Rafael Septien, Danny White, Roger Staubach, Glenn Carano, Doug Dennison, Alois Blackwell, Aaron Kyle, Preston Pearson, Benny Barnes. Second row: Dennis Thurman, Tony Dorsett, Scott Laidlaw, Charlie Waters, Randy Hughes, Cliff Harris, Robert Newhouse, Mark Washington, D. D. Lewis. Third row: Bob Breunig, Randy White, Thomas Henderson, Bruce Huther, Mike Hegman, Guy Brown, Tom Randall, Jim Cooper, John Fitzgerald. Fourth row: Larry Cole, Tom Rafferty, Dave Stalls, Burton Lawless, Pat Donovan, Herbert Scott, Rayfield Wright, Andy Frederick, Ed Jones. Fifth row: Jethro Pugh, Larry Bethea, Harvey Martin, Tony Hill, Golden Richards, Butch Johnson, Jay Saldi, Drew Pearson, Billy Joe DuPree. Top row: Tom Landry, Jim Myers, Mike Ditka, Dan Reeves, Gene Stallings, Ernie Stautner, Jerry Tubbs, Bob Ward, Don Cochren, Buck Buchanan, Ken Locker. (Dallas Cowboys)

other 100-yard rushing game (111) and Staubach another 200-yard passing day (212).

Then something started to go wrong. Suddenly, they no longer looked like the class of the conference. On the field, the enthusiasm had turned to sloth, and the rampage dwindled to not much more than a spirited walk. They began to lose football games. First it was to the Rams, then the Washington Redskins. At midseason, they were 6–2, certainly a respectable record, but they were not the dominating force everyone had expected. They just did not look good; something was wrong. Two games later, it was evident how wrong things were. They had

sunk to a record of 6–4, and it appeared they might not even get into the playoffs that year.

Tom Landry and his cadre of assistants were putting in lots of overtime hours trying to figure out just what was happening to his gold-plated team. He knew part of the problem. There was always a comedown from winning the big one, a deflation the season after Super Bowl success. He remembered: "After we won the Super Bowl in 1971, we never played with intensity the next year . . . the distractions hurt—the endorsements, the appearances, the contract negotiations. You can't stop guys from getting all they can but it's tough to try and run a football team with all of it."

His quarterback agreed. Roger Staubach noted, "I think it was the Super Bowl syndrome, just not giving it everything you've got. We were inconsistent, tentative, as if waiting for the other guy to do something to get us out of the slump."

With the Cowboys reeling and now haunted by the nightmare that they might have to stow their pads and helmets at the end of the regular season, almost unheard of around Dallas for more than a decade, the message to the players was transmitted. Neither Landry nor Staubach were in the mood to accept a comedown that large. On a positive note, both kept reminding everyone else that the Cowboys of 1970 and 1971 also went to Super Bowls V and VI from the midseason pits. In 1970, they were a dismal 5–4 before winning their last five in a row. And in 1971 they were 4–3 before rattling off a streak of seven consecutive victories. Tom Landry retrenched to the basics. "I have no magic solution, just hard work. Cowboys in other years have had to overcome adversity before and they did it. This team has character, but up to now they haven't had to overcome adversity. Now they do, and now we'll find out just how much character they do have."

Having lost in successive weeks to the Vikings and the Dolphins, the next game up in Green Bay became a very meaningful one. Under normal conditions, the Packers would have been considered only nominal competition that year. But under the circumstances, they had to be taken very seriously; the Cowboys simply could not afford to lose to them. Green Bay would have to be the pivotal game if the Cowboys were to nourish any hope for postseason play.

And it was up in that Wisconsin town that the Cowboys regained the form they had evinced at the start of the season. They scored early and then often. The defense was suddenly destroying runners and passers alike. The Cowboys ran up 42 points and gained 537 yards that afternoon, and they allowed the Packers only two touchdowns and a mere 142 yards. Staubach passed for 200 yards, and Tony Dorsett ran for 149. Even Robert Newhouse had his first 100-yard game of the season (101).

Next it was the New Orleans Saints. And again it was a Tony Dorsett day (152 yards on 25 carries). It was an easy 27–7 win. The next week, there was a crucial game with the Redskins. They were always a threat, could rise to the occasion, and there was no team they would rather play spoilers to than Dallas. But they didn't that year. The Redskins, in fact, were never in the game, and the final score was 37–10. The Cowboys' adrenaline was going now, and they surged through the remainder of the season, knocking off the Patriots, the Eagles, and the Jets.

The game with the Eagles was one the Cowboys had wanted sorely, although they were not in real jeopardy of turning over the division title to them that year. The Eagles were a vastly improved team and would be a contender very soon. The Cowboys had managed to barely sneak by them earlier in the year, 14–7 at Texas Stadium, and the Eagles were flying high now behind the passing of Ron Jaworsky, the pass catching of Harold Carmichael, and the running of Wilbur Montgomery. The Cowboys wanted to put them in their place, and they did on a

Tony "Thrill" Hill, two years out of Stanford, became a starter in his second year with the Cowboys in 1978. First with Roger Staubach and later with Danny White, Hill would add some of the most dazzling moments in the history of the Cowboy passing game. He would lead the team in receptions in 1979 and 1980; appear in the Pro Bowl for 1978, 1979, and 1980; and become the only Dallas receiver to gain more than 1,000 yards in two consecutive seasons since Bob Hayes did it back in 1965–1966. (Dallas Cowboys)

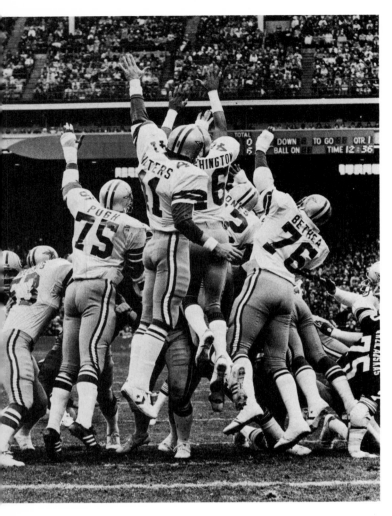

A virtual wall of Dallas Cowboys rises to try to block this Green Bay Packer extra point in 1978. From the left: Bob Breunig (53), Jethro Pugh (75), Charlie Waters (41), Mark Washington (46), Too Tall Jones (72), and Larry Bethea (76). The extra point was good, but the Cowboys mauled the Packers in Milwaukee that day, 42–14. (Vernon Biever)

blustery, cold December day in Philadelphia's Veterans Stadium, 31–13, fully asserting themselves as the division's predominant force and perhaps kindling a fire for revenge which would erupt in flames in the not too distant future.

Once again, the Cowboys had faced the adversity Tom Landry talked about and prevailed, turning a disappointing beginning into a division crown with a six-game winning streak.

When the statistics were all tallied, Roger Staubach headed the NFL ranking of quarterbacks, his rating one-tenth of one point above Terry Bradshaw of the Steelers (84.9 to 84.8). It was the third time he was honored as the NFL's premier quarterback. Tony Dorsett was the third

most productive rusher in the league, trailing only the Houston Oilers' Earl Campbell and Chicago Bears' Walter Payton. Dorsett's 1,325 yards set a club record, and he became only the second Dallas rusher to have back-to-back 1,000-yard years (Calvin Hill did it in 1972–1973).

The Cowboys monopolized both safety positions on the All-Pro team of 1978, with Cliff Harris and Charlie Waters. And Randy "Manster" White, given the nickname because he was such a unique combination of man and monster, was a unanimous selection at defensive tackle.

The Cowboys' first test in the playoffs would be at home against the Atlanta Falcons. In 1978, the postseason picture was changed in the NFL, and now two wild-card teams would go to the playoffs. The Falcons were one of them that year and they qualified to meet Dallas

1978

Preseason

Dallas	(3-1)	Opponents
41	San Francisco (63,736) @ Dallas	24
21	Denver (74,619) @ Denver	14
13	Houston (62,242) @ Dallas	27
16	Pittsburgh (59,747) @ Dallas	13

Regular Season

		(12-4)	
W	38	Baltimore (64,224) (H)	0
W	34	N.Y. Giants (73,265)	24
L	14	Los Angeles (65,749)	27
W	21	St. Louis (62,760) (H)	12
L	5	Washington (55,031)	9
W	24	N.Y. Giants (63,420) (H)	3
W	24	St. Louis (48,991) (OT)	21
W	14	Philadelphia (60,525) (H)	7
L	10	Minnesota (61,848) (H)	21
L	16	Miami (69,414)	23
W	42	Green Bay (55,256)	14
W	27	New Orleans (57,920) (H)	7
W	37	Washington (64,905) (H)	10
W	17	New England (63,263) (H)	10
W	31	Philadelphia (64,667)	13
W	30	N.Y. Jets (52,532)	7
	384		208

Postseason

		Divisional Playoff *(Dallas)*	
W	27	Atlanta (60,338)	20
		NFC Championship Game *(Los Angeles)*	
W	28	Los Angeles (67,470)	0
		Super Bowl XIII *(Miami)*	
L	31	Pittsburgh (78,656)	35

Before Super Bowl XIII

Some random quotes from before Super Bowl XIII:

"They're so good, they're illegal. But I'm the long arm of the law. Do you think the sheriff ever worries?"
—Hollywood Henderson

"It could be an excellent and entertaining contest, for both teams have effective organizations, fine coaches, alert and muscular defensive units, stout running attacks, able quarterbacks who can throw a football and receivers who can catch it and run. It can also be a stinkeroo, as the experience of XII years has taught us. In either case, it will come as an inexpressible release, putting an end to the numbing overkill that precedes this production every winter."
—*Red Smith,* New York Times

"I'm just here to have fun."
—*Terry Bradshaw*

by defeating the other NFC wild card team, the Philadelphia Eagles.

The Cowboys were a heavy favorite, a full 14 points in fact. But the oddsmakers were off that year, and the ship the Cowboys planned to sail to the Super Bowl was almost sunk—by, of all people, the underdog Falcons. The Cowboys trailed at the half, 20–13, but even more disconcerting was the situation involving Roger Staubach, who had been led from the field late in the second quarter after being KO'd by blitzing linebacker Robert Pennywell. Staubach had a concussion and would not rejoin the Cowboys on the playing field for the second half. Suddenly Danny White would have to do something with the football other than punt it.

Tom Landry sent the plays in to White by messenger, but it was White who could take due credit for executing them with the finesse of a veteran quarterback. On their second possession, he had Dallas marching. White maneuvered them 54 yards on seven plays, then rolled to his right on a bootleg from the 2 along with half the Falcon's defense surging toward him. Just before he was about to be dumped for a loss, however, he spied tight end Jackie Smith in the end zone and lobbed the ball over the charging defenders and into his hands.

The Dallas defense became an impenetrable wall in the second half, the players sensing that they were going to have to contribute heavily if the team was to avoid being ousted from the playoffs that afternoon.

In the fourth quarter, the Falcons began to contribute to the Cowboys' cause as well. A punt netted them only 10 yards early in the quarter and gave the Cowboys the

ball at the Falcon 30-yard line. In six plays, Danny White moved the ball to the one and then sent Scott Laidlaw in for the score. As it would turn out, that would be enough to rescue the game. The final score was Cowboys 27, Falcons 20.

There was no 14-point spread to coax the Cowboys into overconfidence when they deplaned in Los Angeles to take on the Rams for the NFC championship a week later. The Rams had posted a record identical to the Cowboys', 12–4, and it was the best in the conference. Most observers called the game a toss-up, maybe even giving a slight edge to Los Angeles because the game was being played in their front yard.

Roger Staubach was back, his head cleared now of the bells and birds that sang there the week before. But he could not get the Cowboys going in the first half. Fortunately for Dallas, Pat Haden could not spur the Rams, either. It was all defense the first half, and when the teams left the field at intermission, the game was a scoreless tie.

In the third quarter, however, the Rams, for some dark,

The starting lineups for Super Bowl XIII:

Offense

Dallas Cowboys		Pittsburgh Steelers
Tony Hill	WR	John Stallworth
Drew Pearson	WR	Lynn Swann
Billy Joe DuPree	TE	Randy Grossman
Pat Donovan	T	Jon Kolb
Rayfield Wright	T	Ray Pinney
Herbert Scott	G	Sam Davis
Tom Rafferty	G	Gerry Mullins
John Fitzgerald	C	Mike Webster
Roger Staubach	QB	Terry Bradshaw
Tony Dorsett	RB	Rocky Bleier
Scott Laidlaw	RB	Franco Harris

Defense

"Too Tall" Jones	E	L. C. Greenwood
Harvey Martin	E	John Banaszak
Larry Cole	T	Mean Joe Greene
Randy White	T	Steve Furness
Thomas Henderson	LLB	Jack Ham
Bob Breunig	MLB	Jack Lambert
D. D. Lewis	RLB	Loren Toews
Benny Barnes	LCB	Ron Johnson
Aaron Kyle	RCB	Mel Blount
Charlie Waters	S	Donnie Shell
Cliff Harris	S	Mike Wagner

A perfect pass, a perfect catch, another Roger Staubach/Drew Pearson touchdown. This one is against the Washington Redskins, and in futile pursuit is cornerback Gerard Williams.   (Dallas Cowboys)

Scott Laidlaw (35) takes advantage of an ample hole in the Redskin defense on his best day ever as a Cowboy. He rushed for 122 yards on 16 carries and scored two touchdowns as the Cowboys easily disposed of the Redskins at Texas Stadium, 37–10. Blocking downfield is Drew Pearson. Other Cowboys in the picture are center John Fitzgerald (62) and guard Tom Rafferty (64).   (Dallas Cowboys)

self-destructive reason, decided to hand the game over to the Cowboys. Pat Haden threw a pass right into the hands of Charlie Waters, who gratefully carried it 20 yards to the Rams 5-yard line. Tony Dorsett then sliced in with it for the game's first score.

A little while later, the Rams were threatening. At the Dallas 15, they disdained a field goal on fourth down and one and Haden handed the ball to Jim Jodat with the mission of picking up the first down. Instead, he ran smack into defensive tackle Larry Bethea and a few other Cowboys and was unceremoniously dumped for a loss, and the Cowboys, their shutout intact, took possession of the ball.

Then Pat Haden threw to Charlie Waters again. Staubach turned this turnover into another touchdown with a little 4-yard pass to Scott Laidlaw. Cullen Bryant then established his presence in the comedy of errors by fumbling the ball over to Harvey Martin at the Dallas 10-yard line. Tony Dorsett got the Cowboys out of that dangerous field position with a 53-yard run, and not long thereafter, Roger Staubach found tight end Billy Joe DuPree in the Rams end zone for the third touchdown of the half. To proverbially ice the cake, Thomas "Hollywood" Hender-

---

Super Trip

Six Cowboy fans from Arlington, Texas, decided to go to Super Bowl XIII in style. The cost of their little weekend junket would be $19,500.

Here's the social schedule. A chauffered limousine would pick them up at their homes and deliver them to Love Field in Dallas, where they would board a Lear jet for the trip to Miami. On board the private jet, they would be served champagne, caviar, and other essential nibbles.

Another limousine would pick them up at the airport in Florida and whisk them to a yacht club in Fort Lauderdale where they would then board the Tulip II, *an 83-foot luxury yacht which would be their home for the next three days. The* Tulip II *had three bedrooms, each with a private bath; a galley and dining room replete with fine crystal, china, and silver; and six color TV sets placed strategically throughout the ship's quarters. A crew of four, including a Cordon Bleu-trained chef, would be on hand to cater to every whim.*

Saturday would be for boating. Sunday would be for cheering on the Cowboys; six tickets were included in the $19,500 package.

After breakfast on Monday, the six would be limoed back to the airport and the Lear jet that would return them to Dallas.

Fandom

Fans from Texas and from Pittsburgh descended on Miami for Super Bowl XIII, and according to many, they were as different as the jersey colors of the two teams. As Allen Pusey, a staff writer for the Dallas Times-Herald, *wrote:*

"Here in Miami, it isn't hard to tell a Pittsburgh fan from a Cowboys' fan.

"The Steelers' fans wave yellow towels when you're talking; Dallas fans wave for the waiter.

"The Dallas fans want white wine and Perrier, a little poached grouper, and a slip for the yacht. Pittsburgh fans can live on Big Macs and beer . . .

"Both Pittsburgh and Dallas fans play their differences up or down, depending on their purpose. But a brief survey of those who have known them best this past week —the maids, cabbies, waitresses, shopkeepers, and bartenders—say the differences are there to be seen.

"Dallas fans generally buy more, but tip less than their Pittsburgh counterparts . . .

"Dallas fans drink better brands of booze, but Pittsburgh fans drink more, said bartenders in a totally unscientific sampling. Dallas fans are quieter but generally more haughty than Steelers fans."

Asked what he thought about the difference between fans, one Dallas partisan shrugged: "I think all this stuff characterizing fans one way or the other is a bunch of bull (bleep)."

---

son picked off still another Rams pass and raced 68 yards with it for a touchdown. When the final gun relieved the Rams of their embarrassments, they could count seven turnovers—five interceptions and two fumbles. And the Cowboys were on the way to their fifth Super Bowl, sporting five conference championships in the nine years since the NFC and AFC began playing Super Bowls.

The Pittsburgh Steelers had posted the best record in the league in 1978 (14–2) and clearly were an extraordinary football machine. The defense, the "Steel Curtain" as they liked to be called, was manned by such luminaries as Mean Joe Greene, L. C. Greenwood, Jack Lambert, Jack Ham, and Mel Blount. The offense was well balanced with Terry Bradshaw and his spectacular receivers Lynn Swann and John Stallworth and a freight train known as Franco Harris.

They had received the AFC bid for the Super Bowl as a result of crushing the Denver Broncos, 33–10, and the next week destroying the Houston Oilers, 34–5.

Super Bowl XIII was the first ever to feature a rematch.

The two teams had met once before when the Steelers beat the Cowboys 21–17 back in Super Bowl X. The game was set for Miami's Orange Bowl, the third time the Cowboys had played in that stadium for the pro football world championship and the site where the two teams had met in their first Super Bowl encounter.

There was a different kind of hype before this Super Bowl. There was very little love between the two teams; in fact, it could be said that they basically loathed each other. And so there were a lot of words and taunts exchanged before either team got to Florida. It was in a way the same kind of posturing and gesturing, name calling and attempts to demean, that usually preceded one of Muhammad Ali's heavyweight championship fights.

At the center of it all was Hollywood Henderson. "I've been babbling for a long time," he said to a *Newsweek* reporter. Then he explained to another, "When my mouth is running, my motor is running." The word war really got going when Henderson proceeded to make some derogatory remarks about a variety of Steelers, from the intelligence of Bradshaw to the looks of Jack Lambert. Retorts came back, and if nothing else, it was entertaining the sportswriters. But blocks and tackles are the only things likely to break some bones on the football field, and soon both teams got down to that piece of business and forgot about all the word bandying.

It rained much of the morning of Sunday January 21, 1979 in Miami. But then, a half hour before the Super Bowl was to begin, it stopped, or as one sportswriter quipped, "Pete Rozelle turned it off and ordered the sun out."

The Cowboys were the first to handle the ball that Super Sunday. They had won the coin toss and were moving the ball on their first possession. They were run-

Danny White (11), coming off the bench to replace an injured Roger Staubach in the 1978 divisional playoff game against the Atlanta Falcons, rolls to his right and throws a perfect strike to tight end Jackie Smith in the end zone. The TD and ensuing extra point tied the game at 20–20. White then led the Cowboys on a later drive for another TD and a 27–20 win, enabling them to keep alive their hopes for a fifth Super Bowl appearance. No. 64 on the Cowboys is guard Tom Rafferty.   (Dallas Cowboys)

The awesome blocking of the Cowboys was never more evident than in this sequence as Doug Dennison (21) takes a handoff from Roger Staubach and blasts in for a TD against the Baltimore Colts. Dennison's corridor is gouged open by the Cowboy line at the right and Tony Dorsett (33) and Robert Newhouse (44), who neutralize the Colts to the left of the hole. This was the Cowboys' first score of the 1978 regular season, and they went on to win the game 38–0.   (Dallas Cowboys)

ning well, but then Drew Pearson had trouble holding on to a reverse, and the ball ended up in the hands of Steeler John Banaszak.

The Steelers opted for the pass in the early going, and Bradshaw led a drive that was highlighted by three completions, the last of which was a 28-yard TD to John Stallworth. The Cowboys came back, however, late in the first period. Harvey Martin broke through to sack Bradshaw, jarring the ball loose, and it ended up under the massive body of "Too Tall" Jones. Roger Staubach, from the shotgun, then found Tony Hill for a 39-yard touchdown, and with Rafael Septien's extra point the Cowboys had evened the score.

In the second quarter, the Doomsday Defense contributed again. This time, Hollywood Henderson got to Bradshaw, and the ball turned up in the possession of Dallas linebacker Mike Hegman, who carried it 37 yards for another Dallas touchdown.

After the Steelers got the ball, they faced a third down at their own 25-yard line. Bradshaw was going just for the first down when he threw a 10-yard pass to John Stallworth. But the fleet receiver made a move and then, with a blazing flash of speed, was suddenly out in front of everybody. He raced 65 yards to put the Steelers right back in the ball game.

Suddenly, the more than 78,000 fans in the Orange Bowl and the tens of millions who were watching their television sets realized they were not witnessing one of the deadly dull Super Bowl games that had become a January tradition. Instead, they were watching an exciting, explosive collision of the two best teams in the league in what would become the most entertaining game in the history of Super Bowls.

The Cowboys were now on the move again. Staubach advanced the ball steadily, cautiously, until he reached the Steeler 32-yard line. Then he went to Drew Pearson at the

Tony Hill, in this sequence, shows the abilities that enabled him to wrest the starting position at wide receiver from Golden Richards and Butch Johnson in 1978. Hill has gone to the Pro Bowl every year since becoming a Cowboy starter. The Eagle defenders he outmaneuvers here are Herman Edwards (40) and Randy Logan (41). (Dallas Cowboys)

THE BATTLE FOR THE 1970S   177

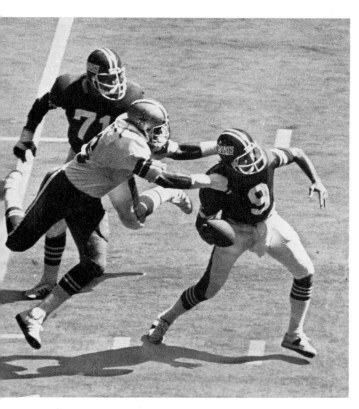

Defensive end Harvey Martin demonstrates how he achieved his reputation as one of the league's most fearsome pass rushers as he collars New York Giant quarterback Joe Pisarcik (9). The blocker who could not contain Martin is tackle Gordon Gravelle (71).   (Dallas Cowboys)

16, but cornerback Mel Blount reached in front of him to record what would be the Steelers' sole interception of the day.

Now Bradshaw was the mover. He guided the Steelers all the way to the Dallas 7-yard line. Then, with only seconds remaining in the half, he rolled to his right and lobbed a little floater just beyond the reach of Cowboy linebacker D. D. Lewis and into the outstretched hands of Steeler running back Rocky Bleier. Pittsburgh led at half-time, 21–14.

Tom Landry had said before the game, "When you have two teams so evenly matched, something could happen that could throw the whole thing off for us. Just one little thing." Actually, it turned out to be three "little things," and they all came in the second half.

The Cowboy defense smothered the Steelers' third-quarter attack; in fact, they did not give them a single first down in their first two possessions. Still trailing by a touchdown, the Cowboys then mounted their own drive, and Staubach maneuvered them to the Pittsburgh 10-yard line. On third and three, he dropped back, eluded

Jack Lambert's raging blitz, and spotted tight end Jackie Smith standing alone in the end zone, no Steeler within 10 yards of him. Staubach lobbed the ball to him, but when Smith, the long-seasoned veteran, raised his hands to accept it, he stumbled. There was not even the sound of a footstep to distract him; the ball was in his hands and then inexplicably went through them, bounced off his body, and fell to the ground. The silence from the grand-stands was attributable to the thunderstruck Dallas fans but then was quickly replaced by the joyful cheers of a group of Steeler fans. No one was perhaps more stunned than Smith himself. It was a mournful way to end an otherwise noteworthy career. The Cowboys settled for a 27-yard field goal from Rafael Septien and still trailed by 4 points.

An inglorious moment in an otherwise fine career. Tight end Jackie Smith is frozen in anguish after dropping an easy touch-down pass in the end zone of Super Bowl XIII. The second-half pass (and extra point) would have enabled the Cowboys to tie the score at 21–21. Instead, they had to settle for a field goal and subsequently were never able to catch the Steelers that after-noon in Miami's Orange Bowl. Except for this grim moment, Smith had an outstanding 15-year career in the NFL.   (John F. Rhodes, Dallas Morning News)

The second "little thing" came in the fourth quarter. The Steelers had the ball, but they were having to work for each yard they were gaining. There was enormous pressure on Bradshaw every time he dropped back to pass. The Cowboys were obviously gunning to get the ball back and make up for the touchdown they lost in the third quarter. On a second down, the Steelers lined up for an obvious passing play. They were at their 44-yard line, with only 9:05 left in regulation time. Lynn Swann lined up on the right and broke down field. The Cowboys blitzed, and safety Cliff Harris came flying in at Bradshaw, who frantically unloaded the ball in the direction Swann was going, an alley-oop pass thrown in desperation into the atmosphere with the hope it might fall into friendly hands. But the ball was thrown short and to the inside, and when Swann cut back to try for it, he tripped over the back of defender Benny Barnes's churning legs, and both players went sprawling. Referee Fred Swearingen grabbed for his yellow flag and threw it. Interference on Barnes was the call. Barnes screamed that *he* was the one who had been tripped. Tom Landry, showing uncharacteristic emotion, ranted and screamed and fumed on the sideline, his lament lost in the cacophony of boos and jeers from the Dallas fans. It had been a bad call—later replays would show that—but it was a judgment call, and therefore it stood. The Steelers, whom the Cowboys felt they were on the verge of stopping, now had the ball on the Dallas 23-yard line with a first down, and the tide was turning.

Tony Dorsett finds it tough going on the ground against the niggardly Pittsburgh Steeler defense in Super Bowl XIII. Dorsett, however, was the game's leading rusher with 96 yards on 16 carries. But the Cowboys, so plagued with bad breaks that day, could not pull off their third and perhaps most coveted Super Bowl victory. No. 70 is Cowboy Rayfield Wright.   (Vernon Biever)

The infuriated Cowboys tried to blitz again, but a shrewd Terry Bradshaw read it, called an audible, and sent Franco Harris through one of the gaping holes left by the blitz. He carried the ball all the way in for a touchdown.

The third of the day's little disasters occurred on the ensuing kickoff. It was short, and tackle Randy White, who was there to block, not to carry the ball, ended up with it, at least momentarily. White, playing with a fractured thumb that was heavily bandaged, started forward but could not hold on to the ball. It bounced on the ground, and Steeler Dennis Winston fell on it. On first down, Bradshaw took advantage of the fervor of the moment and tagged the Cowboys with an 18-yard pass, perfectly placed in the hands of a leaping Lynn Swann, and the Steelers suddenly had a 35–17 lead.

The Cowboys fought back. Staubach had no intention of letting the Steelers off the hook that easily. He scrambled, passed to Drew Pearson, handed off to Dorsett, and finally found Billy Joe DuPree at the Steeler 7-yard line, then watched as the powerful tight end broke two tackles and lurched into the end zone for a touchdown.

The Steelers geared up for the obvious on-side kick. But it didn't help. They swarmed at the bouncing ball, but Cowboy rookie Dennis Thurman was the person who finally ended up with it. The ball was on the Cowboys' own 48-yard line, and time had now become a precious commodity. Staubach passed, was sacked, threw an incompletion, but then found the ever-reliable Drew Pearson with a 25 yarder, which brought the Cowboys to the Steeler 4. A bullet hit Butch Johnson in the end zone, and suddenly the Cowboys were back within 4 points of the Steelers. But only 22 seconds were left on the scoreboard. Rafael Septien tried another on-side kick, and the Cowboys swooped down on the careening ball, but this try was not successful, and the Steelers' Rocky Bleier fell on the ball. The Cowboys had no way now to obtain the ball, and the game ended with Pittsburgh running out the clock. It was truly the finest game ever to entertain a Super Bowl audience.

When it was finally over, Terry Bradshaw had passed for a total of 318 yards (253 of them in the first half), and Roger Staubach had earned 228 yards with his 17 completions. The Cowboys' defense had held Franco Harris to 68 yards, a creditable feat under any circumstances, and Tony Dorsett had garnered 96 yards running with the ball. The two great Pittsburgh receivers, Swann and Stall-

worth, had combined for 239 yards—124 and 115, respectively.

It was a bitter disappointment for a fine Dallas Cowboy team, one which never gave up. They had wanted that game very much, had desired so strongly to show the football world that they were indeed the dynasty of the 1970s. They would have to settle for being a part of the dynastic 1970s, but an integral one because they were the only team up there at the top throughout that entire ten-year period.

After Super Bowl XIII

Some random quotes after Super Bowl XIII:

"It's hell to lose. But we've been here before, and we'll be back."

—Tex Schramm

"Boys, you can't say anything bad about this game. This son of a gun was fun." (and when told of his stats for the day) "Did I do all that?"

—Terry Bradshaw

"I give credit to Dallas because they didn't quit out there today. They kept our defense on the field during the fourth quarter. Man, they really gave us a scare."

—Rocky Bleier

"I'm so upset because this game was so special for us. This was the culmination of nine years when we had been to five Super Bowls. We could have been the first team to win three Super Bowls and it would have been a great climax to an era. But we didn't do it."

—Tom Landry

"They deserved to win. They're the world champions. They were the better team today. The final result is that they beat the best team in football, and now they're the best team in football. It's kinda like Spinks and Ali."

—Hollywood Henderson

"It leaves an empty feeling leaving here a loser. It makes the season incomplete."

—Drew Pearson

16 The End of an Era

THE DALLAS COWBOYS TURNED 20 years old when they suited up for the 1979 season. They had crammed their infancy and adolescence into a brief span of five years and by 1966 were a fully matured professional football team, one that subsequently never strayed very far from the topmost echelon of the league.

The decade of the 1970s was also nearing its end, and the Cowboys had been, if not always the winner, at least the stellar attraction throughout that time. As David Israel wrote in the Chicago *Tribune:*

"When football became television's biggest draw, the Cowboys were football's best show . . . The Cowboys were the ultimate entertainment product of the Seventies . . . as wholesome as 'Little House on the Prairie,' and as titillating as 'Charley's Angels.' They were as human as 'The Rockford Files,' as warm and lighthearted as 'M-A-S-H' . . . They were Roger Staubach and the Dallas Cowboys Cheerleaders. They were vulnerable, they were flawed as Thomas Henderson and Duane Thomas, they were resilient, and thanks to their computerized organization, they were relentlessly successful."

But beyond all the computers and television glitter, the front-office sophistication, and the complex orchestration for on-field performance scored in Tom Landry's play books, the Cowboys were made up of human beings, as vulnerable as anyone else to nature's ills and mortal weaknesses as well as the unpredictable whims of men. Living proof of that would inevitably be found in the Cowboys' 1979 football season.

There were things which no one anticipated. "We ex-

pected to field the same team in '79 but older, wiser, better," Roger Staubach said in his autobiography. "Everything was in place for another Super Bowl run, but it soon began falling apart."

The start of it came about a month before the Cowboys were due to report to Thousand Oaks for training camp. Ed "Too Tall" Jones announced to everyone's surprise that he was not going to play football in 1979. Instead, the 28-year-old defensive end had decided to change careers and become a heavyweight boxer—perhaps the most gargantuan to take to the sport since Primo Carnera hulked about the ring in the 1930s.

Then, during the exhibition season, Tony Dorsett managed to drop a large mirror on his foot and break a toe, which put him out of action, and at that point no one knew how much of the regular season he might have to miss. On an even more disconsolate note, the Cowboys knew exactly how long All-Pro safety Charlie Waters would be out of uniform as a result of all the torn-up cartilages and ligaments in his knee, an injury he suffered in an exhibition game against the Seattle Seahawks. He would be lost for the entire season.

To add to the defensive woes, Coach Tom Landry's reservations about Hollywood Henderson, his attitude and his approach to the game, were daily moving closer to a state of profound disenchantment. Henderson had arrived at the training camp field in a huge limousine and announced he wanted to renegotiate his contract. It fell on deaf ears. He did join the camp finally but later offered the press a scathing criticism of the Cowboy organization. Along with a rash of other minor accidents and injuries, it seemed almost as if whoever it was up there who had liked the Cowboys in the first nine years of the decade had somehow abandoned them, left them to suffer the tribulations of ordinary mortals.

On the brighter side, Roger Staubach was back, putting to rest rumors which had arisen at the end of the 1978 season to the effect that he would retire before the 1979 season. The Cowboys had also latched on to some good prospects in the draft. Their first choice, 6 feet 4 inch, 252-pound center Robert Shaw from Tennessee, was the first offensive lineman to be a Cowboy first-round pick since guard John Niland back in 1966. In addition, the Cowboys drafted running back Ron Springs (Ohio State), cornerback Aaron Mitchell (Nevada/Las Vegas), tight end Doug Cosbie (Santa Clara), and defensive tackle Bruce Thornton (Illinois). Steve Wilson from Howard University, a wide receiver and later a cornerback, was signed as a free agent.

Going after a loose ball. Some dive, some dance; diving here is Aaron Mitchell, dancing is Dennis Thurman.   (Vernon Biever)

"There is nothing particularly modest about the image of the Dallas Cowboys. They tend to consider and project themselves in a fairly grand manner.

"From their diamond-crusted Super Bowl rings to their poster pin-up cheerleaders, from their incredible record of success to their Taj Mahal stadium, they reflect the gaudy dimension of Texas . . .

"The Cowboys, indeed, are something special. Those stars on their helmets carry with them a show biz psychology: 'Inside this chamber resides one of the elite of the profession.' . . .

"Image: The Cowboys are the flex defense and an offense so complicated only Landry seems to understand it. They are Hayes, the world's fastest human, frightening opposing defenders into near nervous breakdowns; they are Staubach and his 'Hail Mary' passes. They are the 'shotgun' on third down, and Cornell Green, the basketball player who became all-NFL."

—Rich Koster, St. Louis Globe-Democrat

The Cowboys were scheduled to play an extra exhibition game in 1979 because they were tabbed for an appearance at the Pro Football Hall of Fame fund raiser in Canton, Ohio, again. The Cowboys lost that one to the Oakland Raiders and another to the Seattle Seahawks but won the other three, including their fifth consecutive preseason victory over the Pittsburgh Steelers—a hallmark they would gladly have swapped for just a single win on that January Sunday earlier in the year.

Even though the Cowboys' defense had been severely depleted before the regular season opened, the team showed surprisingly little effect from it once the season got underway, at least in the sense that they were winning most of their games, albeit they were awfully close ones. In fact, by midyear, the Cowboys had won seven of their eight games, losing only to the Cleveland Browns on a Monday night.

Tony Dorsett came back for the second game of the regular season and by the third game proved that he was no worse for wear by chalking up his first 100-yard game (108) against the Chicago Bears. Roger Staubach threw for more than 200 yards in four of those first eight games, including a 303-yard performance in the losing effort at Cleveland, at that point the fourth most productive passing night of his career. His receivers, Tony Hill and Drew Pearson were on their way to banner years. But the defense was allowing too many points, and if that continued, Tom Landry reasoned, the Cowboys would fall. It was in such a needy state that the Cowboys did something almost unprecedented in their history. They traded away both their first- and second-round draft choices for 1980 to the Baltimore Colts to acquire defensive lineman John Dutton. Not since 1967, when the NFL forced them to give up a first-round choice to settle the Ralph Neely affair with the Houston Oilers, had the Cowboys lacked for an opening-round pick. In only three other years had they given up their top-round choice, and those were in the earliest years when Dallas was just beginning to build.

Although the Cowboys had achieved an impressive midseason record, they were not far from the heat being generated by the strongly contentious Philadelphia Eagles. And there awaited two face-to-face confrontations with them in round two of the season. Not only that, but the Cowboys also had the Steelers and the Oilers on their upcoming schedule as well as two games with the Redskins, who were having a very promising year and were fiercely competing for the same division title as the Cowboys.

The Steelers provided the Cowboys with a poor sendoff into the second half of the season, holding them to a single field goal as they pounded out a 14–3 win. It was the least amount of points the Cowboys had scored since the 1972 season and one of only six games in their entire history of regular and postseason games where they scored that few points.

The ever-steady, ultimately reliable Preston Pearson is about to make one of his more spectacular TD catches, as a luckless defender can do nothing but watch. Pearson ended an impressive NFL career after the 1980 season, having given the Cowboys 6 of his 13 years as a pro. (Dallas Cowboys)

1979

Preseason

Dallas	(3-2)	Opponents
13	Oakland (20,648) @ Canton, O	20
7	Denver (61,192) @ Dallas	6
17	Seattle (59,803) @ Seattle	27
16	Houston (62,803) @ Dallas	13
16	Pittsburgh (64,543) @ Dallas	14

Regular Season

		(11-5)	
W	22	St. Louis (50,855)	21
W	21	San Francisco (56,728)	13
W	24	Chicago (64,056) (H)	20
L	7	Cleveland (80,123)	26
W	38	Cincinnati (63,179) (H)	13
W	36	Minnesota (47,572)	20
W	30	Los Angeles (64,462) (H)	6
W	22	St. Louis (64,300) (H)	13
L	3	Pittsburgh (50,199)	14
W	16	New York (76,490)	14
L	21	Philadelphia (62,417) (H)	31
L	20	Washington (55,031)	34
L	24	Houston (63,897) (H)	30
W	28	New York (63,787) (H)	7
W	24	Philadelphia (71,434)	17
W	35	Washington (62,867) (H)	34
	371		313

Postseason

		Divisional Playoff (Dallas)	
L	19	Los Angeles (64,792)	21

Then, up in Giant territory, the Cowboys came within seconds of losing another. With less than four minutes to go, the Giants led 14–6. But Staubach managed a dazzler to Drew Pearson for a 32-yard touchdown. They fought to get the ball back, and did. There were only six seconds left when Rafael Septien kicked a 22-yard field goal to give Dallas a 16–14 win, which would, as the season wore on, prove to have been absolutely essential.

It may have extracted a toll, however, or at least something did, because the Cowboys sank into a three-game losing streak and were drubbed by division competitors, the Eagles and the Redskins as well as by the Houston Oilers.

During the loss to the Washington Redskins, with only a few seconds left and the Redskins winning by 11 points, the game was totally out of the reach of the Cowboys. But to everyone's shock, their arch-rival called a time-out and sent its field goal unit on to the field. Were they really going to rub it in, the old salt in the wound act? Apparently so because Mark Moseley lined up and before the disbelieving eyes of the Cowboys kicked a field goal to make the final score 34–20. But if they knew at the time how they had fueled the Cowboys' lust for vengeance, they might have had second thoughts. As Roger Staubach later said: "We would be thirsting to get even for what we considered a flagrant insult." And, of course, they would have the opportunity because the Redskins still had to face the Cowboys once more that season. It would be the last game of the year as a matter of fact, and it would not only be a decisive game but one of the most exciting in the history of their rivalry—and certainly one where the Redskins could have benefited if the Cowboys had been a little less bloodthirsty.

During the three-game losing streak, Tom Landry had decided he could no longer live under the same dome as Hollywood Henderson. The flamboyant defenseman's pro football career, at least in Dallas, was over.

For the Cowboys, their season really went on the line December 8 when they went to Philadelphia. It was a must game for the Cowboys; if they lost it, the Eagles would be undisputed champs of the NFL East, and the only hope the Cowboys would have for the playoffs would be as a wild card. But as they had in so many other crucial contests in regular seasons over the years where playoff

"Too Tall" Jones (left) skipped the 1979 NFL season to try his fist at boxing. Although he won all six professional fights that year, his pugilistic career was less than illustrious and he would return to the Cowboys to reclaim his position at defensive end in 1980.   (Dallas Cowboys)

hopes were on the line, the Cowboys came out on top. They led throughout the game, and at the end they had a 24–17 victory that left the division title in a still undetermined state.

As the last game of the season loomed ahead of them, the Cowboys had a record of 10–5. A victory over the Redskins would give Dallas sole possession of the NFC Eastern crown. Even with a loss, they would still go to the playoffs as a wild card. In fact, if they did fail against Washington, the NFC East would send both wild-card

Question: *You were very instrumental in bringing the NFL and the AFL together. What were your initial feelings about the merger? Were you for it from the very beginning?*

Tex Schramm: *Oh, no. No, I wasn't for it. The National Football League even then had been my life, since 1947, so I was a very strong NFL individual. When the league [AFL] first started I would have done anything to stop them. The war between the two leagues continued, and by the midsixties, the AFL had gotten a television contract with NBC. Actually, we got a big contract with CBS first, the biggest in the history of television, and it turned out to be almost a negative rather than an asset. It was a liability because what happened then was that Sonny Werblin was able to go to NBC and say, "Look, you're going to be shut out of pro football unless you come with us and make sure we survive." So they, for the first time, got a television contract, and that's what kept them alive. Otherwise, they were about to sink into the sunset. But by that time it became obvious that players were being drafted and players were being signed no longer on their ability to perform but on the ability of the various teams to sign them. And so the competitive aspect of the game was disappearing. It was rapidly developing into a thing where only those teams that had the money and the willingness to spend it were going to get all of the football players. You had half the teams in the league taking first-round draft choices of people who shouldn't be signed in the second or third round simply because they couldn't afford to get in a bidding war. And the teams that had the money were getting all the best football players. This was one of the reasons that Kansas City was such a strong team in that league in the 1960s and early 1970s, because of all the players they were able to give rich contracts to. The same thing with the New York Jets; same thing with the Oakland Raiders. It wasn't only the AFL but the NFL; there were teams that were heading for destruction. And so it was with that feeling, for that reason, that I finally felt a merger was necessary.*

The only pennant vendor in the NFL who regularly garners national TV exposure is "Crazy" Ray Jones, a fixture in Texas Stadium hawking his wares and occasionally exhorting the fans on behalf of the Cowboys.   (Dallas Cowboys)

teams to the NFC playoffs that year. The Redskins, however, could be excluded from the playoff junket if they lost to the Cowboys and if the Chicago Bears happened to win their last game of the year by at least 33 points. The Bears would then, as a result of the NFL tie-breaking procedure, beat out the Redskins for the wild-card berth. It seemed a remote possibility; the Bears had scored a total of more than 33 points only once all that season and had not beaten any team by close to that margin. A win for the Redskins, on the other hand, could give them the division title, that is, if the Eagles lost that day, too.

The Cowboys would be handicapped by being deprived

Breunig-ism

Bob Breunig: *"Listen, don't say that I'm a mean animal on the field. Say I'm aggressive. Randy White . . . he's the mean animal."*

of the services of Tony Dorsett, who had hurt his shoulder in the previous week's game. Rookie Ron Springs would fill in for him as tandem to Robert Newhouse. But the Cowboys were truly fired up. "Mentally, the Cowboys could not have been more ready to play," Roger Staubach said later. "Moseley's field goal now was working *for* us psychologically. We were committed to play tough; determined to give maximum effort for 60 minutes no matter what happened."

Texas Stadium was filled to the rafters with 62,867 fans, and it was bitingly cold. The Cowboys, who received the opening kickoff, started in a fashion far from the game plan when they turned the ball over to the Redskins on

Television and the Cowboys

Tex Schramm: *"We have always gone out of our way for television exposure. Where most resist television, we sought it. As a result, we would always play whenever they wanted us for a national telecast. We would do it and as a result we got more exposure down through the years than any other team. On the other hand, we wouldn't have been asked so often if we didn't have a successful football team. When the TV people wanted to try Thursday night, we played the first Thursday. Sunday night, we played the first Sunday night. We played Thanksgiving. We moved to 3:00. We did whatever was necessary for national television. Now that's not purely an ego trip. It also provides a great benefit from a competitive standpoint, in three ways. First, we always sign a lot of free agents, and we have had a lot of free agents who have been a success on our football team—Cliff Harris, Drew Pearson, Jay Saldi, and Benny Barnes. We've always had a lot of free agents. Well, when the draft is over, there's competition for free agents. If kids in college have seen the Cowboys on television, that often becomes their team. Then, if they're not drafted and they have a choice of where they want to go, they're going to come to the Cowboys. So we get a lot of help that way. Players who naturally want our football team. Secondly, if they've seen us a lot on television, and they've seen us be successful, then when they come and join us they are much more prone to accept our system, the way we do things. They're going to be believers when they come. And then the third thing is—it's like they used to say about the New York Yankees, that when you put on that pin-stripe uniform, all of a sudden you became a better baseball player—and we think the same thing applies here. Because of the pride and prestige that TV has shown of us, our image, well, our players, when they put on the Cowboys uniform, they just become better football players."*

their second play from scrimmage. Ron Springs fumbled at the Dallas 34, and Redskin quarterback Joe Theismann guided his team in short order to the Dallas 3. But there, on third down, he was sacked by a fired-up old veteran, Larry Cole, and the Redskins had to settle for a field goal. When Mark Moseley came onto the field, he was greeted with a thunderclap of boos from all those who remembered his last field goal against the Cowboys a month earlier. He made it, however, and the Redskins had the lead. They increased it later in the quarter when Robert Newhouse fumbled the ball over to them. This time, Theismann converted the mistake into a Redskin touchdown, the score coming on a bootleg run by Theismann. The quarter ended with the Cowboys in the hole by 10.

In the second quarter, the Redskins struck again, this time on a 55-yard TD pass from Theismann to running back Benny Malone. The score stood at an intimidating

Bob Breunig took over the starting job at middle linebacker in 1977, becoming only the third Cowboy ever to hold down that position (succeeding Jerry Tubbs and Lee Roy Jordan). Here, he keys on quarterback Tommy Kramer of the Minnesota Vikings. (Dallas Cowboys)

17–0. Seven of those points were regained in the second quarter, however, when Roger Staubach executed a picture-perfect drive that netted 70 yards in 13 plays. Ron Springs plunged in for the TD. Staubach engineered another drive during the period, this one 85 yards in all, and

The coaches' tower at summer training camp in Thousand Oaks, California offers a bird's-eye view of what is happening on the playing field.   (Dallas Cowboys)

with nine seconds left in the half, he gilded it with a 26-yard pass to Preston Pearson for the touchdown. So at the half only 3 points separated the two teams.

The Cowboys then took the lead in the third quarter when Robert Newhouse slashed in from the 2. But that was the extent of the scoring in that period of play. It was at this point that everyone in the stadium was treated to a surprising bit of news. It was announced over the public address system that the Chicago Bears had defied the odds and demolished the St. Louis Cardinals 42–6. They had achieved the point differential, and now the Redskins only hope for the playoffs would be if they won the game they were presently losing. The news of the Redskins' now-woeful predicament did not so much inspire them as it seemed to uninspire the once-enflamed Cowboys. The defense let down, and the Redskins got close enough for Mark Moseley to kick a 24-yard field goal, which brought them within a point of the Cowboys. Roger Staubach then threw the ball to Redskin defender Mark Murphy, and Washington was able to capitalize on the turnover by

transforming it into a touchdown. John Riggins carried it in for the score.

After the kickoff, the Cowboys could not move the ball. When they had to return it to the Redskins, John Riggins, on an ordinary running play, burst through the Dallas defense and before a stunned crowd and an astounded Cowboy bench raced 66 yards for a touchdown. Suddenly, the Redskins, who had been losing such a short time ago, now had a commanding fourth-quarter lead, 31–20.

Time was now running out, and it appeared Dallas would have to settle for going to the playoffs as a wild card. But then strange and luminous things can happen in the closing minutes of a football game, especially one in which someone like Roger Staubach is playing.

There were only four minutes left in the game at the point where the gloom in Texas Stadium began to dissipate. It began at the moment Cowboy safety Cliff Harris and the Redskins' Clarence Harmon collided, causing a fumble, with the ball ending up engulfed in the arms of

A quarterback's life is not all glamor. There are also the sacks, blindside hits, and bone-shattering tackles by giant linemen. Here, Roger Staubach is sent to that special dream world which can occur after such an encounter.   (Vernon Biever)

Randy White. Staubach came on to the field to do what he had done so well on so many other desperate occasions. Totally in control, thoroughly unruffled, he moved the Cowboys. First, he threw a 14 yarder to Butch Johnson. Then Tony Hill cut across the middle, and Staubach's pass to him added another 19. The next was for 26 yards to Ron Springs, and he spiked the ball in the end zone. The score was 34–28, with Washington still ahead.

The Cowboys did not try an on-side kick, there was time they felt to rely on their defense, which would somehow have to harness the Redskins' running game and get the ball back for the Dallas offense. It did not look as if that was going to happen, however. There were just 2 minutes left in the game when the Redskins were faced with a third and two situation. The Cowboys had only two time-outs remaining. A first down and they were virtually finished; the Redskins would easily be able to run out the clock. They took their time coming to the line of scrimmage. The Redskins were confident; it was the Dallas Cowboys who had their backs to the wall. And there were only 2 short

yards to gain to clinch the whole thing, and there was powerful John Riggins, who had already toted up more than 150 yards rushing that day. Theismann handed him the ball, and he headed to his right, looking for the gap he could crash through, but suddenly there was Larry Cole, and just as suddenly John Riggins was on his way to the Tartan Turf with a 2-yard loss. The Redskins had to punt, and that took the ball all the way back to the Dallas 25. There was only 1:46 left in the game.

On first down, Tony Hill made a move to the outside, and Staubach delivered the ball to him between two arm-flailing defenders; somehow Hill hung on to it and got both feet in bounds before stepping out of bounds with a 20-yard gain. Then there was the old vet Preston Pearson. He had made so many clutch catches for the Cowboys since he donned that uniform back in 1975. Now there were two more, the first for 22 yards, the second for 25. Suddenly, Dallas had a first down at the Redskin 8-yard line with the clock stopped and a full 45 seconds to go in the game.

Roger Staubach's aerial act for the Cowboys would come to an end with the close of the 1979 season. Here, he rifles the ball over a leaping Washington Redskin defender, tackle Perry Brooks. The Cowboy blockers are center John Fitzgerald (62) and tackle Pat Donovan (67). No. 79 on the Redskins is defensive end Coy Bacon.   (Dallas Cowboys)

A first-down pass was incomplete, as Staubach had to hurry his throw under a furious Redskin pass rush. In the huddle, Staubach said he would go for Billy Joe DuPree in the end zone, but he told Tony Hill that if there was a mad blitz, as he feared there would be, he'd go immediately to him down the sideline. Hill nodded, then lined up out to the right. For the first time in quite a few plays, Staubach did not line up in the shotgun. Instead, he stood right behind the buttocks of center John Fitzgerald. He took the snap and backpedaled; a ferocious Redskin blitz exploded at him. He only had a second to loft what he later called a "semi-alley-oop" pass to Hill streaking down the sideline into the end zone. The first sight that Redskin cornerback Lamar Parrish had of the ball was as it nestled into Hill's hands for the touchdown. With the score tied, Rafael Septien came out and drilled a perfect extra point.

It was enough to win—the final score, the Cowboys 35, the Redskins 34. Roger Staubach called it "a game like no other . . . absolutely the most thrilling 60 minutes I ever spent on a football field." Tex Schramm said, "It was our greatest comeback ever." And Redskin coach Jack Pardee intoned, "One little point takes us from division champs to the outhouse." And that same one little point would take the Dallas Cowboys to their 11th divisional championship.

Roger Staubach had one of his finest hours ever as a football player, and when the day was over, his stats told the story with the happy ending—336 yards passing (24 of 42) and three touchdowns. Tony Hill gained 113 yards on his eight receptions, and Preston Pearson added 108 with his five catches.

It was an incredible way to end a strangely disjointed season. Problems, injuries, disappointments, a losing streak, and a winning streak, and it all came to a climax in an improbable but wildly dramatic way that December afternoon in Texas Stadium.

The Cowboys were at the zenith of an up-and-down, erratic year, but two weeks later, the jubilation subsided, Christmas come and gone, they would plunge from grace.

The Eagles, who had eliminated the Bears in the wild-card playoff game, drew the Tampa Bay Buccaneers, who were making their first appearance in the NFL Playoffs. The Cowboys would host the Los Angeles Rams, who had just barely won the NFC West with a record of 9–7. But there were premonitions of disaster floating around. Tex Schramm was quoted as saying, "Even though we won our division, I just don't seem to feel comfortable. I can't remember experiencing a season in which so many strange things happened to affect us so adversely."

It was a close game. The Cowboys had a 2-point lead in the first quarter when Randy White dumped Rams quarterback Vince Ferragamo in the end zone for a safety. But the Rams came back and worked up to a 14–5 lead

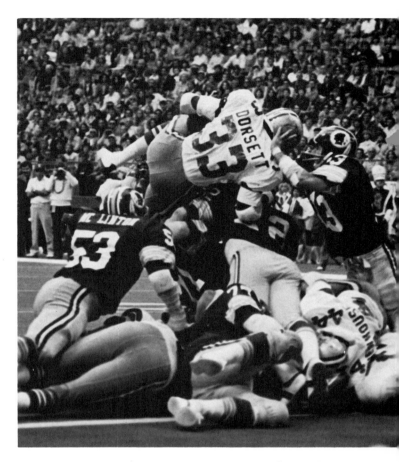

Tony Dorsett, vaulting here over the Redskin defensive line, brought new blood to the Cowboys' anemic rushing game in 1977. The Heisman Trophy winner of 1976, he offered an alternative threat on offense to fellow Heisman winner Roger Staubach (1963) and his passes. Dorsett has gained more than 1,000 yards in every season he has played for the Cowboys. (Dallas Cowboys)

at the half. Ron Springs plunged in for a Cowboy touchdown in the third quarter; another in the fourth quarter on a Staubach to Jay Saldi pass moved the Cowboys into a 19–14 lead. But that day turned out to be Vince Ferragamo's; his destiny was to be the fourth-quarter savior that week. It was he who, with only a little more than 2 minutes left, threw the pass that Cowboy linebacker Mike Hegman barely deflected into the hands of Ram wide receiver Billy Waddy, who ran it in for the game-winning score, a 50-yard, death-dealing play.

So that was it for the 1970s. Ever close, always in contention, the Cowboys had enjoyed a wildly careening ride through the league's stratosphere, tasting the ultimate pleasures of championships and living through the frustration and hell of narrowly losing out. They had been to the Super Bowl five times, an NFL record. And they had been the only team from their conference to win the Super Bowl during the 1970s, and they had done that twice. They had moved from the age of Meredith through the age of Staubach, and that was an era about to end.

17 A New Era Begins

ROGER STAUBACH CALLED EVERYBODY TOGETHER at Texas Stadium on March 31, 1980—the Cowboys kingpins, the press, the media—and made it official. He announced he was retiring from the game. Not just the scribes in Dallas, or even Texas for that matter, queued up to bid him a fond farewell. Throughout the nation, sportswriters and broadcasters addressed themselves to Staubach's retirement. The fact of the matter was they had liked and respected him both as a football player and as a human being. Ray Sons, sports editor of the Chicago *Sun-Times,* wrote it as well as anyone, under the headline, "A Cowboy Hero Rides into the Sunset." He expressed it this way: "It's sad to say goodbye to Roger Staubach. Quarterbacks can be replaced . . . He is, after all, 38 years old. Too many ruffians who outweighed him by 70 or 80 pounds have bounced his head on the floors of too many stadia in the last 11 seasons. He doesn't need another paycheck from the Dallas Cowboys. There is scarcely anything worth doing in football that he hasn't done. Why throw another pass? Should Da Vinci come back and paint another smile?"

And so for the Dallas Cowboys the 1980s would have to be ushered in by another field general. Danny White was the young man; he had been heir apparent for four years and had always been reliable as a reliefer. Now he had his chance.

Staubach was not the only departure that year. All-Pro safety and, at 31, Staubach's junior by seven years, Cliff Harris decided he, too, was giving up the game. Charlie Waters, however, would return to the defensive backfield, his knee now surgically repaired and worked back to a

healthy state. And "Too Tall" Jones decided that boxing, after all, was not the life for him. He had won six matches with second-rate pugs and at the same time had failed to impress the boxing community with his own style and grace in the ring. It did not appear he was on his way to becoming the new Ali, and he was equally disenchanted with boxing.

The question that seemed to transcend everything around Dallas and elsewhere in football circles in 1980 was: Could the Cowboys remain at the top without Staubach? A lot of people seemed to think they couldn't. Jimmy the Greek wrote: "Staubach's retirement is good news for their opponents . . . The Cowboys are at a crisis point in the team's history." And David Israel of the Chicago *Tribune,* who wrote so glowingly of the Cowboys of the 1970s, looked on the 1980s with a dismal forecast: "The Dallas Cowboys are going to get home from work earlier from now on," he wrote. "Coming into the '80s, things are changing for the Cowboys. They may be the team of the immediate past . . . the flaws run all through the marble, intersecting, disrupting its beauty and unity. So carefully constructed over the last two decades, the Cowboys are beginning to crumble around the edges."

Roger Staubach did not feel that way. He wrote: "The way I see it the glory years for the Cowboys haven't ended. I think Dallas will be stronger in 1980 than they were the season before." He had faith in Danny White and said so. And so did Tom Landry and the others in the front office who kept an interested watch on the football scene. It would be a rebuilding year, no doubt, one of adjustment, trial, and, at least for Danny White, on-the-job training.

Bob Lilly is the first Cowboy ever to be inducted into the Pro Football Hall of Fame. Enshrined there in 1980, he asked Tom Landry to be his official presenter.   (Pro Football Hall of Fame)

There was a kind of "wait-and-see" attitude hovering over everyone, and no one—with the Cowboys or among those who covered them for the press and the media—could legitimately predict how it would all turn out.

Without their first two draft choices, the Cowboys were severely limited in the new talent pool for 1980. They did pick up James Jones, a running back from Mississippi State, who would make his mark immediately by returning kicks. And they added another good running back in Timmy Newsome from Winston-Salem State. A few other rookies who showed up at Thousand Oaks would survive the final cut. A third-string quarterback was found in Gary Hogeboom of Central Michigan, to vie with Glenn Carano for the back-up to Danny White; and there was offensive guard Kurt Petersen of Missouri; for the defense, there was safety Dextor Clinkscale (South Carolina State) and linebackers Anthony Dickerson (S.M.U.) and Bill Roe (Colorado).

Just before the exhibition season got underway, Bob Lilly became the first Dallas Cowboy to receive the game's highest honor. He was inducted into the Pro Football Hall of Fame. His presenter that fine day was coach Tom Landry, who had said of him, "A player like Bob Lilly comes along just about once in a lifetime." Being likewise honored that day in Canton, Ohio, was another Cowboy, at least for a part of his career, Herb Adderley.

For Tom Landry and the rest of the coaching staff, the preseason of 1980 was an especially vigilant one. And for the most part, they liked what they saw, at least through the first three games. The Cowboys polished off the Packers, Rams, and Oilers in order, and Danny White looked just fine directing the assaults. But then the Pittsburgh Steelers came to town to shatter the five-year tradition of a Cowboy preseason romp over them. And they made it a walloping lesson, 31–10. As Steve Perkins wrote in the next week's issue of the team newspaper, "The Dallas Cowboys were re-introduced to NFL reality Saturday night." Danny White did poorly that game, the defense was tissue-paper strong, the machine was far from oiled. But it still was only an exhibition game, and Ernie Stautner, defense coordinator, looked on the bright side and hoped he was foreseeing the irony. "We pulled a Steeler trick this game," he said. "We let them win the preseason, now we'll win the Super Bowl."

Then it was the trek to Washington and the introduction of the Staubach-less Cowboys to Howard Cosell and Dandy Don Meredith and Frank Gifford and several million pro-football fans.

Everyone spoke of it as a new era the Cowboys were entering, although there were still plenty of familiar names going out over the airwaves, from Larry Cole, who had been there since 1968, to other long-term veterans like Drew Pearson, Robert Newhouse, Harvey Martin, D. D. Lewis, Billy Joe DuPree, John Fitzgerald, Benny Barnes, and Charlie Waters—all of them had worn Cowboys uniforms for at least eight years. The same crest of popularity was still being ridden—that's why *they* were selected to launch the 1980 season, and that's why more people would watch the game on TV that night than if two other teams were playing. So, new era or not, there were a lot of things which were remaining the same. It was now up to the Cowboys on the field to retain the tradition of winning.

After that Monday night opener, there was not so much speculation about Roger Staubach's successor. Danny White had performed well, leading the team smoothly and posting a win. His passing was fine except for two interceptions, and he generally handled the situations that arose like a veteran more experienced than he actually was.

The next week was not good, however. A lopsided 41–20 loss to the Denver Broncos summoned all kinds of flags from the football pundits; the references now were to things like terminal dreams, fading glories, catastrophic losses, demises. It was hard to tell whether one was reading the sports pages or the obituaries.

The Cowboys had looked awful that day. As Steve Perkins wrote in the *Dallas Cowboys Weekly,* "The clangor of calamitous events began at the opening kickoff." They continued in a depressing blend of turnovers and sloppy catch-up football that didn't catch up, and it had been a team effort. In fact, Danny White had what, at least on paper, could be interpreted as a fine game— 292 yards passing (20 of 34) and two TDs.

It was not the onset of the Dallas decline, however, as so many were speculating. The Cowboys reacted with three straight wins, defeating with relative ease the Tampa Bay Buccaneers, the Packers, and the Giants. Then they opened the doors of Texas Stadium to the San Francisco 49ers and cleared the air for the skeptics and doomsayers. The hapless gridders from the Golden Gate were to be the sacrificial lambs, and when they trotted into the stadium, they might just as well have been entering the Roman Coliseum. The Cowboys attacked with savagery, and the 49ers fell apart completely. Ten San Francisco turnovers helped enable the Cowboys to tie their club record for most points scored in a single game. They racked up 59

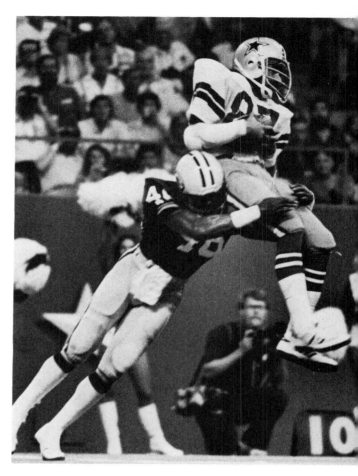

Free agent Jay Saldi goes high to snare this pass from Danny White on the opening night of the 1980 preseason at Texas Stadium. The Packer defender is safety Steve Luke. The Cowboys beat the Packers, 17–14.   (Vernon Biever)

that day and allowed the 49ers only 14. Even when a snap to Danny White in the shotgun formation went right through his legs, the play still became a Cowboy success. He chased it, picked it up, and on the run threw a 43 yarder to tight end Jay Saldi. It was just one of those days. White tossed four touchdowns in the game, three of them to Drew Pearson.

Dallas was 5–1 for the season when they traveled up to meet the stiffest competition in their division that year, the Eagles, who boasted an identical record. Just as in their preliminary encounter the year before, it turned into a moribund afternoon for the Cowboys. The Eagles came out on top of a game that could have gone either way, one that was really played principally between two strong defenses. In fact, the Cowboys' lone TD came when Randy White sacked Eagle quarterback Ron Jaworsky, forcing him to fumble the ball in his own end zone where Mike Hegman fell on it. Both Wilbert Montgomery, who contributed just 23 yards rushing, and Tony Dorsett, who gained only 17, left the game early with injuries. The game did go head to head all the way into the fourth quarter and was not decided until the last six minutes. That occurred when Danny White threw a pass out in the flat intended for James Jones, who tipped it up in the air, and Eagle linebacker John Bunting continued the volleyball action by tipping it to his teammate Charlie Johnson. The Eagles had the ball on the Dallas 20, and a few plays later Ron Jaworsky tossed to Charlie Smith for the Eagles' game-winning touchdown.

That would put the Cowboys in the hole for the rest of the season practically because the Eagles were in the process of running up an eight-game winning streak. Dallas was thrust into a position where they were forced to chase the Eagles all the way through to the next to last game of

the regular season.

The Cowboys fell a game further behind three weeks later when they were totally surprised by a cellar-dwelling but suddenly volatile New York Giant team. The Cowboys were in their luckless blue jerseys that Sunday—the ones Tex Schramm and a few others around Dallas felt had some kind of jinx associated with them; the good Cowboys, after all, always wore white, even rode white horses. Still Dallas posted 35 points that day, certainly enough to win most games, but the Giants, who had scored less than two touchdowns in six of their games that year, somehow managed to rack up 38 against an aghast Cowboy defense. Dallas had led 35–28 going into the fourth quarter but gave up a touchdown and a field goal in that exasperating period. Young Phil Simms, a little-heard-from quarterback in the earlier part of the season, managed to throw for 351 yards and three touchdowns.

The Future

Tex Schramm: *"I've been asked a lot, 'what's going to happen in the '80s.' As far as the Cowboys are concerned we'll be doing different things, and we'll be trying to do more as we have always done; we'll be trying to do more than the other teams are doing, trying to keep ahead of the other teams from an internal organization standpoint. But there are going to be a lot of changes, obviously, in the game, in how you approach scouting, for example, and in how you use current technical technology. You're going to get into the era of much more sophisticated ways of determining people's physical capabilities, their mental capabilities, their emotional capabilities. We are already finding different ways of testing players' reactions. It's getting much more scientific. In the older days, the scouts just went out and looked at a guy and came back and made a judgment and that's what you went on. Well, you don't do that anymore. Now you're going to get much more into the thing of measuring physical capabilities specifically, and in relating those to the predictability of success of a person with certain characteristics and qualities. These are the things that will be done with the computer, all the modern technology. The coaching method will become much more sophisticated because the time and preparation will become much shorter. In some ways, it will be like how they train airline pilots. Hell, they don't even go up in the damn airplane anymore, it's all simulated. Well, you're going to get to the point of where, with computers and films and all this kind of stuff, that you're going to do a heck of a lot of your teaching in that manner. But still you're going to have to get out and get the people who can play the game."*

1980

Preseason

Dallas	(3-1)	Opponents
17	Green Bay (54,876) @ Dallas	14
19	Los Angeles (63,283) @ L.A.	16
20	Houston (63,658) @ Dallas	13
10	Pittsburgh (62,795) @ Dallas	31

Regular Season

		(12-4)	
W	17	Washington (55,045)	3
L	20	Denver (74,919)	41
W	28	Tampa Bay (62,750) (H)	17
W	28	Green Bay (54,776)	7
W	24	N.Y. Giants (59,126) (H)	3
W	59	San Francisco (63,399) (H)	14
L	10	Philadelphia (70,696)	17
W	42	San Diego (60,639) (H)	31
W	27	St. Louis (50,701)	24
L	35	N.Y. Giants (68,343)	38
W	31	St. Louis (52,567) (H)	21
W	14	Washington (58,809) (H)	10
W	51	Seattle (57,540) (H)	7
W	19	Oakland (53,194)	13
L	14	Los Angeles (65,154)	38
W	35	Philadelphia (62,548) (H)	27

Postseason

		Divisional Playoffs (Dallas)	
W	34	Los Angeles (64,533)	13
		(Atlanta)	
W	30	Atlanta (60,022)	27
		NFC Championship (Philadelphia)	
L	7	Philadelphia (70,696)	20

At a press conference in an eerily empty Texas Stadium, Roger Staubach, flanked by his wife, Marianne, announces to the media that his playing days are at an end. For 10 of his 11 years as a Cowboy, Staubach had guided the team's offense, personally quarterbacking them through four Super Bowls and six NFC championship games and compiling a host of team and NFL records on the way. A sure bet for the Pro Football Hall of Fame and one of the most admired quarterbacks ever to play the game, Staubach ironically was never once named All-Pro by either AP, UPI, the Pro Football Writers of America, or Sporting News. (Dallas Cowboys)

Tony Dorsett had the second best rushing day of his career (183 yards), but it did not change the game's outcome or the Cowboys' divisional dilemma.

Philadelphia continued to win, at least until the 13th game of the season. At that point, they had the best record in the entire NFL, 11–1, and the Cowboys with only four games left in the season remained two games behind the Eagles.

Then, however, Philadelphia's little Utopia began to fall apart. First, it was the San Diego Chargers, who nipped them by a point. Then it was the Atlanta Falcons, who edged them by the difference of a lone field goal. And while this was going on, the Cowboys were in the process of humiliating the Seattle Seahawks 51–7 and then outlasting one of the league's premier teams, the Oakland Raiders, 19–13. Suddenly, the Cowboys and the Eagles were tied for the NFC East lead, each with a record of 11–3. Even better, perhaps, was that the Cowboys' destiny was fully in their own hands. All they had to do was win the remaining two games. If they did that, the division crown would be theirs.

"They [the Cowboys] don't simply prepare to play another team. They feed the team into a computer. Piece by piece. Player by player. Situation by situation. The Dallas Cowboys don't just tell their team that No. 43 is big and strong and lefthanded. They say when he likes to do one thing and when he likes to do another and if he gets distracted when someone calls him 'weird.' The Dallas Cowboys tell their team everything because they know everything. Everything there is to know.

"'That's our approach,' they say. 'Preparation, that is our approach to everything. . . .'

"I go to see them play football today the way I always go to see them play football. Uneasy, uncertain. I have the feeling that they know more about me than I know about them."

—Leigh Montville, Boston Globe

The Cowboys, however, had two very fierce encounters awaiting them. Initially, it would be the Los Angeles Rams, gunning for a wild-card berth now that the Falcons had wrapped up the NFC West. Just as the Cowboys could not afford to lose the game, neither could the Rams. And then, of course, there were the Eagles to face in the season's finale. It had all the makings of the classic pro football drama: both teams with equal records meeting on the last day of the season to determine the division championship.

Only it didn't work out that way. The Eagles did what they had to do the next Sunday. They won. But on the following night, the Cowboys failed. And how they failed. It was a rout, as bad and as embarrassing as the mauling the Denver Broncos had given them back at the other end of the season. The Rams could do very little wrong and the Cowboys practically nothing right. The score when it was all over was 38–14. "We just lost the division title tonight," Tom Landry said with pain after the game.

That statement may have been realistically sound, but it was not quite procedurally true. The Cowboys could still win the title if they beat the Eagles by 25 points the following Sunday. The tie breaker would be determined by point differential in the division because both teams had the same overall record, the same record within their

A battery for the 1980s. Danny White now pitches to Drew Pearson. White is fifth in the Cowboy ancestral line of quarterbacks, after Eddie LeBaron, Don Meredith, Craig Morton, and Roger Staubach. (Dallas Cowboys)

After a handoff from Danny White (11), Tony Dorsett spurts through a gaping hole in the New York Giant defense. He carried the ball 24 times and gained 183 yards on the ground in this 1980 game. The only more productive rushing effort in Dorsett's pro career was the 206 yards he picked up for a club record against the Eagles back in 1977. Despite Dorsett's contributions, the Cowboys fell this day at New York, 38–35. (Russ Russell)

division, the same in conference games, the same against common opponents. The Eagles, however, had 25 more net points in divisional games than the Cowboys. If the Cowboys won by 25, the teams would be tied in that category as well. The next tie breaker was net points in all 16 games, and the Cowboys, who had scored the most points in the NFC that year, would come out on top in that tie-breaker category.

The reason it was unlikely that the Eagles would lose by 25 points, and this was what prompted Tom Landry to make his statement, was that they had allowed less than 13 points a game on the average all season, and no team had scored more than 24 points against them in any given game.

It would take some kind of miracle, everyone agreed, but then the NFL had been a proving ground for miraculous events for more than 60 years now. And on that last day of the 1980 season, it looked as if Dallas might add a chapter to that story, for awhile, anyway. It really seemed like they might pull off the miracle. At halftime in Texas

The San Diego Chargers are the victim of this James Jones kick return. A rookie, Jones set club records in 1980 for punt return yardage, 548, as well as the number of punt returns, 54. He accounted for another 720 yards on kickoff returns, with an average of 22.5 yards per.   (Dallas Cowboys)

Stadium, the Cowboys were a mere four points from that magic spread of 25, riding on a 21–0 lead in a game they were totally dominating.

The Eagles came out in the third quarter and got themselves a touchdown. But the Cowboys came right back with one of their own when Danny White hit Drew Pearson for a TD. Tony Franklin, the Eagles' barefoot kicker who had booted a 59-yard field goal against the Cowboys the year before, reduced the lead by three with a 29-yard kick this time. But a short while later, as Danny White handed off to Ron Springs and then took the flea-flicker lateral back and rifled the ball to wide receiver Tony Hill for a 36-yard gain. Two plays later, White hit Billy Joe DuPree in the end zone. Rafael Septien kicked the extra point, and, miracle of miracles, the score was 35–10; the Cowboys had a 25-point margin *and* the division championship if they could hold out . . . for less than a quarter.

If only the game had ended there.

But it didn't. As so often happens, the pendulum of momentum swings, and suddenly it was the Eagles who were doing everything right. Ron Jaworsky threw a 30-yard TD pass. Tony Franklin kicked another field goal. Wilbert Montgomery ran 6 yards for a touchdown. And there went the 25-point advantage. The Cowboys still won

Randy White may be a moment late on this pass rush but he manages to make San Diego Charger quarterback Dan Fouts painfully aware of his presence. Other Cowboys are Too Tall Jones (72) and Harvey Martin (79). This 1980 game was only the second time the two teams have met in regular-season play, and the Cowboys have emerged victorious in both encounters. (Dallas Cowboys)

the game 35–27, but as Eagles coach Dick Vermeil said afterward, "We lost the battle but we won the war."

Still the Dallas Cowboys would go to the playoffs as a wild card. Up to that time, they were the only team in NFL history to have gone to the Super Bowl as a wild card, a feat they accomplished back in 1975. "It was done once, it can be done again," Tom Landry said, but he knew it was a road filled with potholes because after the first game, the wild card eliminator, each game in the playoffs would take place on foreign turf and before hostile crowds, always an advantage for the home team and an especially strong one in playoff action.

With the regular season now over, fans could look with comfort on how the quarterback situation had turned out. Danny White had a fine year, better than anyone would have expected from him in his first year on the firing line.

His 28 touchdown passes set a club record (one more than Roger Staubach had thrown in the previous season). His completion average of 59.6 was third in Cowboy history, and his 260 completions for 3,287 yards had only been exceeded once, and that was by Staubach in 1979. His NFL rating of 80.8 was very impressive.

Tony Dorsett rushed for more than 1,000 yards for the fourth straight year (1,185), and his 11 touchdowns tied Duane Thomas of 1971 for second place in that category and was only one less than his club record of 12 TDs set in 1977.

And James Jones became a Cowboy record holder in his rookie year for punt-return yardage when he gained a total of 548 (an average of 10.1 per return). He also added another 720 yards on kickoff returns.

But now it was time for the playoffs. The first test would

Defensive tackle Larry Cole races 43 yards for his fourth career touchdown here, after stealing one of Joe Theismann's passes in this 1980 game against the Washington Redskins. Cole's other three TDs also were scored against the Redskins—two in 1968 on a pass interception and a fumble recovery return, and another pass interception in 1969. He shares the club record for interception TDs with Mel Renfro and Lee Roy Jordan, not a bad statistic for a lineman. The 1980 season was Cole's 13th and last as a Cowboy. (Dallas Cowboys)

be the Los Angeles Rams, who had handed the Cowboys such a stunning loss only two weeks earlier, the same team that had kicked them out of the playoffs the year before. There was a lot of motivation floating about Dallas and plenty of talk about redeeming themselves before the eyes of another national TV audience.

It was to be played in Texas Stadium, and the Cowboys really wanted this one badly. The game began slowly, with the Cowboys in control for the most part, but at the half all they had to show for it was a 13–13 tie. However, Tony Dorsett had been running well, 73 yards already, and the Dallas defense had been harassing the Rams to the point of distraction.

It was the third quarter when the Cowboys broke the game wide open. Tony Dorsett scored his second touchdown of the day when he caught a 10-yard pass from Danny White. Then White struck again, this time to Butch Johnson, a 35 yarder. The game was never again within the Rams' reach. Another White TD pass was added in the fourth quarter, to Drew Pearson, and the Cowboys had neatly turned around their embarrassment from that Monday night in the regular season, humbling Los Angeles 34–13.

Georgia was the next stop. Football fans down there were riding a high like none they had ever experienced before. The Atlanta Falcons had not only won their division, but they were the team many oddsmakers were favoring to win the NFC and go to the Super Bowl. If that wasn't enough, the home-state folks were basking in the glory of the University of Georgia's football success, the team that had brought them an NCAA national championship.

The Falcons had won the NFC West with a record of 12–4, and they had lost only one game at home all season. The Cowboys would somehow have to get themselves up a little higher than the Falcons already were. Before the game, George Allen, an old Cowboy baiter, sat up in the press box and rated the game a tossup while practically everyone else gave the edge to Atlanta. Perhaps he was haunted by the very personal memories of how the Cowboys got up for crucial games with teams he had coached.

It was clear and sunny and briskly cold when the Cow-

Dallas tackle Randy White in this sequence shows some of his All-Pro talents as he takes Philadelphia Eagle quarterback Ron Jaworsky on a bone-crunching ride to the artificial turf of Veterans Stadium. Many Cowboy observers believe White will one day attain the legendary status as a defensive monument, like Hall of Famer Bob Lilly. (Russ Russell)

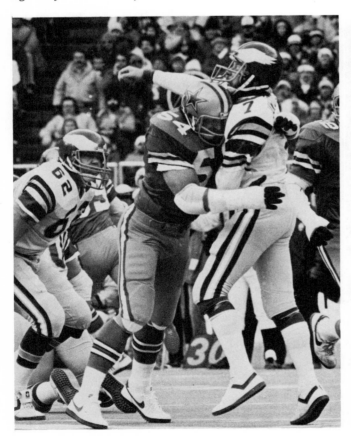

Tony Dorsett fends off the rapacious clawing of Los Angeles Ram defenders Joe Harris (51) and Rod Perry (49) on the way to having the third-best rushing day of his Cowboy career. Dorsett gained 160 yards on 22 carries as the Cowboys, in the postseason battle of the wild cards, decisively eliminated the Rams from the 1980 playoffs, 34–13.   (Russ Russell)

boys kicked off. At the beginning of the game, it did not look as though the Cowboys were up anywhere near where they should be. The Falcons began with a field goal. Then quarterback Steve Bartkowski stung them with a 60-yard pass to wide receiver Alfred Jenkins, and the Cowboys were down by 10 in the first quarter.

The Cowboys came back to tie it with Rafael Septien's 38-yard field goal and a Danny White touchdown pass to Billy Joe DuPree. But just before the half, the Cowboys fell behind again, 17–10. Going into the fourth quarter, it had reached 24–10, and the picture was indeed grim.

The Cowboys were mixing it up, but they hadn't been able to get their running game going until late in the third quarter. Now, thanks to some ground gained rushing and a fine run by Ron Springs on a screen pass, the Cowboys were at the Falcon 17 and threatening. A pass to Tony Hill brought the ball to the 6, and a few plays later, Robert Newhouse carried it in for the touchdown.

The Dallas defense knew what they had to do now that

the game was winding down, and they did it, holding the Falcons and forcing them to punt. But it seemed it would take a mother lode of luck if Dallas were to pull this one out. And that hardly seemed to be in the cards when a ball thrown by Danny White was batted between several players and ended up in the hands of an Atlanta defender. It resulted in a field goal, and the score escalated to 27–17. But then Danny White went to work, and suddenly there were visions of Roger Staubach dancing about Atlanta's Fulton County Stadium. He marched the Cowboys down the field, throwing with precision—to Drew Pearson for 15, then for 24, a 9-yard shot to Tony Dorsett, and finally a 14-yard bullet which Drew Pearson made a great catch of in the end zone.

Once again, the Dallas defense held, and the Atlanta punt sent the ball to the Cowboys at their own 29-yard line with 1:48 left in the game. White hit Butch Johnson, and the Cowboys were at midfield. A pass to Preston Pearson brought them to the Falcon 36. A screen to Tony Dorsett

Drew Pearson's look and the signals of the referee and Cowboy tight end Jay Saldi (87) say it all to Falcon safety Kenny Johnson. The touchdown catch in the 1980 NFC playoff game at Atlanta brought the Cowboys to within three points of the Falcons (27–24) with just 3:40 left in the game. A few minutes later Danny White again hit Drew Pearson in the end zone for the game-winning touchdown, sending the Cowboys to Philadelphia to meet the Eagles for the NFC championship.   (Russ Russell)

and the ball was down to the 24. There were 49 seconds left. Then suddenly there was Drew Pearson racing into the end zone again, and there was the ball spiraling toward him, and there were the defenders, two of them, and they and Pearson were all going for the ball. And finally there was Drew Pearson with it in his hands, a triumphant smile on his face, a touchdown on the scoreboard, and a win for the Cowboys in spectacular fashion. The final score was 30–27.

"It was our third miracle," Tom Landry said. And it was one that would send the Cowboys to Philadelphia to face the Eagles for the NFC championship.

It was a brutal week to patch up wounds and work out tired muscles and to try to keep the adrenaline pumping at the hyperactive rate it had been for three straight weeks now. If they could do it for a fourth game, they would

have a two-week period to rest up for Super Bowl XV.

Everyone had been impressed with the Cowboys' 1980 performance at this point. They were a powerhouse; there was little doubt of that. And there were rumors of an advantage. The Eagles were hurting—"injury-ravaged" was the way their coach Dick Vermeil described them. Their prime running back, Wilbert Montgomery, was allegedly suffering from an injury that might even keep him out of the game altogether.

On the other hand, the Cowboys had to wear their blue jerseys that day, and that struck an ominous chord. Nevertheless, they were considered the favorite even though the game was to be played in Veterans Stadium before a partisan crowd so raucous that sometimes police on horseback and others with large Alsatians on leashes had to patrol the perimeter of the field. Jimmy the Greek favored the Cowboys by one. Roger Staubach, a bit prejudiced perhaps, said the Cowboys would win by 10, maybe 14. Terry Bradshaw, who was doing some TV commentary since his Steelers did not make the playoffs, said he liked the Eagles in a real close one.

It was bitterly cold in Philadelphia that Sunday, a wind-chill factor of minus 16 on the playing field. Even Tom Landry opted for a fur Cossack hat instead of his familiar flip-brim fedora. And for the Cowboys it would remain deadeningly cold all afternoon. As a songwriter once put it, "All dreams must end." The party was indeed over for the Cowboys. The Eagles' defense was overwhelming that day, and the Cowboys were stale and cold and drained from the three weeks of stress-filled games they had soared through in the preceding month. They stayed in it for a half, but then the Eagles took over in the last two quarters and drove to a 20–7 victory.

The Cowboys would not go to Super Bowl XV. But they had come a lot closer to getting there than anyone would have believed in those skeptical days before the regular season. They surprised a lot of people by making it all the way to the conference championship game, an achievement they could now claim *ten* times in the last 14 years. It was their 15th consecutive winning season, and the 15th time in the preceding 16 years during which they had participated in the NFL's postseason festivities (counting the 1965 trip to the Playoff Bowl). It was a record unprecedented in National Football League history.

It was an auspicious way to begin the new decade. And there was little question that people like Clint Murchison, Tex Schramm, Tom Landry, Gil Brandt, and all the others associated with the Dallas Cowboys—now that the 1970s were history—were thinking of the decade that spread before them, thinking of how their team had taken a first step toward becoming *the* team of the 1980s.

18 Profiles

TOM LANDRY

WHEN A TV CAMERA ZOOMS TO A CLOSEUP of Tom Landry on the sidelines, as they have so often during the past two decades, it will rarely reveal even the trace of a smile or a scowl. The countenance it captures is as predictable as heat in a Dallas summer; it is one that has led writers and broadcasters to forever refer to the man's face as "chiseled in stone" or to enlist some other mineralogical metaphor to describe his eternally emotionless expression. Even comedian Don Rickles got into the act when he said of the coach, "There's seventy thousand people going bananas, and there's Tom Landry on the sideline trying to keep his hat on straight. Once he got into a grinning contest with Mount Rushmore, and Mount Rushmore won."

As he stands there or paces back and forth, Tom Landry is a portrait of stark concentration, his mind and senses totally absorbed in the game taking place before him. The complexities and sophistication of his team's manifold offenses and defenses have become legend in the National Football League. And it takes little more than slight intimacy with the game to know that the intricate Dallas orchestration on the field is simply the extension of Landry's football sagacity.

Today, Tom Landry's name is spoken of in the same reverential tones as those of Lombardi, Halas, Brown, Owen, Neale, and Lambeau, After all, by 1981, he had become the third winningest coach in the history of professional football, with 184 regular season victories in 21 years. Only George Halas, whose 320 wins in 40 years of coaching and Curly Lambeau of the Green Bay Packers,

who posted 231 victories in his 33-year career, have won more NFL regular-season games. In addition, Landry has coached in more postseason playoff games than any other man in NFL history—29 games—far ahead of the Vikings' Bud Grant, who is second in that category with 20; and Landry has won 17 of those playoff games, the most victories any coach can claim in postseason play.

Football had always been his life. Born in Mission, Texas, in 1924, he played high school football in that small town and was a highly touted fullback on a team that in his senior year was not only unbeaten but unscored upon. The tote board at the end of the season showed the Mission Eagles had defeated their opponents by a total score of 322 to 0.

One touchdown had been awarded to a team playing against Mission that year, then taken away. The Mission defensive back, Tom Landry, was called for interference on a pass play in the Mission end zone. The referee gave the team a touchdown over the protests of the Mission coach, who claimed correctly that a TD cannot be awarded on such a penalty. Realizing his error the next day, the official canceled the touchdown and thus preserved Mission's perfect record.

Landry spent only one semester at the University of Texas because the United States was swept into World War II. He joined the army air force and eventually became the copilot of a B-17 bomber. Landry flew more than 30 missions over German-occupied Europe, was involved in one crash landing, and had, like so many other fliers in that war, countless flirtations with disaster. But he survived it all. When asked about his wartime experiences,

As a New York Giant, early 1950s. (Pro Football Hall of Fame)

Landry, according to his biographer Bob St. John, with characteristic underplay replied, "Oh, we got a few holes in our bomber every once in a while but nothing much happened really."

After the war, Landry returned to Austin and the state university there. Back in a football uniform, he was converted to quarterback but had to play back-up to a person who would become one of the game's immortals, Bobby Layne. Landry proved to be a superb defensive back and traveled with his nationally ranked team to the Sugar Bowl in 1948, where they defeated the Crimson Tide of Alabama, led by Harry Gilmer. The following year, Texas and Tom Landry went to the Cotton Bowl where they trimmed Georgia.

With the pros, Landry spent one year with the New York Yankees in the All-America Football Conference, a team doomed to play out its last year of existence. When the AAFC was dissolved the following year, Landry was picked up by the New York Giants and became an integral part of one of the finest defensive units in the history of the NFL. Landry was named to the All-Pro team in 1954 as a defensive back, but he played only one season after that.

It was 1956 when he retired and took a job as a Giant assistant coach. He got the assignment to handle one of the NFL's greatest defensive units, peopled with such stalwarts as Sam Huff, Andy Robustelli, Rosey Grier, Jim Katcavage, Dick Modzelewski, and Jim Patton.

That lasted until the end of the 1959 NFL season. Then came the visit from Tex Schramm, and all the rest is Dallas history.

New York Giant defensive back Tom Landry (49) moves in to tackle fullback Leon Heath (24) of the Washington Redskins in this early 1950s game. Landry was named an All-Pro defensive back in 1954. (Pro Football Hall of Fame)

Tom Landry on the sidelines in his regular uniform. (Ron Scribner)

A few reflections on Tom Landry:

Tex Schramm: *"Tom's strengths are confidence in himself and an ability to sell or convey that confidence to all those who are around him."*

Sam Huff (speaking of his rookie year with the Giants, 1956): *"I'd sit in his apartment, and he'd have the projector on, and we'd look at draw plays or circle routes or whatever the hell there was. I learned more in a few hours with Tom than I'd learned playing football all my life."*

Pete Gent (to a rookie regarding Landry's playbook): *"Don't bother reading it, kid. Everybody gets killed at the end."*

Dick Nolan (remembering his days as a Giant cornerback under Landry): *"It was on that club that defense began to be noticed for the first time. The offense would go home, and we'd be sitting there going over the next opponent . . . I remember one time Tom was at the blackboard showing me that if their flanker came out on the strong side on a third-down play, and the fullback flared to the weak side, I was to follow the fullback out a few steps and then race back quickly because they would be bringing the wingback inside me to take a pass. 'But Tom,' I said, 'what if I commit myself that completely and the wingback isn't there?'*

And Tom just looked at me without any change of expression and said, 'He will be.' "

Roger Staubach (*From* Time Enough to Win)*: "I used to sit by my home telephone the night before every Cowboys game at Texas Stadium, game plan spread at the desk. At 8 P.M. the phone would ring, and it would be Landry, calling to make a final review of offensive strategy. Funny, the way he'd do it. I'd pick up the phone and say, 'Hello.' The next thing I would hear was his voice saying, 'Now, you know on that Slant 24, we are going to run it from . . .' He wouldn't say, 'Hello, Roger, this is Coach Landry,' or anything else before starting right in on the game plan. It was as if I were in the room with him."*

THE CHEERLEADERS

In the latter half of the 1970s, a new phenomenon appeared on the sidelines at National Football League games. Where once a few tumblers with megaphones and perhaps a half-dozen schoolgirls with pom-poms jumped up and down to exhort the fans, there were suddenly bountiful troupes of cheerleaders ringing the football field. Decked out in revealing but attractive uniforms corresponding with their team's colors, the best of the acts were carefully choreographed, and the chorus lines were as precise and classy as those of the Radio City Rockettes.

It got its biggest boost in 1976 when the Dallas Cowboys introduced their extravaganza, elaborating on the cheerleading concept. For that regular season, they unveiled an expanded, much more sophisticated, sideline act to inspire game-time cheering and provide pregame entertainment. Other teams throughout the league soon rushed to add their own carbon copies of the Dallas Cowboys Cheerleaders.

Today, according to Suzanne Mitchell, Tex Schramm's former secretary and now the director of the cheerleading team, "the Cheerleaders are a public relations arm of the Dallas Cowboys and therefore must always reflect on the Cowboys' image."

Each year now some 1,500 to 2,000 young ladies converge on Dallas to formally try out for the 36 berths on the cheerleader squad. Letters of application are received in Suzanne Mitchell's offices, and audition appointments are set up. Even returning veterans must try out each year, although they are given a bye to the final selection audition.

The preliminary sessions are held over two weekends in April. At any given session, there may be as many as 250–300 young ladies. They are broken down into groups of four, who will then appear before one of the five or six members of the judging panel. Each individual will talk with and be questioned by a judge and then perform. Beauty is certainly a requisite and so is terpsichorean talent, but the aspirants are also judged on such other traits as poise, personality, intelligence, and the ability to present themselves well in public. The auditions are thorough and demanding and not a lot different from those

(Dallas Cowboys Cheerleaders)

held for a Broadway musical. As Miss Mitchell often points out, "It takes a very special young lady."

The first cut, so to speak, is a large one, and after the initial tryouts, the roster is narrowed to 150 or more semifinalists. They are told what to expect in the ensuing auditions and are often given hints or tips by the judges for individual improvement.

For the second phase of auditioning, the cheerleaders' choreographer, Texie Waterman, takes groups of ten and teaches each a routine, including kicks, splits, and other dance maneuvers. They perform as a group, and each young lady is judged on her ability to learn routines and the precision with which she carries them out.

Finally, the group is narrowed to about 50 finalists. Each of these young ladies must then prepare her own individual performance and choose her own costume. It gives the judges the opportunity to get a look at each person's sense of creativity, taste, and imagination. The young ladies will then again perform in group routines; lastly, each new finalist will have a personal interview with Suzanne Mitchell. The end result is 36 carefully selected Dallas Cowboys Cheerleaders.

Then the real work begins. Rehearsals begin immediately. They are held five nights a week, each session lasting four to five hours. And they continue, with the exception of a two-week layoff in June, all the way up to the opening game of the preseason.

By that time, the cheerleaders have perfected some 40 to 50 sideline routines and 10 to 20 longer ones for pregame shows. The organization provides all uniforms and accessories and a token $15 honorarium per game.

No cheerleading group anywhere, ever, has achieved the broad acclaim that the Cowboys cheerleaders have.

Their name and their uniform design are now trademarked, and the Dallas Cowboys Cheerleaders have become known not only to millions in the United States but to many in other parts of the world as well.

Besides their sideline shows at Dallas home games and Super Bowls in which the Cowboys have played, the cheerleaders have performed live at various other kinds of functions, such as state fairs across the country, and have starred in many TV specials—from "Love Boat" to their own special "The 36 Most Beautiful Girls in Texas." They have performed on TV with such superstars as Bob Hope, Ginger Rogers, the Osmonds, and Douglas Fairbanks, Jr. A made-for-TV movie featuring the cheerleaders aired in 1979, and it became one of the most highly viewed movies made for television in the industry's history, garnering a full 48% of the television audience that night. (A sequel was produced the following year.)

The cheerleaders honored the U.S. government's request to make USO tours to entertain American troops in Korea (1979 and 1980), West Germany (1980), and Greece (1981). They also make many appearances for charity, such as telethons in Dallas, St. Louis, and even Winnipeg, Canada.

In the United States, the cheerleaders have performed in cities as large as New York and Los Angeles as well as in towns like Nacogdoches, Texas, and Grantville, Pennsylvania. They have become a household word on a national level; like their counterparts on the field, they are the only ones in the NFL to have achieved that status.

Requirements for becoming a Dallas Cowboys Cheerleader:

- *Female*
- *Minimum age 18*
- *High school graduate*
- *Employed or full-time student*
- *Live or be willing to relocate in the Dallas–Fort Worth area*

(Dallas Cowboys Cheerleaders)

(Dallas Cowboys Cheerleaders)

Appendix

THE BEST . . .

Scoring

Most points:

Career	Bob Hayes	456	
Season	Danny Villanueva	107	(1966)
Game	Dan Reeves	24	(vs. Falcons, 11/5/67)
	Bob Hayes	24	(vs. Oilers, 12/20/70)
	Calvin Hill	24	(vs. Bills, 9/19/71)
	Duane Thomas	24	(vs. Cardinals, 12/18/71)

Most touchdowns:

Career	Bob Hayes	76	
Season	Dan Reeves	16	(1966)
Game	(same as Most Points above)		

Most points kicking:

Career	Mike Clark	387	
Season	Danny Villanueva	107*	(1966)

Rushing:

Most yardage:

Career	Don Perkins	6,217	
Season	Tony Dorsett	1,325	(1978)
Game	Tony Dorsett	206	(vs. Eagles, 12/4/77)

Best average:

Career	Roger Staubach	5.5	
Season	Amos Marsh	5.6	(1962)

Most touchdowns:

Career	Don Perkins	42	
Season	Tony Dorsett	12	(1977)

Most carries:

Career	Don Perkins	1,500	
Season	Tony Dorsett	290	(1978)
Game	Calvin Hill	32	(vs. 49ers, 11/10/74)

*17 field goals, 56 extra points

Passing

Best NFL rating:

Career	Roger Staubach	83.5	
Season	Roger Staubach	104.8	(1971)

Most completions:

Career	Roger Staubach	1,685	
Season	Roger Staubach	267	(1979)
Game	Don Meredith	30	(vs. 49ers, 11/10/63)
			vs. Giants, 9/18/66)

Most yardage:

Career	Roger Staubach	22,700	
Season	Roger Staubach	3,586	(1979)
Game	Don Meredith	460	(vs. 49ers, 11/10/63)

Most touchdowns:

Career	Roger Staubach	153	
Season	Danny White	28	(1980)
Game	Eddie LeBaron	5	(vs. Steelers, 10/21/62)
	Don Meredith	5	(vs. Giants, 9/18/66)
	Don Meredith	5	(vs. Eagles, 10/9/66)
	Don Meredith	5	(vs. Eagles, 9/29/68)
	Craig Morton	5	(vs. Eagles, 10/19/69)
	Craig Morton	5	(vs. Oilers, 12/20/70)

Most attempts:

Career	Roger Staubach	2,958	
Season	Roger Staubach	461	(1979)
Game	Roger Staubach	49	(vs. Eagles, 10/26/75)

Best completion percentage:

Career	Danny White	58.6	
Season	Roger Staubach	62.6	(1973)

Receiving

Most receptions:
Career	Drew Pearson	378	
Season	Frank Clarke	65	(1964)
Game	Lance Rentzel	13	(vs. Redskins, 11/19/67)

Most yardage:
Career	Bob Hayes	7,295	
Season	Bob Hayes	1,232	(1966)
Game	Bob Hayes	246	(vs. Redskins, 11/13/66)

Most touchdowns:
Career	Bob Hayes	71	
Season	Frank Clarke	14	(1962)
Game	Bob Hayes	4	(vs. Oilers, 12/20/70)

Best average gain:
Career	Bob Hayes	20.0	
Season	Bob Hayes	26.1	(1970)

Kicking

Most field goals:
Career	Mike Clark	69	
Season	Toni Fritsch	22	(1975)
Game	Danny Villanueva	4	(vs. Browns, 11/24/66)
	Toni Fritsch	4	(vs. Cardinals, 11/12/72)
	Toni Fritsch	4	(vs. Rams, 9/21/75)

Most field goal attempts:
Career	Mike Clark	119	
Season	Mike Clark	36	(1969)
	Toni Fritsch	36	(1972)
Game	Mike Clark	7	(vs. Bears, 11/24/68)

Best field goal percentage:
Career	Efren Herrera	.617	
Season	Efren Herrera	.783	(1976)

Most extra points:
Career	Mike Clark	180	
Season	Danny Villanueva	56	(1966)
Game	Danny Villanueva	8	(vs. Eagles, 10/9/66)
	Mike Clark	8	(vs. Lions, 9/15/68)
	Rafael Septien	8	(vs. 49ers, 10/12/80)

Best average punting yardage:
Career	Sam Baker	45.1	
Season	Sam Baker	45.4	(1962)

Most punts:
Career	Danny White	373	
Season	Danny White	80	(1977)

Returns

Most kickoff return yardage:
Career	Mel Renfro	2,246	
Season	Mel Renfro	1,017	(1964)
Game	Mel Renfro	168	(vs. Redskins, 11/22/64)

Most kickoff-return TDs:
Career	Mel Renfro	2	

Best average kickoff return:
Career	Mel Renfro	26.4	
Season	Mel Renfro	30.0	(1965)

Most kickoff returns:
Career	Mel Renfro	85	
Season	Mel Renfro	40	(1964)
Game	Mel Renfro	8	(vs. Packers, 11/29/64)

Most punt-return yardage:
Career	Butch Johnson	1,313	
Season	James Jones	548	(1980)

Best average punt return:
Career	Bob Hayes	11.1	
Season	Bob Hayes	20.8	(1968)

Most punt returns:
Career	Butch Johnson	146	
Season	James Jones	54	(1980)

Defense

Most pass interceptions:
Career	Mel Renfro	52	
Season	Mel Renfro	10	(1969)
Game	Herb Adderley	3	(vs. Eagles, 9/26/71)
	Lee Roy Jordan	3	(vs. Bengals, 11/4/73)
	Charlie Waters	3	(vs. Bears, 12/26/77)

Most pass-interception yardage:
Career	Mel Renfro	626	
Season	Cornell Green	211	(1963)
Game	Mike Gaechter	121	(vs. Redskins, 11/3/63)

Best average-interception return:
Career	Mike Gaechter	20.0	
Season	Randy Hughes	45.5	(1979)

Most interception-return TDs:
Career	Mel Renfro	3	
	Lee Roy Jordan	3	
	Larry Cole	3	

Most tackles:
Season	Bob Breunig	167	(1980)
Game	Lee Roy Jordan	21	(vs. Eagles, 10/28/73)

Most unassisted tackles:
Season	Lee Roy Jordan	100	(1975)
Game	Lee Roy Jordan	14	(vs. Eagles, 10/28/73)

Most assisted tackles:
Season	Jerry Tubbs	101	(1960)
Game	Jerry Tubbs	15	(vs. Bears, 11/27/60)

BEST DAYS . . .

Rushing

206	Tony Dorsett vs. Philadelphia, Dec. 4, 1977 (23 carries).
*160	Tony Dorsett vs. Los Angeles, Dec. 28, 1980 (22 carries).
154	Tony Dorsett vs. St. Louis, Sept. 24, 1978 (21 carries).
153	Calvin Hill vs. San Francisco, Nov. 10, 1974 (32 carries).
152	Tony Dorsett vs. New Orleans, Nov. 19, 1978 (25 carries).
150	Calvin Hill vs. Washington, Nov. 16, 1969 (27 carries).
149	Tony Dorsett vs. Green Bay, Nov. 12, 1978 (23 carries).
147	Tony Dorsett vs. Baltimore, Sept. 4, 1978 (15 carries).
145	Tony Dorsett vs. Minnesota, Oct. 7, 1979 (21 carries).
*143	Duane Thomas vs. San Francisco, Jan. 3, 1971 (27 carries).
141	Tony Dorsett vs. St. Louis, Oct. 9, 1977 (14 carries).
140	Calvin Hill vs. Philadelphia, Oct. 20, 1974 (26 carries).
138	Calvin Hill vs. New Orleans, Sept. 28, 1969 (23 carries).
137	Don Perkins vs. St. Louis, Oct. 28, 1962 (24 carries).
137	Don Perkins vs. N. Y. Giants, Oct. 11, 1964 (17 carries).
*135	Duane Thomas vs. Detroit, Dec. 26, 1970 (30 carries).
134	Duane Thomas vs. Kansas City, Oct. 25, 1970 (20 carries).
133	Don Perkins vs. Green Bay, Oct. 24, 1965 (22 carries).
130	Calvin Hill vs. Chicago, Sept. 16, 1973 (31 carries).
*125	Calvin Hill vs. San Francisco, Dec. 23, 1972 (18 carries).

Passing

460	Don Meredith vs. San Francisco, Nov. 10, 1963 (30 of 48).
406	Don Meredith vs. Washington, Nov. 13, 1966 (21 of 29).
394	Don Meredith vs. Philadelphia, Nov. 6, 1966 (14 of 24).
358	Don Meredith vs. N. Y. Giants, Sept. 18, 1966 (14 of 24).
349	Craig Morton vs. Houston, Dec. 20, 1970 (13 of 17).
345	Eddie LeBaron vs. Pittsburgh, Sept. 24, 1960 (15 of 28).
339	Roger Staubach vs. Baltimore, Sept. 26, 1976 (22 of 28).
336	Roger Staubach vs. Washington, Dec. 16, 1979 (24 of 42).
326	Don Meredith vs. St. Louis, Dec. 11, 1965 (16 of 30).
314	Roger Staubach vs. Philadelphia, Oct. 26, 1975 (27 of 49).
308	Roger Staubach vs. Philadelphia, November 12, 1979 (17 of 28).
307	Roger Staubach vs. St. Louis, Sept. 28, 1975 (23 of 34).
306	Don Meredith vs. Philadelphia, Oct. 13, 1968 (21 of 38).
303	Roger Staubach vs. Cleveland, Sept. 24, 1979 (21 of 39).
302	Don Meredith vs. Philadelphia, Nov. 17, 1963 (25 of 33).

Receiving

246	Bob Hayes vs. Washington, Nov. 13, 1966 (9 catches).
241	Frank Clarke vs. Washington, Sept. 16, 1962 (10 catches).
223	Lance Rentzel vs. Washington, Nov. 19, 1967 (13 catches).
213	Tony Hill vs. Philadelphia, November 12, 1979 (7 catches).
195	Bob Hayes vs. N. Y. Giants, Sept. 18, 1966 (6 catches).
190	Frank Clarke vs. San Francisco, Nov. 10, 1963 (8 catches).
188	Drew Pearson vs. Detroit, Oct. 6, 1975 (6 catches).
187	Bob Hayes vs. Houston, Dec. 20, 1970 (6 catches).
177	Bob Hayes vs. Philadelphia, Oct. 10, 1965 (8 catches).
170	Bob Hayes vs. Pittsburgh, Oct. 22, 1967 (7 catches).
168	Frank Clarke vs. N. Y. Giants, Oct. 20, 1963 (4 catches).
161	Drew Pearson vs. Philadelphia, Sept. 23, 1974 (10 catches).

ALL-TIME LEADERS . . .

Scoring

	TD	PAT	FG	Total
Hayes, Bob (1965–74)	76	—	—	456
Clark, Mike (1968–71, 1973)	—	180	69	387
Fritsch, Toni (1971–73, 1975)	—	119	66	317
Clarke, Frank (1960–67)	51	—	—	306
Perkins, Don (1961–68)	45	—	—	270
Hill, Calvin (1969–74)	45	—	—	270
Villanueva, Danny (1965–67)	—	134	42	260
Reeves, Dan (1965–72)	42	1 (run)	—	253

Rushing

	Att.	Yds.	Avg.	Long	TD
Perkins, Don (1961–68)	1,500	6,217	4.1	59	42
Hill, Calvin (1969–74)	1,166	5,009	4.3	55	39
Newhouse, Robert (1972–79)	1,151	4,638	4.0	54	30
Dorsett, Tony (1977–80)	1,026	4,624	4.5	84	36
Garrison, Walt (1966–74)	899	3,886	4.3	41	30
Staubach, Roger (1969–79)	410	2,264	5.5	33	20
Marsh, Amos (1961–64)	427	2,065	4.8	71	14
Reeves, Dan (1965–72)	535	1,990	3.7	67	25
Thomas, Duane (1970–71)	326	1,596	4.9	56	16

Passing

	Att.	Comp.	Pct.	Yds.	TD	Int.	Rating
Staubach, R. (1969–79)	2,958	1,685	57.0	22,700	153	109	83.5
White, D. (1976–80)	539	316	58.6	4,017	31	31	77.1
Morton, C. (1965–74)	1,308	685	52.4	10,279	80	73	75.5
Meredith, D. (1960–68)	2,308	1,170	50.7	17,199	135	111	74.7
LeBaron, E. (1960–63)	692	359	51.9	5,331	45	52	67.8

Receiving

	No.	Yds.	Avg.	Long	TD
Pearson, Drew (1973–80)	378	6,281	16.6	67	37
Hayes, Bob (1965–74)	365	7,295	20.0	95	71
Clarke, Frank (1960–67)	281	5,214	18.6	80	50
DuPree, Billy Joe (1973–80)	229	3,168	13.8	42	36
Pearson, Preston (1975–80)	189	2,274	12.0	49	11
Rentzel, Lance (1967–70)	183	3,521	19.2	86	31
Garrison, Walt (1966–74)	182	1,794	9.9	53	9
Hill, Tony (1977–80)	168	2,961	17.6	75	24
Howton, Billy (1960–63)	161	2,368	14.7	69	17
Perkins, Don (1961–68)	146	1,310	9.0	39	3
Hill, Calvin (1969–74)	139	1,359	9.8	39	6

Field Goals

	Att.	Made	Pct.	Long
Clark, Mike (1968–71, 1973)	119	69	.580	50
Fritsch, Toni (1971–73, 75)	107	66	.617	54
Herrera, Efren (1974, 1976–77)	65	44	.677	52
Villanueva, Danny (1965–67)	81	42	.519	41
Septien, Rafael (1978–79)	72	46	.639	52
Baker, Sam (1962–63)	47	23	.489	53
Van Raaphorst, Dick (1964)	29	14	.483	43
Cone, Fred (1960)	13	6	.462	45
Bielski, Dick (1961)	9	6	.667	42
Percival, Mac (1974)	8	2	.250	33

*Playoff game

Kickoff Returns

	No.	Yds.	Avg.	Long	TD
Renfro, Mel (1964–77)	85	2,246	26.4	100	2
Harris, Cliff (1970–79)	63	1,622	25.7	77	0
Marsh, Amos (1961–64)	65	1,561	24.0	101	1
Johnson, Butch (1976–79)	79	1,832	23.2	74	0
Garrison, Walt (1966–74)	41	813	19.8	36	0

Punt Returns

	No.	Yds.	Avg.	Long	TD
Hayes, Bob (1965–74)	104	1,158	11.1	90	3
Johnson, Butch (1976–79)	146	1,313	9.0	55	0
Richards, Golden (1973–78)	62	501	8.1	46	1
Renfro, Mel (1964–77)	109	842	7.7	69	1
Jones, James (1980)	54	548	10.1	52	0
Harris, Cliff (1970–79)	66	418	6.3	35	0

Punting

	No.	Avg.	Long	Blk.
Baker, Sam (1962–63)	128	45.1	72	0
Sherer, Dave (1960)	57	42.5	67	1
Widby, Ron (1968–71)	247	41.8	84	2
Lothridge, Billy (1964)	62	40.3	75	1
Villanueva, Danny (1965–67)	192	40.3	58	1
White, Danny (1976–79)	373	40.2	73	3
Carrell, Duane (1974)	40	39.8	59	0
Hoopes, Mitch (1975)	68	39.4	55	1
Bateman, Marv (1972–74)	139	39.3	62	2
Green, Allen (1961)	61	36.7	53	1

Interceptions

	No.	Yds.	Avg.	Long	TD
Renfro, Mel (1964–77)	52	626	12.0	90	3
Waters, Charlie (1970–80)	38	563	14.8	56	2
Green, Cornell (1962–74)	34	552	16.2	59	2
Jordan, Lee Roy (1963–76)	32	472	14.8	49	3
Harris, Cliff (1970–79)	29	281	9.7	60	1
Howley, Chuck (1961–73)	24	395	16.5	58	2
Bishop, Don (1960–65)	22	364	16.5	57	0
Gaechter, Mike (1962–69)	21	420	20.0	100	1
Tubbs, Jerry (1960–67)	15	176	11.7	44	0

YEARLY LEADERS . . .

Scoring

Year	Player	TD	PAT	FG	Tot.	NFL/NFC Rank
1960	Cone, Fred	0	21	6	39	27
1961	Clarke, Frank	9	0	0	54	22
1962	Baker, Sam	0	50	14	92	6
1963	Baker, Sam	0	38	9	65	14
1964	VanRaaphorst, Dick	0	28	14	70	13
1965	Villanueva, Danny	0	37	16	85	10
1966	Villanueva, Danny	0	56	17	107	2
1967	Hayes, Bob	11	0	0	66	T16
	Reeves, Dan	11	0	0	66	T16
1968	Clark, Mike	0	54	17	105	2
1969	Clark, Mike	0	43	20	103	2
1970	Clark, Mike	0	35	18	89	12/8
1971	Clark, Mike	0	47	13	86	13/7
1972	Fritsch, Toni	0	36	21	99	7/3
1973	Fritsch, Toni	0	43	18	97	11/7
1974	Herrera, Efren	0	33	8	57	26/9
1975	Fritsch, Toni	0	38	22	104	3/2
1976	Herrera, Efren	0	34	18	88	6/4
1977	Herrera, Efren	0	39	18	93	3/2
1978	Septien, Rafael	0	46	16	94	5/2
1979	Septien, Rafael	0	40	19	97	8/3
1980	Septien, Rafael	0	59	11	92	13/6

Rushing

Year	Player	Att.	Yds.	Avg.	Long	TD	NFL/NFC Rank
1960	Dupre, L. G.	104	362	3.5	18	3	20
1961	Perkins, Don	200	815	4.1	47	4	6
1962	Perkins, Don	222	945	4.3	35	7	5
1963	Perkins, Don	149	614	4.1	19	7	10
1964	Perkins, Don	174	768	4.4	59	6	5
1965	Perkins, Don	177	690	3.9	43	0	7
1966	Reeves, Dan	175	757	4.3	67	8	6
1967	Perkins, Don	201	823	4.1	30	6	6
1968	Perkins, Don	191	836	4.4	28	4	6
1969	Hill, Calvin	204	942	4.6	55	8	2
1970	Thomas, Duane	151	803	5.3	47	5	8/5
1971	Thomas, Duane	175	793	4.5	56	11	11/7
1972	Hill, Calvin	245	1,036	4.2	26	6	7/3
1973	Hill, Calvin	273	1,142	4.2	21	6	3/2
1974	Hill, Calvin	185	844	4.6	27	7	8/3
1975	Newhouse, Robert	209	930	4.4	29	2	9/4
1976	Dennison, Doug	153	542	3.5	14	6	35/18
1977	Dorsett, Tony	208	1,007	4.8	84	12	9/4
1978	Dorsett, Tony	290	1,325	4.6	63	7	3/2
1979	Dorsett, Tony	250	1,107	4.4	41	6	11/8
1980	Dorsett, Tony	278	1,185	4.3	56	11	6/6

Passing

Year	Player	Att.	Comp.	Pct.	Yds.	TD	Int.	Rating	NFL/NFC Rank
1960	LeBaron, E.	225	111	49.3	1,736	12	25	53.4	8
1961	LeBaron, E.	236	120	50.8	1,741	14	16	66.5	9
1962	LeBaron, E.	166	95	57.2	1,436	16	9	95.3	3
1963	Meredith, D.	310	167	53.9	2,381	17	18	73.2	10
1964	Meredith, D.	323	158	48.9	2,143	9	16	67.3	15
1965	Meredith, D.	305	141	46.2	2,415	22	13	79.7	8
1966	Meredith, D.	344	177	51.5	2,805	24	12	87.7	4
1967	Meredith, D.	255	128	50.2	1,834	16	16	68.6	8
1968	Meredith, D.	309	171	55.3	2,500	21	12	88.3	2
1969	Morton, C.	302	162	53.6	2,619	21	15	85.4	5
1970	Morton, C.	207	102	49.3	1,819	15	7	89.7	5/4
1971	Staubach, R.	211	126	59.7	1,882	15	4	104.8	1/1
1972	Morton, C.	339	185	54.6	2,396	15	21	65.9	15/7
1973	Staubach, R.	286	179	62.6	2,428	23	15	94.6	1/1
1974	Staubach, R.	360	190	52.8	2,552	11	15	68.5	14/7
1975	Staubach, R.	348	198	56.9	2,666	17	16	78.6	8/2
1976	Staubach, R.	369	208	56.4	2,715	14	11	79.9	8/5
1977	Staubach, R.	361	210	58.2	2,620	18	9	87.1	2/1

1978	Staubach, R.	413	231	55.9	3,190	25	16	84.9	1/1
1979	Staubach, R.	461	267	57.9	3,586	27	11	92.4	1/1
1980	White, D.	436	260	59.6	3,287	28	25	80.8	9/7

Receiving

Year	Player	No.	Yds.	Avg.	Long	TD	NFL/ NFC Rank
1960	Doran, Jim	31	554	17.9	15	3	21
1961	Howton, Billy	56	785	14.0	53	4	6
1962	Howton, Billy	49	706	14.4	69	6	15
1963	Clarke, Frank	43	833	19.4	75	10	3
1964	Clarke, Frank	65	973	15.0	49	5	3
1965	Hayes, Bob	46	1,003	21.8	82	12	13
1966	Hayes, Bob	64	1,232	19.3	95	13	4
1967	Rentzel, Lance	58	996	17.2	74	8	6
1968	Rentzel, Lance	54	1,009	18.7	65	6	3
1969	Rentzel, Lance	43	960	22.3	75	12	20
1970	Hayes, Bob	34	889	26.1	89	10	45/26
1971	Garrison, Walt	40	396	9.9	36	1	23/10
1972	Hill, Calvin	43	364	8.5	33	3	18/9
1973	Hill, Calvin	32	290	9.1	29	0	36/21
1974	Pearson, Drew	62	1,087	17.9	50	2	3/2
1975	Pearson, Drew	46	822	17.9	46	8	16/9
1976	Pearson, Drew	58	806	13.9	40	6	4/1
1977	Pearson, Drew	48	870	18.1	67	2	9/3
1978	Pearson, Preston	47	256	11.2	34	0	26/15
1979	Hill, Tony	60	1,062	17.7	75t	10	12/6
1980	Hill, Tony	60	1,055	17.6	58t	8	16/9

Field Goals

Year	Player	Att.	Made	Pct.	Long	NFL/ NFC Rank
1960	Cone, Fred	13	6	.462	45	12
1961	Bielski, Dick	9	6	.667	42	13
1962	Baker, Sam	27	14	.519	53	3
1963	Baker, Sam	20	9	.450	53	12
1964	VanRaaphorst, Dick	29	14	.483	43	8
1965	Villanueva, Danny	27	16	.593	41	7
1966	Villanueva, Danny	31	17	.548	37	8
1967	Villanueva, Danny	23	9	.391	34	14
1968	Clark, Mike	29	17	.586	50	7
1969	Clark, Mike	36	20	.555	47	5
1970	Clark, Mike	27	18	.667	43	7/4
1971	Clark, Mike	25	13	.520	48	19/9
1972	Fritsch, Toni	36	21	.583	54	18/8
1973	Fritsch, Toni	28	18	.643	37	12/4
1974	Herrera, Efren	13	8	.615	39	11/5
1975	Fritsch, Toni	35	22	.629	43	14/8
1976	Herrera, Efren	23	18	.783	46	1/1
1977	Herrera, Efren	29	18	.621	52	12/1
1978	Septien, Rafael	26	16	.615	48	17/9
1979	Septien, Rafael	29	19	.655	51	9/4
1980	Septien, Rafael	17	11	.647	52	13/7

Kickoff Returns

Year	Player	No.	Yds.	Avg.	Long	TD	NFL/ NFC Rank
1960	Franckhauser, Tom	26	526	20.2	46	0	19
1961	Marsh, Amos	26	667	25.7	79	0	13
1962	Marsh, Amos	29	725	25.0	101	1	10
1963	Stiger, Jim	18	432	24.0	66	0	12
1964	Renfro, Mel	40	1,017	25.4	65	0	7
1965	Renfro, Mel	21	630	30.0	100	1	4
1966	Renfro, Mel	19	487	25.6	87	1	9
1967	Garrison, Walt	20	366	18.3	36	0	23
1968	Baynham, Craig	23	590	25.7	40	0	7
1969	Flowers, Richmond	11	283	25.7	30	0	29
1970	Thomas, Duane	19	416	21.9	33	0	23/10
1971	Harris, Cliff	29	823	28.4	77	0	4/4
1972	Harris, Cliff	26	615	23.7	44	0	23/11
1973	Montgomery, Mike	6	175	29.2	63	0	DNQ
1974	Morgan, Dennis	35	823	23.5	43	0	21/11
1975	Pearson, Preston	16	391	24.4	42	0	13/7
1976	Johnson, Butch	28	693	24.8	74	0	11/5
1977	Johnson, Butch	22	536	24.4	64	0	9/5
1978	Johnson, Butch	29	603	20.8	56	0	27/12
1979	Springs, Ron	38	780	20.5	70	0	25/12
1980	Jones, James	32	720	22.5	41	0	11/6

Punt Returns

Year	Player	No.	Yds.	Avg.	Long	TD	NFL/ NFC Rank
1960	Butler, Bill	13	131	10.1	46	0	2
1961	Marsh, Amos	14	71	5.1	19	0	14
1962	Lockett, J. W.	8	45	5.6	17	0	14
1963	Stiger, Jim	14	141	10.1	45	0	6
1964	Renfro, Mel	32	418	13.1	69	1	3
1965	Renfro, Mel	24	145	6.0	35	0	9
1966	Hayes, Bob	17	106	6.2	18	0	7
1967	Hayes, Bob	24	276	11.5	69	1	2
1968	Hayes, Bob	15	312	20.8	90	2	1
1969	Hayes, Bob	18	179	9.9	50	0	3
1970	Hayes, Bob	15	116	7.7	34	0	20/7
1971	Harris, Cliff	17	129	7.6	35	0	11/4
1972	Harris, Cliff	19	78	4.1	21	0	21/11
1973	Richards, Golden	21	139	6.6	46	0	23/10
1974	Morgan, Dennis	19	287	15.1	98	1	3/2
1975	Richards, Golden	28	288	10.3	43	1	12/5
1976	Johnson, Butch	45	489	10.9	55	0	8/4
1977	Johnson, Butch	50	423	8.5	38	0	20/7
1978	Johnson, Butch	51	401	7.9	23	0	18/9
1979	Wilson, Steve	35	236	6.8	13	0	20/7
1980	Jones, James	54	548	10.1	52	0	5/4

Punting

Year	Player	No.	Avg.	Long	Had Blocked	NFL/ NFC Rank
1960	Sherer, Dave	57	42.5	67	1	7
1961	Green, Allen	61	36.7	53	1	14
1962	Baker, Sam	57	45.4	72	0	3
1963	Baker, Sam	71	44.2	64	0	7
1964	Lothridge, Billy	62	40.3	75	1	15
1965	Villanueva, Danny	60	41.8	58	0	10
1966	Villanueva, Danny	65	39.2	58	1	13
1967	Villanueva, Danny	67	40.4	57	0	9
1968	Widby, Ron	59	40.9	84	0	5
1969	Widby, Ron	63	43.3	62	0	2
1970	Widby, Ron	69	41.3	59	1	10/2
1971	Widby, Ron	56	41.6	59	1	8/3

1972	Bateman, Marv	51	38.2	61	0	24/13
1973	Bateman, Marv	55	41.6	62	2	11/7
1974	Carrell, Duane	40	39.8	59	0	11/5
1975	Hoopes, Mitch	68	39.4	55	1	16/9
1976	White, Danny	70	38.4	54	2	20/9
1977	White, Danny	80	39.6	57	1	12/8
1978	White, Danny	76	40.5	56	1	8/5
1979	White, Danny	76	41.7	73	0	4/2
1980	White, Danny	71	40.9	58	0	10/5

Interceptions

Year	Player	No.	Yds.	Avg.	Long	TD	NFL/NFC Rank
1960	Bishop, Don	3	13	4.3	13	0	25
	Franckhauser, Tom	3	11	3.7	9	0	25
1961	Bishop, Don	8	172	21.5	57	0	2
1962	Bishop, Don	6	134	22.3	44	0	9
1963	Green, Cornell	7	211	30.1	55	0	6
1964	Renfro, Mel	7	110	15.7	39	1	4
1965	Green, Cornell	3	49	16.3	43	0	27
	Livingston, Warren	3	5	1.7	5	0	27
	Logan, Obert	3	5	1.7	3	0	27
1966	Green, Cornell	4	88	22.0	41	1	21
1967	Green, Cornell	7	52	7.4	28	0	7
	Renfro, Mel	7	38	5.4	30	0	9
1968	Howley, Chuck	6	115	19.2	58	1	11
1969	Renfro, Mel	10	118	11.8	41	0	1
1970	Waters, Charlie	5	45	9.0	20	0	16/9
1971	Adderley, Herb	6	182	30.3	46	0	9/4
1972	Waters, Charlie	6	132	22.0	56	1	7/3
1973	Jordan, Lee Roy	6	78	13.0	31	1	4/2
1974	Harris, Cliff	3	8	2.7	8	0	42/20
1975	Jordan, Lee Roy	6	80	13.3	38	0	7/4
1976	Washington, Mark	4	49	12.3	22	0	24/11
1977	Harris, Cliff	5	7	1.4	7	0	16/7
1978	Barnes, Benny	5	72	14.4	38	0	25/14
1979	Hughes, Randy	2	91	45.5	68	0	93/45
	Harris, Cliff	2	35	17.5	20	0	
	Barnes, Benny	2	20	10.0	11	0	
	Lewis, D. D.	2	8	4.0	5	0	
	Kyle, Aaron	2	0	0.0	0	0	
1980	Thurman, Dennis	5	114	27.8	78	1	24/10
	Waters, Charlie	5	78	15.6	29	0	

THE LONGEST . . .

Runs from Scrimmage

84   Tony Dorsett vs. Philadelphia, Dec. 4, 1977 (TD).
77   Tony Dorsett vs. St. Louis, Oct. 9, 1977 (TD).
73   Amos Bullocks vs. Chicago, Nov. 18, 1962 (TD).
71   Amos Marsh vs. New York, Oct. 15, 1961.
70   Amos Marsh vs. Washington, Nov. 4, 1962.
68   Les Shy vs. Philadelphia, Oct. 9, 1966.
67   Dan Reeves vs. Washington, Dec. 11, 1966 (TD).
64   Jim Stiger vs. Washington, Nov. 22, 1964.

63   Tony Dorsett vs. New Orleans, Nov. 19, 1978.
59   Don Perkins vs. Pittsburgh, Sept. 27, 1964.
59   Scott Laidlaw vs. Washington, Nov. 23, 1978.
56   Frank Clarke vs. New Orleans, Nov. 12, 1967.
56   Duane Thomas vs. New England, Oct. 24, 1971 (TD).
56   Tony Dorsett vs. New York, Nov. 9, 1980.
55   Calvin Hill vs. New Orleans, Nov. 9, 1969.

Forward Passes

95   Don Meredith to Bob Hayes vs. Washington, Nov. 13, 1966 (TD).
91   Roger Staubach to Tony Dorsett vs. Baltimore, Sept. 4, 1978 (TD).
89   Craig Morton to Bob Hayes vs. Kansas City, Oct. 25, 1970 (TD).
*86   Don Meredith to Bob Hayes vs. Cleveland, Dec. 24, 1967 (TD).
86   Craig Morton to Lance Rentzel vs. Philadelphia, Nov. 1, 1970 (TD).
85   Eddie LeBaron to Amos Marsh vs. Los Angeles, Sept. 30, 1962 (TD).
85   Roger Staubach to Bob Hayes vs. N.Y. Giants, Dec. 12, 1971 (TD).
84   Don Meredith to Pete Gent vs. Pittsburgh, Oct. 30, 1966 (TD).

Kickoff Returns

101   Amos Marsh vs. Philadelphia, Oct. 14, 1962 (TD).
101   Ike Thomas vs. New York Jets, Dec. 4, 1971 (TD).
100   Mark Washington vs. Washington, Nov. 22, 1970 (TD).
100   Mel Renfro vs. San Francisco, Nov. 7, 1965 (TD).
97   Thomas Henderson vs. St. Louis, Sept. 28, 1975 (TD).
89   Ike Thomas vs. Los Angeles, Nov. 25, 1971 (TD).
87   Mel Renfro vs. Pittsburgh, Oct. 30, 1966 (TD).

Punt Returns

98   Dennis Morgan vs. St. Louis, Oct. 13, 1974 (TD).
90   Bob Hayes vs. Pittsburgh, Dec. 8, 1968 (TD).
69   Bob Hayes vs. St. Louis, Nov. 23, 1967 (TD).
69   Mel Renfro vs. Green Bay, Nov. 29, 1964 (TD).
*68   Bob Hayes vs. Cleveland, Dec. 24, 1967.
63   Bob Hayes vs. New York, Dec. 15, 1968 (TD).
*63   Golden Richards vs. Minnesota, Dec. 30, 1973 (TD).
55   Butch Johnson vs. Philadelphia, Dec. 5, 1976.
52   James Jones vs. Washington, Nov. 23, 1980.
51   Mel Renfro vs. Cleveland, Oct. 4, 1964.
50   Bob Hayes vs. Washington, Nov. 16, 1969.

Interception Returns

100   Mike Gaechter vs. Philadelphia, Oct. 14, 1962 (TD).
90   Mel Renfro vs. St. Louis, Oct. 4, 1965 (TD).
86   Mike Gaechter vs. Washington, Nov. 3, 1963.

Fumble Returns

97   Chuck Howley vs. Atlanta, Oct. 2, 1966 (TD).
84   Don Bishop vs. St. Louis, Oct. 28, 1962 (TD).
63   Jim Ridlon vs. Philadelphia, Dec. 6, 1964 (TD).

Field-goal-attempt Returns

94   Jerry Norton vs. St. Louis, Dec. 9, 1962 (TD).
60   Mike Gaechter vs. Washington, Nov. 28, 1965 (TD).

60   Obert Logan vs. New York, Dec. 19, 1965 (TD).

Punts

84   Ron Widby vs. New Orleans, Nov. 3, 1968.
75   Billy Lothridge vs. New York, Oct. 11, 1964.
75   Sam Baker vs. Los Angeles, Sept. 30, 1962.
73   Danny White vs. Los Angeles, Oct. 14, 1979.
71   Billy Lothridge vs. St. Louis, Sept. 12, 1964.
71   Sam Baker vs. New York, Dec. 16, 1962.

Field Goals

54   Toni Fritsch vs. New York, Sept. 24, 1972
53   Sam Baker vs. Pittsburgh, Dec. 8, 1963.
53   Sam Baker vs. New York, Nov. 11, 1962.

IN A ROW . . .

Most Consecutive Games Played
196   Bob Lilly (from 1961 through 1974).

Most Consecutive Passes Completed
12   Roger Staubach (last 11 vs. Baltimore, Sept. 4, 1978, and first one vs. N.Y. Giants, Sept. 10, 1978).

Most Consecutive Passes without Interception
166   Don Meredith (began vs. Philadelphia, Dec. 5, 1965, ended vs. St. Louis, Oct. 16, 1966).

Most Consecutive Games Rush for TD
6   Tony Dorsett in 1977.

Most Consecutive Games Catch TD Pass
7   Frank Clarke (final game of 1961 season, first six games in '62). Bob Hayes (final three games of 1965 season, first four games in 1966).

Most Consecutive Games Intercept Pass
5   Don Bishop in 1961.

Most Consecutive PATs
99   Mike Clark (last 17 in 1969, all 35 in 1970 and all 47 in 1971).

Most Consecutive Games at Least One Pass Catch
58   Drew Pearson (final three games of 1974 season, all of 1975, 1976 and 1977, first 13 games of 1978; ended vs. New England, Dec. 3, 1978).

Most Consecutive Games Kick FG
10   Mike Clark (final nine games of 1969 season, first game in 1970).
Toni Fritsch, twice (final seven games of 1972 season, first three games in 1973; first 10 games in 1975).

AS A TEAM . . .

Season Records

Most points scored:		
	By Cowboys	454 in 1980
	By Opponents	402 in 1962
Fewest points scored:		
	By Cowboys	177* in 1960
	By Cowboys	236 in 1961
	By Opponents	186 in 1968
Most touchdowns scored:		
	By Cowboys	60 in 1980
	By Opponents	52 in 1962
Fewest touchdowns scored:		
	By Cowboys	23* in 1960
	By Cowboys	29 in 1961
	By Opponents	23 in 1968 & 1973
Most first downs:		
	By Cowboys	342 in 1978
	By Opponents	274 in 1962
Fewest first downs:		
	By Cowboys	180* in 1960
	By Cowboys	211 in 1965
	By Opponents	199 in 1974
Most first downs rushing:		
	By Cowboys	147 in 1974
	By Opponents	122 in 1961
Fewest first downs rushing:		
	By Cowboys	57* in 1960
	By Cowboys	87 in 1965
	By Opponents	52 in 1969
Most first downs passing:		
	By Cowboys	195 in 1979
	By Opponents	166 in 1962
Fewest first downs passing:		
	By Cowboys	95 in 1970
	By Opponents	94 in 1977
Most first downs by penalties:		
	By Cowboys	29 in 1978
	By Opponents	27 in 1967
Fewest first downs by penalties:		
	By Cowboys	9 in 1961, 1962 & 1971
	By Opponents	10 in 1969
Most net yards offense:		
	By Cowboys	5,968 in 1979
	By Opponents	5,325 in 1963
Fewest net yards offense:		
	By Cowboys	3,153* in 1960
	By Cowboys	3,704 in 1964
	By Opponents	3,213 in 1977
Most net yards rushing:		
	By Cowboys	2,783 in 1978
	By Opponents	2,242* in 1960
Fewest net yards rushing:		
	By Cowboys	1,049* in 1960
	By Cowboys	1,608 in 1965
	By Opponents	1,050 in 1969
Most net yards passing:		
	By Cowboys	3,593 in 1979
	By Opponents	3,674 in 1962

*12 Games

Fewest net yards passing:

By Cowboys	2,013 in 1964
By Opponents	1,562 in 1977

Most total yards passing:

By Cowboys	3,883 in 1979
By Opponents	3,904 in 1962

Fewest total yards passing:

By Cowboys	2,388* in 1960
By Cowboys	2,445 in 1970
By Opponents	1,991 in 1977

Most times tackled passer:

By Cowboys	60 in 1966
By Opponents	68 in 1964

Most yards lost attempting to pass:

By Cowboys	503 in 1964
By Opponents	442 in 1978

Fewest yards lost attempting to pass:

By Cowboys	229 in 1978
By Opponents	161 in 1963

Most fumbles:

By Cowboys	46 in 1961
By Opponents	44 in 1973

Most fumbles lost:

By Cowboys	21 in 1961, 1971 & 1979
By Opponents	25 in 1971

Fewest fumbles:

By Cowboys	21* in 1960
By Cowboys	21 in 1968
By Opponents	21* in 1960
By Opponents	20 in 1979

Fewest fumbles lost:

By Cowboys	10 in 1966
By Opponents	11* in 1960
By Opponents	10 in 1977 & 1979

Most pass attempts:

By Cowboys	461 in 1979
By Opponents	484 in 1980

Fewest pass attempts:

By Cowboys	297 in 1970
By Opponents	293* in 1960
By Opponents	326 in 1961

Most pass completions:

By Cowboys	267 in 1979
By Opponents	260 in 1967

Fewest pass completions:

By Cowboys	149 in 1970
By Opponents	146* in 1960
By Opponents	154 in 1977

Most passes intercepted:

By Cowboys	29 in 1967
By Opponents	33* in 1960

Fewest passes intercepted:

By Cowboys	15* in 1960
By Cowboys	13 in 1974 & 1979
By Opponents	10 in 1977

Most penalties:

By Cowboys	107 in 1980
By Opponents	106 in 1980

Fewest penalties:

By Cowboys	47 in 1961
By Opponents	38 in 1961

*12 Games

Most yards penalized:

By Cowboys	952 in 1964 & 1971
By Opponents	989 in 1980

Fewest yards penalized:

By Cowboys	427 in 1961
By Opponents	362 in 1961

Most punts:

By Cowboys	83 in 1977
By Opponents	108 in 1978

Fewest punts:

By Cowboys	51 in 1972
By Opponents	43 in 1961

SINGLE-GAME RECORDS . . .

Most Points

Cowboys	59	vs. Detroit (59–13)	September	15,	1968
	59	vs. San Francisco	October	12,	1980
Opp.	54	Minnesota (54–13)	October	18,	1970
Combined	86	vs. Buffalo (49–37)	September	19,	1971

Most First Downs

Cowboys	32	vs. Philadelphia	October	9,	1966
	32	vs. N.Y. Giants	September	10,	1978
	32	vs. Green Bay	November	12,	1978
Opp.	29	Pittsburgh	October	22,	1967

Fewest First Downs

Cowboys	8	vs. Cleveland	October	16,	1960
		vs. Pittsburgh	November	12,	1961
		vs. St. Louis	December	10,	1961
		vs. Green Bay	November	29,	1964
		vs. Philadelphia	November	1,	1970
Opp.	5	Philadelphia	November	6,	1966
		Philadelphia	October	20,	1974

Most First Downs Rushing

Cowboys	17	vs. Green Bay	November	12,	1978
Opp.	15	Cleveland	December	3,	1961
		Pittsburgh	September	23,	1962

Fewest First Downs Rushing

Cowboys	0	vs. Philadelphia	November	1,	1970
Opp.	0	Philadelphia	October	9,	1966
		Pittsburgh	October	30,	1966

Most First Downs Passing

Cowboys	23	vs. San Francisco	November	10,	1963
Opp.	21	Chicago	November	11,	1962

Fewest First Downs Passing

Cowboys	3	vs. Cleveland	October	16,	1960
		vs. St. Louis	December	10,	1961
		vs. Washington	September	26,	1965
		vs. St. Louis	December	4,	1966
		vs. Minnesota	October	20,	1968
		vs. Atlanta	October	11,	1970
		*vs. Detroit	December	26,	1970

*Playoff Game.

		vs. Washington	December	9,	1972
Opp.	1	Chicago	September	16,	1973
		New York Jets	December	21,	1975

Most First Downs by Penalties

Cowboys	5	vs. Detroit	December	11,	1960
		vs. Philadelphia	December	10,	1967
		vs. St. Louis	November	3,	1974
Opp.	5	Cleveland	November	21,	1965
		Cleveland	December	7,	1974

Most Net Yards Total Offense

Cowboys	652	vs. Philadelphia	October	9,	1966
Opp.	527	St. Louis	December	9,	1962

Fewest Net Yards Total Offense

Cowboys	126	vs. St. Louis	December	10,	1961
Opp.	63	Green Bay	October	24,	1965

Most Net Yards Rushing

Cowboys	313	vs. Green Bay	November	12,	1978
Opp.	289	Philadelphia	October	22,	1961

Fewest Net Yards Rushing

Cowboys	41	vs. San Francisco	November	7,	1965
Opp.	7	Pittsburgh	October	30,	1966

Most Net Yards Passing

Cowboys	440	vs. Philadelphia	October	9,	1966
Opp.	437	Chicago	November	18,	1962

Fewest Net Yards Passing

Cowboys	10	vs. Green Bay	October	24,	1965
Opp.	1	Green Bay	October	24,	1965
		New York Jets	December	21,	1975

Most Gross Yards Passing

Cowboys	460	vs. San Francisco	November	10,	1963
Opp.	466	Chicago	November	18,	1962

Fewest Gross Yards Passing

Cowboys	42	vs. Green Bay	October	24,	1965
Opp.	15	New York Jets	December	21,	1975

Most Yards Lost Attempting to Pass

Cowboys	66	vs. San Francisco	November	23,	1972
Opp.	84	Detroit	October	6,	1975

Most Times Tackling Passer

Cowboys	12	vs. Pittsburgh	November	22,	1966
Opp.	9	Green Bay	October	24,	1965
		San Francisco	November	23,	1972

Most Interceptions

Cowboys	7	vs. Philadelphia	September	30,	1960
		vs. Philadelphia	September	26,	1971
Opp.	5	St. Louis	November	5,	1961

Most Fumbles

Cowboys	7	vs. New York Giants	October	11,	1971
Opp.	7	Washington	November	28,	1965
		St. Louis	December	3,	1972
		Kansas City	November	10,	1975

Most Fumbles Lost

Cowboys	5	vs. New Orleans	November	3,	1968
		vs. New York Giants	October	11,	1971
		vs. Kansas City	November	10,	1975
Opp.	5	New York Giants	October	11,	1971

		Chicago	September	16,	1973
		San Francisco	October	12,	1980

Most Penalties

Cowboys	14	vs. New York Giants			
			November	6,	1977
		vs. San Francisco	September	9,	1979
Opp.	11	Chicago	November	1,	1964
		St. Louis	October	9,	1977
		Washington	November	23,	1978

Fewest Penalties

Cowboys	0	vs. St. Louis	December	10,	1961
Opp.	0	Pittsburgh	October	21,	1962
		Philadelphia	December	5,	1965
		*Detroit	December	26,	1970
		*Miami	January	16,	1972
		*Pittsburgh	January	18,	1976

Most Yards Lost on Penalties

Cowboys	161	vs. Washington	November	22,	1970
Opp.	166	St. Louis	October	9,	1977

Most Punts

Cowboys	10	vs. Pittsburgh	November	12,	1961
		vs. Detroit	October	13,	1963
		vs. Cleveland	October	17,	1965
		vs. Buffalo	November	15,	1976
Opp.	11	Los Angeles	September	30,	1962
		Atlanta	September	15,	1974
		Buffalo	November	15,	1976

Fewest Punts

Cowboys	0	vs. Cleveland	December	3,	1961
		vs. Detroit	September	15,	1968
		vs. Baltimore	September	4,	1978
Opp.	0	Philadelphia	October	22,	1961

*Playoff Game.

THE ALL-PROS . . .

The Dallas Cowboys listed below have been named All-Pro by either one or several of these rating sources: Associated Press (AP), United Press International (UPI), Newspaper Enterprise Association (NEA), Professional Football Writers Association (PFWA).

	Position	Number of Years Selected
Bob Lilly	DT	7
Chuck Howley	LB	5
Mel Renfro	S	4
Cornell Green	CB	4
Rayfield Wright	OT	4
Cliff Harris	S	4
Ralph Neely	OT	3
John Niland	OG	3
Drew Pearson	WR	3
Randy White	DT	3
Bob Hayes	WR	2
Calvin Hill	RB	2
Charlie Waters	S	2
Don Perkins	RB	1
Frank Clarke	WR	1
Blaine Nye	OG	1
Lee Roy Jordan	LB	1
Harvey Martin	DE	1
Efren Herrera	K	1
Herbert Scott	OG	1

DALLAS COWBOYS ALL-PROS

BOB LILLY

Photo Credits: *The Dallas Cowboys*

JOHN NILAND

CHUCK HOWLEY

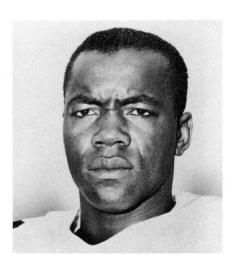

CORNELL GREEN

RANDY WHITE

CHARLIE WATERS

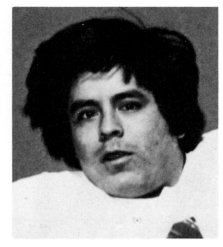

EFREN HERRERA

RALPH NEELY

RAYFIELD WRIGHT

CLIFF HARRIS

BLAINE NYE

HARVEY MARTIN

HERBERT SCOTT

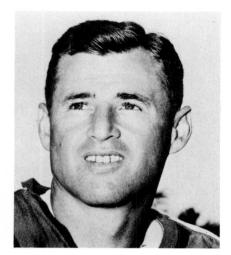

EDDIE LeBARON

DAN REEVES

CRAIG MORTON

DUANE THOMAS

DREW PEARSON

LEE ROY JORDAN

WALT GARRISON

ROBERT NEWHOUSE

L. G. DUPRE

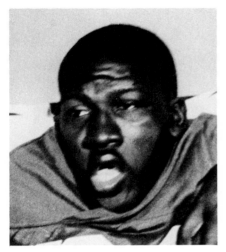

AMOS MARSH

DON MEREDITH

TONY DORSETT

BOB HAYES

MIKE GAECHTER

DON PERKINS

LANCE RENTZEL

DANNY WHITE

DANNY VILLANUEVA

SAM BAKER

FRANK CLARKE

MIKE CLARK

CALVIN HILL

LEE ROY JORDAN

MEL RENFRO

ROGER STAUBACH

JAMES JONES

TONI FRITSCH

Index